Be A Shining Star Daily Devotional

Patricia Dunn

Dedicated in Loving Memory
to the love of my life, Ted
(1968-2019)

*"So that you may become blameless and
pure, children of God without fault in a crooked
and depraved generation, in which you shine
like stars in the universe." (Philippians 2:15 NIV)*

All scripture is from the New Kings James Version unless so noted.

Table of Contents

Author's Note

When God called me to write a devotional at the end of 2017, little did I know how the words He gave me during 2018 would be used to carry me through my darkest days in 2019. My prayer is that you will allow God to speak to you through the words on these pages. God is real, my friend. We are not promised tomorrow. Seek Him, draw closer to Him. Allow Him to not only become your Savior, but also your Lord.

beashiningstardevotional.com

January 1
Let there be light
Genesis 1, Matthew 1

"In the beginning God created the heavens and the earth. The earth was without form, and void; and darkness was on the face of the deep. And the Spirit of God was hovering over the face of the waters. Then God said, "Let there be light"; and there was light." (Genesis 1:1-3)

Out of the darkness and void, God spoke: "Let there be light." What was once without form, over the next six days, became the beautiful, organized world Creator God spoke into being. The perfect world He envisioned for His creation and the people made in His image. However, if you read through Jesus' genealogy in Matthew 1, you realize that God's created world and created people did not remain perfect. You may even wonder how some of the names on that list end up as part of Jesus' genealogy.

Some of Jesus' earthly ancestors were deceivers, prostitutes, and murderers. They were those who had lost their way or were just blatantly evil. The world Jesus came into did not look like the Garden of Eden. The world once again had void and darkness and disorder.

Referring to Jesus, John states "In Him was life and the life was the light of the men and the light shines in the darkness and the darkness did not comprehend it." (John 1:4-5)

Once again, God seems to be saying "Let there be light." There had not been any word from God for four hundred years. Can you even imagine the loneliness, hopelessness, and emptiness?

But God still said, "Let there be light." Jesus: the hope, the purpose, the fulfillment for all humanity. Jesus: the way to restore God's creation and His people back to that state of perfection. JESUS. And in today's world, God is still saying. "Let there be light."

We as Christ-followers are now that light. Matthew 5:14 says, "You are the light of the world. A city that is set on a hill cannot be hidden." Just as those listed as Jesus' ancestors, our lives may be marred by past mistakes, deep wounds, darkness. But God still used those people to bring Light to the world. Men and women who chose to follow God. Becoming the light in their own dark world.

Will you join with me as we recommit, or perhaps even begin, being the "light of the world"? Being the light that is so desperately needed?

Lord, no matter how little my light may be right now, let it shine in the dark world around me for Your glory and for Your kingdom purpose. Your kingdom come, Your will be done! Amen!

January 2
Light shines in the darkness
Psalm 23

When was the last time you read Psalm 23 and absorbed all that is in those six verses? Verse four is one that often hits home. At some point in time, most of us have probably felt like we were walking "through the valley of the shadow of death." This valley may look different for each of us. You or a loved one may be walking through an illness or a loss. Natural disasters, terrorist attacks, war, addiction, the list that brings death seems endless. Where can we find the light in such darkness? The answer is found in verse four: "You are with me."

God sent His Son to earth to be the light in the darkness. No matter what we are facing, the most significant time of darkness was when Christ was on the Cross. The Hope of all creation was dying. Jesus was saying, "My God, My God, why have you forsaken me?" (Matthew 27:46) The world was losing their Light. Jesus chose to bear the pain and agony of the cross for us, in our place. He did it all for you. He did it all for me. During our valley of the shadow of death, we may feel forsaken. But "You are with me." Because of what Jesus did on that cross, we are never forsaken. He is with us. He understands our grief, our confusion, our anger. He is the Light in our darkness. He serves as a reminder that we are not completely alone in the dark. And He brings hope that the darkness will one day be over. There is coming a Day when Christ will return, and Heaven will be our home. And "there shall be no night there." (Revelations 22:5) But while we await that glorious day, God is with us. We do not have to face these dark days here on the earth alone.

"The Lord is my Shepherd; I shall not want. He makes me to lie down in green pastures; He leads me beside the still waters. He restores my soul; He leads me in the paths of righteousness for His name's sake. Yea though I walk through the valley of the shadow of death, I will fear no evil; for You are with me; Your rod and Your staff, they comfort me. You prepare a table before me in the presence of my enemies; You anoint my head with oil; My cup runs over. Surely goodness and mercy shall follow me all the days of my life; and I will dwell in the house of the Lord forever." (Psalm 23) Dear friend, whatever your valley looks like today, He is with you. You are not alone. What a great comfort to know we don't have to face anything within our own strength and wisdom. The God of all creation is with you and me each day. That's the message we need to shine to the world that sits in darkness and who needs His light.

Father God, thank You for Your promise never to leave us or forsake us (Hebrew 13:5). That no matter how dark our days seem, You are with us. Thank You for the promised eternity where there will be no more valleys of the shadow of death. Guide us to shine Your light to those who sit in darkness today. May we be the light of the world until the day of Your glorious return!.

January 3
Guide our feet to peace
Luke 1

"To give light to those who sit in darkness and the shadow of death, to guide our feet into the way of peace." (Luke 1:79)

Peace seems like some unattainable state. We can't even seem to find peace in our own lives, let alone in our family, church, country, and world. Peace seems hard to come by, yet Christ came "to guide our feet into the way of peace." David, while being pursued by Saul, says in Psalm 3:5 "I lay down and slept, I awoke for the Lord sustained me." In Psalm 3:3, he says, "But You, O Lord, are a shield for me, My glory and the One who lifts up my head." In Psalm 34:14, he gives us the answer to having peace. "Depart from evil and do good. Seek peace and pursue it." We try to work for peace however Jesus said: "Peace I leave with you, My peace I give to you." (John 14:27) Jesus is our guide to peace. He is our answer to peace. You probably know the chorus to the song Trust and Obey: "Trust and obey for there's no other way to be happy in Jesus but to trust and obey." ("Trust and Obey"/John Sammis) It seems to be such a simple song. But the concepts are not that simple. Trust - There are times that we can easily say "Yes, we trust You, Lord." However, what about those times when we are struggling to want to know why or how. We all have those times when things are not going our way, when we can't see the answer and are starting to feel that desperation. "God, I need You to move NOW!" Not quite so easy to trust then. However, it's a decision that we make to say "God, You are my Creator, my Father. You have a bigger plan for me than what my limited vision can see, so I choose to trust You, my good Father." Obey - Another concept that we would like to control. We like to think "God, lay out the options and I will choose which I want to obey." We can't just choose to obey when it's easy. We must decide to obey every time. We are not perfect. We will not always make the right decisions. God understands us better than we do ourselves. A favorite verse is Psalm 103:14 "For He knows our frame, He remembers we are dust."

Christ came to be our Prince of Peace. So, in a world full of chaos, He can still "guide our feet into the way of peace." The last verse says "Then in fellowship sweet we will sit at His feet or we'll walk by His side in the way. What He says we will do, where He sends we will go, never fear, only trust and obey." ("Trust and Obey"/John Sammis)

Father, guide us to the way of peace. Amidst whatever we are facing right now, help us remember that You are the Prince of Peace. Help us to trust and obey even when we can't see the outcome. "And let the peace of God rule in your heart." (Colossians 3:15) Amen.

Trust God
Proverbs 3

"Trust in the Lord with all your heart, and lean not on your own understanding, in all your ways acknowledge Him, and He shall direct your paths." (Proverbs 3:5-6)

God made us with a free will. And we, like Adam and Eve, want to exercise that will. We want to trust our own instincts, opinions, desires, and thoughts. We want to think we have our lives figured out. But the truth of the matter is, without God, we end up just like Adam and Eve who made a mess of their lives by trusting their way over God's way. Adam and Eve's story is one of the most well-known from the Bible. From our perspective, we want to say, "No, Eve. Don't take the fruit. You don't understand how this one action will impact the rest of your life (and ours by the way!). However, how many of us have those looking in at our story who are thinking the same thing about us? "No, (insert your name here), don't do that! You don't understand how (insert action/decision here) will impact the rest of your life."

We have all been there. We have all made decisions that we wish we could "undo." If we carefully examined those decisions, we would find at the core that we were leaning on our own understanding.

Our Creator God, who knows and sees everything, has a much better view of our lives than we do. He is better equipped to guide us from His vantage point. Trusting Him with all our hearts is still not going to be a "perfect" life, because face it, we are all still human, and we still live in a fallen world. However, we can save ourselves disappointments and negative consequences if we make it a practice of trusting and acknowledging Him as the Lord of our life. If we submit our day, schedule, attitude over to Him for His kingdom purpose, how much richer our lives would be. If we are not living our lives just for ourselves and are willing vessels, God can use us in someone else's life today. Jesus says on the Sermon on the Mount in Matthew 6:33 "But seek first the kingdom of God and His righteousness, and all these things shall be added to you." If we allow our lives to be kingdom purpose lives, then we realize how limited our own understanding is and why we need to trust God will all our heart so that He can direct our paths.

Lord, may we daily live our lives by trusting You with all our hearts and lean not on our own understanding. May we acknowledge You in all our ways so that You can direct our paths. Amen.

January 5
Seek His righteousness
Matthew 5-7, Isaiah 64

Today, most people seem to have their own definition of being "moral." It appears that people want to "rewrite" the truth to fit their opinions, experiences, etc. They also want to try to adapt the divine law to accommodate their plans and actions. They want their righteousness to be self-defined. They use the events and other people around them to justify how righteous they are. However, Isaiah 64:6 says, "and all our righteousness are like filthy rags." God's response: 2 Corinthians 5:21 "For He made Him who knew no sin to Be sin for us that we might become the righteousness of God in Him." The Message paraphrases that verse like this: "In Christ, God put the wrong on Him who never did anything wrong, so we could be put right with God." Christ took our filthy rags to the cross, so that we might become right with God. Instead of pursuing our own ideas of right and wrong, we need to pursue our relationship with God. Matthew 6:33 says, "But seek first the kingdom of God and His righteousness and all these things shall be added to you." Psalm 23:3 says "He leads me in paths of righteousness for His name's sake." Too often we are like children; we want to see how close we can get to that line of right and wrong before we get "in trouble." To seek God's righteousness does not mean we stay close to the "right-side" of that line and then look back every so often to see where we are in relation to it. In our pursuit of Christ, we let Him become the focus.

We will fail, we are human. Our righteousness is as filthy rags however the God of all creation has made us right through the blood of His Precious Son. "For all have sinned and fall short of the glory of God, and are justified freely by his grace through the redemption that came by Christ Jesus. God presented Him as a sacrifice of atonement, through faith in His blood." (Romans 3: 23-25 NIV) We should not take it for granted. "What shall we say then? Shall we continue in sin that grace may abound? Certainly not! How shall we who died to sin live any longer in it?" (Romans 6:1-2) Instead, we should pursue how He wants us to live for Him.

Our lives are not our own. They are His. You and I should "present (our) bodies a living sacrifice, holy, acceptable to God which is your reasonable service. And do not be conformed to this world, but be transformed by the renewing of your mind, that you may prove what is that good and acceptable and perfect will of God." (Romans 12: 1-2)

Father, thank You for sending Jesus to die in our place. May we never take that gift for granted. Help us to live our lives for Your glory. Amen.

Missed blessing
1 Kings 11:26-14:20

When we think of the evil kings of Israel and Judah, we often think of Ahab and Manasseh. However, in 2 Kings, the following statement was made about eight different kings including Ahab's son: "And he did evil in the sight of the Lord, he did not depart from the sins of Jeroboam the son of Nebat, who made Israel sin." If you don't remember Jeroboam's story, he was one of King Solomon's servants. One day, he met a prophet who prophesied to him about Israel and Judah becoming divided. God said to Jeroboam through the prophet, "Then it shall be, if you heed all that I command you, walk in my ways and do what is right in my sight, to keep My statutes and My commandments, as my servant David did, then I will be with you and build for you an enduring house as I built for David and I will give Israel to you." (1 Kings 11:38) When the division happened, Jeroboam became king of Israel.

David's descendants did not always follow God. However, because of David's own relationship with God, God promised "And your house and your kingdom shall be established forever before you. Your throne shall be established forever." (2 Samuel 7:16)

God was offering to make a similar promise to Jeroboam. However, Jeroboam decided to do what was right in his own eyes. He did not want the people to go to Jerusalem to make their sacrifice to God, so he created idols that were closer. He also allowed anyone to become priests. Because he chose his righteousness over God's, all his family was destroyed. Baasha kills Jeroboam's son, Nadab, and claims the throne. "And it was so, when he became king, that he killed all the house of Jeroboam anyone that breathed until he had destroyed him, according to the word of the Lord which he had spoken by His servant Ahijah the Shilonite because of all the sins of Jeroboam, which he had sinned and by which he had made Israel sin because of his provocation with which he had provoked the Lord God of Israel to anger." (1 Kings 15:29-30) Such a sad story. To be offered an "enduring house" if he kept God's commandments, but failing to recognize what he had been offered. How often do we miss out on what God has for us because we want to do things our own way? We all have reasons that seem right to us for following our own path. But God "leads me in paths of righteousness for His name's sake." (Psalm 23:3) What treasures are waiting for us if we trust and obey?

Father, may we, like David, have a heart for You. May we seek to follow You as You lead us on the paths of righteousness. May we bring glory to Your name. "Do not lead us into temptation but deliver us from the evil one. For Yours is the kingdom and the power and the glory forever." (Matthew 6:13) Amen!

January 7
Draw near to God
James 4

The book of James is one of those books everyone needs to read when they think they have "being a Christian" all figured out. James reminds us of how filthy our righteousness rags are in our own strength. But thank God, He took our filthy rags and replaced them with Jesus' shed blood!

In James 4:7-8, and 10 we read about drawing near to God:
"7 Therefore submit to God. Resist the devil and he will flee from you. 8 Draw near to God and He will draw near to you. 10 Humble yourselves in the sight of the Lord, and He will lift you up."

We do this initially at our conversion, however, it should also become a daily habit. We often refuse to daily submit our schedules and plans to God. He knows our schedules, He knows what we think needs done, but He also knows what He desires to be done that day. There may be someone who needs a kind word, a friendly smile, or simply a prayer. How many opportunities do we have to shine a light into someone's dark world? "Whom shall I send and who will go for Us? Then I said "Here am I, send me." (Isaiah 6:8)

God is not asking all of us to be foreign missionaries. He is not asking each of us to leave our jobs to minister to the poor. But He is asking us to be willing to be His hands and feet each day, a light that shines in someone's dark world. How can we be ready to answer that call? By drawing near to God so He will draw near to us. We can go through our own schedule with renewed eyes and hearts that are opened to God's direction throughout our day. We are human and not perfect. God understands that however, that doesn't mean we give up trying. We continue to draw near and submit to God.

"Resist the devil and he will flee from you." (James 4:7) Satan seems to use a lot of different techniques however one of his proven ones is distraction. If he can distract us from the work God has called us to do, then he doesn't have to worry about his world of darkness.

However, we can't always use the devil to excuse all our actions and thoughts. Sometimes it is just our human nature. But again, if we submit to God, no matter how we are feeling today or what is going on around us, God will draw near to us. The closer we are to God, the more we become aware of His promptings. How do we draw near to God? Spend time with Him. "Humble yourself in the sight of the Lord and He will lift you up." (James 4:10)

Father, I am available to be Your hands and feet today. Amen!

Jesus, Savior of the world
Luke 2

Back before Jesus' birth, the people were waiting for the Messiah, their Savior. Perhaps their expectation was one of a mighty soldier who would single-handedly swoop in and stop their oppression. The words of the prophets had been passed down from generation to generation. Was God ever going to fulfill His promise for a Savior?

Then an angel appeared! To Zacharias, to Mary, to Joseph, to the shepherds. And the angel brought "good tidings of great joy which will be to ALL people." (Luke 2:10) Jesus!

He did not come as the mighty warrior some expected but as a helpless newborn. Throughout the Christmas story we see the verse, "But Mary kept all these things and pondered them in her heart." (Luke 2:19) Simeon even prophesied that "a sword will pierce through your own soul." (Luke 2:35) Did she realize the precious child in her arms, the Savior of the world, would one day face a cross? We look around today at the sorrow, the pain, the sickness, the death, and the evil that surrounds us and wonder "where is the Savior"? Where is our perfect world? Jesus came to die on the cross so that we can again have access to God, so one day we can live in a perfect world called Heaven. Jesus came to die so that this world of sorrow, pain, sickness, death, and evil is ONLY temporary! Jesus came to die so that we do not need to face this world ALONE!

"For God so loved the world that He gave His only begotten Son, that whosoever believes in Him should not perish but have everlasting life. For God did not send His Son into the world to condemn the world, but that the world through Him might be saved." (John 3:16-17)

Have you experienced salvation? Do you live with the knowledge that even though you live in this world, you have a Savior who will never leave you to face it alone? Do you know there is a promised day when our Savior will return as King? A day when He will wipe every tear from our eyes. When there will be no more sorrow, no more pain, no more sickness, no more death. And evil will be defeated!

Father, we can celebrate Christmas every day in our hearts as we experience the abundant life Jesus came and died to give us. Thank You that because of the Savior of the world, we can still experience joy and peace during the troubles of this life. Thank You that we can stand on Your promises that you will never leave us nor forsake us. Thank You that someday we will call Heaven our home and will finally experience that perfect world You designed for us. I love You, Lord and lift Your praise as the Only One worthy to receive all praise. Amen.

January 9
Walk worthy
Colossians 1

How often do we forget where Paul was in the early part of Acts? Saul truly believed that he was doing God's will by destroying the Christ-followers. He believed Jesus was a false prophet. However, as you read through Colossians 1, you see the remarkable transformation that happened in his life. Now, Paul could not say or do enough for the name of Jesus.

Paul could have lived his life recalling his past and his guilt. He could have dwelt on all his sufferings since he had become a minister for Christ. However, Paul focused on Jesus and sharing Him with everyone he could. Paul used his past and his current sufferings as a testimony for Jesus. He decided to follow Jesus even when life would have been easier had he compromised. Paul fully committed his life to Jesus. Paul was not a superhero. He did not have super strength nor super wisdom. He was not invincible when harm came his way. He was a human that was committed to sharing Jesus to the world. That was his calling in life. Paul was not perfect; his own words prove that. But his desire was "that in all things He (Jesus) may have the preeminence." (Colossians 1:18) Merriam-Webster Online Dictionary defines preeminent as "having paramount rank, dignity or importance." Jesus was most important to Paul. His own life, his own sufferings, his own friends, and his own past were not as important to Paul as Jesus was. And that was what he desired for all of us: to know and experience Jesus as he did. That desire motivated his prayer for the Colossians: "that you may be filled with the knowledge of His will in all wisdom and spiritual understanding; that you may walk worthy of the Lord, fully pleasing Him, being fruitful in every good work and increasing in the knowledge of God; strengthened with all might, according to His glorious power, for all patience and longsuffering with joy; giving thanks to the Father who has qualified us to be partakers of the inheritance of the saints in the light." (Colossians 1:9-12) Paul recognized that "He (God) has delivered us from the power of darkness and conveyed us into the kingdom of the Son of His love, in whom we have redemption through His blood, the forgiveness of sins." (Colossians 1:13-14) Paul lived forgiven, and he did not lose sight of that. He knew his past deserved judgment from God. Instead, he found mercy and was considered worthy of sharing Jesus with the world.

Again, Paul was not supernatural. What he was, was a willing vessel to be used by God for his kingdom purposes. Not just when Paul felt like it. Not when it fit into Paul's schedule. Not when it benefited Paul. But in all things!

Dear friend, Paul's prayer for the Colossians is my prayer for me as well as you. May Christ fill our daily lives. Amen!

January 10
Rest and companionship
Genesis 2

Often chapter 2 of Genesis is overlooked. Genesis 1 tells the Creation story, and Genesis 3 tells the story of the Fall. And between is Genesis 2 which just seems to be a recap of Genesis 1. However, two essential concepts are introduced in Genesis 2.

The first is rest. "Then God blessed the seventh day and sanctified it, because in it He rested from all His work which God had created and made." (Genesis 2:3) God rested. And we, who were created in His image, need to rest also. We live in a world where working to gain more prestige, to earn more money, and "to move up the ladder" seem to be the standard. God says to rest. In a society where giving 110% with everything you got seems to be expected, God says to rest. You may think: "Well, God did not rest until His work was finished and I can't see any end to my work." There are seasons of our lives where it seems impossible to rest. However, eventually, our bodies reach the place where they demand rest. If we allow ourselves to find the time to rest, we will be better prepared for the seemingly endless tasks before us. We need to recognize the importance of rest. We need to realize that it is ok to say "no" to that one more thing to add to our to-do list. Ask God to teach you how to rest.

The second concept from Genesis 2 is companionship. We need each other. Even though Adam had all the animals around, it was not enough. He needed another human. Only another human could meet his need for companionship. Even the most introverted people need other humans in their lives. We need people to communicate with and share life. Other people can challenge us to become better humans. They provide a community where we can be a part of something larger than ourselves. Different viewpoints, opinions, experiences help us learn more about the world around us than just from our limited perspective.

When we have the choice, we need to choose our community wisely. We need to seek companions who will lift us up and challenge us to live the life God has for us. When we choose unwisely, we can be pulled off course and follow the crowd instead of God.

If you have a healthy safe community of people around you, be thankful for them. Offer them the support and security that you receive from them. "Therefore encourage one another and build each other up." (1 Thessalonians 5:11 NIV) If you do not, pray God will send those people to you.

Creator God, we thank You! You know what we need and have designed a plan to provide for our lives. Amen!

Sin, the separator
Genesis 3

The Garden of Eden was a true paradise. Adam and Eve were at peace with each other and creation. Most of all, they were able to walk with God physically. Creation was beautiful. All was as it should be! Then sin entered the picture. Because of sin, we, as humans, no longer live peacefully together. We no longer trust each other. We are hard-pressed to find peace and harmony in the world around us. But most of all, we are separated from God. Many spend their whole lives trying to find something to fill that missing piece in our lives. Some call it religion and try to work their way back to God. Some fill it with more "things" - possessions, people, hobbies, habits.

But we can never find anything that fills that hole in our lives until we connect again with God. Because of the shed blood of Jesus who took our sins to the cross and died in our place; we can once again approach the Holy God. In response to sin entering His perfect world, God created a redemption plan. "And I will put enmity between you and the woman, and between your seed and her Seed; He shall bruise your head and you shall bruise His heel." (Genesis 3:15)

There were consequences for Adam and Eve's sin just as there are for us today. But God took upon Himself to make the way to salvation. We can be saved from our sins. Our sins no longer need to separate us from knowing and approaching the throne room of God, our Father, who will welcome us with loving arms. Matthew 11:28-30 says "Come to Me, all you who labor and are heavy laden, and I will give you rest. Take My yoke upon you and learn from Me, for I am gentle and lowly in heart, and you will find rest for your souls. For My yoke is easy and My burden is light." We do not need to live a life separated from Him. He will once again come and walk with us through life.

Even amidst the consequences of our sin, He will be with us. For those who choose to be their own "god," they are missing out on the best relationship of their lives. Our Father God loves us unconditionally. We have an active God who pursues us. We don't need "religion" to try to find our way to God. He is right here waiting for us to accept His precious gift of forgiveness.

Father God, thank You that You love us so much. You made a way of escape from our sins. You sent Your only begotten Son to die on a cross for our sins. We can come and confess, and You will forgive. We can approach Your throne and lay all our concerns at Your feet. For Yours is the kingdom and the power and the glory forever. Amen!

Legacies
Genesis 4-5

In Genesis 5, we get our first genealogy of the Bible, a list of Adam's descendants. We read several verses of "he begot... had sons and daughters, … and then all the days of." Until "Enoch lived sixty-five years, and begot Methuselah. After he begot Methuselah, Enoch walked with God three hundred years, and had sons and daughters. So all the days of Enoch were three hundred and sixty-five years. And Enoch walked with God; and he was not, for God took him." (vs 21-23) Why, of all the names listed, did Enoch get described as walking with God? Hebrews 11:5 says: "By faith, Enoch was taken away so that he did not see death "and was not found, because God had taken him;" for before he was taken he had this testimony, that he pleased God." Wouldn't we all like to leave the legacy "that we pleased God?" I am sure that like me you can think of those who have already reached their heavenly Home. Those who it could be said "they pleased God." People who showed God to those around them. Their legacies encourage me to live my life so that I may please God. "Therefore we also, since we are surrounded by so great a cloud of witnesses, let us lay aside every weight, and the sin which so easily ensnares us, and let us run with endurance the race that is set before us, looking unto Jesus, the author and finisher of our faith, who for the joy that was set before Him endured the cross, despising the shame, and has sat down at the right hand of the throne of God." (Hebrews 12:1-2)

If we go back and look at Genesis 4, we see another kind of legacy. Cain and Abel brought their offerings before the Lord. Cain's was unacceptable. God told Cain "sin lies at the door and its desire is for you, but you should rule over it." (Genesis 4:7) Cain had a decision to make regarding sin. God said that he "should rule over it." However, Cain let his anger lead to the sin of taking his brother's life. Cain and his descendants then had to bear the consequences of that sin. One of Cain's descendants, Lamech also took a man's life and seemed more worried about himself than sorry for the life he had taken. Cain's descendants became productive people in life, but something was missing. We are told that the descendants of Cain's younger brother, Seth, are the first to seek God. "Then men began to call on the name of the Lord." (Genesis 4:26). When we seek God and look unto Jesus, our lives take on a purpose that can be carried down from generation to generation. We can leave the testimony "that we pleased God."

Lord, we thank You for those cloud of witnesses both from Your Word and from our own lives who have left a legacy of seeking You with all their heart. Help us to reflect on how their service to You has changed our lives. May it challenge us to take up the mantel and seek Your will in our own lives. Your kingdom come, Your will be done.

You are loved
Job 38-39

I love the description in Proverbs 8:22-31 of how God created the heavens and the earth from the viewpoint of "wisdom." Often, we read through Genesis 1 too quickly. It is such a familiar passage we almost glance right through it. We no longer stop to marvel "For He spoke, and it was done; He commanded, and it stood fast." (Psalm 33:9)

When was the last time you read through Job 38-39 and marveled at the details of God's handiwork? The Creator God tells "the sea its limit" (Proverbs 8:29), knows when "the deer gives birth" (Job 39:1), and knows when the sparrow falls (Matthew 10:29). He is the same God that knows your name (Isaiah 43:1), knows the number of hairs on your head (Matthew 10:30), knows each tear that falls (Psalm 56:8) and knew us in our mother's womb (Jeremiah 1:5). That same God knows us and loves us!

Oh, that we could grasp how much He loves us. Those lonely days, brokenhearted days, those unloved days when our Abba Father is waiting with outstretched arms to hold us close and whisper "You are loved."

How different our days are when we feel loved and accepted here on this earth. But we all have days when we feel unloved and unlovable. But our Father in Heaven is still whispering "You are loved." You and I are more precious to Him than all His other creation. He sent His only Son to die to make a way that He could be reunited with us. Choose today to accept that Love and live in the freedom that Love brings to your life.

Father, thank You for loving me even on my most unlovable day. Your love is not conditioned on what we do. It is freely given and extravagant. May we share with everyone we meet about Your unconditional love and how that love helps us live an abundant life. Amen.

January 14
Seek wisdom
Proverbs 8-9, Deuteronomy 10:12-22

We spend our lives seeking. Seeking education, the perfect mate, the perfect job, more possessions, and the "ideal" future. Even when we seem to attain what we have sought, we quickly grow dissatisfied and begin seeking again for something more. Sometimes we forget this is our temporary home, that the perfection we are seeking will not be found in this life but in the life to come. In all our seeking, hopeful we remember to seek God. "But seek first the kingdom of God and His righteousness, and all these things shall be added to you." (Matthew 6:33)

God is offering us something more precious than rubies. Proverbs 8:11 says, "For wisdom is better than rubies, and all the things one may desire cannot be compared with her." And has promised "And those who seek me diligently will find me" (Proverbs 8:17)

How do we seek for wisdom? "Ask, and it will be given to you; seek, and you will find; knock, and it will be opened to you. For everyone who asks receives, and he who seeks finds, and to him who knocks it will be opened." (Matthew 7:7-8) Psalm 111:10 says: "The fear of the Lord is the beginning of wisdom; a good understanding have all those who do his commandments. His praise endures forever." Proverbs 9:10 says: "The fear of the Lord is the beginning of wisdom, and the knowledge of the Holy One is understanding."

What is "fear of the Lord"? In the commentary portion for Proverbs 1:7 in the Life Application Bible (NKJV), it states "to fear the Lord - to honor and respect God, to live in awe of His power; and to obey His Word." There are innumerable examples from the Bible, where God tells whoever He is speaking to, not to fear man. The Israelites did not have to fear the Canaanites, David did not need to fear Goliath, the Hebrew boys did not need to fear the fire, Jonah did not need to fear the Ninevites. But we are told to fear God. Fear, but not be afraid of, because He is our good Father. When Christ died on the cross, the veil separating the Holy of Holies was rent into, thereby giving us access to God. I think God expects our awe and reverence. Our respect that we don't lose sight of who He is. Our understanding that He has a plan for our lives and desires for us to follow Him and allow Him to be the Lord of our lives.

Father, we bow in awe of You. The Creator of the universe who cares for and loves us. Who knows us by name. Who pursues us. Who adores us. You tell the oceans and seas where to stop and yet You know my name. I love You, and I lift my hands in praise to You the King of kings and Lord of lords. May I live my life surrendered to you. Amen!

January 15
Longing for Home
Philippians 2-4

Have you ever noticed that we seem to focus on the negative aspects of life? That some of our stronger memories are the painful ones? Life seems to get us down. Our hearts and mind long for our promised peaceful Home. They long to be permanently reunited with their Maker. They want to toss off these imperfect bodies. Our souls long for Home.

We look at the world around us and dwell on all that is wrong with it. Romans 8:21-23 says: "because the creation itself also will be delivered from the bondage of corruption into the glorious liberty of the children of God. For we know that the whole creation groans and labors with birth pangs together until now. Not only that, but we who have the firstfruits of the Spirit, even we ourselves groan within ourselves, eagerly waiting for the adoption, the redemption of our body." We long for Home.

Yet, here we live in our fallen world with its heartaches, pain, sickness, loneliness, death, and sin consequences. It is easy to sit and ponder all that's wrong in our lives. However, Paul wrote to the Philippians: "Finally, brethren, whatever things are true, whatever things are noble, whatever things are just, whatever things are pure, whatever things are lovely, whatever things are of good report, if there is any virtue and if there is anything praiseworthy - meditate on these things." (Philippians 4:8) Colossians 3:2 says: "Set your mind on things above, not on things on the earth." God wants us longing for Home.

While we are here on this earth though, we can meditate on the truth, on what is praiseworthy. We can live this imperfect life also thinking about all the many blessings, promises and hope He has given us. And do the work He has for us. Paul says in Philippians 3:13-14: "Brethren, I do not regard myself as having laid hold of it yet; but one thing I do: forgetting what lies behind and reaching forward to what lies ahead, I press on toward the goal for the prize of the upward call of God in Christ Jesus." (NASB) When life gets us down, and it will, here are some reminders from Philippians to face those times. Hold fast to the Word of life. (2:16) Stand fast in the Lord. (4:1) Look out for the interest of others. (2:4) Rejoice in the Lord always. (4:4) Be anxious for nothing. (4:6) Pray and give thanks. (4:6) Let our requests be known to God. (4:6) And remember: "I can do all things through Christ who strengthens me." (4:13) "And the peace of God which surpasses all understanding, will guard your hearts and minds through Christ Jesus." (4:7) "And my God shall supply all your need according to His riches in glory by Christ Jesus." (4:19)

"Now to our God and Father be glory forever and ever. Amen." (4:20)

January 16
Call to praise
Psalm 46-48; 146-150

"Let everything that has breath praise the Lord." (Psalm 150:6)

Too often, we limit praise time to that hour of worship on Sunday morning. Where we can come together with our church family and praise God. Too often, we offer praise just as a thank you for a blessing or answered prayer. Too often, we praise when we feel like it. However, as you read through Psalms, you realize we have been called to praise period. It is not based on where we are, how we feel, if things are going our way, or who we are with. We are called to praise. "Great is the Lord, and greatly to be praised." (Psalm 48:1) Psalm 47:7 says: "For God is the King of all the earth; sing praises with understanding."

"Sing praise with understanding." Sometimes, I think we lose sight of God in our daily lives. We get busy with our routines and commitments that God is no longer the King of our hearts. When we have struggles or heartache, we are so burdened down in the darkness that it's hard to acknowledge that the God of the universe is still in control. But even amid the battle, we are called to praise. "And when he had consulted with the people, he appointed those who should sing to the Lord, and who should praise the beauty of holiness, as they went out before the army and were saying: "Praise the Lord, for His mercy endures forever." Now when they began to sing and to praise, the Lord set ambushes against the people of Ammon, Moab, and Mount Seir, who had come against Judah; and they were defeated." (2 Chronicles 20:21-22)

Not only are we called to praise. We are called to praise specifically. Read through the Psalms and you see that the praise being offered up often praise God specifically for what He has done, what He is doing, what He is going to do and for who He is. We also are called to praise Him with what we have. We may not have the greatest singing voice or know how to play an instrument. We may be a little shy about raising our hands. But we can still praise, whatever that looks like for each of us individually. When Jesus was coming into Jerusalem for what is called His Triumphal Entry, when ask to silence the crowd, Jesus responded. "I tell you that if these should keep silent, the stones would immediately cry out." (Luke 19:40) If the stones can praise, so can you! Get in on the praising! He is worthy! "Be still, and know that I am God; I will be exalted among the nations, I will be exalted in the earth!" (Psalm 46:10) "Therefore by Him let us continually offer the sacrifice of praise to God, that is, the fruit of our lips, giving thanks to His name." (Hebrews 13:15)

Inspired by "Praise the Lord" by Russ Taff

January 17
On time God
Daniel 3, 6

Some of my favorite Bible stories are found in Daniel: the three Hebrew boys in the fiery furnace and Daniel in the lion's den. God did not save Daniel, Shadrach, Meshach, and Abed-Nego from being thrown in either the lion's den nor the furnace. He saved them once they were inside. Why did they have to experience being thrown in the fire or den? Because God had nations that needed to learn about Him. Daniel and his friends had decided that they would only serve God and that was the exact reason they experienced the den and furnace. Shadrach, Meshach, and Abed-Nego refused to bow to King Nebuchadnezzar. Daniel refused to NOT bow to his God. All went in with the confidence that God would deliver right on time. The Hebrew boys looked at King Nebuchadnezzar and said "If that is the case, our God whom we serve is able to deliver us from the burning fiery furnace, and He will deliver us from your hand, O king" (Daniel 3:17) In Daniel's story, though it is the king himself, King Darius, who states "Your God, whom you serve continually, He will deliver you." (Daniel 6:16) What were the outcomes? The kings praised! "Nebuchadnezzar spoke, saying, "Blessed be the God of Shadrach, Meshach, and Abed-Nego, who sent His Angel and delivered His servants who trusted in Him, and they have frustrated the king's word, and yielded their bodies, that they should not serve or worship any god except their own God! ... because there is no other God who can deliver like this." (Daniel 3:28-29) King Darius states: "I make a decree that in every dominion of my kingdom men must tremble and fear before the God of Daniel. For He is the living God, and steadfast forever; His kingdom is the one which shall not be destroyed, and His dominion shall endure to the end." (Daniel 6:26) Does that amaze anyone else? These powerful kings, who expected people to worship them, end up acknowledging and worshipping God! Why did that happen? God showed up on His timeframe and not man's. We would love God to move in those situations where we want everything fixed now. When Lazarus died, Jesus told his disciples: "Lazarus is dead. And I am glad for your sakes that I was not there, that you may believe." (John 11:14) God has a purpose for His timing. 2 Peter 3:8-9 says "But, beloved, do not forget this one thing, that with the Lord one day is as a thousand years, and a thousand years as one day. The Lord is not slack concerning His promise, as some count slackness, but is longsuffering toward us, not willing that any should perish but that all should come to repentance." *Father God, may we, like Daniel and his friends, hold fast to what we believe. Help us not compromise but be ready instruments for You to display Your glory. Have Your kingdom purpose in our lives that we may see others praising You for the work You are doing in our lives. Amen.*

17

Wait on the Lord
Psalm 27, 100 Isaiah 40

"Rest in the Lord, and wait patiently for Him." (Psalm 37:7)

We are not born with patience. Have you ever watched a newborn wait patiently to be fed? We, as adults, are not much better. We spend our lives anxiously waiting for the next step in our lives. We assume the next life phase will be better. Or perhaps we are just ready to get out of our mundane routine of life. Waiting is not something we like to do. That seems especially true if we are waiting for God to move. Read through the Bible and you can find impatient people. But we also learn of the consequences of their impatience. How many of them tried to do things their way instead of God's only to realize that they really messed it up? Probably the most familiar Bible passage on waiting on the Lord is Isaiah 40:28-31: "Have you not known? Have you not heard? The everlasting God, the Lord, the Creator of the ends of the earth, neither faints nor is weary. His understanding is unsearchable. He gives power to the weak, and to those who have no might He increases strength. Even the youths shall faint and be weary, and the young men shall utterly fall, but those who wait on the Lord shall renew their strength; they shall mount up with wings like eagles, they shall run and not be weary, they shall walk and not faint." With a promise like that, why do we still get impatient? The answer is simple; we want to know the outcome and time frame. Because something deep inside is longing for our perfect life - ultimately, we are impatient to be reunited with God our Maker. What should we do when we get impatient? Seek God. That's one of the benefits of our salvation. Through what Jesus did on the cross and through the presence of the Holy Spirit, our souls can reunite with their Maker. "One thing I have desired of the Lord, that will I seek: that I may dwell in the house of the Lord all the days of my life, to behold the beauty of the Lord, and to inquire in His temple." (Psalm 27:4) We should take advantage of the gift that has been given. "Make a joyful shout to the Lord, all you lands! Serve the Lord with gladness; come before His presence with singing. Know that the Lord, He is God; It is He who has made us, and not we ourselves; we are His people and the sheep of His pasture. Enter into His gates with thanksgiving, and into His courts with praise. Be thankful to Him and bless His name. For the Lord is good; His mercy is everlasting, and His truth endures to all generations. (Psalm 100) We can communicate with God anytime, anywhere about everything! What a gift. When the waiting gets rough, remember "our soul waits for the Lord; He is our help and our shield. For our heart shall rejoice in Him, because we have trusted in His holy name. Let Your mercy, O Lord be upon us, just as we hope in You." (Psalm 33:20-22)

January 19
AM I enough?
Luke 9, 18

Have you had times in your life when you knew God was trying to get your attention, but you continued to ignore Him? Maybe it was because of something He asked you to do for Him, and you didn't want to commit to doing it. Maybe it's a sin that He asked you to finally give up, but you wanted to hold on to it a little longer. Maybe it's an opinion or thought you had about yourself or others that He asked you to set aside so that you would be open to the truth. Do you ever sense Him saying "AM I enough?" AM I enough to provide for your needs? AM I enough for you to feel loved? AM I enough for you to trust and follow me?

The rich young ruler came to Jesus asking, "what shall I do to inherit eternal life?" (Luke 18:18) When Jesus confirmed what he was doing right, he was comfortable with his standing. However, when Jesus confronted the issue that was preventing the ruler from following Him, the ruler didn't like the answer. He chose his riches over Jesus, over eternal life, and walked away. The ruler could not say that Jesus was enough. Jesus says in Luke 14:26 and 33: "26 If anyone comes to Me, and does not hate his father and mother, wife and children, brothers and sisters, yes and his own life also, he cannot be My disciple. 33 So likewise, whoever of you does not forsake all that he has cannot be My disciple." Sounds harsh, doesn't it? But knowing God is love, and God is good, we can read these scriptures in the right context. Jesus was saying that He needs to be above all things. He needs to have our heart's throne. Is the Great I AM enough in your life?

AM I enough when the storm rages? AM I enough when My ways are higher than yours? AM I enough when you walk through the valley of the shadow of death? AM I enough when you lost your way? AM I enough to sustain you? AM I enough? Yes, Lord, You are enough!

Father thank you that You are enough for whatever we are facing right now. You are enough for our past and our future. You are enough to see us safely Home. Amen!

January 20
How quickly we forget
Jonah, Nahum

Do you remember the story of Jonah? Not just the fish part but the before and after? God gave His prophet, Jonah, a job to do. Go and preach to the Ninevites. After God gets his attention in the belly of the fish, he goes. And the message he preaches is: "Yet forty days, and Nineveh shall be overthrown." (Jonah 3:4) The next verse says: "So the people of Nineveh believed God, proclaimed a fast, and put on sackcloth, from the greatest to the least of them." (Jonah 3:5) The people responded to the Word of the Lord and repented. Since they repented, God did not destroy them. Jonah was not happy with this. How could he not rejoice when they repented? Jonah knew how evil the Ninevites were and that they truly deserved God's judgment. He had so quickly forgotten his own second chance at life. He forgot the great lengths that God took to bring him back to where he needed to be. He almost seems to have shared God's Word with Nineveh begrudgingly. It is almost if he did not want them to respond to God. He wanted to see God's judgment instead of His mercy. Mercy he had just again received before arriving in Nineveh. Nineveh also forgot. According to The Life Application Bible, the time frame between Jonah and Nahum is around 100 years and then after Nahum's prophecy, it was only another 50 years before Nineveh was destroyed. So, it took less than 100 years for them to forget God's mercy and be back to the place where God was ready to bring judgment on their wickedness again. How often do we forget? How often do we forget the many times that God proved Himself faithful? How many times do we forget His promises? How many times do we forget to lay it all at His feet? How often do we forget to pray? If we are honest with ourselves, we will admit to allowing our own way of living to sometimes get in the way of seeking God. We become too busy and distracted. How many times in our life has God given us our own "fish" so that we will again focus on where He needs it to be? For those, like the Ninevites, who can say "You should see what God saved me from," how often do we go back to old habits, old places, old emotions? Take time to remember. Take time to remember how God saved you. Take time to remember His faithfulness. Take time to remember how He has moved in your life. Take time to remember how much you are loved! Jonah lost sight of God's mercy. Nineveh lost sight of God's forgiveness. Both lost sight of God's promises. Hold on to God's truth. Remember how much He loves us. Remember He is there waiting to be our refuge and our strength.

Thank You, God! You don't give up on us, even when we lose our way. You love us enough not to leave us where we are but pursue us until we are back in the fold. Amen!

January 21
Praying for the lost
Jonah, Colossians 4

If someone came to your town and began telling people a Word from God, what reaction would you expect? Would you expect everyone to respond to the truth of God's Word? Not the response I would expect. Some to accept, but all to bow? How guilty am I of not praying for ministers and missionaries that their message will change the hearts of unbelievers? The very reason Jesus came to earth was to save the lost. "For the Son of Man has come to seek and to save that which was lost." (Luke 19:10) Do we pray for the ones who cause violence in our towns? Pray that they may hear the Word and repent? Or are we like Jonah and would rather they get justice instead of the opportunity to hear about God's grace and mercy? When was the last time we prayed for our pastor or local and foreign missionaries?

Paul asks the church in Ephesus: "praying always with all prayer and supplication in the Spirit ... - and for me, that utterance may be given to me, that I may open my mouth boldly to make known the mystery of the gospel, for which I am an ambassador in chains; that in it I may speak boldly, as I ought to speak." (Ephesians 6:18-20) He asked the church of Colossae: "meanwhile praying also for us, that God would open to us a door for the word, to speak the mystery of Christ, for which I am also in chains, that I may make it manifest, as I ought to speak." (Colossians 4:3-4)

We need to pray. Often, we pray just for the sick or for the troubles in the lives of our family and friends. When we do pray for the lost, typically it is for our own lost family members. We also need to pray for those who answered the call to share God's Word. And we need to pray for more people to answer that call. Matthew 9:37-38 says: "Then He (Jesus) said to His disciples, "The harvest truly is plentiful, but the laborers are few. Therefore pray the Lord of the harvest to send out labourers into His harvest." But most of all, we need to pray for those who need salvation. We anxiously await Christ's return, and God wants to be reunited with us. However, He desires for all souls to come to Him. "The Lord is not slack concerning His promise, as some count slackness, but is longsuffering toward us, not willing that any should perish but that all should come to repentance." (2 Peter 3:9)

Father God, place the desire in us for "all to come to repentance." That we will never cease praying for the lost in our families, in our sphere of influence and even into the uttermost parts of the world. Guide us to shine the light of Your Truth to all we encounter that we may see more come to the saving knowledge of You. Thank You for saving us and may You find us faithfully serving Your kingdom purpose until Your return. Amen!

January 22
Relying on God
Genesis 6-9

When we think of Noah, we think about the ark and the flood. Perhaps we think more about the "story" than we do the man. Put yourselves in Noah's shoes for a minute. First, he was living in a world full of evil. "Then the Lord saw that the wickedness of man was great in the earth, and that every intent of the thoughts of his heart was only evil continually." (Genesis 6:5) "But Noah found grace in the eyes of the Lord." (Genesis 6:8) Noah was the only one walking with God in a corrupt world. Do you think he ever felt like giving up and joining the crowd? Then he is given an enormous task from God. He is given specific instructions on how to build an ark. Noah took God at His word and did what He asked even though it appeared strange and futile work. The flood did not come immediately after the declaration that there would be one. While Noah and his family waited for the promised flood, they had work to do. They build the ark, and they stored up food. When it was time to enter the ark, they were leaving everything they knew and entering a boat build with their own hands. And then God shut the door. Do you think they wondered if the ark was going to hold? Would there be enough space, enough food, etc.? Do you think they ever thought "are we ever going to get off this boat"? When the rains stopped, and the water receded, can you imagine how anxious they were to get off the ark? Only to have to wait some more before God told them it was finally time. What about the world they were stepping back into? All land life forms were on the ark. They were stepping out into an isolated world. One they were then given the charge to fill. Every step of the journey, Noah and his family had to trust God and do the work that He appointed for them. The tasks they were given were bigger than they were and out of their knowledge base. They had no choice but to rely on God.

Have you ever found yourself in a situation where you had no control? You had no idea what to do? Have you ever had a time where all you had was God? It is times like this where God can use us most. Paul says: "And He said to me, "My grace is sufficient for you, for My strength is made perfect in weakness." Therefore most gladly I will rather boast in my infirmities, that the power of Christ may rest upon me. Therefore I take pleasure in infirmities, in reproaches, in needs, in persecutions, in distresses, for Christ's sake. For when I am weak, then I am strong." (2 Corinthians 12:9-10)

Father, thank You for being Someone I can rely on for every situation in life. There is nothing out of Your control. There is never a time when You don't know what to do. There is never a time when You are surprised. I praise You my faithful Lord for Your care of me! You are completely trustworthy and will equip us for the work You have for us. Amen!

22

January 23
Living expectantly
Matthew 24-25, 1 Thessalonians 5, 2 Peter 3

We live under a promise today. One day, Jesus will return. "For the Lord Himself will descend from heaven with a shout, with the voice of an archangel, and with the trumpet of God. And the dead in Christ will rise first. Then we who are alive and remain shall be caught up together with them in the clouds to meet the Lord in the air. And thus we shall always be with the Lord. Therefore comfort one another with these words." (1 Thessalonians 4:16-18) After Jesus gives the signs to watch for in Matthew 24, He then warns about being ready and what we are to do as we wait. "Where is the promise of His coming? For since the fathers fell asleep, all things continue as they were from the beginning of creation." (2 Peter 3:4) Even in Peter's lifetime, there were those getting impatient for Jesus' return. We need to recognize that no one knows when His coming will be. Even though we have been given the warning signs, we don't know when He will come. Are we living our lives in such a way that, when He does come, He will find us faithfully watching and waiting? And working? In the parable of the talents, we see the master giving each of his servants some talents. Upon his return, they were to give an account of what they did with those talents. Those who used what they received to gain more talents were rewarded. But the one who hid his talent was condemned, and the one talent he did receive was taken away. God wants us to be using what He has given us for His kingdom purposes. In the last section of Matthew 25, the Lord comes to judge. The criteria that He uses to judge is based on how others were treated. "The King will reply, "I tell you the truth, whatever you did for one of the least of these brothers of mine, you did for me." (Matthew 25:40 NIV) How often do we take the time to see how much Jesus loves the person beside us, across the hall from us, in the car in front of us? Too often, we look at how they may have offended us or how wrong they are living their life. But God desires for us to open our eyes to see how everyone we meet needs Jesus. He wants us to shine the light of His love into the darkness of those around us. God wants all to come to repentance. Are we doing our part in sharing that message? *Father, I know I am often guilty of selfishly wanting Your return to be today when there are those in my sphere of influence who still do not know You. Father, may I be Your hands and feet to those around me so that I may hear "Come, you who are blessed by My Father; take your inheritance, the kingdom prepared for you since the creation of the world. For I was hungry and you gave me something to eat, I was thirsty and you gave me something to drink, I was a stranger and you invited me in, I needed clothes and you clothed me, I was sick and you looked after me, I was in prison and you came to visit me." (Matthew 25: 34-36) Amen!*

Acceptable sacrifice
Malachi

Throughout the book of Malachi, when God confronts a sin, the response is "In what way have we despised Your name?" (1:6) "In what way have we defiled You?" (1:7) "In what ways have we robbed You?" (3:8) Do you think that they were asking God because they didn't know? Or was it just a way to try to cover the sin? Do you think that they had grown so complacent with their worship and service of God that they fail to notice when it was no longer acceptable? Do you think it was just a quick decision one day to say "We are in a hurry, just grab a lamb and come on!" "God's not going to notice this one time." However, how quickly, this "one time" may have led to a routine or habit where they were no longer careful or deemed it necessary to bring the acceptable offerings to God. God even said they had gotten to the point of "you have said, 'It is useless to serve God; what profit is it that we have kept His ordinance…?'" (Malachi 3:14) They lost sight of the purpose of the sacrifice. "Has the Lord as great delight in burnt offerings and sacrifices, as in obeying the voice of the Lord? Behold, to obey is better than sacrifice, and to heed than the fat of rams." (1 Samuel 15:22)

God has a plan for how we live our life. All through the Bible, we read of how He desires our worship and service. How He wants us to trust and obey. How often do we get complacent in our worship and service? How often do we make compromises in what we give back to God? If we are honest, we will all acknowledge that there have been times in our lives where we have grown complacent and have compromised. Yes, we are imperfect humans, and we make mistakes. However, if we look back, we can see where we had to deal with the consequences of that complacency or that compromise.

Take a moment with me and let's evaluate the places in our lives where we may have made worship or service routine. Are we just serving out of obligation? Are we just serving for recognition? Let's get back to worshipping and serving with an obedient heart. With a heart that has returned to our first love.

Father, forgive me for the many times I serve and worship out of habit by just going through the motions. Forgive me when I put the sacrifice before the purpose. Open my eyes to see the areas of my life where I have become complacent in my worship of You. Give me an obedient heart "that (I) will present (my) body a living sacrifice, holy, acceptable to God." (Romans 12:1) Amen!

He hears our cries
Psalm 40, 44

In many of the Psalms, David was praising God. However, there was also much crying out. David cried his heart out to God. He shared how he was feeling with the God of the universe. Many times, David asked: "How long, O Lord? Will You forget me forever? How long will You hide Your face from me?" (Psalm 13:1) There are times in our lives, where we too feel like crying "How long, O Lord?". The heartache and pain that we are experiencing seem to have no end in sight. We seem to have one thing after another hit us, often unexpectedly. As much as God wants our praise, He wants our cries also. He wants us to turn to Him when our hearts are broken, when we don't understand, when we can only say, "how much more, Lord?" Often in the Psalms, there would be praising and crying out in the same Psalm. David knew that "You are my help and my deliverer," even while he was crying out "Do not delay, O my God." (Psalm 40:17) By doing both praising and crying, David was giving it ALL to the Lord. He was not just praising God, pretending all was fine in his life. He was praising God despite what was going on in his life. And he learned not to hide his feelings from God. God knows and understands us better than we do ourselves. He knows how we are feeling, and He wants us to be willing to be honest with Him. Do you ever imagine climbing up onto your Father's lap and crying your heart out to Him? Do you ever imagine His loving arms surrounding you and holding you close? Don't hide from God. Share your thoughts, feelings, and emotions with Him. He will hear you and answer. Perhaps it will not be in the way or timeframe you want. But we still can hold fast through His promises. We may still be in a place of "how long" but when we release and trust Him with our thoughts, will, and emotions, He can shine the light of His truth in our situation. And sometimes just knowing we are not alone can bring peace and joy amidst the trial. David didn't get an immediate answer to his cries. He often repeated the same pleads to God. However, he recognized how God was with him through it all. "He also brought me up out of a horrible pit, out of the miry clay, and set my feet upon a rock, and established my steps, He has put a new song in my mouth - Praise to our God; many will see it and fear, and will trust in the Lord." (Psalm 40:2-3) He recognizes how God was there amidst the heartache and pain.

Father, I am so glad You hear our cries even when we can't put voice or words to the ache inside. You know each tear that falls. May we always come to You with both our praise and our cries. And trust You to complete the work You began in us. Amen!

White as snow
Isaiah 1, Psalm 51

One of the verses I remember memorizing as a child is Isaiah 1:18: "Come now and let us reason together," says the Lord, "though your sins are like scarlet, they shall be as white as snow; though they are red like crimson, they shall be as wool." When snow first falls and covers the ground, it is so bright and beautiful. For that brief time before someone walks through it or the snowplow comes and pushes it to the side, the world outside our window looks clean. However, it does not take long before the bright brilliance of the snow turns to slush. If asked to describe our lives, we would probably compare it more to the slush than the freshly fallen snow. But in the verse from Isaiah, God is comparing our repented sins to the freshly fallen snow.

You may be one of those people who met God later in life and have a wonderful testimony of how God saved you. You have a past that Satan likes to keep throwing in your face and reminding you about how bad you had been. You may be a person who was raised in church and never really did anything that "bad." Can I say we are all the same in God's eyes? "For all have sinned and fall short of the glory of God." (Romans 3:23) And when we all repent, "As far as the east is from the west, so far has He removed our transgressions from us." (Psalm 103:12) We all are as white as snow. We are all covered with the same blood and look the same in God's eyes. Maybe you are still living in the ugliness of your sin. You have never yet asked God for forgiveness. May I say, dear friend, you are missing out! God is able to take your filthy life with all its scars and brokenness and make you clean. David says in Psalm 51:10: "Create in me a clean heart, O God, and renew a steadfast spirit within me." He also says: "The sacrifices of God are a broken spirit, a broken and a contrite heart - these, O God, You will not despise." (Psalm 51:17) No matter what ugliness you carry, no matter how evil you have been, God wants you. He loves YOU! He wants you to come to Him just as you are, so He can make you clean.

Father, I pray that if anyone is tired of living in the ugliness of their sin, that they will decide to come to You to receive that clean heart and clean life. Place those around them to shine Your love into their lives. Thank You that You came for "whosoever." "For God so loved the world, that he gave his only begotten Son, that whosoever believeth in him should not perish, but have everlasting life. For God sent not his Son into the world to condemn the world; but that the world through him might be saved." (John 3:16-17 KJV) Thank You for making us white as snow. Amen!

January 27
Hold on to truth not tradition
Galatians 1-4; John 8

The Book of Galatians starts with Paul asking the Galatian Christians to remember the gospel that was first delivered to them. Some Jewish Christians had come and were convincing the Gentiles that they also required to become Jewish to be Christians. Paul reminded them that all that was needed was accepting what Christ did on the cross. He wanted them living in the freedom of Christ instead of being enslaved to traditions. Paul was so worried about the Galatian Christians that he said: "I am afraid for you, lest I have labored for you in vain." (Galatians 4:11) Paul was a faithful Jew and observed Jewish traditions. However, he made sure that those traditions were observed in the right context and did not take the place of God in his life.

We sometimes get hung up with our traditions and forget that it's about God and not us. Don't get me wrong; our traditions are an important part of our lives. But if we start serving the traditions, they can become detrimental to the work God has for us. Sometimes our families or churches become so focused on the traditions that have been passed down from generation to generation, that we miss out on what God is trying to do through us. We get set in our ways and think that everyone should follow our traditions. Paul describes this as being led by the flesh instead of the Spirit. Even Peter got off course with this. Paul had to confront Peter when he returned to the tradition of only eating with Jewish people. Peter had allowed the influence of other Jewish leaders to replace the freedom that God had given him to eat with the Gentiles. And what more, he was leading others astray with the return to that tradition. In John 8, Jesus is speaking with the Jewish leaders who did not believe He was the Son of God. They were holding so tightly to their traditions and their personal beliefs that they didn't even recognize when the God they supposedly serve was in their midst. "Then they asked him, "Where is your father?" "You do not know me or my Father," Jesus replied. "If you knew me, you would know my Father also." (John 8:19 NIV)

My dear brothers and sisters let us hold fast to the truth and not just our traditions. The Pharisees were all about their traditions. They seem to love their traditions more than people. When our tradition gets in the way of our loving others, we need to rethink the purpose of that tradition.

Father, may we always hold fast to Your truth and love others as You commanded us. Help us to lay aside anything that stands in the way of our love for You and others. Amen.

January 28
What are you reaping?
Galatians 5-6

When we accept Jesus into our lives, the Holy Spirit begins to live in us. The more we allow the Holy Spirit to lead us, the more we will be bearing the fruit of the Spirit which is "love, joy, peace, longsuffering, kindness, goodness, faithfulness, gentleness, self-control." (Galatians 5:22-23) Have you ever wondered why it is a singular fruit instead of plural if there are nine traits listed? This fruit is not a list where we can pick and choose. "Lord, I can do the love, joy, and peace but the longsuffering, gentleness, self-control, those are not for me." All these characteristics will be exhibit if we are surrendered to the Spirit. And they are not something we will have to "work" at. These will be the natural consequences of our submitted lives.

If we are choosing to live our life by the flesh, meaning we are doing what we want to do and make decisions on what feels right, we will not be exhibiting these characteristics. We will be missing out on peace amidst the turmoil in our lives. We will not be displaying as much self-control. We will not be as longsuffering, or kind, or good. Paul wrote: "Do not be deceived, God is not mocked; for whatever a man sows, that he will also reap." (Galatians 6:7) When we choose to lean into our own understanding, we may lose our way. We may make choices that hinder our walk with God.

Sometimes when we look at the world around us, we decide that we just want to give up. What's the purpose of trying to live a Godly life? But remember "Let us not grow weary while doing good, for in due season we shall reap if we do not lose heart." (Galatians 6:9) Sometimes it seems like doing good is getting us nowhere. But don't lose faith. It is God working through us, not we ourselves. And He will see us through. "Being confident of this very thing, that He who has begun a good work in you will complete it until the day of Jesus Christ." (Philippians 1:6)

So, what are you sowing in your home, in your church, in your workplace? What about in the world around you? Are you sowing love, joy, peace? Or are you sowing disharmony, anger, and condemnation? You will reap what you sow.

Father, may we see the fruit of the Spirit in our lives, in our families, in our churches. May we carry that fruit into the world who need to know Your love, Your peace, and Your faithfulness. Amen.

January 29
Love is an action
1 Corinthians 13, 1 John 3-4

God loves us so much He demonstrated His love by sending His Son to die for us - the greatest example of Love. How often do we tell people we love them? How well do we demonstrate it? When Jesus was asked about the greatest commandment, His reply was "You shall love the Lord your God with all your heart, with all your soul, with all your mind, and with all your strength. This is the first commandment. And the second, like it, is this "You shall love your neighbor as yourself." (Mark 12:29-31) In Luke 10, Jesus then goes into the parable of the Good Samaritan. In this parable, we anticipate the "religious" people will stop and help the injured man. However, they both looked and "passed by on the other side." (Luke 10:32) How sad! They looked and avoided. Perhaps they thought they were too busy or perhaps they didn't want to get dirty. However, the Samaritan, stopped and helped and went out of his way to take care of the injured man. A Samaritan who the Jews deemed beneath them. How well do you show love? We all can probably name the people in our lives who we think exhibit love well. We also know those who are more reserved with showing love. Love is not just an emotion; it is also an action, a decision. If we rely solely on the emotion of love, we are going to be confused. Because face it, all sorts of things can impact our emotions at any given time on any given day. However, the action of love, although not always easy, is what God calls us to do. "Love is patient and kind; love does not envy or boast; it is not arrogant or rude. It does not insist on its own way; it is not irritable or resentful; it does not rejoice at wrongdoing, but rejoices with the truth. Love bears all things, believes all things, hopes all things, endures all things. Love never ends." (1 Corinthians 13:4-8 ESV) One of the most significant ways we can put love in action is to take our eyes off self and notice what is going on around us. This is an area where I struggle. I can get so busy and caught up in my own life that I lose track of what others are facing or take them for granted. Sometimes I get overwhelmed by all the hurting people around me and pull into my safe "shell." Is anyone else with me? Sometimes all that people want is to be acknowledged, listened to, and valued. They want to know you care. They may just need a listening ear, a hug, or a prayer. Though there may be times where God is asking us to do more. God may want to show them His love through us by our time, our money or our presence. "Let us not love in word or in tongue, but in deed and in truth." (1 John 3:18) *Lord, open our eyes to see those who need to know we love today, but more importantly, that need to know that You love. Father, may we never take Your love for granted. Help us to love more like You! Amen.*

I AM A CHILD OF GOD
John 15, Romans 8

How many of you remember your teenage years? Those years when you were still trying to figure out who you were; while being pressured into becoming what everybody else thought you should be? And typically, if you made one person or one group of people happy, then another group would be there saying you should do things differently. And you were never sure who you were supposed to be pleasing. I remember times I would be walking the halls of my high school and had to remind myself that I am a child of God! When Jesus came into the world, He presented us the opportunity to become children of God. "But as many as received Him (Jesus), to them He gave the right to become children of God, to those who believe in His name: who were born, not of blood, nor of the will of the flesh, nor of the will of man, but of God." (John 1:12) How many times do we still get to the point where we are insecure with who we are? Or we don't like ourselves very much? Or we feel like we have messed up so much that we do not deserve anyone's love? Sometimes we are our own worst enemy. Romans 8:31 says: "What then shall we say to these things? If God is for us, who can be against us?" Sometimes we just need an identity check. Yes, we have days that we have messed up, we have days where we feel worthless, days we ask, "what's my purpose?" However, God reminds us – "You are talking about My child." A child that can be secure in her/his Father's love knowing she/he is adored by the Father. Jesus told his disciples in John 15:9 "abide in My love." One of the definitions from the Merriam-Webster Online Dictionary for the word abide is: "to remain stable or fixed in a state." So, remain fixed in God's love! "For I am persuaded that neither death nor life, nor angels nor principalities nor powers, nor things present nor things to come, nor height nor depth, nor any other created thing, shall be able to separate us from the love of God which is in Christ Jesus our Lord." (Romans 8:38-39) My Father loves me! And it is not based on me and what I do, but it's all about Him.

My friend, hold your head up high, Your Heavenly Father adores you. He is the King of the universe. He doesn't just love you when you live life "perfectly." He doesn't just love you when you get it right and deserve that love. "But God demonstrates His own love toward us, in that while we were still sinners, Christ died for us." (Romans 5:8) We are loved!

God, I am so thankful that I can call You Abba Father! Thankful that I am a joint-heir with Jesus. Thankful that someday I will get to come Home. Thank You for Your unconditional, unfailing love. Amen.

January 31
What a day that will be
1 Thessalonians 4, Revelation 21-22

One of my favorite hymns growing up was "What a day that will be." But the older I get, the more precious that song becomes. The more we experience life with all its heartache and disappointment, the more we desire to be released from this sinful, painful world. How we long for the New Jerusalem! "Then I, John, saw the holy city, New Jerusalem, coming down out of heaven from God, prepared as a bride adorned for her husband. And I heard a loud voice from heaven saying, "Behold, the tabernacle of God is with men, and He will dwell with them, and they shall be His people. God Himself will be with them and be their God. And God will wipe every tear from their eyes; there shall be no more death, nor sorrow, nor crying. There shall be no more pain, for the former things have passed away." (Revelation 21:2-4) I love reflecting on what will be missing there. We long to be with Jesus! We long to be with our loved ones who have gone on! But my friend, do you long for the day when there will be no more pain, no more sickness, no more death, no more war, no more hatred, no more divisions, no more fighting, no more hurting, no more sin? Have you ever sat at the bedside of someone who was going Home? Shortly before my mother-in-law pass, she was brought back to the nursing home from the hospital. As we walked into the room that day and began to visit, she started singing and asking us to sing with her. We couldn't make out the words, but the smile and happiness she exhibited made me think she was hearing the angel choir. She was looking forward to going Home. It reminded me of a song I used to sing with my family. "Oh look what I've traded for a mansion, oh look what I'm leaving behind, oh look who will be there to greet me when I step in God's sweet paradise. I'm leaving behind all my sorrow; I'm leaving behind all my care. I've traded it all for a mansion that Jesus has gone to prepare." ("Look what I'm trading for a mansion"/Paul and Beverly Chitwood) What a promise that we can live in daily! This world is not our permanent home! There will be a day when our tired and weary souls will walk on streets of gold! "What a day that will be when my Jesus I shall see, when I look upon His face, the One who saved me by His grace; when He takes me by the hand and leads me to the Promised Land, what a day, glorious day that will be!" ("What a day that will be"/Jim Hill)

Father, we thank You that one day there will be a reunion day. There will be a day when we lay down the heavy load of this life and put on a glorified body. There will be a day when Heaven will be our Home. What a day that will be when I get to look on Your face! Until that day, Lord, may you find me faithfully loving and serving You. Amen.

February 1
Answer the call or stay in the boat
1 Samuel 3, Matthew 14

When they heard the call: Young Samuel did not recognize God, Moses felt unequipped, Esther was afraid. Too often, we read the Bible stories and picture the characters as superheroes. We don't think of them as flesh and bone, imperfect people such as us. Could it be that we want to put them on a pedestal so that when we receive a call from God, we can say "but I'm just a normal person, there's nothing special about me?" Everyone who stepped out on faith and answered God's call probably felt the same way. Gideon was the least in his family. David was a shepherd. Mary was a young girl. Peter, Andrew, James, and John were fishermen. None felt extraordinary; still, each had to respond to the call. Moses explained to God why he was not the right man for the job. Gideon negotiated to verify that the call was from God. Eli had to tell Samuel God was speaking and to respond: "Speak Lord, for Your servant hears." (1 Samuel 3:9) Isaiah responded first with "Woe is me, for I am undone! Because I am a man of unclean lips." (Isaiah 6:5) Then with "Also I heard the voice of the Lord, saying: "Whom shall I send, and who will go for Us?" then I said, Here am I! Send me." (Isaiah 6:8) They answered the call. When Jesus came walking out on the water to the disciples in the boat, "Peter answered Him and said, "Lord, if it is You, command me to come to You on the water." (Matthew 14:28) And he stepped out of the boat. What about the other disciples? Why didn't they decide to step out? Yes, Peter was the impulsive one who often spoke before he thought. But they only watched as Peter experienced. Were they just waiting to see what happened to Peter before they decided to step out? No matter what our calls may look like from God, whether "big" or "little," we have the choice of how we will respond. We may have the insecurities of so many of our forefathers. We may want to double or triple check that it really is a call from God. We may decide we want to wait for a more convenient time. In whatever situation, we need to remember "Because He who is in you is greater than he who is in the world." (1 John 4:4) What made our Bible "heroes" memorable was their willingness to answer the call. For some it took a little longer, for some they gained more courage as they watched God move. There were mistakes made along the way. There were times when eyes were taken off God. But God accomplished the work He had planned and used the people He called. When God calls, will you stay in the boat or will you be able to say: "Spirit lead me where my trust is without borders. Let me walk upon the waters wherever You would call me. Take me deeper than my feet could ever wander and my faith will be made stronger in the presence of my Savior?" ("Oceans"/Hillsong United) *God, we need to remember that You are God and if You have called us, You will equip us.*

February 2

Joy to the world
Luke 2

"Then the angel said to them, "Do not be afraid, for behold, I bring you
good tidings of great joy which will be to all people." (Luke 2:10)

Have you put away all your Christmas decorations yet? Too often we put
the Christmas story away with all the lights, garland, and Nativity set. Then
don't pick it up again until next December except maybe at Easter when we
tell the beginning of the story before we tell the end. Every year, there are
debates on when it is an acceptable time to begin listening to Christmas music.
However, there are many Christmas carols that I believe we should be singing
all year long. "O, come let us adore Him." "O come Emmanuel" "Silent
Night" "Joy to the World" Unlike the rest of the Christmas music, these songs
have meaning for us all the time. God did not send His Son so that we
would celebrate it during one season of the year. The "Christmas spirit" of
hope, peace, love, and joy should be felt and shared all year long. But
sometimes we seem to lose sight of that as we go back to our mundane
routine lives. At Christmas, it almost seems like the whole world stops to
hope for peace and love and joy. Some will even acknowledge that it's because
we are celebrating Jesus' birth. And even make that one of the few times that
year they enter the church doors. However, as God's children, we should
have the "Christmas spirit" daily. Merriam-Webster Online Dictionary defines
joy as "the emotion evoked by well-being, success, or good fortune or by
the prospect of possessing what one desires." When you think of how joy
is mentioned in the Bible, you may think of verses such as: "Weeping may
endure for a night, but joy comes in the morning." (Psalm 30:5) "Do not
sorrow, for the joy of the Lord is your strength." (Nehemiah 8:10) "Restore
to me the joy of Your salvation." (Psalm 51:12) However, it is also included
in the fruit of the Spirit. We may experience joy when we are enjoying
"well-being, success or good fortune." Often that depends on what is
currently going on in our lives. But because God sent His Son to be born
in a manager, we always have "the prospect of possessing what we desire."
Even though externally we may not be experiencing "joy" in this moment of
life; we can still have the joy that one day we will possess our Heavenly Home.
We will be able to worship at the throne of God Himself. "Joy to the World
the Lord has come, let earth receive her King, let every heart prepare Him
room and heaven and nature sing." ("Joy to the world"/Isaac Watts)
*Lord Jesus, thank You for coming to earth as a babe to bring hope, love,
peace, and joy into the world. I pray that we never take that gift for granted
and that we help spread the "Christmas spirit" all year long.*

February 3
Sing a new song
Psalm 33, 96

Music has always been an important part of my worship time with God. I am amazed how people can poetically write and sing words that so deeply touch my soul. They use what God has taught them or has done in their lives to share with millions who need to hear that truth and encouragement. Even in our Bible reading, we often turn to the Psalms when we need encouragement. However, we each have our own heart song. We may not sing or play an instrument, but we each have a unique "song" to share with the world. We each have our own life experiences with God. And every so often, I believe we need to let Him hear it. Sometimes we need to sit quietly and talk to God about what He has done in our lives. We can look at both the mountaintops and the lowest valleys. Recognize what He has brought us through, how He has been faithful and true. How He has been patient and kind. How He has never left us (even when we thought He had). It does not need to be just a praise song though. We can also "sing" of our hurts, frustration, or even our anger. God knows our hearts. Sometimes we need to be willing to sit down with Him and examine the deepest parts of our hearts. There are also times when we may need to share our song with others. People need encouragement. People need to know that they are not alone in how they feel. People need to know that God is still active in our daily lives. They need to know we can still worship God amidst our darkest days. David encourages us to: "Oh, sing to the Lord a new song! Sing to the Lord, all the earth. Sing to the Lord, bless His name; proclaim the good news of His salvation from day to day. Declare His glory among the nations, His wonders among all peoples. For the Lord is great and greatly to be praised; He is to be feared above all gods. For all the gods of the people are idols, but the Lord made the heavens. Honor and majesty are before Him; strength and beauty are in His sanctuary. Give to the Lord, O families of the peoples, give to the Lord glory and strength. Give to the Lord the glory due His name; bring an offering, and come into His courts. Oh worship the Lord in the beauty of holiness! Tremble before Him, all the earth. Say among the nations, "The Lord reigns; the world also is firmly established, it shall not be moved; He shall judge the peoples righteously." Let the heavens rejoice, and let the earth be glad; let the sea roar, and all its fullness; let the field be joyful, and all that is in it. Then all the trees of the woods will rejoice before the Lord. For He is coming, for He is coming to judge the earth. He shall judge the world with righteousness, and the people with His truth." (Psalm 96) *Father, I raise my heart song to You. A song full of hope that You give even when the world seems to be falling apart. You are an awesome God! Holy is Your name in all the earth. Thank You for always being there. Thank You for being my Father and my Friend.*

February 4
Truth shall set you free
John 8, 10

"Then Jesus said to those Jews who believed Him, "If you abide in My word, you are My disciples indeed. And you shall know the truth, and the truth shall make you free." (John 8:31)

We have been taught early in our Christian walk that Satan is the father of lies. We are also warned, "your adversary the devil walks about like a roaring lion, seeking whom he may devour." (1 Peter 5:8) However, we still fall so easily into his traps. There needs to be a daily effort on our part to hold on to Truth. We all have that little voice in our head that tells us we don't measure up and that we are worthless; feeding us false information about ourselves and others. We could also be misled by the voice of a friend or something in the media. We are surrounded by lies every day. To be able to combat the lies, we need to have a firm grasp on the Truth. Time with God is so important. We need to be reading His Word and listening to Him daily. Because if we do not have a firm grasp of the Truth, we are so easily led away. That's why Jesus calls us sheep. We need to know the voice of our Shepherd. The Good Shepherd "calls His own sheep by name and leads them out and when He brings out His own sheep, He goes before them, and the sheep follow Him, for they know His voice." (John 10:3-4) There were many times when I had thoughts that kept running through my head. I had to consciously recognize them as lies and counter them with the truth. However, there are also times that I allowed those thoughts and emotions to cause me to become upset and angry. I believed the lies. Satan always seems to know when we are most vulnerable. When we are tired, sick, sad, anxious, or feeling alone; that's when he loves to attack. I often pray "Lord, open my eyes to see the truth" or help me "hear the voice of truth." Lies can look so much like the truth sometimes. Our emotions or even previous experiences may make the lie seem true. Peter reminds us to "be vigilant." (1 Peter 5:8) James tells us "Therefore submit to God. Resist the devil and he will flee from you." (James 4:7) My friend, don't let your guard down because when you least expect it, you will realize that you are following a path based on lies and not on the truth of God's Word. Daily communication with God is essential to being able to distinguish the lies from the truth. Let us pray for one another that we will be able to withstand the lies of the evil one. Pray for yourself that "Out of all the voices calling out to me, I will choose to listen and believe the voice of truth" ("Voice of Truth"/Casting Crowns). *Father, in a world where everyone wants whatever they believe to be the truth, remind us that You are "the Way, the Truth, and the Life." (John 14:6) Help us to examine everything through the lens of Your Truth. May Your Voice be the one we heed.*

February 5
When we don't get our way
Matthew 21 and 27

It has always kind of amazed me how quickly the Jerusalem crowd went from "Hosanna to the Son of David! Blessed is He who comes in the name of the Lord! Hosanna in the highest!" (Matthew 21:9) to "Let Him be crucified!" (Matthew 27:22) Why did they change their cry so quickly? One of the reasons, I believe, is that Jesus was not following their plan. As they were cheering Him into Jerusalem, I think they believed they were cheering on their conquering Redeemer who would save them from the Romans. However, Jesus came with a much bigger plan. He came to redeem all people not just the Jerusalem crowd. He came to free us all from the guilt of our sin and shame. But because the crowd could not see their Redeemer for the Conqueror He was, they walked away from Him. When Pilate asked the crowd which prisoner they wanted to be released, "the chief priests and elders persuaded the multitudes that they should ask for Barabbas and destroy Jesus." (Matthew 27:20) Pilate asked "Why, what evil has He done? But they cried out all the more, saying "Let Him be crucified!" (Matthew 27:23) They did not seem to know or need a reason. Perhaps they were angry that Jesus did not free them; He did not live up to their expectations. They seem to have forgotten about the miracles He performed; the love and compassion He had shown everyone. Even Peter seems to get a little confused. He was a witness to all that Jesus had done. Peter had even acknowledged Jesus as the Son of God. However, as Jesus was facing the crowd and the accusers, Peter was denying. Can we identify with the crowd or Peter? Are there times in our lives when our planned script does not happen the way we want? When God did not move the way we thought He should? Do we forget "For as the Heavens are higher than the earth, so are My ways higher than your ways, and My thoughts than your thoughts."? (Isaiah 55:9) When that happens, do we turn as quickly as the crowd did from praising God to grumbling and complaining against Him instead? How we would all like to understand what happens in our lives. How we all would like a life of ease and contentment. But if here on earth, we lived the ideal life where everything always went our way, we would not long for our true Home. The life we are living now is not our perfect life; that is what awaits us on the other side. My friend, don't lose hope when things don't go your way. Your Heavenly Father is preparing a perfect place where we will no longer need to be rescued from the oppression in this life. But while we are here, Jesus is with us. He will sustain us in this life as we wait for our Heavenly Home. *Father, often there are times in this life where we just don't understand. But You are there with us through it all. Thank You for guiding and providing during those times of uncertainty. Thank You for loving us even when we, like the crowd, grow angry. Thank You for Your patience.*

February 6
Don't worry
Psalm 139, Luke 12

Worry seems to be one of our favorite pastimes. Do you know anyone that can't wait to find out how the story ends before they even finish the book or movie? Often, we want to know the outcome of our current situation. Will it eventually get better? Will we have enough? Enough time, money, wisdom? What does the next chapter of our lives look like? We envision a million different outcomes. We think "I will say this if this person says that." We plan "this is how we make the money last." Sometimes we get caught up in our envisioned future that we miss out on the present. Jesus tells His disciples: "And do not seek what you should eat or what you should drink, nor have an anxious mind." (Luke 12:29) Don't have an anxious mind? Some of us live in that anxious state. Why? Control. We desire to have more control over our lives than we do. We would love to just be able to live life in our "perfect" way. Our kids will be "angels." We can buy whatever we want. Everyone will stay healthy. Everyone will love us. However, when we open our eyes, we see that is just not the world we live in. There is too much out of our control. And since we can't control, we worry. What has worry accomplished in your life? If you are honest, you will admit "nothing." Our worry does not change our circumstance, but it does change us. By worrying we are taking our eyes off the One who is in control. We keep our eyes on the situation and not on our Savior. If we are not careful, we can begin "worshipping" the problem and not the Provider. God is our Father. He is All-Knowing, All-Present, All-Powerful. And He is faithful! "Therefore humble yourselves under the mighty hand of God, that He may exalt you in due time, casting all your care upon Him, for He cares for you." (1 Peter 5:6-7) Prayer is the key. We need to take everything that worries us and lay it all at His capable feet. Allow Him to fill our worried hearts with His peace. Jesus says: "And which of you by worrying can add one cubit to his stature? If you then are not able to do the least, why are you anxious for the rest?" (Luke 12:25-26) We need to recognize and release our anxious thoughts. We need to acknowledge that we have no control over certain things anyway. We can give them to our Father who is faithful to meet all our needs. Releasing our worry is not easy, especially the more responsibility we have. It is hard not to worry about our children, our finances, and our future. But if we keep reminding ourselves of God's promises, we will be able to release the worry a little more easily. If you have things that you specifically worry about all the time, ask God to give you a verse to use to help you overcome the worry.

God, we still try to take control of situations instead of trusting You with everything in our lives. May we learn to trust You a little more each day. Amen!

Do your part
Nehemiah 1-7, Romans 12

When Nehemiah learned about the destruction of Jerusalem, God laid a burden on his heart to see it rebuilt. First, Nehemiah prayed. Not just a five minute, "bless this project" prayer but a "many days fasting and praying before the Lord" prayer. He also developed a plan. Nehemiah trusted God to move the heart of the king. He trusted God to provide. He trusted God to protect. However, he entrusted the actual work to the people.

Nehemiah came to Jerusalem with the vision, the supplies, and the motivation. He was passionate about the calling from God to see the wall rebuilt. But it took the people working side by side to accomplish this huge job. It took them watching and working. It took their dedication to see the job done. They came with a common goal. They each had to do their part. Most worked on the wall where they lived.

We need all kinds of "workers" to build a successful community/church. There seems to be a lot of recognition for those with "visible" jobs. However, we also need the prayer warriors, those who check up on others, those who prepare the meals, those who make the repairs, and those who clean. We all must do our part to have any success.

Paul reminded the Romans: "so we, being many, are one body in Christ, and individually members of one another." (Romans 12:5) He then goes into gifts: prophecy, ministering, teaching, exhortation, giving, leading, and showing mercy. (Romans 12:6-8) Different jobs need to be done and all are important. Paul uses how the physical body works in 1 Corinthians 12 to show us how valuable all our "jobs" are to the kingdom.

Each of us has a kingdom job to do. We offer all sorts of reasons why we can't do our part. We are tired. We have been working for a long time. We are inexperienced. We don't know what we are doing. We don't know where to start. We have failed too many times. No one appreciates my "job." As you see, the list is endless.

Jesus says in John 9:4 (ESV): "We must work the works of Him who sent Me while it is day; night is coming, when no one can work." God is not going to ask you to do something He will not equip you to do. He won't leave you on your own. He just needs your willing hands and feet. Seek Him and listen. Is there a thought that pops in your head every so often about something you see that needs done in your community? If you are the one noticing something, you may be the one God would like to help address it. Don't let the "workers" in your community/church be the only ones who receive the blessings from their labor. Join your brothers and sisters in service for our King.

February 8
Good, good Father?
Psalm 37

If we are honest with ourselves and God, there are times we do not "feel" the truth of God's Word. We may feel forsaken, so find it hard to believe: "I will never leave you nor forsake you." (Deuteronomy 31:6) We may feel unloved, so can't accept "But You, O Lord, are a compassionate and gracious God, slow to anger, abounding in love and faithfulness." (Psalm 86:15 NIV) We may feel God doesn't care, so refuse to "cast all your care upon Him, for He cares for you." (1 Peter 5:7) There may be many reasons why we may not be "feeling" the truth of God's Word. Are we, like the children of Israel, in the wilderness based on a decision we made? Are we, like David, in a tough situation because of the decision of others? Are we, like Mary and Martha when they lost Lazarus, in a place that God needs us to be, so He can show up and say "Arise."? None of those places may feel good. God never promised an easy life. Just read through the Bible. You will recognize that even those who were doing what God wanted did not have it easy. Can you imagine being Ezekiel when God asked him to lie on his left side for 390 days and then on his right for another 40 to bear the iniquity of Israel and Judah? (Ezekiel 4:4-6)

When we take our eyes off God, we, like Peter, start to sink. When we look at our lives through the natural eyes, it is easy to think "how is God good when all this is going on in my life?" However, we need to remember to look through spiritual eyes, where we can see the Master of the winds and the sea amid our storms. When we lose hope through the natural eyes, we can look through the spiritual ones to know God is still on the throne. He is still with us. In the wilderness, He still provided. In David's situation, He still protected. In Mary and Martha's situation, He still promised. Not the way any of them wanted, but the way that would bring Him glory. We are not living our lives for our own purposes but for His. He wants to bring glory to His name through our lives. "Everyone who is called by My name, whom I have created for My glory; I have formed him, yes, I have made him." (Isaiah 43:7) "Therefore, whether you eat or drink, or whatever you do, do all to the glory of God." (1 Corinthians 10:31)

Lord, even when we don't "feel" like You love us, You have a plan for our lives. Even when it seems our world is falling apart, You are still working. Father, our current situation doesn't affect who You are eternally. We may not be able to see or understand how our current situation is being used for Your glory. But we will trust in You and recognize that You ARE our good, good Father no matter what the circumstance. Amen.

February 9
March around the walls
Joshua 6

Joshua inherits the responsibility of leading the Israelites to the Promised Land. They have already been on this journey for 40 years overcoming many obstacles along the way. Now, Joshua must face one of the largest obstacles, the impenetrable city of Jericho. Can you imagine Joshua standing across the Jordan and looking into the distance toward Jericho and thinking "how are we going to get past that?" Even though he was leading a multitude, he was not leading a military army. He thought that they did not have the weapons needed to conquer the city. However, God had equipped them with the weapons they did need: their feet, their voices, and trumpets. Doesn't seem much like a battle plan, does it? However, God gives this battle plan to Joshua who probably does not know exactly what the final victory will look like. Joshua does obey and leads the Israelites into obedience as well. Can you place yourself there marching quietly around the wall? Walk around the wall and then go back to camp. Next day, walk around the wall and go back to camp. You get the picture. I imagine there were those who grew impatient for the victory, they wanted to continue moving on their journey. There were probably those who thought the plan would never work. There were those who were probably fearful. But still they marched in obedience to God. They may not have known what the outcome would look like, but they obeyed. They may have had doubts and were afraid, but they obeyed. What walls are in your way? God has a plan. God has a timeframe. (It may not be just seven days. Remember this had already been a 40-year journey for the Israelites.) And He will equip you with your weapons. We often quote Joshua 1:9: "Have I not commanded you? Be strong and of good courage: do not be afraid, nor be dismayed, for the Lord your God is with you wherever you go." What an awesome promise! However, I think we also need to remember verse 8: "This Book of the Law shall not depart from your mouth, but you shall meditate in it day and night, that you may observe to do according to all that is written in it. For then you will make your way prosperous, and then you will have good success." When we try to follow our own battle plan, the result is often just more confusion and unsuccessful attempts. But if God can use feet, trumpets, and voices to level Jericho's walls, He can use what little you feel you have to offer. So, my friend, begin "marching around your walls" whatever that looks like for you. Meditate on God's Word and listen to God's plan and watch your walls come tumbling down.

Father, as we face the Jericho in our lives, lead us to victory for Your name's sake. Help us to recognize the "weapons" you have given us. Help us to remember to meditate on Your Word. And may we acknowledge: "for the battle is not (ours), but God's." (2 Chronicles 20:15) Amen!

February 10
God loves us all
Acts 10-11

As the Israelites are preparing for Jericho, a man suddenly appeared before Joshua. Joshua wants to know: "Are you for us or for our enemies?" The response is "Neither, ... but as commander of the army of the Lord I have now come." (Joshua 5:13-14 NIV) If I were Joshua, I would be hoping to hear that the man was for us. Do you wonder why he said "neither?" Sometimes in the disagreements in our lives, we want to be so "right" that we forget that the other person is also loved by God. Division plays such a huge, unfortunate role in our world today. But we should remember, even if we don't agree, that we are still called to "love one another." (John 13:33) We should not look on "them" as less than we are. While Jesus was on the earth, He loved everyone: women, Samaritans, the diseased, the rich, and the religious. In Acts 10, Peter had a lesson to learn about this. God sends Peter a vision telling him he can now eat of the previously forbidden foods. Immediately, Cornelius' men show up. God sends Peter back with them where he leads Cornelius and his entire household to God. Sounds great but why is this so significant? My friend, because of Cornelius' conversion, you and I are also partakers of God's kingdom. Cornelius and those with him were the first Gentiles to receive the Holy Spirit. (Acts 10:44) Before this, Jews felt they had the only connection to God. Now, God is opening it up to all people. Are we like the Jewish people walking through life thinking because we are Christians we are better than anyone else? Do we shun people that don't "measure" up? Those who don't live the "perfect" Christian life?

My friend, let us all remember: "for by grace you have been saved through faith, and that not of yourselves; it is the gift of God, not of works, lest anyone should boast." (Ephesians 2:8-9) God may be doing a work in the other person's life. We may be in their path to plant or water, so God can give the increase. (1 Corinthians 3:8)

Thank God, He loves us all unconditionally. I am sure there are areas in all our lives that others view as "not measuring up." We need to remember as we interact with others that God only sees two types of people: those covered by the blood and those who still need to be. And He loves us all. "There is neither Jew nor Greek, there is neither slave nor free, there is neither male nor female; for you are all one in Christ Jesus. And if you are Christ's, then you are Abraham's seed, and heirs according to the promise." (Galatians 3:28-29) *Lord, open our eyes to see everyone as You see them. Even though we may disagree with someone, help us to see how precious they are in Your sight. Help us to love like You. Amen!*

41

Fighting our battles Part 1
Judges 7, 2 Chronicles 20

There are seasons in our lives, (sometimes long seasons), when we feel like we are in a daily battle with self, with others, or with circumstances. We dread getting up in the morning because we know we are heading into the same old war zones. We may feel like we are losing. But my friend, at times like this, remember the ultimate war has already been won. I like reading through the "battle scenes" of the Old Testament. Some battles were won in the most unique ways. Joshua's army marched around a wall. God decreased Gideon's army and then sent him into battle with torches, trumpets, and pots. David went up against Goliath with just a sling and a stone. Sometimes the army itself would just stand and watch God move. "And when he had consulted with the people, he appointed those who should sing to the Lord, and who should praise the beauty of holiness, as they went out before the army and were saying: "Praise the Lord, for His mercy endures forever." Now when they began to sing and to praise, the Lord set ambushes against the people of Ammon, Moab, and Mount Seir, who had come against Judah; and they were defeated." (2 Chronicles 20:21-22) "And when the servant of the man of God (Elisha) arose early and went out, there was an army, surrounding the city with horses and chariots. And his servant said to him, "Alas, my master! What shall we do?" So he answered, "Do not fear, for those who are with us are more than those who are with them." And Elisha prayed, and said, "Lord, I pray, open his eyes that he may see." Then the Lord opened the eyes of the young man, and he saw. And behold, the mountain was full of horses and chariots of fire all around Elisha." (2 Kings 6:15-17) Don't we wish that all our battles could be fought from the sidelines? However, where we should be fighting the battle is on our knees. On our own, we are never equipped for what life throws at us. But "nothing is impossible with God." (Luke 1:37 NIV) "For Your Father knows what you need before you ask Him." (Matthew 6:8 NIV) Seek Him, my friend, in all the "battles" of your life whether big or small. Then trust and obey. "Some trust in chariots, and some in horses, but we trust in the name of the Lord our God." (Psalm 20:7 NIV) "He who is in you is greater than he who is in the world." (1 John 4:4) Hold on to His promises even in your toughest battles. Allow God to fight for you.

Lord, You know that we get tired from our battles. You know that we grow discouraged when we lose some ground. You know we get scared. You know we lose sight of what we are fighting for. But through it all, help us to remember that "those who are with us are more than those who are with them." Lord, You are with us every step of the way. Thank You for not deserting us in our time of need. Amen!

February 12
Fighting our battles Part 2
Ephesians 6

"For our struggle is not against flesh and blood, but against the rulers, against the authorities, against the powers of this dark world and against the spiritual forces of evil in the heavenly realms. Therefore put on the full armor of God, so that when the day of evil comes, you may be able to stand your ground, and after you have done everything, to stand. Stand firm then." (Ephesians 6:12-14 NIV)

Most of our battles are fought on the spiritual realm. And these are battles that are not to be taken lightly. "The thief does not come except to steal, and to kill, and to destroy." (John 10:10) Often, he takes us unaware and unprepared, we may not even realize we are in a battle. We find our weapons for battle in Ephesians 6: "Having gird your waist with truth, having put on the breastplate of righteousness, and having shod your feet with the preparation of the gospel of peace; above all, taking the shield of faith with which you will be able to quench all the fiery darts of the wicked one, and take the helmet of salvation, and the sword of the Spirit, which is the word of God." (14-17) We often stop here, however verse 18 may be the most important piece of our armor: "praying always with all prayer and supplication in the Spirit." We have assurance of the outcome of this spiritual war, Jesus has already won. However, here on earth, before he is bound and throw into the bottomless pit (Revelation 3:2-3), he "walks about like a roaring lion, seeking whom he may devour." (1 Peter 5:8) Sometimes we take that verse too lightly. He has come to DEVOUR. He takes the battle more seriously than we do. Yes, we are confident of the ultimate victory, but while we still live on this earth, we need to "be vigilant." (1 Peter 5:8) In "The Daniel Prayer", Anne Graham Lotz quotes Oswald Chambers: "prayer is not preparation for the battle, it is the battle." How's your prayer life? Most of us will probably admit that it is not what it should be. However, we need to be like the disciples when they ask Jesus to "teach us to pray." (Luke 11:1) To be able to resist the devil, we need to be submitted to God. (James 4:7) That involves time with God. My friend, especially as we see the day of the Lord approaching, we need to be diligent in our prayer life. "Look up and lift up your heads, because your redemption draws near." (Luke 21:28) But until that day comes, pray without ceasing. (1 Thessalonians 5:17) Commit to prayer. Specifically ask God to grow your prayer life - to teach you to pray. Prayer is your best offensive and defensive weapon. You need to know how to use it! "Ask, and it will be given to you; seek, and you will find; knock, and it will be opened to you." (Matthew 7:7)

Father God, teach us to pray: prayers that are effective against the evil one and prayers that move Heaven. May we boldly approach Your throne and seek Your face. For thine is the kingdom, the power, and glory forever. Amen!

February 13
He knows my name
Isaiah 43, 62

For me, one of the most touching scenes from the Bible is when the newly Risen Savior reveals Himself to Mary in the garden. Mary does not recognize Him in His glorified body; she thinks He is the gardener and even asks where He took Jesus' body. When He first speaks to her, she still does not know who He is. However, when He calls her name, she recognizes her Lord. (John 20:14-16) Throughout life, we have many "names." There are our given names but we also have nicknames, roles in life such as mommy or daddy, and perhaps, even our occupation creates a new name for us. Our names have been called out in many different tones: out of love or anger. They have been called out by different people and we respond differently depending on the tone and who is doing the calling. If you are a parent, do you remember the feeling when your child first said dada or mama? You felt like you were the most important person in the world. Names seem to be important to God too. In the Bible, people's given names were very significant. God also changed people's names when He had a new role for them. Abram (father is exalted) became Abraham (father of a multitude) when God made His covenant promise with him. Jacob's name means "he grasps the heel" or "he cheats, supplants." (Holman Bible Dictionary) God changes his name to Israel: "for you have struggled with God and with men, and have prevailed." (Genesis 32:28) Remember your conversion, when you became known by a new name: Christian or Christ-follower. "Thus says the Lord, who created you, O Jacob, and He who formed you, O Israel; "fear not, for I have redeemed you; I have called you by your name; you are Mine." (Isaiah 43:1) Does that still bring a thrill to your heart? To know that God knows your name and you are His? In whatever circumstance in life, our loving Heavenly Father calls our name out in love. He tenderly calls our name when we are hurting. He cheers our name to victory. He speaks our name in discipline. But no matter when it is called, it is always in love. When we accept Christ in our hearts, some of our new names are redeemed and holy. "And they shall call them The Holy People, The Redeemed of the Lord; and you shall be called Sought Out, A City Not Forsaken." (Isaiah 62:12) We receive an everlasting name: "I will give them an everlasting name which will not be cut off." (Isaiah 56:5) Do we even recognize and walk according to our "new" names? As excited as I get when I think about those new names, I still want to hear my Father tenderly calling my name. In those times when it is just He and I. When I take the time to listen to Him, and He just wants to tell me how much I am loved. My friend, take some time today to go to your Father and allow Him to whisper your name. *Father, Thank You that I am Yours. Amen.*

February 14
He will quiet you with His love
Zephaniah

Don't you just love it when you seem to find a "new" scripture? Zephaniah is about the great Day of the Lord and the destruction that will occur. Part of me gets a little excited when I read about how evil will be destroyed one day. However, in chapter 3, there is a verse that makes me sad. This verse was written about Jerusalem, but I think there are times it may apply to us as well. "She has not obeyed His voice, She has not received correction; She has not trusted in the Lord, She has not drawn near to her God." (3:2) Toward the end of chapter 3 is a different type of verse: "The Lord your God is with you, He is mighty to save, He will take great delight in you, He will quiet you with His love, He will rejoice over you with singing." (3:17) This verse is for the remnant in Jerusalem that had remained faithful to God. See the difference. Which verse would you rather be spoken about you? "He will take great delight in you" Wow! Think about the Creator of the Universe, who hung the stars in place and sees the seemingly endless galaxies and all the wonders of His creation. That same Creator looks at me with great delight. Of all the countless beauties He has created, He still looks at me with delight. Can you imagine Him pointing us out to His angels - "that one is Mine!"? "He will rejoice over you with singing." We sing of our great love of God. But can you imagine Him singing of His love for us? He rejoices over us. To be honest, I can't get my head around that. Am I worth rejoicing about? God thinks so! How does that change your outlook today? God is rejoicing over you. And then this part of the verse: "He will quiet you with His love." My friend, do you need to hear that as much as I do? When everything is chaos around us, and everything seems to be falling apart, He quiets us with His love. When I picture this verse, I imagine a newborn baby who is upset when in a stranger's arms. However, when placed in a parent's arms, calms down immediately. That infant knows he/she is safe, loved, and at home. My Heavenly Father can quiet me the same way. I do not have to allow the chaos of this world, or the chaos of my mind to have control. I can lie quietly in the loving arms of my Father. My friend, do you need to be quieted today? Allow Your Father to love on you. Lay down all the reasons for not turning to God in your times of trouble and just run with outstretched arms into His.

Father, "For I am persuaded that neither death nor life, nor angels nor principalities nor powers, nor things present nor things to come, nor height nor depth, nor any other created thing, shall be able to separate us from (Your) love." (Romans 8:38-39) Amen!

February 15
What type of "church" are you?
Revelation 1-3

At the beginning of the Book of Revelation, Jesus tells John to write to the seven churches in Asia. These churches were in different spiritual conditions, and Jesus wanted to address each of them. The Bible refers to them as loveless, persecuted, compromising, corrupt, dead, faithful, and lukewarm. The loveless church had left their first love. The persecuted church was being attacked by Satan. The compromising church was allowing false doctrine into the church. The corrupt church allowed immorality. The dead church was not truly experiencing God. The faithful church had "kept My (Jesus) command to persevere." (3:10) The lukewarm church became too content with their life. We sometimes find our own lives reflected in these churches. We have probably been in similar places at one time or another in our own lives. We may have become satisfied with life, so do not seek God as we should. We may have allowed "popular" mindsets into our way of thinking without measuring them against the word of God. We may have decided "to enjoy the pleasures of sin for a short time." (Hebrews 11:25) Perhaps we have lost our initial excitement about being a Christian.

Where are you currently? Have you lost your first love? Are you on the frontlines of the battle with Satan? Are you compromising your beliefs so as not to offend? Are you allowing sin to control you? Is the Spirit alive and well in your life or are you living in a way that the Spirit does not have much say in your life? Are you satisfied with your relationship with God even though you know He is calling you to go deeper with Him? Or are you holding fast to God's Word and His promises? The good news is we do not have to stay where we are. Jesus gave each of the churches instructions on how to return to where He desired them to be. Then He gave them a promise if they listened and overcame.

Friends, God has given us His Word, His promises, and His Spirit living in us to guide us in the right path. Most of the time, where we are at spiritually is based on our own decisions. If you are not satisfied with where you are, seek Him. He desires for us to listen.

Jesus, as You did with the seven churches, speak to us about our spiritual condition. Instruct us in the way we should go. Give us the "ears to hear" that we can be overcomers in this life. Amen!

February 16
Lift them up
Mark 2

My favorite movie scene in "The Lord of the Rings" trilogy is when Sam tells Frodo, "I can't carry it for you, but I can carry you." I am almost sure that we all can think of someone in our lives right now that we would say "I wish I could carry it for you." It's hard to watch loved ones go through something that we have no power to do anything about. We can't change the circumstance. We can't change the outcome. Our words and actions seem worthless. But what we can do is "carry" them. Remember when the Israelites were in the battle where Moses' hands needed to be raised to ensure the victory? Moses got tired and needed Aaron and Hur to help "carry" him by holding his hands up for him to claim the victory. (Exodus 17:10-13) We can look for ways to help our hurting loved ones. Perhaps its running errands for them, cleaning their house, helping with the kids. Perhaps it's just a note to let them know you are thinking and praying for them. Sometimes, it may be being there. You may not even need to speak but simply hold a hand and listen. Of course, the best thing we can do is take them to the Father. In Mark 2, the paralytic's four friends brought him to Jesus and did not let any obstacles get in the way. They were not able to physically help their friend walk, but they knew Someone who could. They did not give up when it got hard or when they got tired. They did not give up when it seemed impossible. "And let us not grow weary while doing good, for in due season we shall reap if we do not lose heart." (Galatians 6:9) They made a way to get their friend to the Master.

We need to remember that God loves our loved ones even more than we do. He is moving in their lives even without our help. "Blessed be the God and Father of our Lord Jesus Christ, the Father of mercies and God of all comfort, who comforts us in all our tribulation, that we may be able to comfort those who are in any trouble, with the comfort with which we ourselves are comforted by God." (2 Corinthians 1:3-4)

Father, we bring (ENTER NAME HERE) to You. You know their needs. You know what they are going through. Father, we are unable to do anything within our own strength to ease this burden they are carrying. But Father, we stand here willing to do our part to help "carry" them through this trial. Remind them and us of Your unfailing love. Remind us all "My grace is sufficient for you, for My strength is made perfect in weakness." (2 Corinthians 12:9) We are Yours God, and You love us. You are our Provider, our Comforter, the Healer. Amen.

February 17

Not my plan
Genesis 11 Acts 2

Back in Genesis 11, the people had spoken the same language, lived in the same area, and had the same history and traditions. However, because they were the same, they relied on each other and not God. They decided to build a tower up to Heaven so they could make a name for themselves. God then separated them by creating new languages and sending them to the uttermost parts of the world. In Acts 2, the disciples received the Holy Spirit and began sharing "the wonderful works of God" (Acts 2:11) in Jerusalem. Everyone in the multitude heard in their own tongue. How could this be? The men who were speaking were just common men. They did not hold linguistic degrees. They had not been trained in languages of the world. The Holy Spirit provided the words. And they were so filled with the Spirit that they had to tell everyone they met. God brought the nations together again to hear in their own languages about His plan for them. Here is the difference to Babel. The people were coming together to live for God and not themselves. When we make plans, even as a service to God, "we" often get in the way. If we are not careful, we make the plan more about us than about God.

When the disciples entered the upper room, they really had no idea of what they were waiting for; they just obeyed Jesus. When the Spirit fell, they were compelled to open their mouths. The Spirit was moving, and the crowd listened. The church began to grow quickly. They were meeting together, taking care of each other and winning souls for Christ.

Along the way, we have sometimes lost sight of God's plan. We make church more about us and our priorities than about winning souls for Jesus. We institute worship plans and programs to meet our needs. When did we lose sight of God's plan "that none should perish?" Have we resorted back to Babel, where we are building to make a name for ourselves and not for God? When did we start leaning into our own understanding about how church should be and ignored how the Holy Spirit wants it to be? My friend, if you make going to church about you, you are going for the wrong reasons. Yes, we need the corporate worship time to support us along our Christian walk. However, if every Sunday we come and say, "fill me up Lord" and don't seek to offer encouragement to our brothers and sisters who may need it, we make coming to church all about what we can get out of the service and not what we can offer back to God.

Lord, as we enter Your house of worship, may we return to the early church's model. May we take care of one another. May we pull our resources to further your kingdom plan. May we seek and bring in those who are lost. Your kingdom come, Your will be done. Amen.

February 18
The ups and downs of our Christian walk
1 Kings 18-19

Don't we all wish that we could live our Christian walk on Mount Carmel and experience victory after victory? When you read these two chapters in 1 Kings, does it make you wonder why Elijah could face 450 prophets but run from one woman? Why are there times in our own lives when we are ready to face anything that comes our way and then at other times just a tiny word sends us running in the opposite direction? Perhaps it's because we trust God to move in the "big" things in our lives but think He leaves the "little" things to us. Or we feel like Elijah did; we are the only One left serving God. Or we could simply be tired and need a time of refreshing. We tend to seek God when the big things come our way in life. Those times when we know we are way over our heads and need divine intervention. But many of us take the day to day activities and think we will handle them ourselves. This reminds me of a song by Charles Johnson and the Revivers: "I can't even walk without you holding my hand." We don't like to admit weakness or that we are totally dependent on God. But my friend, when we realize that every breath we breathe is from God; it puts into perspective how much we need Him. Maybe you are in a situation where you are the only Christian in your family or in your workplace. You daily feel the pressures of trying to live out your faith amidst a world that does not recognize their need for a Savior. You may be ridiculed or looked down on because of your faith. You may even be in a position where you are looking at other Christians around you and realize they are not living out what they profess to believe. You feel ready to give up and give in. My friend, hold on! There are others who are seeking God and His will for their lives. You are not alone. Ask God to guide you to someone who can encourage you along the way. There are also times in our lives where we just need to rest. These are times when we have just been through a tough "battle," experienced loss or have not taken time for ourselves lately. As God had Elijah hide away for a little while, we too need that time. We may need to lay aside some of our responsibilities and just focus on ourselves. Spend time with God and let Him refresh you. No matter what stage we are in life, God is with us. If we are on the highest mountain, He is there. If we are in the lowest valley, He is there. We are never alone. "No matter what I have, Your grace is enough. No matter where I am, I'm standing in Your love."
("Hills and Valleys"/Tauren Wells) *O Sufficient God, where I am, there You are also. Just as You did with Elijah, let us hear from You. Give us what we need whether we are on the Mount Carmels in our lives or in the wilderness. Open our eyes to see where You are working in our lives. Amen.*

February 19
Pass on the mantle
2 Kings 2

"And Elisha the son of Shaphat of Abel Meholah you shall anoint as prophet in your place." (1 Kings 19:16)

In a society where everyone wants the truth to be how they define it, we as Christ-followers need to do a better job of passing on the mantle. In schools, our young people are taught the world's perspective of what the truth should be. As adults, we are pressured to join someone's "bandwagon" to validate their truth. We are surrounded by so many different "right in their own eyes" philosophies, from our entertainment to our politics, to even our churches. As parents and grandparents, we need to "train up a child in the way he should go" (Proverbs 22:6) We need to actively be living out our own faith, so our children and grandchildren can see it. Our actions need to match our words. They need to see God in us. We need to have conversations with them about what they are being taught in schools. We need to have an open dialogue about how what the world teaches is often contrary to the Word of God. Daily pray for your children. Pray they have other good Christian influences around them whether it is friends, teachers, or youth leaders. Pray they will hold to the truth and will recognize the lies. Pray for their relationship with God that they will not just view themselves as God's "grandchild" but as a child of God themselves.

In our churches and for our ministries, we also need to raise up and train those who can take up the mantle after us. Look around your church, who would be able to lead in the next 5 or 10 years? Who would even lead next year? Pray for your church and ministry leaders. Pray that God begins raising up the people that He wants in these positions. Pray for yourself. Ask God to direct you in the work He has for you in His kingdom. Leaders, ask God how He wants you to begin passing on the mantle.

Father, we thank You for the wonderful people in our lives who mentored us. Those who had set an example that was worthy of being followed. We pray that we will be worthy mentors to those who are coming up. Raise up the next generation to carry on Your name. Your kingdom come, Your will be done. Amen!

Who is your king?
1 Samuel 8-13

In 1 Samuel 8, after the Israelites demanded a king, Samuel tells them they will be giving up some of their lands, crops and even family members and will become servants themselves. After all God had brought them through, why did they still demand a king? There are probably several answers, however, perhaps a simple one is they wanted to be like everyone else. Perhaps without a "real" king, they did not feel they were recognized as a "real" nation. Perhaps they would be more unified under a "real" king. God told Samuel to go ahead and anoint Saul the first king of Israel. However, it did not take long for King Saul to fail. Throughout the rest of the Old Testament, we see the consequences of having human kings. We often judge the Israelites. We think if we had seen all the miraculous works they had, if we had experienced all His mercy, we would always trust Him. Oh, but I think we judge too quickly. "First take the log out of your own eye, and then you will see clearly to take the speck out of your brother's eye." (Matthew 7:5 ESV) If we take an honest evaluation of our own lives, we can see there are times in our lives where we have allowed people, things or even self to become the king in our lives. And what are we willing to sacrifice to have a king other than God? God's blessings: His provision, His plan, His purpose, His Presence. Yes, we do still experience them; however, we may never know how much more we are missing out on. Back before Israel crossed the Jordan, God told Joshua: "this Book of the Law shall not depart from your mouth, but you shall meditate in it day and night, that you may observe to do according to all that is written in it. For then you will make your way prosperous, and then you will have good success." (Joshua 1:8) If we could examine our own lives like we do the Israelites', we may see a lot of similarities. We may see some failed battles when we were fighting without God by our side. We may see grumbling and complaining when we were not getting our way. We may see times we became "captives" so that God could once again get our attention. When we try to become too self-sufficient or too dependent on people and things, we can lose sight of God. God created you with a purpose. "For I know the plans I have for you," declares the Lord, "plans to prosper you and not to harm you, plans to give you hope and a future." (Jeremiah 29:11) Part of God's plan could still take us through the "fire," but it would be for His kingdom purpose.

Lord, when our sin nature leads us to think we have life in control,
that we do not need divine direction or intervention, we are so wrong.
Forgive us when we worship another "king." Guide us quickly back to You.

February 21
Where your treasure is
Matthew 6

"Do not lay up for yourselves treasures on earth, where moth and rust destroy and where thieves break in and steal; but lay up for yourselves treasures in heaven, where neither moth nor rust destroys and where thieves do not break in and steal. For where your treasure is, there your heart will be also." (Matthew 6:19-21)

Let's face it; our earthly "treasures" do not always stay very valuable. Our bodies age, develop aches, pains, and diseases and ultimately, they die. Our relationships are not perfect. We hurt each other and let each other down. Our houses and cars need maintenance after something breaks or wears out. Our money is not always secure. We could experience job loss or make poor investments. However, we experience treasures through God every day. We experience His love which is unconditional and unfailing. We experience His grace which is amazing and sufficient. We experience His great mercy which is new each morning. We experience His hope which is eternal. We experience His rest when we are weary. And that is just to name a few. What treasures await us when we accept Jesus as our Savior!

But my friend, just imagine the treasures awaiting us over yonder! We will get to be reunited with those who have gone before us! We get to sit down with the saints throughout the ages and hear their redemption story and share ours. We get to experience the "no mores" from Revelation 21:4. But most of all we get to see Jesus, the One who gave His life for ours! Those are treasures we anticipate. But there will also be the treasures we are storing up. These treasures will be the ones where we gave of our time or our resources for the kingdom purposes. Can you imagine someone walking up to you to say "thank you" for the part you played in their redemption story? "And let us not grow weary while doing good, for in due season we shall reap if we do not lose heart." (Galatians 6:9)

As we live our earthly lives, let us not lose sight that we have a higher calling. We are not here are earth for the sole purpose of living our lives for ourselves. We are here to live kingdom purpose lives.

Father, thank You for the treasures You have provided both here on earth and in our heavenly home. May we choose to lay up more treasures in Heaven than here on earth. Thank You for the ultimate treasure, Your beloved Son who gave Himself for us. May we share that good news with all we meet. Amen.

February 22
When we pray - Part 1
Acts 12,16

"Ask, and it will be given to you; seek, and you will find; knock, and it will be opened to you. For everyone who asks receives, and he who seeks finds, and to him who knocks it will be opened." (Matthew 7:7-8) "If you ask anything in My name, I will do it." (John 14:14)

How bold have your prayers been lately? How many of you have ever been "surprised" when God answered a prayer? Prayer is such a precious gift however I'm not sure we have its full potential all figured out. Some of us have our standard prayers that cover the "essentials" in our lives. Some of us just approach the throne when we have problems or concerns. Some of us may feel unworthy. However, when we accepted Jesus into our lives, prayer became one of the benefits.

In Acts, those in the early church were given the opportunity to demonstrate the power of prayer. As the church witnessed the miracles prayer produced, their confidence in the power of prayer grew. Some of us may believe that the miracles that occurred back then no longer happen in today's world. However, the same Spirit resides in us today, meaning we have the same access to the Spirit's power.

The early church learned a lot about the power of prayer. When they were praying for Peter in Acts 12, they were probably praying that God would spare his life. However, they were not expecting the way that God answered. God sends an angel to lead Peter out of prison. He then shows up at the prayer meeting. However, when told he was there, they did not believe. Some believed he was already dead: "It is his angel." (Acts 12:15) They were praying for deliverance, but initially, do not recognize the answered prayer. My guess is that all of us could admit to being in the same place at some point in our lives. We don't recognize the answer, the power, or the provision.

Lord, open our eyes to see how You are moving in our lives. Show us how "the effective, fervent prayer of a righteous man avails much." (James 5:16)

February 23
When we pray - Part 2
Acts 12,16

Remember where Paul and Silas were in Acts 16. They were praying and singing to an audience of inmates and a jailer. They had such faith in God that it did not matter what the outcome was going to be, they knew God was in control. So, they prayed and praised because they knew that God would faithfully answer according to His kingdom purposes. And they did so vocally. This prayer time was not mumbled prayers or silent prayers from the heart. Paul and Silas wanted all to recognize the power of prayer when the answer came.

I trust that we have all witnessed the power of prayer at some point in our lives. I know I have. However, I can also say that I have not always prayed with the eager expectation of receiving an answer. Those were more of an "if You want or choose to answer" kind of prayers. If we take a moment to reflect on our prayer life, we will recognize the many ways we approach the throne. It may be a "drive-thru" type of prayer: "Lord, I need this, this, and this and make it quick." It may be a lack of faith type of prayer: "I don't see how You are going to answer this." It may be a prayer of desperation. It may be a prayer from a broken heart. But I hope we can also recall the prayers where we prayed in the full power of the Spirit; where we boldly approached the throne with our request. These are not the type of prayers where we approach God as if He was a genie to grant our wishes. These are the prayers where we come before God with His kingdom purposes in mind; where the answers will bring glory to His name.

Father, may we get in the habit of bringing everything to You in prayer. As we walk through our day, may we become aware of what we need to pray about: not only in our lives, but in the lives of those around us, the lives of those in our city, country, and the world. May we stand in the gap. May we recognize the power in our prayers and what You want to do through our prayers. Lay upon our hearts and minds today those circumstances You want us to pray for. Grow our prayer life to be what You would have it be. Amen.

Ruth's love story
Ruth

When we read the Book of Ruth, we often think of the love story between Boaz and Ruth. However, what about Ruth's great love for her mother-in-law Naomi or her trusting love for God? "Entreat me not to leave you, or to turn back from following after you; for wherever you go, I will go; and wherever you lodge, I will lodge; your people shall be my people, and your God, my God. Where you die, I will die, and there will I be buried. The Lord do so to me, and more also, if anything but death parts you and me." (1:16-17) Naomi had explained to both her daughters-in-law that she really did not have anything to offer them. She tells Ruth: "look, your sister-in-law has gone back to her people and to her gods; return after your sister-in-law." (1:15) From Ruth's response, it seems that she not only wanted to remain with Naomi; she also wanted to remain with God. Ruth could have easily thought that God was not a good God. He had taken away her husband as well as her security. Without a man in the family, they really had no provider. However, she decided to follow.

When they return to Bethlehem, Ruth obeys whatever Naomi tells her to do. It appears that she doesn't even question. Perhaps the time spent with Naomi while her husband was alive had built such a trust. However, I think it was also her choice to follow God that lead to her devotion and obedience. God blesses her faithfulness to Naomi by providing Boaz. Ruth would also eventually become part of Jesus' lineage.

Another love to be recognized is God's provisional love for Naomi. When Naomi lost her husband and her sons, she felt God had "gone out against me." (1:13) However, God had not forgotten Naomi. He used Ruth to help provide for her. Perhaps He also used Ruth's faith at this point to strengthen Naomi's weakened faith. Naomi felt she had lost it all and had nothing left to give, yet God gave her Ruth, Boaz, and a grandchild.

Do you have people in your life that you walk your "faith walk" with? People who encourage you along life's journey? God puts people in our lives to support us. "Two are better than one, because they have a good reward for their labor." (Ecclesiastes 4:9) Fellow believers lift us up, challenge us, and perhaps even help carry us.

God, thank You for those people You have placed in our lives who make us better people. May we also be that person to someone else. Amen.

February 25
Fulfill your calling
1 Timothy

"Who saved us and called us with a holy calling, not according to our works, but according to His own purpose and grace which was given to us in Christ Jesus before time began." (2 Timothy 1:9)

What do you feel is your calling in life? Are you even able to identify it? Who or what is it based on? Sometimes, I think we take our calling as Christians too lightly. Sometimes, because of the freedoms that we have in Christ, we can be almost too casual in our relationship with God and others. "Now the purpose of the commandment is love with a pure heart, from a good conscience, and from sincere faith." (1 Timothy 1:5) "Be an example to the believers in word, in conduct, in love, in spirit, in faith, in purity." (1 Timothy 4:12) We can read these verses and think since Paul wrote them to Timothy, a minister, they only apply to our pastors or spiritual leaders. However, shouldn't we all try to live by those standards? To love with a pure heart: To love without strings attached, to love without conditions. To love with a good conscience: To love free from deception, guilt, shame, ulterior motives. To love from a sincere faith: To love based on who we are in Christ.

What kind of example do we set? Do our words and actions exhibit the same thing? Do we speak and act out of love? Do we allow how we believe dictate our actions? God created us with a purpose. That purpose is for His kingdom work. He has called us to be a shining light to a lost and dying world. We are to encourage our brothers and sisters. Our purpose is to glorify God in all we say and do.

Father, You are the Potter, we are the clay. May we recognize the work You have for each of us to further Your kingdom. Equip us for the work You set before us. That everything we do will be for Your glory. Amen.

February 26
Not ashamed
2 Timothy

"For I am not ashamed of the gospel of Christ, for it is the power of God to salvation for everyone who believes." (Romans 1:16)

Raise your hand if you have ever done something that caused you to be ashamed. All hands raised? We have all done or said something in our lives that we look back on with shame. You have probably done something in your Christian walk that made you ashamed of how you acted as a Christian. However, because of Christ's gift on the cross, we do not need to continue to live in that shame. "As far as the east is from the west, so far has He removed our transgressions from us." (Psalm 103:12)

God also does not want us to be ashamed to be Christ-followers. In today's world, where what we believe feels like it is constantly challenged, we need to be even bolder declaring the Truth in love. Our goal is to share God's salvation plan with a world who wants to devise their own plan. We, as Christians, need to be careful not to fall into that trap ourselves. "I marvel that you are turning away so soon from Him who called you in the grace of Christ, to a different gospel, which is not another; but there are some who trouble you and want to pervert the gospel of Christ." (Galatians 1:6-7) However "be diligent to present yourself approved to God, a worker who does not need to be ashamed, rightly dividing the truth." (2 Timothy 2:15) "For this reason I also suffer these things: nevertheless I am not ashamed, for I know whom I have believed and am persuaded that He is able to keep what I have committed to Him until that Day." (2 Timothy 1:12)

Father, when we are called Home, may we be able to say: "I have fought the good fight, I have finished the race, I have kept the faith. Finally, there is laid up for me the crown of righteousness, which the Lord, the righteous Judge, will give to me on that Day, and not to me only but also to all who have loved His appearing." (2 Timothy 4:7-8) Amen.

Don't give up
Numbers 13-14

Can you imagine being on the threshold of the Promised Land and then stop? The Israelites had been out of Egypt for about a year. They had already seen God do miraculous things. They had also received discipline from the Lord. However, here they stand ready to head into the land that God had already promised them back in Egypt. And when the spies come back, they choose to listen to the ones who say it is impossible. They are convinced that the obstacles are bigger than their God. How could they have forgotten the Red Sea? How could they have forgotten the manna? How could they have forgotten Moses' shining face after he had been with God?

Why in our lives do we think our current obstacles are any bigger than the ones God has already brought us through? How many times in life do we feel like giving up on our loved ones, ourselves, or even God? Life seems to get too hard, the obstacles too big, our faith too small. But hold on. "If you have faith as a mustard seed, you will say to this mountain, 'Move from here to there,' and it will move; and nothing will be impossible for you." (Matthew 17:20) God can slay our giants, part the waters, calm the storms. When He has not yet done those things in our current situation, we sometimes decide to stay in our wilderness or head back to our Egypt.

My friend, this world is not our Promised Land. We may experience some benefits of the Promised Land here in this life, but until we reach that Heavenly shore, we will not have the full view of the Promised Land. God has proven Himself faithful and true. "Being confident of this very thing, that He who has begun a good work in you will complete it until the day of Jesus Christ." (Philippians 1:6)

So, hold on to His promises! Hold on to what He has already done in your life! Hold on to the assurance that He is always with you! Hold on to His Word!

Father, if we are at a place in our lives where we feel like giving up, send someone to encourage us on our journey. Give us a glimpse of our future Promised Land. Remind us that this is only our temporary home, we are just passing through. Remind us that our current cares, hurts, and burdens are here for only a little while. And while we are in the wilderness, You are there providing and guiding. Father, until that day when we see Your face, may we stay faithful to the journey You have laid out for us. Amen.

February 28
Thank You, God
Acts 7

Throughout the Bible, we come across scripture that is basically a "recap" of what God had already done. Whether it's Moses reminding the Israelites, David singing Psalms of remembrance, or Stephen testifying before he was stoned to death. Being reminded of what God has done offers encouragement for our current situations and for others.

We also have our own unique story of what God has done in our lives. Today, let's walk through our own Christian journey and thank Him for all He has done.

Take a moment to:

Thank God for the people in your life who first taught you about God.

Remember how God saved you from your past sins, mistakes, and failures.

Thank God for the people who are helping you along life journey.

Reflect on the times you saw God move.

Reflect on the times when God held you when your heart was broken.

Acknowledge how God is currently moving in your life.

Look around you at what God has given you.

Look outside to see His glorious creation.

Thank Him for the cross.

Thank Him for our Heavenly Home.

Lord God, You are so good to us and we can never thank You enough for all You do. I am sorry for not saying thank You enough. Today, I bow, not with requests, but with gratitude for Your countless blessings. AMEN!

Inspired by "Say Amen" by Finding Favour.

I shall not be moved
Psalm 62

"He only is my rock and my salvation; He is my defense; I shall not be moved." (Psalm 62:6)

I shall not be moved from my Father's Love: (Romans 8:38-39)
"For I am persuaded that neither death nor life, nor angels nor principalities nor powers, nor things present nor things to come, nor height nor depth, nor any other created thing, shall be able to separate us from the love of God which is in Christ Jesus our Lord."

I shall not be moved from my Father's Presence: (Matthew 28:20)
"And lo, I am with you always, even to the end of the age."

I shall not be moved from my Father's Provision: (Philippians 4:19)
"And my God shall supply all your need according to His riches in glory by Christ Jesus."

I shall not be moved from my Father's Protection: (Joshua 1:9)
"Be strong and of good courage; do not be afraid, nor be dismayed, for the Lord your God is with you wherever you go."

I shall not be moved from my Father's Promise: (John 11:25-26)
"Jesus said to her, "I am the resurrection and the life. He who believes in Me, though he may die, he shall live. And whoever lives and believes in Me shall never die."

I shall not be moved from my Father's Peace: (John 14:27)
"Peace I leave with you, My peace I give to you; not as the world gives do I give to you. Let not your heart be troubled, neither let it be afraid."

I shall not be moved from my Father's Plan: (Philippians 1:6)
"Being confident of this very thing, that He who has begun a good work in you will complete it until the day of Jesus Christ."

I shall not be moved from my Father's Power: (Philippians 4:1)
"I can do all things through Christ who strengthens me."

Amen!

Follow Jesus
John 14

"Let not your heart be troubled; you believe in God, believe also in Me. In My Father's house are many mansions; if it were not so, I would have told you. I go to prepare a place for you. And if I go and prepare a place for you, I will come again and receive you to Myself; that where I am, there you may be also." (John 14:1-3)

If people were asked where they wanted to go when they die, almost everyone would say Heaven. However, if asked, "How do you get there?," they would probably provide a variety of answers. Some would probably talk about how you need to live a good life, others may assume that everyone gets to go there, some may think your good deeds need to outweigh your bad. People seem to think their actions dictate their destination. These people need to recognize that it's not our actions, but the action Jesus took on the cross that is the key to Heaven. "Jesus said to him, "I am the way, the truth, and the life. No one comes to the Father except through Me." (John 14:6) To make Heaven our Home, all we need to do is accept Jesus' precious gift of salvation. We need to repent of our sins and allow Him to become our Savior and Lord. Although, this does not mean we should live the rest of our lives any way we want. Jesus as our Savior means that "If we confess our sins, He is faithful and just to forgive us our sins and to cleanse us from all unrighteousness." (1 John 1:9) His death on the cross means we no longer face the death penalty. "For the wages of sin is death, but the gift of God is eternal life in Christ Jesus our Lord." (Romans 6:23) Jesus as our Lord means we live submitted lives to Him. We give Him control. This is where we struggle. Yes, we like to think of Jesus as our Savior. But when it comes to accepting Him as Lord, that becomes more of a problem. We like being lord of our lives. Living by our own standards and plans. But accepting Jesus means we also acknowledge that we need Someone else to be the Lord of our lives. My friend, you can't work your way to Heaven. You can't bypass Jesus and what He has done for you and get to Heaven. You need to recognize that you need a Savior and Lord. And Jesus is the only One qualified to be that Savior and Lord. Do you know with complete assurance that when you die, you will awake in Heaven? If not, simply accept Jesus' gift. Admit you are a sinner and ask forgiveness for your sins recognizing not only that you need a Savior, but you also need a Lord. Believe that Jesus is God's Son and that what He did on the cross was enough. Then confess your faith in Him as your Savior and Lord.

God, thank You for making a perfect plan for us to be able to enter Heaven.

March 2
Jesus, You just made my day
John 20

Can you imagine Mary early on that Resurrection Day? Before she got to the tomb? Her whole world was crushed. Not only did she mourn Jesus, but she also mourned all the hope He had provided. She probably did not know what she was going to do next. Resume the life she had before? After all she had learned, would she be able to? But then she gets to the tomb and everything changes. Hope is restored! The risen Jesus just made her day! She could turn her mourning countenance into one of joy. She could continue living with a bigger purpose in mind.

Our front door faces east. Every morning when I go to work, I step out and see the sunrise. It is always unique. Some days the beauty is just mind-blowing. We serve a creative God! But just as I recognize that as God made each unique sunrise, He has also made the day before me as well. And just as Mary, I can acknowledge "Jesus, You just made my day." Not only can I face each day knowing He knows what that day holds. But I can recognize, because of the Resurrection Day; even my worst day can be filled with hope and joy. If I can recognize that the Risen Jesus made my day, I can relinquish control of my day to Him and allow His kingdom purposes to be the focus of my day. I can remember that the problems of today do not affect who I am in Him. My identity is not found in who I am at home or work but is found as His child.

Lord, thank You for Your new mercies each morning! (Lamentations 3:23) Thank You for the day you have made for me today. And because of Your Resurrection, my hope is in You. Father, You have given me today and I give it back to You to be used for Your kingdom purposes. Amen.

Our Deliverer
Matthew 8-9, Psalm 18

In Matthew 8 and 9, we see Jesus deliver. He delivered the disciples
from the storm. He delivered from demon possession. He offered
deliverance from the bondage of sin. The disciples were seasoned fishermen,
yet they were frightened by the storm. They were fearful that they would not
survive unless the Master was able to rescue them. Does that make you think
of any of your life storms? Or do we just assume that since the Master is
with us, it will all be smooth sailing? No matter how long we have been a
Christian or how strong our faith, we still face life storms that require us to
"awake the Master."

There are also times in our lives where we need to be delivered from a
problem that has us worrying. Or perhaps we need to be delivered from
an addiction or depression. Some of us might even need to be delivered
from some demonic oppression in our life. But most of all, we have a
Deliverer who stands ready to forgive our sins and "will cast our sins into
the depth of the sea." (Micah 7:19)

Aren't you glad we have a Deliverer that cares for us? One "who makes
a way in the sea and a path through the mighty waters." (Isaiah 43:16) One
who says "Peace, be still" (Mark 4:39) and the winds and waves obey. One
even the demons themselves recognize and obey. (Mark 1:24-26) And most
of all, One "who Himself bore our sins in His own body on the tree, that we,
having died to sins, might live for righteousness - by whose stripes you were
healed. For you were like sheep going astray, but have now returned to the
Shepherd and Overseer of your souls." (1 Peter 2:24-25)

*He is our Deliverer, so we say: "I will love You, O Lord, my strength.
The Lord is my rock and my fortress and my deliverer; My God, my
strength, in whom I will trust; My shield and the horn of my salvation,
my stronghold. I will call upon the Lord, who is worthy to be praised; so
shall I be saved from my enemies." (Psalm 18: 1-3) Amen.*

March 4

All in
Colossians 2-3

Have you seen the sports slogan "All In?" This slogan implies that the players put everything they have into the game. No matter which sports team is your favorite, you can tell when they are not giving it their all. They make simple mistakes and are not playing with their normal energy. When they do come to play, it's obvious. They are ready and focused. They know what is going on in the game and are ready to do their part. Their heads and hearts are only in the game.

My son's school uses "All In" in reference to Colossians 3:23: "And whatever you do in word or deed, do all in the name of the Lord Jesus, giving thanks to God the Father through Him." The goal is to teach the students that every aspect of their lives, including their school day, should be done for God. They want the students to put forth their best in the classrooms and on the fields because they are representing God in all they do.

Have many of us live our Christian life "all in?" Do we give our everything in our walk with God? "Set your mind on things above, not on things on the earth." (Colossians 3:2) Do you think about God just on Sunday or when you are having problems? Or do you recognize and acknowledge His work in your life every day? Just as we know when our favorite sports team is not "all in" their game; people can tell those who just say "I'm a Christian" from those who are walking with Christ.

Father, I desire to live my life "All In" for You. Let the cry of my heart be: "I can't stop, I can't quit. It's in my heart. It's on my lips. I can't stop, no I can't quit. It's in my heart, yeah I'm all in." ("Til the Day I Die"/TobyMac)

March 5
Fear not
Isaiah 41

We live in a society where there seems to be much to fear. We have fears which we acknowledge as being a little irrational. However, we recognize there are also legitimate fears. We fear for our safety as well as our children's. We fear sickness. We fear financial issues. But as we read through the Bible, how many times do we come across a "fear not" or "peace be still?" How do we apply those to the fears in our own lives?

Hold on to His Word! "But now, thus says the Lord, who created you, O Jacob, and He who formed you, O Israel: "Fear not, for I have redeemed you; I have called you by your name; You are Mine." (Isaiah 43:1)

Hold on to His promises! "Fear not, for I am your God, I will strengthen you, yes, I will help you, I will uphold you with My righteous right hand." (Isaiah 41:10)

Hold on to His power! "For God has not given us a spirit of fear, but of power, and of love and of a sound mind." (2 Timothy 1:7)

Hold on to His timing! "Therefore do not worry about tomorrow, for tomorrow will worry about its own things. Sufficient for the day is its own trouble." (Matthew 6:34)

Releasing our fears is not easy. Life is uncertain and bad things happen. But recall the many times in your life where you have heard "fear not" or "peace, be still." The same God who spoke *to* the fears of your past is the same God who still speaks. "Be strong and of good courage; do not be afraid, nor be dismayed, for the Lord your God is with you wherever you go." (Joshua 1:9) God hasn't promised that bad things won't happen; He has promised to be there when they do.

My friend, please do not allow your fears to paralyze you. Ask God to help you overcome your fears. He is able. Find a "fear not" verse or two and keep them close. Allow God's Word to calm your fears and shine the light on the truth.

Father God, when the fears in life assail, speak "Peace, be still" into our storms. Remind us that You left us peace for our weary souls. "Peace I leave you, My peace I give to you; not as the world gives do I give to you. Let not your heart be troubled, neither let it be afraid." (John 14:27) You love us Lord and will be with us no matter what comes our way.

March 6

Revive us
Psalm 119

Have you ever experienced a time when it had been a while since you read your Bible and when you finally sit down to start reading, it feels like water to a thirsty soul? You just can't get enough? You wonder why you allowed other things to get in the way of taking the time to read?

Psalm 119 is the longest chapter in the Bible. What is the major theme of Psalm 119? The value of the Word of God to our life! One of the repetitive words used in this chapter in the NKJV is revive. Other translations use: KJV – quicken, NIV - preserve, ESV - gives life. God's Word revives, quickens, preserves, and gives life.

Here are the definitions from the Merriam- Webster Online Dictionary:
Revive: "to return to consciousness or life: become active or flourishing again; to restore from a depressed, inactive, or unused state: bring back"
Quicken: "to cause to be enlivened; to cause to burn more intensely; to shine more brightly"
Preserves: "to keep alive, intact, or free from decay; to keep up and reserve for personal or special use"
Life: "a principle or force that is considered to underlie the distinctive quality of animate beings; spiritual existence transcending physical death"

Does that put into perspective how important the Word is to our lives? The imagery in these definitions of a given life revived, quickened, and preserved is one I want. How many of us would like to feel like our life was flourishing again, that it would shine more brightly, and that it would be kept intact? The Word also promises eternal life that transcends our physical death.

Dear friend, will you join me in praying that we can get to the point where we can honestly say: "O, how I love Your law! It is my meditation all the day?" (Psalm 119:97) Can we recognize it as a life source that we need as desperately as water, food, and the air we breathe?

Father, thank You for Your Word. Forgive us for not valuing it as much as we should. Make us thirsty for Your Word, Lord. Place on our hearts the desire to take some time out of our day, to read and meditate on Your Word of life. Amen.

March 7
Persistent faith – Part 1
Luke 18

As we read through Luke 18, we encounter a variety of people. The very first line of Luke 18 is: "then He spoke a parable to them, that men always ought to pray and not lose heart." (vs. 1) The woman in this parable recognized that she had to continue to approach the judge to get her desired justice. Do we pray until we hear from God? Until we get some answer, even if it takes years? "But how much of that kind of persistent faith will the Son of Man find on the earth when he returns?" (vs. 8 MSG)

The next parable is about two men who come to the temple. The "righteous" man comes to tell God all about what he does and does not do. However, the tax collector comes with a humble heart to ask for mercy. Have we ever stopped to listen to or think about what our prayers sound like? Do most of our prayers revolve around us and those we love? Or do our prayers go beyond our small world to the much bigger one in need of a Savior?

In Luke 18, there are three different approaches to Jesus as He is teaching. The rich young ruler comes to Jesus, wanting assurance that what he is doing will get him to Heaven. When told the one thing he lacked, he left. He was not willing to give up his possessions to follow Jesus. Aren't we like that sometimes? Don't we want to pick and choose how we serve God? "God, I'll do this, but I would rather not do that." Aren't you thankful that "and those who heard it said, "Who then can be saved?" But He said, "The things which are impossible with men are possible with God." (v26-27)

March 8
Persistent faith – Part 2
Luke 18

In Luke 18, the other two approaches were people that others discouraged from disturbing Jesus. They were deemed unimportant. The first group was children. Persistent parents wanted their children to see Jesus. They were probably also hoping that Jesus would bless them. When Jesus rebukes his disciples for sending them away, He states: "for the kingdom of God belongs to such as these." (Luke 18:16 NIV) Jesus let the world know that even the small children were important to Him.

The last person we meet in Luke 18 is the blind man. People were trying to quiet him down, but he had a mission. He knew that he needed a touch from the Master. So, he persistently and loudly cried out. He knew that Jesus was his only Hope.

Luke 18 seems like a random chapter will all these different people we meet. And then we come across verses 31-33 where Jesus predicts his death and resurrection. Could it be that these verses tie the whole chapter together?

Can you find yourself somewhere in this chapter? Are you the woman who constantly seeks justice? Are you the "righteous" man who thinks about all YOU do for God? Are you the humble tax collector who feels unworthy to approach the throne of God? Are you the rich young ruler who knows there is one thing you should give up and follow God completely? Are you like the children where others may not see your worth? Or are you like the blind man who needs a miracle and persistently seeks the Master's touch?

Because of verses 31-33, because of Jesus' death and resurrection, He sees each as worthy. He makes it possible for us to lay everything down to follow Him. We can persistently come to Him with our needs.

Don't lose heart in your prayers, my friend! God wants to hear your persistent prayers. He also wants you to recognize your worth comes from Him, not based on who or what you are here on earth.

Father, thank You for Your love. Thank You for making us worthy to approach Your throne. Thank You for hearing us when we call. Jesus, thank You for dying in our place. Thank You for Your resurrection power. Amen!

Light into our path
Psalm 119

Have you ever been in a situation where you had to decide what to do? Of course you have. We face decision-making every day. However, there are some decisions that are bigger than others. Some that are life-changers. I am so glad that my Maker has a plan for my life so that I can seek His face when those decisions come my way. One of my first "big" decisions in life was whether to go to college. I recognized at even that age I needed God's direction in that decision, I was unequipped to make it on my own. However, there have been other decisions in my life, where I felt equipped to decide under my own strength, and then ended up making the wrong one.

God gives us His Word and His Spirit to guide us. We don't have to live life trying to guess the right path. God wants to be our Guide. He has a plan for our life, however, if we do not seek Him and spend time with Him, how are we going to know His direction? We also need to wait on His timing, which is not always easy.

In today's world with all its "truths," what a comfort to know there is an Absolute Truth. What a peace knowing there is an Authority amidst all the voices calling out "truth, truth." When we are in the Word, we can more clearly identify the partial truths and half-lies that come our way. Satan knows the Word better than we do, and he knows how to use it against us. We need to be plugged into the Source of Absolute Truth so He can shine a light into our path. "I will choose to listen and believe the voice of truth… because Jesus You are the voice of truth." ("Voice of Truth"/ Casting Crowns)

Father, "Your word is a lamp to my feet and a light to my path." (Psalm 119:105) Forgive me for those times I stumble down paths in the darkness because I have not been in Your Word. Help me to trust when I can only see a little part of where You are leading. Thank You for the gift of Your Word so I can know Your Truth. Amen.

March 10
Finish strong - Hezekiah and Manasseh
2 Chronicles 29- 33

Father and son lived very different lives. They were both powerful leaders, one leading in the right direction while the other did not. Both are kings we usually remember. King Hezekiah is often remembered as one who worked to turn the children of Israel back to God. He brought Israel and Judah together in Jerusalem to celebrate the Passover. His prayers accomplished much. The Bible also mentions some technological advancements during his time as king. King Manasseh is remembered for all the evil that he did. "So Manasseh seduced Judah and the inhabitants of Jerusalem to do more evil than the nations whom the Lord had destroyed before the children of Israel." (2 Chronicles 33:9)

Those reading how they lived their lives might then be surprised at the end of their stories. When Hezekiah was sick unto death and prayed for more time, God granted him fifteen more years. However, "but Hezekiah did not repay according to the favor shown him, for his heart was lifted up; therefore wrath was looming over him and over Judah and Jerusalem." (2 Chronicles 32:25) Hezekiah became prideful. The prophet Isaiah told Hezekiah that everything that was in his house would be carried away to Babylon. (2 Kings 20:16-18) Hezekiah had taken his eyes off God and put his faith in his possessions. "Then Hezekiah humbled himself for the pride of his heart, he and the inhabitants of Jerusalem, so that the wrath of the Lord did not come upon them in the days of Hezekiah." (2 Chronicles 32:26) Manasseh, on the other hand, when he was carried off to Babylon, then humbled himself before the Lord. God heard his cries and prayers. God delivered Manasseh back to Jerusalem. Manasseh took away the foreign gods, repaired the altar of God and commanded Judah to serve the Lord God of Israel. (2 Chronicles 33:15-17)

What should we take away from these two kings? Even though we think that we are being "good" Christians, we can still allow things to come into our lives that may hinder our walk with God. Or if we have spent our lives apart from God and enjoyed the "evil" life, we can still be forgiven when we humble ourselves and repent. Both kings received God's forgiveness.

God, thank You for Your mercy and forgiveness. May we always seek Your face! Father, we pray for those in our lives who may be living away from You right now. We pray that You would get their attention, so they will turn their hearts to You and seek Your forgiveness. Put people around them who will share Your love with them. Amen!

March 11
Broken but usable
John 4

Let's face it. We have all had to deal with some brokenness in our life. Some of us might feel more "broken" than others. And because of that brokenness, we feel unworthy or incapable of being used by God. Shall we do a Heavenly "roll call" to disproof that feeling? Abraham lied, Moses killed, David committed both adultery and murder, Peter denied, and Paul was an active participant of the persecution of the early church. That's just to name a very few. When you think of the "great" men and women of the Bible, most have something in their story that reflects their brokenness. We live in a fallen world. We experience brokenness in various ways and times in our lives. Perhaps you feel too broken to be usable. Remember God is the Potter and we are the clay. (Isaiah 64:8) He can use the broken places in our lives to make a masterpiece. He can use your broken pieces to touch someone else's life. Look at the Samaritan woman at the well. Here we see a woman coming to draw water at a time she knows she can avoid everyone. Perhaps she was banished from coming with the other women. Perhaps she was tired of all the stares and mumbling. Perhaps she was ashamed and avoided the crowd. I imagine she was aware of her brokenness. But then she met Jesus.

Jesus did not avoid her. Jesus spoke to her. Jesus acknowledged her. Isn't that all we desire? To be seen beyond our brokenness to the hurting person underneath? The person desperate to feel loved, to feel valued, to feel whole again. After her encounter with Jesus, she hurriedly returned to the city. This time she did not avoid the crowd, she called for them. She had found the Messiah and wanted to share it with the world. From her broken place and her broken story, Jesus used her to draw many to believe in Him. "And many of the Samaritans of that city believed in Him because of the word of the woman who testified, "He told me all that I ever did." (John 4:39) My friend, my prayer is that you allow Jesus to acknowledge you, to speak to you, to love you. Don't avoid Him. Come to the well. He knows all that you ever did. Yet He loves you and He wants to be with you! He wants to take your brokenness and use it for His glory. Will you allow Him to be the Potter in your life?

Father, thank You that You do not need people to be "perfect" before they deserve Your love and forgiveness. You don't need them to be "perfect" before You use them for Your purposes. "For all have sinned and fallen short of the glory of God." (Romans 3:23) "For God did not send His Son into the world to condemn the world, but that the world through Him might be saved." (John 3:17) Father, use our brokenness for Your glory!

71

Love Mercy
Micah 6

"And what does the Lord require of you but to do justly, to love mercy, and to walk humbly with your God? (Micah 6:8)

When Jesus was asked what the most important commandment was, His response was: "You shall love the Lord your God with all your heart, with all your soul, and with all your mind." This is the first and great commandment. And the second is like it: 'You shall love your neighbor as yourself.'" (Matthew 22:37-39) How we treat others is very important to God. Do you seek ways that you can do justly and show mercy to others? Do you practice submission to God?

Paul challenges us to "put on tender mercies, kindness, humility, meekness, longsuffering, bearing with one another, and forgiving one another." (Colossians 3:12-13) Too often, we do the opposite. We are impatient, set too high expectations, hold grudges and judge too quickly. How would our world change if we were more patient with the people around us? How would our view of others change if we recognized that we all are flawed people, leaving in a flawed world? How would we change if we remembered how much God forgave us when dealing with those who have hurt us? Colossians 3:23 says we should be "doing all in the name of the Lord Jesus." This includes how we treat others. The cries we frequently hear in our world are about how unjust people are being treated, how their needs are not being addressed, how everyone should agree with their opinions. At the heart of these cries, I believe, is a call to be loved. We, as God's people, need to spread His love to all we meet. And sometimes that means we should look past how we are feeling about the person and their actions, and just love like Jesus.

God, You have called us to "do justly, love mercy, and walk humbly with (You)." We need Your help to do this. A lot of times, we would rather just see justice without any mercy. But You came so that everyone would have the opportunity to come to the saving knowledge of You, to experience Your love and forgiveness. Help us to put aside how we feel and show Your love to all those we meet. Amen.

Valley of dry bones
Ezekiel 37

Do you ever feel like you are living in the valley of dry bones? That you are among those dry bones? Or that the church and the world seem to be spiritual dry? Do you feel that we need God to breathe life on us, on our churches, and on our world again? "Our bones are dry, our hope is lost, and we ourselves are cut off!" (Ezekiel 37:11)

Now imagine being Ezekiel, when God asks if the bones can live again. These are VERY dry bones. The skin and sinews that held them together are long gone. Considering that when God made man initially, He only used dust, we should not be surprised at His ability to give life to these bones. He breathed life into Adam. He did it again with these bones. And He can do it with our "dry bones".

Are there dry bones in your life that you have given up on? That you have discarded in the valley? Which of these would God like to breathe life into again? Or how about your local church? Are there some dry bones there? Some aspects that need the breath of God? Are there people in your life or church who are no longer seeking God?

Bring these "dry bones" before the Lord. Ask Him, if it's His will, to breathe life back into your dry bones that they will come alive. These requests should not just be for our benefit but for His glory.

Lord, come breathe on us! Breathe on those dry places in our lives that need Your touch. Breathe on our loved ones who are no longer serving You; that they will return to Your love and forgiveness. Breathe on our churches that they will come alive in their worship and service for You; that being alive they will draw the lost and dying world to You. Breathe life into our prayers so that they become ones full of life. "We call out to dry bones, come alive. So breathe, oh breath of God, now breathe." ("Come Alive"/Lauren Daigle) Amen!

Don't lose your glow
Exodus 34

When our son's fiancée was a new Christian, she had something laying heavy on her heart and didn't know what to do about the situation. She prayed and told God that she needed to hear from Him. The next day, He showed up in a mighty way! As she was sharing her story with us, her face was aglow. It made me think of Moses when he came down from the mountain after being with God. Think about a time when you noticed someone "glowing": a bride, an expectant mother, a proud father. They did not have to say a word about their happiness and love; it was evident on their face.

Do you remember when you first got saved? Do you remember the first time you experienced God answering a "big" prayer? You probably couldn't wait to tell everyone you met. Can you say with all honesty that you still get that excited over an answered prayer? I hope so. I hope there is still that amazement each time you see God move.

However, I think that sometimes, as we mature as Christians, we either don't pay as much attention or take for granted answered prayers. I think sometimes we grow complacent in our appreciation for what God does in our lives. Yes, we face trials, valleys, disappointments. But God has given us eternal life. He is with us now and forever. He loves us even when we seem unlovable. He enjoys providing blessings along the way. Yet we let the temporary cares of this world reflect more on our faces than the fact that we are loved unconditionally and have the assurance of an eternal life with God. This world is looking for something different. They are seeking something that can bring joy and peace back to the chaos of life. When they look at you, do they see a difference? Is there a "glow" that is reflected because of time spent with God?

My friend, don't lose your glow. We need to spend time with the Father to bask in His love. Then we can shine our light into this dark world. "Let your light so shine before men, that they may see your good works and glorify your Father in heaven." (Matthew 5:16)

God, place a hunger in us to spend time with You and Your Word. Remind us that it not only benefits us, it benefits those around us as well. You have called us to be the light in the world. Help us to shine for You.

March 15
When God changes your plans
Acts 8-9

Do you know someone who is a planner? Who lives by their calendar and does not like unexpected last-minute changes? I am one of those people. However, one thing I have learned over time is that sometimes my plans need to change to make room for God's plans. My plans tend to be self-centered or focused on my small world, whereas God's plans are more focused on the needs of others. I must decide to lay aside my selfishness and allow Him to do a greater work in my life.

Saul had a plan. He was on his way to Damascus to persecute the new Christians that were spreading a "false" religion. On that Damascus road, however, God interrupted his plan. Jesus revealed the truth to Saul. Saul had to decide whether to follow his original plan or begin following God's. Little did he realize on that road, the impact his life would have on the new Christian faith.

Philip was in Samaria preaching and performing miracles. "Now an angel of the Lord spoke to Philip, saying, "Arise and go toward the south along the road which goes down from Jerusalem to Gaza." (Acts 8:26) God had a divine appointment for Philip that He did not want him to miss. Philip shared the gospel with an Ethiopian and led him to the saving knowledge of God. And as much rejoicing as he was doing, I'm sure he went on to share about God's love and forgiveness when he got home.

Do you see a pattern? When God changes our plans, He does so for His kingdom purposes and His glory. When our plans don't go our way, we may feel inconvenienced and put out or frustrated and upset. When God changes our plans, more important things happen. Would you be willing to give up your plan, so someone could come to the saving knowledge of God? Most of us would say "of course." But even if we never fully witness the impact of God changing our plans, we need to be open to His leading.

Lord, have Your Will in my life today. I lay my plans and my schedule at Your feet to be available for the kingdom work You have for me today. Amen!

Seeking reconciliation
Philemon

You have probably flipped past the New Testament book of Philemon a time or two. We learn a lot about Paul in this book. If you have read much of the New Testament, you know that Paul was bold and spoke what he thought. He lived in the freedom of Christ and shared the Good News to everyone. Now imagine receiving this letter from Paul. It sounds like Philemon and Paul were good friends. Paul was already aware of the good works that Philemon was doing. However, Paul asks Philemon to show grace to Onesimus. Paul states that he could command Philemon, but he instead appeals to him in love. (8-9) Onesimus was Philemon's runaway slave. Paul shared his faith with Onesimus and he too accepted Jesus as Lord. It sounds like Paul spend some time mentoring Onesimus. Paul calls him his son. (v10) Paul was in chains at this point and could have used Onesimus. He knew, though, that Onesimus had to return to Philemon even if he faced a potential death sentence. So, Paul sent this letter to Philemon. Paul had faith in both Philemon and Onesimus that both would handle the situation God's way. He expected that there would be reconciliation. He expected grace to be given. When we think about Paul, we think of the boldness of his faith and his willingness to go wherever God sent. Sometimes we miss out on how much he loved people. People were important to Paul. He knew his message was for all people and he wanted to make sure that everyone he met had the opportunity to learn about Jesus. Paul rarely chose an easy path. Even in this book, he could have kept Onesimus with him with no one thinking anything about it. However, he knew the right thing to do was to seek reconciliation. Have you ever been in a situation where you had to go back and right a wrong? Perhaps it was something minor and the only thing hurt was your pride. However, maybe it was something more significant, something where you needed to seek someone else's forgiveness. Going back can be difficult. When you face a situation where you need to seek forgiveness, find someone to pray with and for you. Prepare your heart with love and acceptance. Pray for the person, asking God to go before you and work in that person's life. Trust God that He is in control. You do your part to reconcile; the rest will be the responsibility of the other person. Jesus taught: "Therefore if you bring your gift to the altar, and there remember that your brother has something against you, leave your gift there before the altar, and go your way. First be reconciled to your brother, and then come and offer your gift." (Matthew 5:23-24)

Father, owning up to our mistakes and failures is something we often like to avoid. Our relationships with others are important to You. Strengthen and guide us as we seek reconciliation for Your name's sake.

March 17
What's your motivation?
Judges 13-16

Samson was set apart to be used by God before he was even conceived. He is named as a judge. He single-handedly killed many Philistines. However most of the time, everything he did was because of a woman instead of God. His parents did all they could to ensure that Samson was living the consecrated life, which was his calling. However, Samson decided he wanted a Philistine wife. Because he was set apart, his parents tried to convince him to find a "nice" Israelite woman. "But his father and mother did not know that it was of the Lord - that He was seeking an occasion to move against the Philistines." (Judges 14:4) Samson was able to get closer to the Philistines because of his relationship with the Philistine women. Samson chose women who were not loyal to him and who tried to bring him more harm than good.

Samson was able to come against the Philistines. Most of the time, though, it was for selfish reasons. Samson chose to try to please the women in his life more than God. Yet, the Spirit of the Lord still gave him the strength to defeat the Philistines. Samson came against the Philistines out of anger for what they had done to him. He didn't seem to consider how they were treating the other Israelites or that they were enemies of God. Even when he called on God to give him the strength to tear down the pillars, he did so for partial selfish reasons. "Then Samson called to the Lord, saying, "O, Lord God, remember me, I pray! Strengthen me, I pray, just this once, O God, that I may with one blow take vengeance on the Philistines for my two eyes." (Judges 16:28) God was able to use Samson to accomplish His plans even when Samson was focused more on his own desires. Do you ever wonder how much more Samson could have achieved if he had sought God? What is your motivation in life? Are you more worried about pleasing the people in your life than God? Perhaps you are motivated by your accomplishments and your possessions. Whatever it is, God can use us despite our flaws and weaknesses.

Father, even in our selfishness and our weakness, You still use us for Your kingdom purposes. Thank You for not seeking "perfect" people to do Your will, just willing ones. And even when we come with selfish motivations, You can still accomplish Your plan for our lives. Amen!

March 18
Joseph: an unexpected journey
Genesis 37, 39-48

Not many of us would want to be Joseph. At the beginning of Genesis 37, we find a confident, if not arrogant, young man who believed he knew his place in the family. Joseph may have been one of the youngest, but he (and everyone else) knew he was his father's favorite. And when he began to have visions where his father and brothers bowed down to him, he felt confirmed of his role in the family. However, his life did not go the way he anticipated. At the end of Genesis 37, we find him starting an unexpected journey that would be years and years of unpleasant experiences. He begins as a slave and prisoner. Joseph was 17 at the beginning of Genesis 37. (v 2) He was 30 when he interpreted Pharaoh's dreams. (41:46) For 13 years, he leads a life where others had command over him. Where was his value? Where was his greatness? Instead, he faced a life where he was lied about and forgotten. Do you think he gave up hope? Do you think he dreamt of what he would do if he ever saw his brothers again? Do you think he ever cried out to God that life wasn't fair? Joseph's story doesn't end in Genesis 40. He doesn't remain in prison. He eventually is exalted to second in command. And when his brothers come looking for food, he is the one who provides. It is easy for us to read through Joseph's story and realize how God was working. However, it is not so easy, when we feel like the ones in prison. In Joseph's story, we see how he had to be sold to get to Egypt; then lied about so he ends up in prison where he begins interpreting dreams. He is summoned to interpret Pharaoh's dream so that he is granted the power to oversee the distribution of food; where he will be able to provide food for his family during the famine. God is orchestrating our lives to accomplish His plan for His glory. Our story may not seem to end with a "happy ever after" like Joseph's. We may wish that life was easier. But remember this life is only temporary. One day, when we pass from death into life, we will begin to live the life God had for us from the beginning. We will be living in a perfect world where sin and death no longer exists. Throughout Joseph's slave and prison days, he knew God was with him. And God blessed him and all that he did. If you feel like you are in the prison days of your life, look around for the ways God is providing, guiding, and loving you.

Father God, how often we wish we could see the end of our story. How the struggles and trials we are currently facing will be used for Your plan and Your glory. But Father, that is where we must stop and trust in Your love and Your Word. "Being confident of this very thing, that He who has begun a good work in you will complete it until the day of Jesus Christ." (Phil. 1:6) "And the Lord, He is the One who goes before you. He will be with you, He will not leave you nor forsake you; do not fear nor be dismayed." (Deut. 31: 8)

March 19
Teaching our children
Exodus 15, Judges 5

In Biblical days, storytelling or songs were the forms that were used to spread God's word. There was not a Bible on every night stand or a hymnal in every temple pew. Word of mouth was how God's Word was spread. These songs would be passed on from generation to generation. "Hear, O Israel: the Lord our God, the Lord is one! You shall love the Lord your God with all your heart, with all your soul, and with all your strength. And these words which I command you today shall be in your heart. You shall teach them diligently to your children, and shall talk of them when you sit in your house, when you walk by the way, when you lie down, and when you rise up. You shall bind them as a sign on your hand, and they shall be as frontlets between your eyes. You shall write them on the doorposts of your house and on your gates." (Deut. 6:4-9) Do you sense the expectation in these words? The command to live out and share your faith everywhere but especially in your home. What conversations happen in your home? I'm sure there are discussions about your favorite sports teams and tv shows. However, are your children hearing and having conversations with you about what God's Word says and what God is doing in your life? We worry about the future of our children. We hope we have equipped them with essential life skills. However, we also hope that we have equipped them with the Truth. All of us, but especially our young people, are being bombarded with lies. They need to know God's Truth. Sharing our faith story and our faith journey with them is crucial. Share with them what God is doing in your life, when He answers prayer, etc. Then when the time comes, those conversations can be brought back to their remembrance. We should not just rely on our churches to teach them about Jesus and God's Word. It is our job. So, sing your song of victory to them. Teach them God's Word. "Train up a child in the way he should go, and when he is old he will not depart from it." (Proverbs 22:6) At some point in their lives, your child needs to realize that they are not God's grandchild, but His child. This may happen when they are younger; however, I observe that happening more when they are out on their own. Yes, we still see children raised in church pursue the things of this world instead of God. But as God is continually working on us, He is also working on them. Your children will need to experience God for themselves. And decide for themselves who God is in their life. *Father, my prayer is that our children and young people will come to know You on a personal level. They need to experience You for themselves. I pray that our families will pass down Your truth and love from generation to generation. Amen.*

March 20

Judge not
Matthew 7

"Judge not, that you be not judged." (Matthew 7:1)

Judging is one of the areas of my life with which I struggle. And if I had to guess, I'm not alone. We so quickly judge a person with just a glance. We may judge because of the outward appearance. We may judge based on how they are choosing to live their life. It is easy to judge from the outside looking in. However, have you had the experience where once you got to know the person and their situation, you had a better understanding of why they looked or lived the way they did? Why don't we take the time to get to know people before we begin judging? One of the answers to that question is we are too busy with our own lives to stop and take the time to get to know others. How sad! Knowing that Jesus desires for us to love others, why are most of our friendships still at surface level? Friendships where we are not complete honest with each other. Relationships where we don't take the time to really get to know one another. We need relationships in our lives where we support one another, advise one another, and pray for one another. The more time we get to know people, the less likely we are to judge. Because as we get to know people, we start seeing them the way Jesus does. We need to get to a place where our first instinct is to love and not judge.

Lord, give us Your eyes to see the actual worth of people we encounter. Eyes that do not allow our preconceived notions to blind us to the real value of the people You love. Forgive us for our shortcomings in this area. Teach us to love like You. Amen!

Inspired by "Give me Your eyes" by Brandon Heath

March 21
Just let go!
Genesis 12

What is that one thing you are still holding on to that has become your "safety net?" What is that one thing you need to let go of so You can follow God completely? You sense God moving in a specific direction. You have prayed about it. You have sought advice about it. You have turned to His Word about it. But you have not been able to move out in faith. There is something you are still holding on to whether for security or sentiment. It's time to let it go!

Imagine being Abram (Abraham). He is 75 years old. Loves his wife. Sees his family often. Has many possessions. God tells him to go. He doesn't tell him where. He just says go. Abram must let go of the security of his life. He must let go of being comfortable. But still, Abram goes. He becomes the father of a great nation which God uses to bless the whole world through His Son, Jesus. But for all that to come to pass, Abram had to let go.

Fear of the unknown is one of the reasons we have for holding on. God may not be asking you to give up the thing you are holding on to. He just needs your willingness to move in the direction He wants you to go. We have a good Father. One who is Faithful and True. However, we do not always understand Him and the way He chooses to move. That's when we accept that He is God: the Creator of everything, the Lord of lords, and King of kings. We take Him at His Word.

Father, help us to clearly see what we need to let go of so You can accomplish Your plan for our life. May we trust You more. God, You have proven Yourself so many times. Thank You for the many ways we have already seen You move. Father, here is our prayer: "Take my life and let it be consecrated, Lord, to Thee; Take my moments and my days, let them flow in ceaseless praise. Take my hands and let them move at the impulse of Thy love; Take my feet and let them be swift and beautiful for Thee. Take my voice, and let me sing always, only, for my King; Take my lips, and let them be filled with messages from Thee. Take my silver and my gold; not a mite would I withhold; take my intellect and use every power as Thou shalt choose. Take my will and make it Thine; it shall be no longer mine. Take my heart, it is Thine own; it shall be Thy royal throne. Take my love; my Lord, I pour at Thy feet its treasure-store. Take myself, and I will be ever, only, all for Thee." ("Take my life and let it be"/Frances Ridley Havergal, 1874 Public Domain) Amen!

March 22
Whose story do you want to hear?
Hebrews 11

Have you ever thought about what you want to do first when you get to Heaven? I imagine the first stop will be at the feet of Jesus praising and thanking Him for all He's done. I imagine the next stop would be to reunite with friends and family who had gone before. But where would your next stop be? Would you like to find those that had been an inspiration to you on your faith journey? Those you knew personally or whose song or story touched your life? What about the men and women whose stories are shared in the Scripture? Would you like to sit down and chat with Daniel and his three friends? Would you want to sit down with blind Bartimaeus? Would it be Moses, Abraham, Elijah, or Peter? Would you like to hear the rest of the Bible stories; the details that were left out and the thoughts or emotions of those involved? I'm sure we each have our "favorite" stories that we would like to hear firsthand.

The Bible is full of real people and real events. It is not a book of fairy tales and make-believe. We will have the opportunity to one day spend eternity with people from the Bible. However, we will also have our own story to share with them. The people from the Bible are not any more important than you in God's eyes. The work that God did in the life of those from the Bible, He can still do today. It may look different because of the different landscape, timeframe, and culture. But He still moves in mighty ways. He still works miracles. He still uses ordinary people to do extraordinary things.

So, when we all get to Heaven, who will want to hear your story? Who will seek you out for the inspiration you provided for them? We will have all of eternity to listen to the testimonies of what an Awesome God we serve!

Father God, as we praise You here on earth, we look forward to the time when we can praise You face to face for all eternity. "When we all get to Heaven, what a day of rejoicing that will be! When we all see Jesus, we'll sing and shout the victory." ("When we all get to Heaven"/E.E. Hewitt) AMEN!

March 23
Jesus, our Lighthouse
Psalm 46

The definition for a lighthouse according to the Merriam-Webster Online Dictionary is "a structure (such as a tower) with a powerful light that gives a continuous or intermittent signal to navigators." Lighthouses were used as both navigational and safety instruments. They could be both beacons of hope and of warning. Imagine being on a boat in the middle of the sea. The winds and waves are tossing to and fro. The darkness surrounds you to the point you cannot determine where the sky ends, and the water begins. You have no way of knowing which way to go or how far the journey. Then out of the darkness, a tiny beam of light shines forth as a small beacon of hope.

As you read the description of being in the boat, did it bring back memories? Or are you there in the storms even now? Life can sometimes seem like we are in the dark with everything pulling us to and fro. We don't know where to go. We don't know who to turn to for direction. We don't know how long we will be in the storm. Yet, there is a glimmer of light shining out in the darkness. It is God, our Guide and Provider, the lover of our soul. He is our Lighthouse in the storms of life. "The name of the Lord is a strong tower; the righteous run to it and are safe." (Proverbs 18:10) "Then Jesus spoke to them again, saying, "I am the light of the world. He who follows Me shall not walk in darkness, but have the light of life." (John 8:12) Through your darkest days, through your fiercest storms, head to the Light of His love for you. "God is our refuge and strength, a very present help in trouble. Therefore we will not fear, even though the earth be removed, and though the mountains be carried into the midst of the sea; though its waters roar and be troubled, though the mountains shake with its swelling." (Psalm 46:1-3) "Fear not, for I am with you; be not dismayed, for I am your God. I will strengthen you, yes, I will help you, I will uphold you with My righteous right hand." (Isaiah 41:10) When you feel like giving up, and all hope is lost, hold on to His promises.

Lord, thank You that we do not have to navigate life on our own. You are there to guide us and lead us safely Home. You are still God even amidst the storms of life. May we seek Your light instead of determining our own direction. Amen!

A prodigal daughter – Part 1
by my sister, Peggy Rowan

I returned to God on a sunny October day. I hadn't stepped foot inside a church, for church, in almost twenty years. There was nothing wrong with my life; no tragedy had struck, no bad relationship I was trying to get out of, no unhealthy addiction I couldn't let go of. I just knew there was something missing. I stepped inside a church in Mason, Ohio. It was called Rivers Crossing, and how appropriate because I was crossing a "river" back to God. I wasn't sure what to expect when I went inside. I remember being slightly nervous. I sit in the back in hopes that I could get to the door quickly should I need to run out. There was no quick, safe way back to the doors since there were about ten individuals in blue "welcome team" shirts between me and the door. I wouldn't be able to escape and not have one of them in the way. As I listened to the music of the worship team, I was waiting for something and found myself getting anxious that I didn't feel a "knock" on my heart. I didn't feel an invitation as I did all those years before. I started to panic, what if I had strayed too far? What if the mistakes I had made in my life were unforgivable? As the pastor got up and started talking about "recovering the purpose in your life", I started to feel a peacefulness inside. As open arms spread wide and a still small voice said; "I have been here this whole time, waiting for you." He had left the ninety-nine to come find me.

If you have walked away, God will come after you. He is relentless in pursuing His prodigals. If you think you have strayed too far...you haven't. If you think He doesn't love you anymore...He does. I encourage you to step back inside a church. I encourage you to open your heart. I encourage you to come home.

> "What man of you, having a hundred sheep, if he has lost one of them, does not leave the ninety-nine in the open country, and go after the one that is lost, until he finds it?" Luke 15:4

March 25
A prodigal daughter - Part 2
by my sister, Peggy Rowan

When I first found my way back to God, I asked him point blank to change my life. I was feeling stuck. It felt like life was circling around me while I had been standing still for years. My career had been the focal point of my life, the one consistency. It was true that I had been enjoying my life; traveling places, attending events, doing what I wanted to do, but still my life felt empty. Five months after stepping back inside a church, I turned in my resignation and threw off the security blanket I had been holding on to for so long. I was leaving; the city, the state, the career, the life I had. God told me to move, so I took the biggest leap of faith I had ever faced. It was simply time to go. So, I moved to Dallas. I didn't know I would only be there for 5 short months when I moved, but I will never forget my time there. I spent those warm sunny days walking with Jesus. Those walks were a time of restoration, renewal, and reawakening. My soul opened up and I began to blossom. Even now whenever I feel defeated or lonely, I hear Jesus say; "come on, let's take a walk". And it was in those quite moments that I learn to trust him. He gave me back something I had lost. He lightened my heart and broke down the wall I had built up around it. While I was in Dallas, God led me to a church called "Covenant". Every time the doors were open I wanted to be there. Every time I walked through those doors I would grow closer to Him. I know what the purpose was to move so far away only to find myself moving back a few months later; it was to build my covenant with God. I had carried all my baggage to Dallas with me, and I left it there. I was free now, and there was no turning back. I was committed to living my life for Him.

Jesus loves to spend time with us, He loves to walk with us in our daily lives. Time spent with Him is NEVER wasted. I encourage you to take time out from your day, no matter what, and spend it in quiet moments with Him. Praying, singing and just talking with Him about whatever is on your mind. Go ahead…lie down in those green pastures, let Him lead you beside still waters, it will RESTORE your soul!

March 26
A prodigal daughter - Part 3
by my sister, Peggy Rowan

Regardless of your level of faith, change and uncertainty can be scary. A lot of people choose not to move away from their current situation because of not knowing what awaits on the other side. Giving up control of your life and letting God lead may feel like you are jumping off a cliff. I spent many days wondering where I would live and when I would get a new job. The one thing I never had to wonder about was where I was going to attend church. When I got back to Columbus, I had a list of four churches in Grove City. The first one was named the same as the one I had left in Dallas, so I thought I would start there. I went one morning, and they had someone in speaking on a social issue, and although at any other time I would have stayed and listened, it was Sunday morning. Sunday mornings are for worship and being "fed." I ended up leaving and going to the second church on that list which is where I am today.

Thanks to a church called "Rivers Crossing", I had crossed a river back to God. Thanks to a church called "Covenant", I had made a covenant with God as he transformed my heart into something new. Although my journey is far from over, I know that this first phase is completed.

Oh...and the name of the church I attend now? VICTORIOUS LIVING!

Inspired by "Reckless Love" by Cory Asbury

A mother's faith
Exodus 2

Imagine the prayers and tears as the mother prepares to let her son go. There was no other way to save his life, even though this does not seem safe either. She double and triple checks her work. Makes sure her daughter knows what to do. And with a final prayer and a kiss, she places him in the basket. In three short verses, we meet a trusting mother. Moses' mother had to release her son into the Father's care. Moses had a death sentence, so she devised a plan to save him. She placed her three-month-old into a handmade basket and placed it in the reeds on the Nile River's banks. As she lay him down, she may have pondered all the things that could go wrong. The dangers that her son could still face while in the basket. The basket could leak, and her son could drown. He could be found by a snake or crocodile before someone saw him. Cruel people could find him. But she had to let go and let God.

How many times in our own lives, do we play the "what if" game? As we send our loved ones out the door for the day, do we stop to think what harm could befall them? Most of us will probably admit to doing this at some point in our lives. Yet, we, like Moses' mother, continue to send them out into the world as we should. Yes, we would love to be able to protect our families from the bad things in this world. We don't want to see our kids bullied. We don't want to answer the doctor's call. Bad things happen in our society. We sometimes feel powerless to protect our loved ones from harm and bad news.

Like Moses' mother, we do what we can to protect our loved ones from the dangers in this world. And then, we too must let go and let God. Remember God was the one who gave us our family. Remember He loves them more than we do. Remember He is always with them. Tragedies still happen, and lives are broken and forever changed. As much as we would like to live in a safe bubble, we can't. Not here in this life. But one day we will! So, what can we do when we can't seem to find the courage to send them out that door? Pray for them. Pray for yourself. Pray with them. Be specific about your fears and concerns. Then let them walk out that door with the Father. He will be with them (and you) no matter what comes their way.

Father, we know You do not want us bound by fears. You know this world is a scary place. May we trust You with our families. May we trust You with our future. We anxiously wait for the day when we get to our Heavenly Home and will have nothing more to fear. Amen!

March 28
The Father's love for us
Psalm 139, Romans 8

The theme of the Bible is how God loves us. This love is something we know. This love is something we count on. This love is something for which we thank Him. How often, however, do we stop to see how He is loving us now? How often do we take the time to bask in that Love? Our Father adores us. When we think of love, we often associate it with a quiet, calming emotion. We quote 1 Corinthians 13. However, that is not always how God's love is portrayed. "For the Lord your God is a consuming fire, a jealous God." (Deuteronomy 4:24) We often view jealousy with a negative connotation. However, God is jealous for us. Two of the definitions for jealous from the Concise Oxford English Dictionary are: "fiercely protective of one's rights or possessions" and "(of God) demanding faithfulness and exclusive worship." "I am the Lord, that is My name; and My glory I will not give to another, nor my praise to carved images." (Isaiah 42:8) God loves us with a fierce passion. And He desires our love in return. He sacrificed His Son because He loved us. He fights for us against the enemy because He loves us. He leaves the 99 to pursue us because He loves us. He also disciplines us because He loves us.

Yes, He is the loving Father with arms open wide for us to climb into His lap and be loved. But He is also the passionate Father who will go to the ends of the earth to bring us back into the fold. So again, how are you seeing or feeling God's love right now? Don't just recall how You have experienced His love in the past. How are you currently experiencing it? Take some purposeful time to allow God to love you. It's not just about how "good" life is right now because we go through seasons of trials where He doesn't love us any less. Go beyond just thinking about how He is blessing you right now. (Yes, that is part of His love for us.) But how does He love you when your world is falling apart? Climb into His "lap" and just be held. Listen to His loving words to you.

Father, may today we spend some time to bask in Your awesome love for us. At times, You love us gently. Still other times, You release Your power to show Your love for us. Thank You that Your love is not dependent on how we measure up today, but simply because You love. Abba Father, may we never take that love for granted. Amen.

March 29
Cloud watching
1 Thessalonians 4-5

As the storms rolled in, I must admit for a second my heart started racing. One cloud had caught my eye, and I began to wonder, "could this be the day of the Lord's return?" Sometimes we need to stop and search the clouds. We get so caught up in life that we lose sight that this is not our forever home. One day Jesus will return! "For the Lord Himself will descend from Heaven with a shout, with the voice of an archangel, and with the trumpet of God. And the dead in Christ will rise first. Then we who are alive and remain shall be caught up together with them in the clouds to meet the Lord in the air. And thus we shall always be with the Lord. Therefore comfort one another with these words." (1 Thessalonians 4:16-18) We love to quote the first part of those verses! However, I think the last statement is one we need to hold on to also. "Therefore comfort one another with these words." There are times in life when there is no earthly comfort to offer. But thank God, we can comfort each other with the promised future. "Then they will see the Son of Man coming in a cloud with power and great glory. Now when these things begin to happen, look up and lift up your heads, because your redemption draws near." (Luke 21:27-28) When your world seems to be growing darker and darker, lift up your head. Spend some time gazing expectantly into the clouds to acknowledge that there will come a day when our King of kings and Lord of lords will return. We will then leave this dark world behind and stand in the brilliance of our Risen Savior.

Don't get discouraged as the days pass with no sign yet of His return. Remember God wants all to come to repentance. As you gaze into the clouds, pray for a lost loved one who needs to accept God's gift of salvation before His return.

Lord, we are so thankful that one day, we will see You face to face. Whether we are coming forth from the grave or watching the clouds roll back to reveal Jesus, we will all be reunited with You. As we ponder your return Lord, lay upon our hearts those who have not yet received Your precious gift. Renew in us a passion to continue to pray for and seek ways to share Your love with them. Amen!

March 30
More of You, God
John 3

If asked what you remember about John 3, most of you would probably tell the story of Nicodemus and explain John 3:16. However, there is a meaningful conversation at the end of the chapter that we sometimes forget. John the Baptist's disciples, and the Jews they had been arguing with, approach John. When they confront him about Jesus also baptizing people (although it was Jesus' disciples doing the baptizing), John again confirms that Jesus is greater. He uses the illustration that Jesus is the bridegroom and he is the joyful friend. John states: "He (Jesus) must increase, but I must decrease." (John 3:30) We, like John, need to decrease so Jesus may increase. We need more of God in our lives, in our churches, in our communities, and in our world. We need less of our own selfish opinions and desires and more of His love for others.

Lord, how different would our world look if we allowed You to be the Lord of our lives entirely? How different would we speak and act? Too often, we respond to situations with our own sense of right and wrong. We want to justify our actions and emotions. We want to get people to come around to our way of thinking. But what happens when those words and actions come from an angry, misguided heart? What happens when we view a situation from our perspective and judge based on our opinion instead of truth? Lord, with so many voices wanting to be heard in our world today, help us to hear Your voice of truth and compassion. Help us to see and listen to others as You do. Open our eyes to see past the poor judgments and arrogant persona to the scared, lonely person that's hiding behind a wall. Instead of just hearing the angry, hateful words, help us to hear the hurt and uncertainty underneath. Help us also to see ourselves through Your eyes, Lord. We may be someone who feels unworthy and unlovable, help us to see how precious we genuinely are. Guide us during those times when we think we have it all together, but, we are pursuing a path that is taking us farther away from You. Draw us back to You. More of You Lord! Less of me. Less of my judgmental attitude and more of Your love. Less of my opinions and more of Your truth. Less of my anxiety and more of Your promises. Lord, when people look at me, may they see more of You and less of me. Amen.

March 31
Help my unbelief
Mark 9

Have you ever done a trust fall? You must relinquish all control and trust others not to let you down or let you get hurt. Self-preservation is something we all have; relinquishing control and simply trust is not something we do naturally. Unfortunately, at times, the same is true about trusting God. We say we believe and trust, yet when asked to let go of our security (whatever that looks like - a person, a defense mechanism, a possession), it seems more natural to hold it closer. Jesus tells the father in Mark 9: "If you can believe, all things are possible to him who believes." (v:23) The father recognizes that he is not able to believe entirely. His response? "Help my unbelief" (v 24) The fate of his son was in the balance. Yes, he trusted that Jesus was able to touch him. But he also knew there were areas where doubts remained.

We too have areas in our lives where doubts may reside. We have an enemy who plants uncertainty in our minds. We may not even be able to identify the unbelief in our lives. We view God with our limited, finite minds and think "there is nothing God can do about my situation." We may also think: "God may not want to do anything about this situation since I am not serving Him as I should." We don't know the mind of God. We don't know what tomorrow holds. We may not see how God is already moving in our situation. What we do know is that we need to surrender to God. We need to relinquish what control we think we have and cry out "help my unbelief."

Lord, help our unbelief. Move us past "things will never change" to waiting with eager anticipation for what You are going to do. Forgive us for the times we are surprised when a prayer is answered. Reveal to us the areas of unbelief in our lives. Thank You for still working on us. Thank You for not giving up on us. Amen.

April 1

Hope amid the storm
Acts 27

When storms rage around us, when we are battered and bruised, when there seems no end in sight, where is hope? Life's storms can damage, even cause life-changing, permanent destruction.

Paul had warned about continuing the journey in Acts 27. However, some of the crew decided to press on. Perhaps they just wanted to get home. Perhaps they misread the winds and the waves. Perhaps they trusted in their own skill. But they find themselves in the middle of a seemingly never-ending fierce storm. They are lightening the load as much as they can. In a storm like this, three days would seem like an eternity. This storm, however, was now in its 14th day. All hope is lost. . . until God. God sends an angel to Paul to let him know that all lives will be saved. The sailors have a plan to abandon ship now that land is in sight. The soldiers have a plan to kill the prisoners, so they won't escape. But God has a better plan. First Paul has everyone eat to strengthen themselves for the swim. Once overboard, everyone makes it to shore the best way they can. Some are strong swimmers and swim for shore. Some must grab hold of something and float to shore. However, everyone still makes it safely to shore.

Yes, sometimes our storms leave us with a broken home and a broken heart. Sometimes it seems like the storm will never end and we are too exhausted from the battle to stay afloat. Some days the darkness is too overwhelming. But no matter how dark, how damaged, how exhausted we are, there is still hope. We may, like Job, ask "Where then is my hope? As for my hope, who can see it?" (Job 17:15) Paul's response to that question may be: "If in this life only we have hope in Christ, we are of all men most miserable." (1 Corinthians 15:19 KJV) Yes, we face many damaging storms in this life, that leave us in various stages of devastation. But thanks be to God; these storms are limited to this side of Heaven. Someday, our lives will be peaceful without damaging storms. As we ride out the storms of life, may we seek for the Hope that is always there. There is the Hope in His presence, His protection, His provision, and His promise. God is with us no matter what the storm looks like or the outcome. Sometimes, we can see how He is protecting us through the storms. Sometimes, we understand how He is providing for us through our storms. But sometimes, the only Hope we can hold on to is His promises.

Lord, sometimes life's storms leave us alone, bruised and exhausted. We look around and all we can see is the damage left behind. At times like this Lord, help us to find that ray of Hope amid the devastation. Help us to trust You in the eye of the storm and its aftermath. Amen!

How are you loving?
1 John

In today's world, there seem to be many people who associate God with hate. They seem to think He is a wrathful judge who has all these rules and is ready to zap them when they sin. Satan has spread his lies and distorted the truth to where it seems he is the "good" guy and God is the "bad" guy. Some people seem to be convinced that God hates the sinner. Why do people believe that? Because, we as God's people, have not done a very good job of loving. God is love! Everything God does is based on His love for all of us. "But God demonstrated His own love toward us, in that while we were still sinners, Christ died for us." (Romans 5:8) His message of love is written on every page of the Bible. Yet here we are trying to convince people that God loves them. If you talk with people who don't believe God loves them, you will probably find that they know a Christian who did not exhibit God's love very well. There may have experienced more of a tone of disapproval and condemnation from them than one of love and mercy. Yes, we want people to turn from their sinful ways, but immediately passing judgment is not the answer. We must love them to God. He is more equipped to convince them to turn from their sinful ways than we are. And if we do need to confront them about the sin in their lives, we need to do so in love.

People need to be loved in life. They need to be loved on by the Father. But as a representative of God, we may be "delivering" the only message they are "hearing" from God right now. What message are you delivering? Take some time to earnestly and prayerfully reflect on that question. Think about your interactions both with your Christian brothers and sisters and with those who have not yet found their way to God. Is love at the core of your words and actions toward them? If you asked others, what would they say? We are imperfect people living in an imperfect world. Sometimes our hurt and anger get the better of us and we start reflecting our own heart, instead of God's. But for people to see how much God loves them, we as His people need to be His hands and feet and love people to Him.

Father, forgive us when love is not our first response. Teach us to love more like You. May others realize how much You love by the love reflected in our own lives. Amen.

Lazarus' story
John 11

Do you ever wonder why Lazarus' resurrection seems to be more significant than Jairus' daughter and the widow's son? Was it because he was a friend of Jesus? Was it because he was dead "longer?" We are told several times about how much Jesus loved his friends. But I don't think that is what makes Lazarus' resurrection story stand out. Jesus waited until the sickness took Lazarus' life before going to Bethany. Then He headed there to raise Lazarus from the dead so "that the Son of God may be glorified through it." (John 11:4) When Martha comes out to greet him, she states that she knows Lazarus will rise again in the resurrection. (John 11:24) But Jesus tells her: "I am the resurrection and the life." (John 11:25) When He gets to the tomb, tells them to remove the stone, then calls Lazarus back from death and the grave! This is the first time someone has been called out of the grave. I think part of the significance of Lazarus' resurrection is what is going on in the background of this story. It was dangerous for Jesus to return to Bethany. The Jewish leaders were already angry with him. "Then Thomas, who is called the Twin, said to his fellow disciples, "Let us also go, that we may die with Him." (John 11:16) They believed that they were headed to their death. Jesus alone knows He is coming close to the end of His ministry here on earth and will be facing His own death and resurrection before too long. Toward the end of John 11, we see the religious leaders now desperate to stop Jesus. Lazarus' resurrection seems to be the "final straw." "Then, from that day on, they plotted to put Him to death." (John 11:53) Jesus has tried to prepare His disciples for His death however they still do not fully comprehend the impact of His words. With Lazarus' resurrection, Jesus has now revealed His authority over death. He has revealed Himself as "the Resurrection and the Life." He is exhibiting His Resurrection Power. But first He must die. At Lazarus tomb, before He calls him forth, Jesus weeps. Yes, I believe that Jesus shares our sorrow. But I believe there were more in those tears than just the current sadness. As He thinks ahead to His own death, I believe He weeps for people everywhere. He recognizes the sorrow His death will bring to those close to Him. He is heartbroken for the ones who will still not believe; those people who so quickly will turn their "Hosanna" into "Crucify Him." He came to love and forgive everyone. He came so that all may have eternal life. He knows that there will be those who will reject Him and not accept His precious gift of salvation. Do you think there could be some tears for Lazarus too? Jesus chose to leave Paradise for us to sacrifice His life for us. Lazarus is being summoned from that peaceful place to become a living witness to the Power of our Savior! *Father, we thank You for Your Resurrection Power!*

Who is Jesus to you?
Matthew 16

"He asked His disciples, saying, "Who do men say that I, the Son of Man, am?" (Matthew 16:13)

As we are getting ready to celebrate the final days of Jesus' earthly ministry, we recognize the importance of this question. The question is not just to those whom Jesus was asking, it is the question for all eternity. Everyone must one day answer this question. For some, Easter and Christmas may be the only time that they give serious thought to this question. Some will choose to debate it, some will choose to ignore it, some will choose to identify Jesus as the Son of God but state that He has no impact on their lives. It is not a question to be taken lightly. If you believe Jesus is who He says He is, you decide how who He is impacts your life. Do you only acknowledge Jesus by your words? Or do you live your life in the acknowledgment of what Jesus has done for you? Do you live knowing you have a Redeemer who took your place and faced death, Hell, and the grave so that you can one day live for all eternity with your Heavenly Father? Do you admit He is your Savior, yet spend your days doing your own thing instead of seeking His will for you? Do you just want to ignore who He is and believe that it has no impact on your life or eternal future? This question might be easier if the Resurrected Savior was not still moving among us. If the Holy Spirit did not give proof of the answer to this question. It might be easier to ignore if you did not see evidence of a greater Power at work in this world today. It might be easier if the earth itself did not bear witness to the truth of God's Word. It might be easier if God was not actively pursuing all to come to repentance. You feel the tug, you know it's real, but you would rather ignore and push it away, then address the question: "Who do (INSERT YOUR NAME HERE) say, that I, the Son of Man, am?" My friend, there will be a day when you will be confronted with the answer you give to this question. It is one you need to answer today.

My Father, I pray that You reveal Yourself to all those who have not yet answered this question in their life. That as they walk through the week, that everywhere they turn, everything they hear, will point them back to the sacrifice that Jesus gave on that cross for them. Make it personal for them God. "For God so loved the world that He gave His only begotten Son, that whoever believes in Him should not perish but have everlasting life. For God did not send His Son into the world to condemn the world, but that the world through Him might be saved." (John 3:16-17) Father, I pray they answer "You are the Christ, the Son of the living God." (Matt 16:16)

95

Cries of Hosanna!
Matthew 21, Mark 11, Luke 19, John 12

Have you ever anticipated something in your life that you thought would make everything better? Perhaps it was a new home or a new job. Maybe it was a future spouse or children. We think "my life will be better when ...", you fill in the rest of the sentence. As Jesus entered Jerusalem, everyone in the crowd probably was also thinking, "now my life will be better because ..." They may have had different expectations for what Jesus was going to do now that He seem to be taking on the role of their King. When we read about the Triumphal Entry, we focus on the shouts of praises and the feeling of celebration. However, according to the Holman Bible Dictionary, their Hosanna cries were taken from Psalm 118:25-26: "Save now, I pray, O Lord; O Lord, I pray send now prosperity. Blessed is he who comes in the name of the Lord! We have blessed you from the house of the Lord." According to the Merriam-Webster Online Dictionary, the origins of the word Hosanna is from the Hebrew meaning "pray, save (us)!" Their shouts of praise were for salvation. The salvation they were expecting was not the same that Jesus was coming to bring. They wanted to be saved from Roman authority. Perhaps they wanted salvation from their taxes. Since they knew that Jesus healed, perhaps they wanted salvation from sickness and even death. Jesus' plan of salvation was for their spiritual lives rather than for their physical lives. He came to save them from the penalty of sin. He came to save them from the shame of sin. He came to free them from the bondage of sin. And that salvation would be for all people. Jesus did not enter Jerusalem to be just the King of the Jews; He entered Jerusalem to be the King of kings and the Lord of lords. He entered Jerusalem amidst the Hosannas to save a dying world, to bring the redemption plan to all people.

Father God, today we offer up our own "Hosanna! Blessed is He who comes in the name of the Lord!" (Mark 11:9) We offer up our own cries of "save us!" We thank You for Your plan of salvation where once again we could be counted worthy to be in Your Presence. Not through anything we have done, but because of Your Son's gift of salvation on the cross. We sing "Worthy is the Lamb who was slain to receive power and riches and wisdom, and strength and honor and glory and blessings." (Revelations 5:12) Amen!

Confused and alone
Matthew 26, Mark 14, Luke 22, John 18

What do you do when your life with Christ is not turning out the way you thought it would? You may have anticipated a life with Christ as a life of ease. You envisioned a life with no problems or quick solutions. You planned for a life where all your "needs" would be met. You would have perfect children, the ideal job, financial security, and good health. Imagine the Jewish people who were expecting a Conquering King to rescue them from Roman rule. Imagine Jesus' disciples as the soldiers led Him away. Life was not working out as they anticipated. All they were left with was confusion and the feeling of being abandoned. What happens next? How do they go on? Hope is gone. Evil has won. It seems all they believed were lies. A sense of emptiness and loneliness had surrounded them. The Jewish people grew angry at Jesus and, with encouragement from their spiritual leaders, turned to angry cries of "Crucify Him." While some of the disciples did not know what to do, some just returned to their life before Christ. Peter even ends up denying Him. When our expectations of God are not met, we sometimes react the same way. We grow angry at God. We return to life before. We deny Him.

We sometimes face desperate situations where the answer from God is not what we want or expect. We are left feeling confused and alone. We wonder what happens next? How do we go on? There is no easy answer. And it's may be hard to trust God when that happens.

But Resurrection Day did come for the disciples and the Jewish people. The disciples' confusion and fear turned to joy and faith. Many of the Jewish people began to see Jesus as their Eternal King who conquered sin, death and the grave. Someday, we too will experience our "Resurrection Day." We too will have the curtain removed so we can see the way "all things work together for good to those who love God." (Romans 8:28) We will understand: "weeping may endure for a night, but joy comes in the morning." (Psalm 30:5) Until then, we trust. We hold on to the faith the size of a mustard seed. We wait for His glorious appearing when He will wipe away all our tears.

Lord, give us the faith to stand on Your Word and promises during those darkest days when all hope seems lost. When we feel alone and forsaken, remind us You are there. When we feel let down, take our minds back to Calvary's cross and the empty tomb. Father, we know You love us and that You are good so even when we don't understand, and we don't like the answer, may we still trust in You. Amen.

When friends forsake
John 13, 18, 21

At some point in your life, you have probably been hurt by a friend. They may have spread lies about you, betrayed a confidence, or even worse. People let us down. They are human and make mistakes or have bad judgment. And sometimes they are downright mean and hurtful.

Jesus experienced friends letting Him down during His final week. Judas betrayed, and Peter denied. Jesus predicted the betrayal and the denial so was not taken by surprise. But the results were the same. Yet, He still showed compassion. Jesus did not have a couple of the disciples throw Judas out of the Last Supper. He never refused to talk to Peter again. He knew they both would bear the consequences of their actions.

We are not Jesus who was perfect. Compassion may not be our first reaction, if we are even able to get there at all. When we have been hurt, we experience a wide range of emotions often dependent on the circumstance. There seems to be no way to undo the damage done. Time can mend some of the brokenness, but trust and forgiveness maybe be tough to offer back. But know that Jesus understands what it means to be hurt by a friend. You can turn to Him with all those emotions and the hurt.

There was no restoring a relationship with Judas. However, Peter was another story. After the Resurrection, we find some of the disciples back out fishing. As they fish, Jesus prepares breakfast. There is then a conversation between Jesus and Peter where Jesus ask Peter "do you love me?" three times. Here Jesus commissions Peter as a spiritual leader for the early church.

When we have been hurt, we need to look past the emotions to the bigger picture. How important is this relationship to us? What was the motivation of the person who hurt us? If the person comes to ask for forgiveness, we need to really listen to what they are saying and take some time to process. For some situations, we may very quickly forgive and began to restore the relationship. For others, we may need to step away from the relationship. But in whatever the situation, we need to seek Jesus' help to be able to forgive.

Lord Jesus, You know how much we sometimes hurt each other. You know how painful it can be to be betrayed by a friend. However, You also know how meaningful relationships are in our lives. Help us to forgive and restore those relationships that we still need in our lives. Help us to know when we need to forgive but let go. Please guide us through the forgiveness process and teach us more about Your grace and mercy during that time. Amen.

Jesus prayed for us
John 17

In John 17, we read about Jesus' final instructions to His disciples before heading to the Garden. He ends those instructions with prayer. What was one of the central themes of His prayer? Unity. In the first part of the recorded prayer in John 17, Jesus is asking God, His Father, to glorify Him. He knew He was headed to the cross to pay the sin debt for all. And by doing so, will provide the way to eternal life. The second part of the prayer is directly for His disciples. He prays that God would guide and protect them. During that prayer though, we find "that they may be one as We are." (John 17:11) The unity theme continues in the last section of the prayer where Jesus is praying for all believers. He again prays "that they all may be one." (John 17:21) Jesus knows He is getting ready to face the agony of the cross and His death. And with that weighing heavy on His heart and mind, He still prayed for us. We might anticipate a prayer for God to guide and protect us. But why pray for unity? Jesus knew that disunity would be one of the most significant problems we as Christian people would face. If we take a quick look back through history, or at current events, we can see the effect the unity or disunity of the Christian faith has on the world around us. If Satan can have the Christian believers spend their time fighting amongst themselves, he knows they will not be as effective in the battle against him. When Jesus prayed that we would be one, He added: "as We are one." How can we, as a body of believers, be as "one" as the Father and Son? "That they may be made perfect in one, and that the world may know that You have sent Me." (John 17:23) Yes, we will have disagreements about many things. But we should not allow the "minor" stuff to take away from the calling of all believers. "Go therefore and make disciples of all the nations, baptizing them in the name of the Father, and of the Son and of the Holy Spirit, teaching them to observe all things that I have commanded you." (Matthew 28:19-20) When we as a body of believers come together in unity, we accomplish so much for the Kingdom. It is when we allow Satan's seeds of disharmony to grow that we become less effective. We take the focus off our kingdom purpose. When God's people come together to pray and work toward a common goal of sharing the Good News to a lost and dying world, things begin to change. Jesus prayed for us that through us all "the world may believe that You sent Me." (John 11:21) He also prayed: "Father, I desire that they also whom You gave Me may be with Me where I am." (John 11:24) Jesus prayed for you and me. Let us go forth in unity to bring the message of salvation to the world.

We are Barabbas
Matthew 27, Mark 15, Luke 23, John 18

Do you think we will see Barabbas in Heaven? I almost expect to see him there. To be the one deserving of death and then have an innocent Man take your place, I think that would change your outlook on life. Perhaps, Barabbas stood in the background of the cross pondering how he missed the death sentence. He may have even been the prisoner with the most extensive list of crimes, yet, he finds himself free. Wouldn't you like to hear the rest of his story? How did he choose to live his "new" life? The Bible, however, doesn't give any more information about Barabbas, so we are left to wonder.

The reality is any one of us could have been in Barabbas' shoes that day. Jesus came to take our place on that cross. You may think "well, I'm not a murderer." Have you ever read the Sermon on the Mount? "You have heard that it was said of those of old, 'You shall not murder, and whoever murders will be in danger of the judgment.' But I say to you that whoever is angry with his brother without a cause shall be in danger of the judgment." (Matthew 5:21-22) We are borne into a sinful world. None of us escape sin. We could spend time justifying our sin or comparing our "little" sin to everyone else's "big" sin. The reality, however, is: "for all have sinned and fall short of the glory of God." (Romans 3:23) Most of us have seen the images of Jesus being beaten and whipped, of Him carrying His cross, of Him being nailed to the tree, and finally hanging between the thieves. These images are not pleasant. We often prefer to turn away from them. Now imagine standing at the foot of that cross with the realization that cross was meant for you. No matter how "good" we think we have been, "but we are all like an unclean thing, and all our righteousnesses are like filthy rags." (Isaiah 64:6) But Jesus steps in and takes our place. Barabbas walked out of those prison doors into a life of freedom. He became only an observer of all the preparation for the crucifixions. We don't know what he chose to do with his freedom. But my friend, we too can live in that freedom. Our sin has imprisoned us, but we also can walk out of our prisons into freedom through Christ. How we choose to live that freedom life is up to us. Do we still live like we are prisoners? Or do we enjoy our freedom life with the assurance that our sins are covered by the blood of Jesus?

Jesus, there are no words or actions that will ever be enough to thank You for taking our place. Teach us to live in the freedom into which You have called us. Amen!

Oh, what a gift
Genesis 3, Hebrews 9-10

The events of Good Friday have their beginning all the way back in
Genesis 3. They are motivated by love for each life lived between Genesis 3
and the cross; and each life between then and now. God had created a
perfect world for us to live in with Him. However, Adam and Eve sinned
and were no longer able to be in the perfect place and walk beside the Holy
God. God knew then He would need to make a way to restore their
relationship. One where they could once again be clean and worthy to be
in His presence. God looked down through history at the many men and
women whom He loved. They were hopelessly lost in their sins with no
means of escape. So, God institutes the Law. Have you ever tried to read
through Leviticus with all the laws and sacrifices? How difficult would it
have been to live up to those expectations on your own? Have you ever
imagined being a priest back then? All that blood! Back then, animal
sacrifices were the payment for sin. "Indeed, under the law almost
everything is purified with blood, and without the shedding of blood there
is no forgiveness of sins." (Hebrews 9:22 ESV) Once a year, the high priest
was permitted to enter the Holy of Holies into the presence of God. And
only after he had gone through an extensive procedure to make himself
acceptable. Sacrificing was not a one-time event. There were sacrifices for
various reasons. God knew this system would only serve in a temporary
capacity. He needed a sacrifice that could take the sins of all humanity, so
they would once again be worthy to be in His presence. God knew the only
One worthy was His only begotten Son. However, that meant that His Son
would have to leave the splendor of Heaven and take on a human form. He
would have to experience pain and agony and yes, even death. The spotless
Lamb would have to lay down His sinless life for the sin of all humanity.
"For God so loved the world that He gave His only begotten Son, that
whoever believes in Him should not perish but have everlasting life."
(John 3:16) After Jesus takes His final breath, "the veil of the temple was
torn in two from top to bottom." (Matthew 27:51) The need for a high
priest was thereby removed. We all may now enter the Holy of Holies and
approach the mercy seat. My friend, thank God that we do not need to offer
up sacrifices anymore. Thank God for the gift of His precious Son who
bleed and died for you and me. Thank Him, that we no longer need a high
priest to be our mediator. That by accepting Jesus' gift of salvation, we are
counted worthy to approach God ourselves. *Lord Jesus, thank You for
your sacrifice and for taking my place. Worthy are You, Lord, to receive all
our praise!* Inspired by "O Come to the Altar" by Elevation Worship

April 11
What now?
Matthew 27, Mark 15, Luke 23, John 18

I am almost sure that a sleepless night followed the Crucifixion for many
in Jerusalem. For some who witnessed the horrific scene, they were unable to
close their eyes. For others, they may have laid pondering many questions.
Still others may have been wondering how they could have been so wrong.
Others may have been anxious for what the next few days would bring.
Do you envision some of the men and women who had been part of the
"Crucify Him" crowd now wondering "what have we done?" What about the
centurion? He had taken part in many crucifixions and had never had an
earthquake or sky darken before. What about the religious leaders who
worried about what would happen at the tomb in the next few days? The
disciples who were now facing both an identity crisis and feared for their
lives? What about Mary, the heartbroken mother? As they lay sleepless in their
beds or up pacing in their rooms, were they trying to determine "what
now?" With Hope dead and in the tomb, perhaps the question of the night
was "what do we do tomorrow?" The disciples lost their identity. The soldier
lost his truth. The mother had lost her son. And the religious leaders were
afraid they would lose their victory. The disciples, who had followed the
Master for over three years, now are without a Shepherd and without a
purpose. The centurion had to acknowledge "truly this was the Son of God."
(Matt 27:54) and now must decide how he will choose to live his life? Mary
who had been told "yes, a sword will pierce through your own soul also"
(Luke 2:35) now is painfully aware what that prophecy means. The religious
leaders are afraid of the consequences if someone gets past their guards and
steals the body. Have you ever had a time where you seem to have lost your
purpose? Or discover the "truth" you were following had all been lies? Have
you ever been afraid of what tomorrow will bring? Have you, like Mary, had
to face your unbearable, darkest days of sorrow and emptiness, without a
certain presence to comfort? Or have you reached a place in your life,
where you recognize the truth about Jesus and now must decide how you
let that knowledge influence your life? The night of the Crucifixion, there was
no Hope for an answer. There was no Presence to comfort and guide. But
THANK GOD, we know the rest of the story. My friend, for all those
situations we may face in our lives, we have the assurance of an empty grave!
We do not have to face life's problems alone or forsaken. *Our loving Father,
who sacrificed His only Son for us, loves us. He is waiting with open arms to
carry us through our darkest days and nights. Father, we bow humbly before
You to thank You for Your loving Presence and the assurance that Sunday is
coming! Every burden, care, heartbreak, tear will never to be endured again!*

April 12
Believing the impossible – Part 1
Matthew 28, Mark 16, Luke 24, John 20, 1 Corinthians 15

Life went on. They had survived the crucifixion scene and the initial few hours that followed. But the disciples never knew when soldiers might be knocking on their door. When the knock sounded, however, it was not what they had expected. The women stood in disbelief of what they had just witnessed: an empty tomb. As word of the empty grave grew, speculation abound, even among the disciples. What amazes me a little is in Matthew 28:11-15, when the soldiers told the chief priests what had happened, there did not seem to be disbelief. There did not seem to be a discussion about what they really saw. They just decided to pay the soldiers off and told them to say, "His disciples stole the body."

As Jesus began appearing to more people, then the truth of that Resurrection morning became real. Jesus had tried to prepare His disciples for His death and resurrection, but the disciples' human minds could not comprehend. Now God's plan was being revealed in such a way that it left no doubt. Hope returned, as did a passion for sharing the Good News of a Resurrected Savior. The first-hand accounts made the difference. Who could argue with the still frightened soldiers about what they saw? When He spoke Mary's name, there was no denying the call of her Master. As people began to see Jesus face to face, none of them could doubt His return. "He is risen, He is risen indeed" began to ring throughout Jerusalem. Many spent time with the glorified Savior. The effects of a Resurrected Lord could be felt as they walked down the street. The religious leaders tried to discredit those who spread the News. But lives were changed, and Power was revealed. And the truth of the Message was hard to refute. And even though we have not yet seen Jesus face to face, we too can give first- hand accounts of what a Risen Savior has done in our own lives. We can shout with all authority: "He is risen, He is risen indeed." We are living a life in the knowledge that the grave has been defeated! Death and Hell have no power. We know with all assurance that our Savior and Lord died, was buried, and came forth from that grave!

April 13
Believing the impossible – Part 2
Matthew 28, Mark 16, Luke 24, John 20, 1 Corinthians 15

How does the knowledge of the Resurrection impact our lives? We know we are loved. Jesus loved us so much He was willing to lay down His life for us. "For God so loved the world that He gave His only begotten Son, that whoever believes in Him should not perish but have everlasting life." (John 3:16) We know we are never alone. "I will never leave you nor forsake you." (Hebrews 13:5) We know the grave is not our final resting place. "O Death, where is your sting? O Hades, where is your victory?" (1 Corinthians 15:55) And we know He will return! Not as our Humble Sacrifice but as our Reigning King! "Behold, He is coming with clouds, and every eye will see Him, even they who pierced Him." (Revelation 1:7)

As we celebrate the Resurrection, may we continue to spread the Good News. There is a Savior who died in your place and my place. A Redeemer who was buried in a new tomb. A Risen Lord who defeated death, hell and the grave. And because of His sacrifice and victory, we can live with the promise of eternity reunited with a God who loves us. "Oh, what a Savior, isn't He wonderful? Sing Hallelujah; Christ is risen. Bow down before Him for He is Lord of all. Sing Hallelujah; Christ is risen." ("O come to the altar"/ Elevation Worship)

Lord, we raise our redeemed hands up to You for all You have done for us. Father, may we, with the boldness of the early church, share the Good News. Jesus died, was buried, and rose again and will one day return to take us Home with Him! "Blessing and honor and glory and power be to Him who sits on the throne, and to the Lamb, forever and ever!" (Revelation 5:13)

April 14
God of all comfort
John 14

"And I will pray the Father, and He shall give you another Comforter, that He may abide with you for ever." (John 14:16 KJV)

We often think of the world's darkest day as being the day of the Crucifixion. However, I think the day between the Crucifixion and the Resurrection was just as dark, if not more so. Up until Jesus took His final breath, some may have held on to hope that He would still be rescued from the cross. However, the following day, Hope seemed gone forever. There was no Comforter for Jesus' mother, the other women, or the disciples. It was not yet time for the Holy Spirit to be revealed. So, they each faced that day entirely alone with no word from God, no presence of Jesus and no appearing of the Holy Spirit.

Sometimes we may take for granted the Holy Spirit's presence in our lives and the many ways He helps us. John 14:16 in the Amplified Bible reads: "And I will ask the Father, and He will give you another Helper (Comforter, Advocate, Intercessor-Counselor, Strengthener, Standby), to be with you forever." Jesus knew that when He physically left, that His disciples would still need guidance, provision, teaching, and comforting. They would need Someone to pray for them when the words would not come. They would need Someone with them always.

God provided a Presence that resides in us. Someone to comfort us on our darkest days. One who helps us to follow God's plan by letting us know when we sin, guiding us to the right path, strengthening us to keep on going.

Thank You, Holy Spirit, for being our daily Companion. For understanding us even better than we know ourselves. Thank You for interceding on our behalf when our hearts have no words, only cries of despair and anguish. Amen.

April 15
He still rolls away the stone
Mark 16

"And they (the women) said among themselves, "Who will roll away the stone from the door of the tomb for us?" (Mark 16:3)

When the stone was placed across the tomb, it seemed to signify the locking away of all their hopes and their future. It seemed to be the finale to a horrifying day. On the morning of the third day, when the women approached to anoint the body, they wondered who would move that stone for them. They knew they were powerless to remove it themselves. When they got to the tomb, the stone had already been rolled away. God had rolled away the stone, not to let Jesus out, but to let all who came, find an empty tomb. Hope was alive! Death had been defeated!

How many of us seem to have buried all our hope? How many of us have covered it with a stone, perhaps of bitterness, disappointment, or grief? We feel like we will never experience joy or peace again. But hold on, it's not the end. The God who rolled away the stone to reveal the power of His Son, is still able to roll away the stones in our life too. When life seems to kill all hope, God's resurrection power can raise it up again. When life leaves us heartbroken and alone, God's presence remains.

In those first days after our world has been shaken, we feel like we are in the tomb and the stone is too large to move. We are too weak to move it. Perhaps we decide that we rather stay in the "tomb" than try to move on with life. But as God is still working, pursuing, and loving us, we begin seeing little rays of light piercing into our darkness. Over time, God's healing hand begins moving the stone. Until one day, we find it only halfway across the "tomb." Eventually, we get to the point where we are feeling stronger and more willing to try to live again. Only God can roll away those massive stones in our lives. Only God can restore hope, joy, and peace. Only God can promise us that eventually there will be a day when broken heartedness, loneliness, pain, and death will be wiped away.

Our loving Father, You are the only one who can roll away the stones that lock us away from truly living. We are too weak, and the stones are too large. You love us enough not to leave us there. Lord, if there are stones that are trapping us inside an overwhelming darkness, shine the light of Your love. Roll away the stones so that we may live in the abundant life You have for us. Amen!

Pass on the joy
1 Peter 1

"Whom having not seen, ye love; in whom, though now ye see Him not, yet believing, ye rejoice with joy unspeakable and full of glory."
(1 Peter 1:8 KJV)

Several of my family members and friends are going through some difficult times. Our prayer lists always seem longer than our praise lists, would you agree? There seems to be more negativity in our world than positivity. Yes, life is hard. We live in a fallen world with fallen people. We live in a world of hate, disease, and death. But amidst that, we have "joy unspeakable and full of glory." And we need to spread that joy!

What does it mean to have joy unspeakable or inexpressible? We sometimes act like that means we are not supposed to talk about what God is doing in our lives. We don't want to offend someone. We don't want to upset someone who is going through a tough time by expressing our joy. But we also understand the true meaning of that scripture. No mere human words can accurately and adequately express the joy that we possess all because of Christ. We experience it but fully explaining it to someone else is impossible.

But pass it on! When we share what Christ is doing in our lives and when we share the joy only He can give, we are spreading not only joy but also hope. What happens if we turn our praise list into the focus instead of our prayer list? Yes, praying for one another is essential but sometimes that list gets so long, that it leaves little room for praise. Start with your praise list both in your prayer life and when you share requests with others. Invite them to "rejoice with those who rejoice." (Romans 12:15) When sharing with someone a prayer request or a burden on your heart, consciously also mention a reason you are thankful or joyful. I think we can all agree that we need more joy in life. So, pass on the joy! The joy of living with your sins forgiven! The joy of never being alone! The joy of a Reunion Day! The joy of the peace amid your storms. The joy of your daily blessings. Make your joy list today and share it with someone.

Father, may our hearts be filled with "joy unspeakable" today! That we take some time away from all the worries of this life and just bask in Your love and mercy! Recognizing that You are worthy of all our praise no matter what our life looks like right now! You are our Hope, our Peace, our Provider, our Healer, our Redeemer! Let Your name be glorified! Amen!

Moldable clay
Jeremiah 18

Thank God that He is the Potter of our lives. I am not an artist. What I envision and what comes out are never the same. I may try to make changes to my artwork, add more color here, erase this, etc., but the result is usually the same. When I try to cover up the flaws, it only seems to make them worse. Doesn't that sound like life too? Life never seems to turn out the way we envision it. We try to make changes but still run into the same problems. We try to cover up mistakes and make them right, only to realize we are just making a bigger mess. However, we have Hope. The Creator of the universe is eagerly waiting for us to hand over our ruined clay. He takes His loving hands and begins to reshape us. He covers up cracks and smooths out the rough edges. He tenderly molds us into one of His masterpieces.

No matter how "messed up" your life is. The One who laid the foundations of the world, who hung the stars in the sky, who creates each new day, wants to be creative in your life. Are you moldable clay in the Potter's hands? The artwork does not get the credit for becoming a masterpiece. It has no power to make itself beautiful. But the skillful hands of the Creator can take the most ordinary art and transform it into a priceless treasure.

Father, You are the Potter, we are the clay. Mold us into what You would have us to be. Amen!

Days go by
Ecclesiastes 1, 3

Are you ever like me and find yourself "wishing away" days? Wishing for a family, wishing the kids were a little older, wishing the kids were younger, wishing for warmer weather, wishing for cooler weather: an endless wishing list. How many "perfect" days can you remember? Perfect weather, time to enjoy what we want to do, spending time with family, etc. Yes, we have those days however they seem a lot fewer than our "regular" days. But what about ALL those days where we are just trying to "get by?" How quickly we forget and take for granted: "This is the day that the Lord has made; we will rejoice and be glad in it." (Psalm 118:24) God made each day! Those days where the weather's not perfect. Those days where there is too much to do and not enough time to do it. Those days we feel tired and alone. How do we reclaim our days "for rejoicing and being glad in (them)?" By recognizing that God made those days also. God walks with us through the mundane days as well as the mountaintop and valley days. How we view each day is often a decision. We can look at our long to-do list. We can dread getting out of bed and heading to work. We can try to gear up to face another exhausting day with the kids. Or we can decide to be thankful for another day to do kingdom work. Start your day in communication with your Father. When you get tired of doing the same old thing all the time, decide to seek ways to be a blessing to someone that day. We can live in a state where we allow our thoughts to bring us down or we can "take captive every thought to make it obedient to Christ." (2 Corinthians 10:5) Have you had days where you have to tell yourself to "stop thinking along those lines?" We can get in the pattern of allowing our thoughts to follow a negative path, one often mixed with lies, exaggerations and frustrations. Many times, when my thoughts start down those same old paths that lead to anger, disappointment and hurt, I must stop and speak Truth. When I speak God's Truth and His Love into those thought patterns, I am the one who changes. My outlook changes. My control of the day changes. My attitude changes. When you start down your worn out thought path, ask God to speak His truth into those thoughts, ask Him to remind You of His Love for you. Then we can say: "This is the day that the Lord has made; we will rejoice and be glad in it." (Psalm 118:24) *Lord, thank You for living life with us. That You never leave us to face any day alone. In our darkest days, You are there. When we are basking in Your blessings, You are there. And when we encounter those countless routine days, You are there! In every day, may we be reminded of who we are in You and that we are loved.*

Boast in the Cross
2 Corinthians 11, Philippians 3, Galatians 6

If you ask my boys which scripture they remember me quoting to them over the years, their first response would probably be the paraphrase of Proverbs 16:18: "Pride comes before a fall." Most children and teens think they have all the answers. However, we as adults, are just as bad even though we have more life experience to know better. We have a hard time changing our minds about something. We get set in our ways (because we believe they are always "right"). We take pride in our accomplishments. We will share lessons learned through our experiences whether others want to hear them or not. None of these are necessarily a bad thing. We should stand up for what we believe. We should take pride in what we have achieved in life. The problem is when pride keeps us from hearing others, accepting our limitations, and hinders our willingness to learn. It is also an issue when we take credit for it all without recognizing we are nothing without Christ.

In 2 Corinthians 11, Paul lists his qualifications as a minister of Christ. However, he seems to do so reluctantly. Why? He does not want any credit for his ministry. Paul has a lot to boast about, even outside of his ministry. In Philippians, he states that if he chose to boast in the flesh, he could. Paul was an intelligent, highly-respected man. He had the education, the family lineage, the confidence, and the ministry. However, he concluded, that none of that was worthy of his boasting. Paul tells the Galatians: "But God forbid that I should boast except in the cross of our Lord Jesus Christ." (Galatians 6:14)

Let us, like Paul, recognize that who we are and what we have accomplished is only by the grace of God. When we boast, let it be as a testimony of what God has done in our lives. He made us. He adores us. He lifts us up. He thinks we are worthy of boasting. So, share your story of what you know and what you've done, but let it ring like an anthem to what a great God you serve.

Inspired by "Boasting" by Lecrae

We'll understand it by and by
Job

May I be honest? When I sing lyrics about not being disappointed with God or that He will never let us down, it causes me to pause. The reason is that there are times in my flesh, that I do feel disappointed or let down. From my human perspective, I wish the answer had not been "no" or I had gotten my way. However, I have been a Christian long enough to trust God with the "nos" even when I would have preferred a miracle. But even during the "disappointment," I still know my God is faithful and good. I recognize that His ways are higher than mine. I realize I do not see the full picture. I only see from my perspective. I don't know His plan or His purpose. I also understand that this world is not my Home.

The Book of Job has 42 chapters. In most of those chapters, Job and his friends are trying to figure out why all these bad things had happened to him. In their limited knowledge, they find reason upon reason for all the misfortune. The conversation had gotten so out of hand, that God joined in. "Who is this that darkens counsel by words without knowledge?" (Job 38:2) What they did not see was how God was using this for His glory. What they did not see was the end of the story. Job's friend, Elihu, states: "Behold, God is exalted by His power; who teaches like Him? Who has assigned Him His way, or who has said, 'You have done wrong'?" (Job 36:22-23)

So, in times when we don't understand, we trust. In times that we hurt, we hold. We hold on to His truth, His promises, and His love. For whatever the outcome, He is there. And one day, we will get to go Home, to the world God desires for us all to live. Home, where we will experience freedom from pain and loss. "Farther along we'll know more about it, farther along we'll understand why: cheer up, my brother, live in the sunshine, we'll understand it all by and by." ("Farther Along"/ W. B. Stevens)

Father, You hold the world in Your hands, yet You know each name. You see each tear that falls. We may never understand on this side of eternity why things happen as they do. But we trust that Your love will never forsake us. We trust that Your promises are true. We trust that You are somehow using our hurt for Your glory. We are Yours! Use our experiences for Your kingdom purpose. Though we cannot see Your purpose, we will trust in You. Amen.

April 21
The Son will shine again
John 20

This is the time of year, at least in my part of the world, where we anxiously await sunny days. At this point, we don't even mind the temperatures (sort of) if the sun is there to behold. The sun brings the hope of warmer days, color and beauty to the land, and longer days to enjoy with family and friends. In our Christian walk, we have times where we anxiously await the Son. We have been through the cold dark "winter" of life or the seemingly endless "rainy" season. We long for some brightness, some warmth, some beauty, some hope.

The reality is that even during the winter when it seems farther away, we still know that the day begins with the rising of the sun. Through it doesn't feel like it, the sun is still providing heat to the earth during even the coldest days. The fullness of the sun may be hidden by the position of the earth, but eventually, spring arrives!

The same is true for our Christian walk. We know that Jesus is there even in those "seasons" where we can't see Him. He is still providing even when we can't feel it. His Truth and Love never changes even amidst our current "position" in life. And eventually, in this life or the next, the "Son" will shine again.

Father, we know that the cold dark days of winter give us a deeper appreciation of the warmth and light of the sun. We pray that we can see how You are still there during those cold dark days in our lives. You are our never changing Love. You are our everlasting Hope. You are our Peace amid life storms. Thank You for Your provision, Your power, and Your promise. Amen!

Alone
Ruth, Genesis 37, 47

Like most families, Naomi and her husband sought a better life for their family. To escape the famine, they went to Moab. However, their "better" life was short-lived. Within ten years, Naomi had lost it all: her family, her livelihood, her security, her identity. There was no hope for a "better" life now. The only future Naomi could see was a lonely future with no love, no peace, and no purpose. But God had other plans. A plan to bring a young Moabite woman to Bethlehem to become a part of the lineage that would bring the Savior into the world.

Young Joseph was the apple of his father's eye. He had more family than he probably knew what to do with. He was one of the youngest, so at the time, probably enjoyed a little more freedom from family responsibilities. God even seem to be on his side, giving him dreams where his father and brothers would bow down to him. But then jealously arose, Joseph lost his freedom, his identity, and his home. Joseph may have looked ahead at the lonely days he would be living out as a slave. But God had other plans. A plan that would bring a young betrayed brother to Egypt to provide a home and food for His people.

My friend, you may be feeling alone or forsaken. You may be looking into a future that has no love, no peace, and no purpose. A future bound to your past or your situation. But God has other plans. "For I know the plans I have for you," declares the Lord, "plans to prosper you and not to harm you, plans to give you hope and a future. Then you will call upon me and come and pray to me, and I will listen to you. You will seek me and find me when you seek me with all your heart." (Jeremiah 29:11-13 NIV) Too often we read these words and assume that they mean to say we will be living a carefree life where everything is sunshine and roses. But these words were written to a people that were captives. "This is what the Lord says, "When seventy years are completed for Babylon, I will come to you and fulfill my gracious promise to bring you back to this place." (Jeremiah 29:10 NIV) No matter what is going on in your life, God is there. No matter what future you see for yourself, God is there. He knows you. He sees you. He loves you. No matter how alone you feel, you are NOT! Even if you are in a place where you feel forsaken by Him, He is there. We may never know this side of eternity what God brings about through our pain and suffering. We may never understand the reason for our tears. But God hears our cries. He sees each tear that falls, and He is holding us in His righteous hands.

Thank You, God that we are never alone or forsaken! Amen.

April 23
Living in Resurrection Power
Romans 8

When we think of living in Resurrection Power, many of us think only of the promised eternity after we die. We relish in the thoughts of reuniting with our family and friends who have gone on before. We envision Jesus waiting for us with outstretched arms when we say our final goodbyes here in this life. And that is something to be excited about! However, how many of us recognize that we are living with that Power right now? How many of us are still bound by the chains of our past mistakes or our current situation? How many of us fall into the same traps all the time? How many of us try to handle life in our own strength? How many of us forget that we are not alone? "But if the Spirit of Him who raised Jesus from the dead dwells in you, He who raised Christ from the dead will also give life to your mortal bodies through His Spirit who dwells in you." (Romans 8:11) Jesus says in John 10:10: "The thief does not come except to steal, and to kill, and to destroy. I have come that they may have life, and that they may have it more abundantly."

What are you allowing the enemy to steal, to kill, and to destroy in your life? Your family? Your church? Your joy? Your peace? Your hope? You have the Resurrection Power living in you. If He was able to raise Jesus from the dead, He can raise what needs to be resurrected in you also. Too often, once we see the effects of the enemy attacks, we think there is nothing we can do. It's too late. It's too hopeless. It's not worth the fight. My friend, it is time we stop allowing the devil to come in and destroy our lives. It is never too late. It is never too hopeless. And it is always worth the fight. "You are of God, little children, and have overcome them, because He who is in you is greater than he who is in the world." (1 John 4:4)

Put on your Ephesians 6 armor! "Pray without ceasing!" (1 Thessalonians 5:17) Allow the Holy Spirit to fight for you. You are not in the battle alone! Fight from your knees submitted to God and the work He wants to do in your life.

Father, stir in us a reminder of who we are in You. We are Your children. We are children of the King of kings and the Lord of lords. We are the children of the Almighty God, the Everlasting Father, the Alpha and the Omega, the Beginning and the End, the First and the Last! Teach us to live in Your Power. Amen!

Calling out His name
Matthew 9

There are times when our children are young, that we would like 5 minutes without hearing a "Mommy" or "Daddy" one more time. Because we know that what comes after the mommy or daddy part, is something we are going to have to take care of or fixed or clean up. But we answer the call and meet the need because our children rely on us and we love them. No one can meet the needs of a young child like a parent.

Everywhere Jesus went, people knew His name. Most called out for Him to heal, save, or forgive them. Most of the time there was always a large crowd surrounding Him. "But when He saw the multitudes, He was moved with compassion for them, because they were weary and scattered, like sheep having no shepherd." (Matthew 9:36)

When Jesus answered the call, He knew that what was needed was more than what was being asked. Even amid the crowds, He would answer the rich man, the blind man, the woman in need, the children. Jesus loved His children and knew that He was their only Hope. No one could meet their needs like Him.

Jesus took the time to go off alone to be with God. But when He was with people, it appears He almost constantly heard His name. Even when we read of Him trying to get some rest, we read "And they came to Him, and awoke Him, saying, "Master, Master, we are perishing." (Luke 8:24) And He always responded! There was no "come back later, I'm busy." No "your need isn't big enough for Me to pay attention to." No "you're not important enough." Jesus answered their calls while He was on earth. And He still answers our calls today!

Lord, You are never too busy to hear our cries. You never think our requests are too small. You never think we are never important enough. You hear our calls and response because You know we rely on You and Your love for us. Amen.

Our cheering squad
Hebrews 12

"Therefore we also, since we are surrounded by so great a cloud of witnesses, let us lay aside every weight, and the sin which so easily ensnares us, and let us run with endurance the race that is set before us, looking unto Jesus, the author and finisher of our faith, who for the joy that was set before Him endured the cross, despising the shame, and has set down at the right hand of the throne of God." (Hebrews 12:1-2)

If you watch football or basketball, you probably can recall games where the cheerleaders and pep band really got the fans pumped up to encourage their team to victory. There are times when that encouragement becomes a game changer. Recognizing that they are playing for more than themselves rejuvenates the players to play their best. In Hebrews 11, we read what is often referred to as the "Hall of Faith." The writer of Hebrews recalls the faith that our forefathers had to further the kingdom of God. We don't see perfect people on this list. We don't see people who made the right decision every time. What we do see is those, that despite their human weakness, chose to trust God. After we read about those listed in Hebrews 11, the writer starts the next chapter with "since we are surrounded by so great a cloud of witnesses." The author paints the picture of us running a race. You can almost envision Abraham and Moses in the stands cheering you on. Who else is in your stands? Who in your life has finished their race and received their reward? Can you hear them shouting your name and saying "You can do it. Don't give up. It will be worth it after all."?

What about your "teammates" in life that are running their races with you? Can you hear their encouragement? And look up ahead to the finish line! There's Jesus! Waiting with outstretched arms!

My friend, if life's race is getting you down and you feel like giving up, look up! "Your redemption draws near." (Luke 21:28)

My God, when I think of all those who fought the fight and kept the faith, it encourages me to keep running; during those times I get tired, when I lose sight of the finish line, when I get off track. You are always there to strengthen me enough to take that next step, to jump that next hurdle, to stay the course. Thank You for providing our cheering squad to encourage us Home!

Walking on water
Matthew 14

God is so faithful! When we can't, He can. When we doubt, He doesn't give up. When we fall, He picks us up. When He calls us, He provides. When Peter asked Jesus to call him to come out on the water, he steps out of the boat and walks on water. This was something beyond Peter's power to do. Something that was humanly impossible. But Peter starts walking until he notices the winds. He shifts his focus back to his natural surroundings instead of his supernatural experience. He begins to sink. May I take this time to testify about what God is teaching me about His faithfulness? When God called me to write a devotional, I assumed it was to enhance my bible study. When I noticed that the devotionals were being written for an audience, I thought I would write a year's worth and then find a way to publish it. However, God had other plans. At the beginning of the process, I tried to have some control. At first, I had written enough in advanced, that I had plenty of opportunities to reread and edit the devotional before I had to post. I sought perfection. I would send my devotions to family to make sure it made sense before I posted. I would double check to make sure I hadn't already written something on the topic of the day or had not used the Bible reference before. Did you notice a lot of "I's"? Even though God was giving me the words to write and even though I was holding on to His promises, I still felt like I needed some level of control. Before God called me to the devotional, I had prayed: "Spirit lead me where my trust is without borders, let me walk upon the waters wherever You would call me, take me deeper than my feet could ever wander and my faith will be made stronger in the presence of my Savior." ("Oceans"/Hillsong United) God is teaching me what this means. God has been teaching me so much through this devotional. I have had to release my control and trust God. You know the old cliche "If God leads you to it, He will lead You through it." My friend that statement is SO true! He has never failed to give me words. Even when I feel too weak, too tired, or too incapable, HE still moves. Even when I feel like I am running out of time, He moves in His timing. My friend, if there is something that God is asking you to do and you feel unequipped to do it, trust Him! Step out onto the water. If He is directing you to do something, it is for His glory. He only needs an obedient heart.

Father God, we are nothing without You. You give us life and breath. You surround us with Your creation and Your Presence. You direct our paths. When we start to sink in life's waves, You are there to pick us up. Thank You for Your care and love for us. Use us for Your glory! Amen.

April 27
Listening to words of wisdom
Exodus 18, 2 Samuel 12

Thank God for those people in our lives that speak truth and wisdom to us! Too often we want to think we know it all. Too often we don't want to listen to the advice of others. However, God has us living life with other people for a reason. We need different perspectives to be able to know what we are missing.

In Exodus 18, Jethro, Moses' father-in-law, watches as Moses is wearing himself out trying to meet all the needs of the people. Moses, who knows it's his job to lead, just assumes he must do it all on his own. Jethro points out that some situations are not worth Moses' time and that someone else could resolve. The wisdom of Jethro eases some of Moses' burden.

In 2 Samuel 12, Nathan has the tough job of confronting the king. King David had sinned. Nathan bravely must face him with the truth of his actions. When confronted, David acknowledges and repents of his sins.

Do you readily accept advice from other people? Do you seek Godly wisdom from those you trust? Or do you think you have all the answers? Your way is the right way. Your way is the only way. Other people can see where we are blinded. They perceive the truth we refuse to see. If you do not have someone like this in your life, you need to ask God to send you a Jethro or Nathan. Someone who will share the truth with you no matter how hard. Someone who is looking out for you and has sound advice to help you better walk life's road. Are you a Jethro or Nathan? Before confronting someone, pray for guidance. Remember to offer biblical advice. Remember to do so in love. "He who speaks truth declares righteousness." (Proverbs 12:17)

Lord, thank You for those in our lives who speak truth to us. Give us ears to hear the wisdom of others. Give us a heart that is willing to respond. Thank You for Your Word and the Holy Spirit who bear witness to the Truth. Amen.

Enjoying life
Ecclesiastes 3

For those of us who have the weekends off, we can't wait until Friday. However, if your family is like my family, your weekend to do list is almost as long as your week-long list. There always seems to be something to do. People seem to have to plan weekends away or vacations just to take a break from "life." And many do not even have the opportunity to do that. As you read through Ecclesiastes 3:1-8, you realize that there are times of hardships, work, and pain. However, there are also times of healing, laughing, and dancing. You may feel like you on the hamster wheel of life, an endless cycle that leads nowhere. There are always dishes, laundry, grocery shopping, car repairs, house maintenance, . . . However, life does not revolve around our chores list (even though it seems to). Our life revolves around the relationships in our lives, including our relationship with God. The primary reason people get away and take vacations is to spend time with the people in their lives. But we should be doing that every day! How can we enjoy and build up those relationships in our lives with all our "to-dos"? Evaluate your priorities. Are you rushing away from family time to try to get another thing marked off your list? Or are you sitting around the table slowly sipping your coffee listening and sharing with those you love? Are you so busy running through life that you don't stop to visit with friends just to laugh and play? Are you working so hard to "win" at life that you forget those you live life with? My friend, life is not about work and possessions, it is about God, family, and friends. They should be at the top of your "to do" list every day.

God, You have blessed us with the people in our lives. Forgive us for those times we are too "busy" to take care of them, to just be with them, to lift them up. Lord, reveal the times in our lives where we place our to do list before them. Help us to love like You. Amen.

April 29
Plug into the Power Source
Ephesians 3

Take a moment to look around your home. Notice all the items that are plugged directly into the power. Think about how ineffective these items would be if they became unplugged. What good is a lamp if it is not plugged in? Now think about those items that sit unplugged until you need to use them. What good are they until you plug them in?

God is our Power Source. "Now to Him who is able to do exceedingly abundantly above all that we ask or think, according to the power that works in us." (Ephesians 3:20) Do you stay connected to the Power? Are you like a vacuum cleaner and only plug in when you need to clean up a mess? Are you like a cell phone and run on the Power you connected to in the past and only reconnect when you need to recharge? Or are you like the refrigerator that stays connected because you realize you can do nothing without God? We like to think of ourselves as self-sufficient. We like to think we have it all together, that we only need to tap into the Power Source for the bigger problems in life. My friend, in a world where lies and hate seem to be around every corner, we need to stay connected. Connected to the Power, we can recognize the lies and respond with Love and Truth. Connected to the Power, we remember to walk in grace and mercy. Connected to the Power, we realize we have a higher purpose in this life.

"I pray that out of His glorious riches He may strengthen you with power through His Spirit in your inner being, so that Christ may dwell in your hearts through faith. And I pray that you, being rooted and established in love, may have the power, together with the saints, to grasp how wide and long and high and deep is the love of Christ, and to know this love that surpasses knowledge-that you may be filled to the measure of all the fullness of God."
(Ephesians 3:16-19 NIV) Stay connected my friend!

Inspired by "I Can't Even Walk (Without You Holding My Hand)" by Charles Johnson and the Revivers.

April 30
Praying for the prodigal
Romans 10

We had prayed for my sister, "The Prodigal Daughter," for over 20 years. As long as there is breath in their bodies, it is never too late for our loved ones to come to repentance even if we feel like it is hopeless and feel like giving up. One of the first things I had to learn when my sister walked away from God was to love her, not judge her. Sounds simple, right? However, every time I talked to her, it was about God. It got to the point, where she stopped talking to me and I did not hear from her for months. Why? Because I think I made her feel like I did not love her, I was just more concerned about her getting back into church. God helped me realize that I was not the one who should be working at "winning" her back to Him. I just needed to love her unconditionally. She finally got to the point where we could have open conversations without her feeling condemned by me. My family still prayed for her though. When she returned, she told our sister and I that she knew we were praying for her because there were times that she should not have come through as safely as she did. God was still watching over her. Having said that, there were also times I had prayed that "Lord, You know what it is going to take for her to come back to You." I would ask God to show me how to pray for her. Some days it would be: "Lord, everywhere she turns today, help her be reminded of You." Some days, I would pray that God would send someone to talk to her about Him and to demonstrate His love for her. And then there were days that I boldly approached the throne to plead that He would move in a mighty way to bring her back. You know what? God wanted her back more than I did. He never stopped pursuing her. Pray scripture over the prodigal in your life. Acts 26:18 says: "to open their eyes, in order to turn them from darkness to light, and from the power of Satan to God, that they may receive forgiveness of sins and an inheritance among those who are sanctified by faith in Me." I also prayed the song "Come Alive" by Lauren Daigle over her, boldly asking God to breathe on her dry bones. My friend, I don't know when your prodigal will return. But as hopeless as it may seem, don't give up. Keep on praying, keep on loving, keep on believing. You never know the work that God is doing "behind the scenes" in someone's life. "The effective, fervent prayer of a righteous man avails much." (James 5:16) *Father God, we come before You and ask You "to open (your prodigal) eyes, in order to turn (their name) from darkness to light, and from the power of Satan to You, that (name) may receive forgiveness of sins and an inheritance among those who are sanctified by faith in You." Lord, renew in us a passion to fervently pray without ceasing for our prodigal that Your power may fall in their lives.*

Don't give up the fight
1 Samuel 17

Sometimes we forget that there is a constant spiritual battle raging around us. Sometimes we act like the battle does not affect us. There are times we may feel like we are on the sidelines while other times we are in the heat of the battle. Sometimes we feel strong enough for the battle while other times we feel too weak or afraid to fight. No matter what, we must remember the battle is the Lord's. In 1 Samuel 17, we tend to focus on little David taking on mighty Goliath. But today, let's focus on Saul and his army. Why had they allowed the insults to go on as long as they had? Why did they sit on the sidelines afraid to engage in battle? Did they forget the reason for the battle? And why did Saul allow a young boy to take on the giant when his strongest and fiercest warriors were sitting quaking in their boots? Once Goliath fell, why was the army then ready to fight even though the Philistines were still fierce? We know that God orchestrated the fight between David and Goliath for several reasons. This battle would introduce Israel to its future king. But more importantly, God wanted to demonstrate, once again, that it was by His might the battle was won. Isn't it sad that not one member of the army trusted God enough to go into battle for Him? Saul and his army had 40 days to seek God's help in the battle. And in comes a young shepherd boy with the faith to take down the giant. David recognized the battle for what it was whereas Saul and his army just saw the physical impossibility of the battle. David acknowledged the greater spiritual battle. He knew that his God was bigger than the giant.

Have you been like Saul's army in the battles in your life? Spending days, months, years wondering what you are going to do about the "giant" in your life. Have you looked at the people around you hoping one of them will step up and fight? Your God is bigger than any obstacle! Your God will deliver! Your God will fight for you! However, you need to have the faith to step off the sidelines and into the valley with your giant. God could have taken down Goliath the first time he called out against Israel. However, God needed someone to step forth in the faith He could use to bring down the Philistines.

God, how many times have we looked around asking who will fight for us? How many times have we pointed out our "giant" to everyone we meet asking "what am I going to do?" Forgive us for thinking that our problems are bigger than You. Give us the faith like David to say "I come to you in the name of the Lord of hosts, the God of the armies of Israel, whom you have defied. This day the Lord will deliver you into my hand." (1 Samuel 17:45-46) Amen!

Watch where you build
Matthew 7

You probably remember the parable of the wise man who built his house on the rock and the foolish one who built it on the sand. When the winds and the water came, both men realized the impact their foundation had on their life. Jesus had spent three chapters telling the gathered crowd about a "new" way to live, a "new" way to love. He even tells them: "unless your righteousness exceeds the righteousness of the scribes and Pharisees, you will by no means enter the kingdom of heaven." (Matthew 5:20) Can you imagine their initial reaction? Jesus was referring to their spiritual leaders. How were they supposed to be more righteous than them? The verses leading directly into the parable of the builders are: "Not everyone who says to Me, 'Lord, Lord,' shall enter the kingdom of heaven but he who does the will of My Father in heaven. Many will say to Me in that day, 'Lord, Lord, have we not prophesied in Your name, cast out demons in Your name, and done many wonders in Your name?' And then I will declare to them, 'I never knew you; depart from Me, you who practice lawlessness!'" (Matthew 7:21-23) Now some may think that is harsh or even a little frightening. They appear to be sincere people who tried to serve God yet are being rejected. Why? They were building on the sand. They were trying to work their own way into Heaven. They were trying to establish their own rules or twisting God's rules to their liking just like the scribes and Pharisees. When we set our beliefs on an "interpretation" of scripture that pleases us, (leave in the blessings, take out the parts we don't want to have to follow), we are building on the sand. We may initially leave in rules we can live by only to find someone else who may convince us that we should take that rule out also. Still, others may leave in all the mercy and take out the judgment part. We are fickle people and let emotions or experiences dictate the "truth" in our lives. But those who build on the foundation of the truth of God's Word will stand. We are to be examples of God's love. We are to seek His will for our lives, not just choose to live life any way we want. We are to treat others with love and mercy. We are to live with Kingdom purpose. God's Word stays the same. It does not shift based on our feelings or experience. It is something we can hold on to when everything else in our world seems to be falling apart. *Father, why do we think we can pick and choose the truths from Your Word to live by? Why do we rely on our knowledge, experience, and feelings when we know we are weak and are prone to change our minds? We are self-centered people, Lord. We need Your Truth and Love to show us how to live for more than just ourselves. Guide us to be the wise man or woman built on You. Amen!*

God's Masterpiece . . . YOU
Psalm 139

"I will praise You, for I am fearfully and wonderfully made." (Psalm 139)

When was the last time you took time to think about YOU: about how complicated your body systems are or how your body works together for you to function properly? Look at your fingertips. How intrinsic and unique they are. No one on the earth has fingerprints precisely like yours. Listen to your heartbeat and ponder all the life-providing work that is being done by that one little organ. Think of the trillions of individual cells in your body that come together to form YOU.

God, Creator of the vast solar system, Creator of Heaven and Earth, created YOU unique and precious. "How precious also are Your thoughts to me, O God!" (Psalm 139:17) And He's not finished yet! He is not rushing through the process to be "done" with you. He is not giving up on you nor thinks you are hopeless. Look at how He still designs in the world around us. The beauty to behold that is different each morning. No two days are the same. Reread Genesis 1. "God saw everything that He had made, and indeed it was very good." (Genesis 1:31)

My friend, don't waste away your days wishing that you looked different. Yes, there are times we may need to make changes to be healthier but even then, Your Creator, Artist Father looks on you with adoration and declares you "very good." Unless we are a biologist, I'm not sure we can comprehend how wonderfully God has made us. I don't understand how blood flow works. I can't define every bone, muscle, organ in our bodies. I don't understand how the brain communicates to the rest of our bodies. I don't know how our skin heals from cuts or bones from breaks. But I do know the Creator of the whole universe made us too. He treasures YOU! YOU are His handiwork! Praise Him for YOU are fearfully and wonderfully made!

Look up the YouTube clip of "Louie Giglio talks about Laminin (short)" and watch it to the end. It is about 6 minutes but will amaze you, what an excellent reminder of how much thought God put into making us.

God's family
Acts 10

What do you envision when you think about that first day in Heaven, specifically about who will be there? In your mind, you are probably picturing Jesus and those who you knew in this life or perhaps even some of the saints of old. If you look beyond them, who else do you see? Envision looking around; there will be people from every nation! Brothers and sisters that live in other parts of the world. Since we will have all of eternity, wouldn't it be awesome to hear all the salvation stories of our brothers and sisters from around the world?

Here in this life, when something happens to one of our loved ones, it impacts us. We rejoice or weep with them. However, we have brothers and sisters around the world. If we could remember that when we hear about world events, how would that change our reaction to those events? To know that a brother or sister is impacted by them? Would you spend a little more time in prayer? Would you seek ways to help?

God opened Peter's worldview in Acts 10. Up to that point, Peter was focused on sharing Jesus with the Jewish people. He perceived non-Jewish people as ones to be avoided (even though Jesus Himself had shown him otherwise). After a vision from God and an encounter with Cornelius, Peter states: "In truth I perceive that God shows no partiality. But in every nation whoever fears Him and works righteousness is accepted by Him." (Acts 10:34-35)

When we think of our Church family, we too need to expand our worldview. Members of our family are in war-torn countries, in impoverished nations, in oppressed lands across the earth. We need to lift each other up in prayer daily, and that includes our family members who we have never met, in places we have never been.

Father, You know which of our brothers and sisters are most in need of a touch from You today. In our daily prayer times, reveal to us specific areas or situations that need to be covered by prayer. When we hear of news from both home and around the world, remind us to stop and pray. Guide us to be Your hand and feet in any of those situations that we need to be. Thank You for giving us such a large family! Teach us to better love one another. Amen.

Homeless and bound
Psalm 68

My favorite verse in Psalm 68 may be "God sets the lonely in families, He leads forth the prisoners with singing." (Psalm 68:6 NIV) Don't you love that imagery! God gives those alone a family, a home. He leads prisoners out of their prisons with singing. However, we know that not everyone has the "ideal" family life. There are widows, orphans, children in foster homes and the homeless who may look at this verse and wonder how it applies to them. There may be those who are still in "prisons" of abuse, addiction, or physical captivity. They may all read this verse and think "what about me?" I don't know the answer. Perhaps God has provided a "family," but it doesn't look like what you imagined. Perhaps He has opened the prison door; you just haven't walked out yet. Or perhaps the answer is found in scripture. "A father of the fatherless, a defender of widows, is God in His holy habitation." (Psalm 68:5) "Now, the Lord is the Spirit, and where the Spirit of the Lord is, there is freedom." (2 Corinthians 3:17) Maybe right now in your life, God alone is Your family and Your freedom.

I don't know why it seems like God has not fulfilled Psalm 68:6 in your life yet. But I do know that if you have received Him as your Lord and Savior, you are free and not alone. This life is temporary; we are not Home yet. One day, you will experience family and freedom. You may think: "Yes, but what about this life?" Again, there is no easy answer. Seek God, read His Word, hold on to His promises, don't give up on Him. Be honest with God about your situation, ask Him to open your eyes to how He is working Psalm 68:6 into your life. Just know that you are not forgotten, that you are loved, and there are brothers and sisters praying for you.

Father, my heart breaks for those who seem to face life alone, for those who are held captive whether physically, emotionally, or spiritually. How we long for Home! But we live in a fallen world where evil destroys families and bounds the innocent. Father, I pray for my brothers and sisters who are not currently experiencing family and freedom. Remind them You are near and they are loved. "Heal the brokenhearted and bind up their wounds" (Psalm 147:3) Amen.

New life
Ephesians 2

Spring is the time of year we celebrate new life. The bare cold ground gives way to green grass, yellow daffodils, and red tulips. Animals come out of hibernation and bring forth new offspring. It's a long-awaited time of the year. Friends and family reconnect around a grill and good food. All feels right in the world after a long cold winter. When we accept Jesus, we also gain new life. "Therefore, if anyone is in Christ, he is a new creation; old things have passed away; behold, all things have become new." (2 Corinthians 5:17) What does new life look like for a believer? You may be someone who has not yet surrendered your life to Jesus. You may be wondering "why should I become a Christian?" A new life means you begin life again with a clean slate. All your past mistakes and failures can be left at the cross entirely forgiven by God. No matter how you had chosen to live your life, it is ALL covered by the blood. When God looks at you, all He sees is His child. A new life means your life now has a purpose. Before Jesus, there may seem to be little or no purpose to life. You are just trying to get by. With a new life, God becomes your purpose for living. He will direct your path. A new life means you are never alone. When it seems that everyone has forsaken you, know that God never will. A new life brings peace amidst whatever storm you are facing. God is your anchor. A new life reveals unconditional love. God loves you so much that He sent His own Son to die for YOU. There is nothing you can do or not do that will make Him stop loving you. A new life brings a Constant Companion. The Holy Spirit resides in you. He is your Ever-Present Friend who will never betray you, never leave you, and you can trust without reserve. A new life brings the promise of eternity in Heaven. It brings a promise of a reunion with your loved ones who believe. There are no permanent goodbyes between believers. While a new life in Christ is not perfect and trouble still comes a Christian's way, you never have to face any of it alone. Even though there is still heartache and pain, you are never without hope. The God who loves you is there with you every step of the way.

God, today I come before You in petition for those who are facing the decision to choose You or to walk away. Father, I know how much You love them and are drawing them to You. Father, give them the courage to lay down the heavy load they are carrying and come to You. You alone can save. You alone can heal their brokenness. Raise up prayer warriors around them to stand in the gap. Send those to show Your love for them. Let today be their day of salvation. In Jesus' precious name I pray. Amen.

Let us pray
2 Chronicles 7

"If My people who are called by My name will humble themselves, and pray and seek My face, and turn from their wicked ways, then I will hear from Heaven, and will forgive their sin and heal their land." (2 Chronicles 7:14)

Father, we come before You today with our brothers and sisters across our country. May we approach your throne in one accord praying for unity, peace, love, and direction. Move our prayers to what You desire to do in our families, churches, communities, and country. Lord, we raise our voices in praise for the many blessings You have bestowed on our nation and in our own lives. We thank You for the freedoms we have here in America. We thank You for providing and making a way when there seems to be no way. We thank You for Your new mercies. We praise You for the gift of Your Son who brought salvation to all who will receive. Father, we come before You on bended knees to seek forgiveness for the lies we have allowed to be manifested in our lives. We ask forgiveness for laying down in the battle and permitting the enemy to destroy our relationships, our reputation as Your people, and our responsibility to share Your truth with a lost and dying world. Father, we pray comfort and healing for the brokenhearted in our land. We pray for Your divine provision for those who need Your touch whether it be physical, mental, emotional, or spiritual. Only You can meet our deepest needs. Only You loved us enough to send Jesus to take our death sentence and give us life. Lord, we pray that You help our unbelief. May those who are Your people rise up and offer Your love and mercy to our fellow man. Give us the courage to step out in faith to accomplish what You want to do in our lives. Open our eyes to the hurting around us that we may be Your hands and feet. Revive us again! Let Your Church arise to love and serve those in our homes, our churches, our communities and our world. May we boldly proclaim Your truth and way of salvation in love and mercy. May we "wake up! (and) Strengthen what remains." (Revelation 3:2 NIV) God, give us all the wisdom and desire to discern and follow Your will. Lord, we pray for Your protection and Your guidance. Help us not to be "tossed to and fro and carried about with every wind of doctrine... but, speaking the truth in love." (Ephesians 4:14-15) May we, as a family, church, nation, seek Your face. "And this I pray, that your love may abound still more and more in knowledge and all discernment, that you may approve the things that are excellent, that you may be sincere and without offense till the day of Christ, being filled with the fruits of righteousness which are by Jesus Christ, to the glory and praise of God." (Philippians 1:9-11)

God is not defeated
Revelation 20

In a world where evil seems to reign and being a Christian almost seems like a bad thing, know that our God is not defeated. Satan may like to boast about all the wars, hate, and anger running throughout the earth. He may want to brag about all those abused, abandoned, and rejected. He may give voice to lies that everything goes, we can be our own "gods" and live by our own rules. He may be destroying our homes, our churches, and our countries. But my friend, let me tell you, our God is not dead and He is not defeated! Our God won the war 2000 years ago when Jesus hung on a cross bearing all our sins and paid the sacrifice and atonement for them then arose victorious over death, hell, and the grave on the third day! The final battle scene has already been written and God wins!

Satan may want us living defeated lives. He may want to bombard us with our past mistakes and failures constantly. He may want us to be fighting amongst ourselves. He may want petty arguments to lead to division. He may want to make our sin "look right in our own eyes." But my friend, he already knows the outcome. He just wants you to believe his lies to keep you from the abundant life God has for you. You do not need to buy into his lies. "Therefore submit to God. Resist the devil and he will flee from you." (James 4:7) "The thief does not come except to steal, and to kill, and to destroy. I (Jesus) have come that they may have life, and that they may have it more abundantly." (John 10:10)

God is still moving in our world today. He is not on the sidelines waiting for the final day to come. He is actively pursuing people to bring them into His fold. He is fighting for His children. Souls are still being saved. Homes are still being restored. Hope still reigns. Satan may like to be louder to try to convince the world he is winning, but thanks be to God, the battle is the Lord's and He is victorious!

Father God, You have "given Him (Jesus) the name which is about every name, that at the name of Jesus every knee should bow, of those in heaven, and of those on earth, and of those under the earth, and that every tongue should confess that Jesus Christ is Lord, to the glory of God the Father." (Philippians 2:10) Jesus is the King of kings and the Lord of lords. He is victorious! Lord, help us to remember that we too can live in victory because of Christ. Amen!

May 9
What is God doing in your life?
John 4

If you look past all the struggle and pain in your life, what is God doing in your life? What blessings are you enjoying every day? How is He moving in your life and the lives around you? But wait, do you have to look past the problems in your life before you can see God? Can you find Him in your struggles and your pain? We like to acknowledge God in the good times of our lives. We sing about how good He is, how great He is. But what about those days when nothing seems good about our lives? Those seasons of endless trials and heartache? What is He doing then? Is He any less good? Is He any less great? What about those times when we pursue our own sinful desires instead of following His path of righteousness? Does He walk away from our lives until we figure it out? Does He say, "I'm done."?

God is not just God when everything is going our way. He is not always heaping blessings on top of blessings on us. (Although, we really like when He does.) God is a God in the trenches of our lives. He is there when we don't know how we are going to make ends meet. He is there when the unexpected happens in our lives. He is God when the pain is more than we can bear. Does He love us any less during those times? Are we too much of a mess for Him to gaze on with love? Have we made too many mistakes for Him to still be good in our lives? Of course not!

Look at your struggles and pain, can you find God there? In what ways is He guiding and providing? What ways is He your Comforter and Healer? My friend, God is never going to give up on His child. Rest assured that even though you may not sense His Presence, refuse to acknowledge His Power, and ignore His Provision, He is near. "The Lord is near to the brokenhearted and saves the crushed in spirit." (Psalm 34:18 ESV)

Start each day with at least one reason you can be thankful. Take the time to acknowledge He is there.

God, Who You are is not based on how we feel. You are not just doing things in our lives that we can see. You are working in so many ways to take care of Your child. Forgive us for not trusting You are there. Thank You for loving us! Amen.

God of all my days
Psalm 90

"So teach us to number our days, that we may gain a heart of wisdom."
(Psalm 90:12)

Wake up. Work. Go to bed. Wake up – a seeming endless routine of life! The older we get, the more we wish we could take the knowledge we have now and start our adult life over again. Right our wrongs, make better decisions, choose a different life path, pursue our dreams. We often overlook the fact that we have this knowledge because of our life experiences. Psalm 90:10 says: "The days of our lives are seventy years; and if by reason of strength they are eighty years, yet their boast is only labor and sorrow; for soon it is cut off, and we fly away." If you knew that your days were numbered, how would that impact how you are currently living your life? Would you try something new? Would you make some life changes? Would you spend more time with family and friends? The truth of the matter is that: "For what is your life? It is even a vapor that appears for a little time and then vanishes away." (James 4:14) We all know people that have died too early and those who are still living in their nineties. We need to learn to live a balanced life between work and play. There is so much beauty in the world around us. So many opportunities to try new things. God has given us life to enjoy. So find something you enjoy doing and make sure to take plenty of time to do it. Yes, we have responsibilities. However, take time to play. Take time to relax. Take time to laugh. Could it be that part of what Psalm 90:12 is trying to tell us is that life is short so don't keep putting off life's pleasures? Learn how to live life not just through the lens of work but also through play. Learn to live life less self-centered, and more through our relationships with others and God. We should not be too busy to spend time with God daily. Communicate with Him by reading, praying, and listening. Serve Him by serving others. Take time to seek His heart. We need to learn to live our short life with Kingdom Purpose in mind. There are days we are providing for and taking care of our families. But even those days can be lived with a focus-shift. What ways can you fulfill your Kingdom Purpose at home and work? How can you find time to play, laugh and love throughout your day?

Father, sometimes we work so hard to achieve a goal only to discover that we have missed out on living. You desire for us to build up the relationships in our lives. You want us to seek You every day. Teach us to live life beyond on to-do list. Teach us how to "gain a heart of wisdom" so that our days fulfill a Kingdom Purpose. Amen.

May 11

Who is Heaven for?
Luke 23

Can we revisit Good Friday today? Gaze upon Jesus. Physically, He is experiencing excruciating pain. He has been whipped, beaten, and is now hanging on a cross. Every breath He takes results in more pain. Mentally, He is weary. The crowd, who He loves so much, is shouting anger and hate at Him. His friends have forsaken and denied. Spiritually, He is carrying the weight of every sin from all generations. His own Father must turn away. He is sacrificing His life for you and me. And yet, we see the tender exchange found in Luke 23:40-43. While waiting to die and in unbearable pain, Jesus takes the time to accept a sinner's repentance and welcome him home. When we picture the people in Heaven, we envision angelic appearances with beautiful faces. We envision folded innocent hands with peaceful smiles. We see perfect people. I don't know how we will actually look in Heaven.

However, I do know that all those destined for Heaven here on this earth do not look so innocent or good. From reading the Bible, we already know that Heaven's roll call will include deceivers, prostitutes, murderers, and yes, thieves. Here on earth, the world tends to think there is a level of goodness that will get you to Heaven. You haven't committed any "big" sins. You are nice to everyone you meet. You help your fellow man. And then they look at those who live with messed up lives made from bad choices and unfortunate circumstances and condemn them to hell. My friend, Heaven is not going to be only made up of those who are "sweet and innocent." There will also be those who had been in prisons here on earth. Those that may have hurt you or those you love. Because, my friend, Jesus died on that cross for EVERYONE. And those who come to repentance, no matter what they have done in their past, will be welcomed into Heaven's door.

Lord Jesus, I am thankful that there is not some human standard that we have to all measure up to before we get into Heaven. I am grateful that You paid the price so that I can freely enter. All that is required of me is to accept Your gift of salvation, repent of my sins, and allow You to be Lord of my life. Jesus, You accepted the repentance of a dying man. You are calling all to repentance. I pray for those who are struggling to accept that gift. I pray that grace wins, and they will experience Your love and forgiveness. Amen.

Inspired by "Come to the table" by Sidewalk Prophets

May 12
What do you need to surrender?
Proverbs 3

Do you feel like you are stuck in a rut? That your life seems to be one never-ending cycle? You know something needs to change, but no matter how hard you try, you are still in the same place? You have prayed. You have sought counsel. Yet, here you are still stuck in the struggle and the dissatisfaction. How long have you been there: days, months, years? Perhaps you even know what you need to do to break out of the rut. However, you decide to try other ways to make it work. Maybe it's a new direction God is leading you, but you hope He changes His mind. Perhaps it's a situation that God has told you needs addressed, yet you continue to ignore, hoping it will go away. Maybe you need to let go of something.

Not obeying is disobedience. You are still making a choice not to heed the voice of God. It may seem like a little thing. However, it may be preventing you from experiencing complete freedom. You know you need to surrender to God and His plan. You know you can trust Him with the details and the results.

Sometimes we need to relinquish our control, so God can take control. Sometimes we need to recognize God's answer instead of waiting for the more desired response. We may not like change. We may wonder what's going to happen to our routine, to our relationships, to our dreams. "Trust in the Lord with all your heart, and lean not on your own understanding; in all your ways acknowledge Him, and He shall direct your paths." (Proverbs 3:5-6)

Lord, You have a plan for our lives, but we are a stubborn people. We like to stay in our comfort zone. We don't want to change even when we are feeling the effects of living life in a rut. You have called us out of a life of complacency into abundant life. Father, give us the courage to step out of the boat and into the life that fulfills Your kingdom purpose for us. May we seek to honor You in all that we do. For Yours is the kingdom and the power and the glory forever. Amen.

Manna for today
Exodus 16

Why do we want all the answers today? Why is it so difficult to trust God with the future? Our human nature wants to be in control. We want to know what to expect so we can be prepared to handle it.

When the children of Israel tried to hold on to the day's manna so they would be guaranteed food for the next day, it spoiled overnight. God had told them the manna was for that day and, except in preparation for the Sabbath, they were only to gather enough for the day. If we are honest, many of us would have probably been out there gathering the extra manna. The children of Israel were out of their comfort zone. They did not know what challenges they would face tomorrow. The knowns of Egypt were looking more promising than the unknowns in the wilderness.

The issue, at its core, was whether they truly trusted God to provide for the next day. Now early in the journey, before they began to learn about how God moved, you can understand the doubt. They were in a "new" relationship with God and, like any other relationship, it took time to build trust. However, one would expect that the more they experienced God's faithfulness, the more they would trust. Throughout the rest of the Old Testament, we see how often their lives did not reflect trust. In the "big" battles, sure we read of a recommitment to trust God more, but how quickly they forgot. They forgot God's goodness, His faithfulness, His miracles. Isn't that true for us also? For those of us who have been Christian for a while and have experienced His faithfulness, shouldn't trust come more easily? But we find ourselves still trying to store up manna for the "what ifs" in our lives. Jesus said: "Therefore do not worry about tomorrow, for tomorrow will worry about its own thing." (Matthew 6:34) He knew that would be an area in our lives where we struggled.

When we begin to worry about life's uncertainty, we need to hold on to God's Word. We need to recall His faithfulness. We need to trust that there will be manna tomorrow.

Father, thank You for not giving up on us. Even when we still try to do things our way. Even when we have witnessed Your faithfulness time after time and still worry about our tomorrows. Thank You for Your Word to remind us and teach us that You are all we need. Amen.

We will serve the Lord
Joshua 24

"But as for me and my house, we will serve the Lord." (Joshua 24:15)

Families experience change during the various seasons of life. As Christian parents, we hope to establish a spiritual foundation for our children that they will take with them as they begin building their own homes. However, we have no control over the decisions they make as they venture out on their own. We hold on to: "train up a child in the way he should go, and when he is old he will not depart from it." (Proverbs 22:6) Or, maybe you did not raise your family in a Christian home. No matter the situation, we often feel some responsibility for their decisions. However, our children are not God's grandchildren. Ultimately, their decision is between them and God. Everyone must make their own decision about what they are going to do with God. "Now therefore, fear the Lord, serve Him in sincerity and in truth, and put away the gods which your fathers served on the other side of the River and in Egypt. Serve the Lord! And if it seems evil to you to serve the Lord, choose for yourselves this day whom you will serve, whether the gods which your fathers served that were on the other side of the River, or the gods of the Amorites, in whose land you dwell. But as for me and my house, we will serve the Lord." (Joshua 24:14-16) Yes, as parents we have a responsibility to teach our children the ways of God. But as they grow and become responsible for other aspects of their lives, they also become more accountable for their spiritual life as well. Again, if we step back and look at how God works and moves in our lives, we realize, He works and moves in our children's lives also. God wants a personal relationship with our children. And at some point, we need to recognize that we do not bear the sole responsibility for our children's spiritual decisions. They need to experience God for themselves. Pray for your children. Continue to seek ways to "train" them. However, do not think that you bear all the responsibility for their relationship with God. They need to build that up themselves. And you can trust God that He is working on them also. You do not want your child's only experience with God to be through you. God loves them more than you do. They are His. They need to experience God for themselves. *Father, we love our children, and we wish we could guide them through life without them making mistakes and bad choices. However, we know that at some point we are no longer responsible for decisions they make. Help us to train them up in the way they should go, but then trust You to work in their lives. We pray they serve the Lord.*

Find your way to shine
Philippians 2

You may wonder how you can "shine as lights in the world." (Philippians 2:15) You may be feeling too weak, too worn out, too unequipped, too young, too old, etc. You daily wonder how God can use you. Know that as long as there is breath in your body, God can. When my mother was living, there were several years before she passed, when she would ask why she was still here. She was on dialysis and limited to what she could do. She could no longer see a purpose for her life. Her daughters, on the other hand, knew we had someone to listen to us, offer advice, pray for us.

Sometimes we get so wrapped up in what we can't do, that we cannot see what we can do. God has work for us all. He can use our story to lift someone else up. He can use us to stand in the gap for someone in prayer. Even at our weakest, there are still ways we can be a blessing. Have you ever been to visit a nursing home and find yourself the one being blessed? You may not have the resources or time to minister to someone on a regular basis. However, you can wake up each morning and ask God who needs your prayers that day. You can ask God who needs a phone call or note to say, "I'm thinking about you." You can ask God who needs to hear your testimony of His faithfulness. Your prayers are appreciated. Reaching out to let someone know you care may be the one thing to brighten someone's dark day. Sharing your testimony will serve as a reminder of hope to someone who has about given up. Earnestly seek God about how you can shine. "For it is God who works in you both to will and to do for His good pleasure." (Philippians 2:13)

Lord, You can take our smallest offering and use it tremendously for Your Kingdom. You just need us to be willing to offer it. The reasons we have for not doing so are often lies that we accept as truth. Even at our weakest, we are still children of the Almighty. Father, we offer up what little we have, to be used by You in someone's life today. "Your kingdom come. Your will be done on earth as it is in heaven." (Matthew 6:10) Amen.

Sacrifice of praise
Jeremiah 33

Sacrifice is defined by Merriam-Webster Online as "an act of offering to a deity something precious; especially, the killing of a victim on an altar." In both the King James Version and New King James Version, Jeremiah 33:11 uses the phrase "sacrifice of praise." When we think of sacrificing, part of what comes to mind is the actual act of sacrificing. We envision an animal being slaughtered on an altar or Christ's battered body on the cross. That imagery does not seem to match a picture of a "sacrifice of praise." We recognize that there are different types of sacrifices. However, almost always, it seems to require "giving something up" which often gives it a negative connotation. But what are we "giving up" when we offer praise to God? We are acknowledging that we are not the king or queen of our lives. We are not the ones who are calling the shots. We cannot do it all on our own. And, yes, sometimes that may be hard to do. The act of sacrificing may sometimes "feel" negative, but the purpose of the sacrifice isn't. The reality is we are not giving something up; we are giving something back. God has given us everything. When we offer something back to God, we are acknowledging that truth. Praise seems to be an easy thing to "sacrifice." It doesn't cost anything. We can offer it at anytime and anywhere. It feels "good." But if we are honest, sometimes praise isn't so easy to offer. Sometimes we don't feel like praising. We may think our current situation is not praiseworthy. Then it becomes a "true" act of sacrifice when we still acknowledge God is God and He is good. "Among the gods there is none like You, O Lord; nor are there any works like Your works." (Psalm 86:8) And for times when we think we have life figured out and we have it all together, that sacrifice of praise may also be difficult to offer. We like to think that it's all about us and how awesome we are.

Giving praise to God during those times requires admission to the truth that we are nothing without Christ. As you offer your sacrifice of praise today, take some time to make it more than words from a song you are singing along with in the car. Acknowledge the sacrifice aspect of it. Think about the many reasons you are praising God: for who He is, for what He is doing in your life, and for the ultimate sacrifice of His Son.

Lord, we praise You for You are good and Your mercies endure forever. (Jeremiah 33:11) As we bring You praise, may it not be with empty words, but with heartfelt thanks for who You are and what You have done, are doing and will do in our lives. May we daily acknowledge that You alone are worthy of our praise! Amen.

Steadfast Love
Psalm 86

How many of you are thankful for steadfast love? Love that never changes? Love you can rely on no matter what comes your way? Hopefully, you have those in your lives that you experience steadfast love with. As humans, though, because we are imperfect people, sometimes we make mistakes within our steadfast love. Parents steadfastly love their children but do not always make the best decisions in demonstrating it. Spouses may love steadfastly but experience times of selfishness that makes it seem to waver. Ultimately, the truest steadfast love is God's. How do we experience steadfast love daily? Do we take it for granted? Do we forget to express it to those around us because we assume they know? When we receive it, do we no longer appear grateful because it is always there for us?

How do we experience God's steadfast love? Do we take it for granted? Do we enjoy the benefits of His steadfast love so much that we forget to be thankful for it every day? How do we love Him in return? Can you say you steadfastly love God? What a blessing to live life loved! Loved by our family and friends! Loved by a God who was willing to sacrifice His own Son to show it! When we live in the security of being loved, we are able to face whatever comes our way. We can meet challenges, make mistakes, express our true feelings and emotions, and know that when we fail, there will be those who are with us every step of the way. God's steadfast love for us ensures us that we are never too much of a failure, too messed up, too weak, for Him to love. Even when we feel the most unlovable, He is there. When we feel the most unloved, His love is a truth we can hold on to.

"For I am persuaded that neither death nor life, nor angels nor principalities nor powers, nor things present nor things to come, nor height nor depth, nor any other created thing, shall be able to separate us from the love of God which is in Christ Jesus our Lord." (Romans 8:38-39)

Thank You for Your steadfast love, O God. A love that lifts us up and carries us through whatever comes our way. We love You, Lord! Amen.

Take God's Word for it
2 Timothy 3

"All Scripture is given by inspiration of God, and is profitable for doctrine, for reproof, for correction, for instruction in righteousness, that the man of God may be complete, thoroughly equipped for every good work." (2 Timothy 3:16-17)

At the heart of everyone's decision about God is whether they take Him at His Word. Do we believe "In the beginning, God created?" (Genesis 1:1) Do we believe Jesus was who He claimed to be? Do we believe there is a God who is active in our lives? Do we believe that "so then each of us shall give account of himself to God."? (Romans 14:12) If we choose not to take God at His Word, then we live life by our own rules and desires. We believe there is no ultimate consequence. And once we die, that's the end. Even if we try to live a "good" life, we may decide to pick and choose which parts of God's Word we want to live by. We may choose to enjoy all the blessings and assurances but refuse to accept God's way of living so we can pursue our own plans and desires. Ultimately, we are still not taking God at His Word. "No one can serve two masters; for either he will hate the one and love the other, or else he will be loyal to the one and despise the other." (Matthew 6:24) But if we choose to take God at His Word, we believe that our lives have been fashioned by our Creator God. That we are loved beyond all measure. That our eternal Home is our destination. We believe "For God so loved the world that He gave His only begotten Son, that whosoever believes in Him should not perish but have everlasting life." (John 3:16) We believe that we "can do all things through Christ who strengthens (us)." (Philippians 4:13) But that also means that we acknowledge that God has a plan and a purpose for our lives. It means we accept that the Bible contains God's laws for how we live our lives and we submit to His authority over us. There will come a day when everyone will know the Truth. If those of us who take God at His Word are wrong, then we would have "wasted" this life, but since there is no afterlife, it doesn't matter. However, if those of you who do not take God at His Word are wrong, then you will have an eternity to face without God. "Choose for yourselves this day whom you will serve, . . . But as for me and my house, we will serve the Lord." (Joshua 24:15) *Father God, one of the greatest gifts You gave us was our free will. You are "not willing that any should perish but that all should come to repentance." (2 Peter 3:9) But the decision is ours to make. Father, I pray for those who are not sure where they would spend eternity, that today would be their day of salvation. Amen!*

Give thanks for another day
Psalm 9

"I will give thanks to the Lord with my whole heart; I will recount all of your wonderful deeds. I will be glad and exult in you; I will sing praise to your name, O Most High." (Psalm 9:1 ESV)

Perhaps you woke up this morning wondering how this verse applies to your life today. There are too many things that are weighing heavy on your heart. Perhaps you have again watched the news with all the world's heartache and have seen your life reflected in the despair. When we live in such a fallen world where is our reason to be thankful?

The Message paraphrases Psalm 9:1: "I'm thanking You, God, from a full heart, I'm writing the book on your wonders. I'm whistling, laughing, and jumping for joy; I'm singing your song, High God." Living in a world of hate, war, disease, and death, that imagery is something many of us just can't picture doing right now. All the emotions and heaviness we are feeling are too real and our hearts too full of grief, hurt or anger. At times like this though, we need to remember that we still have a Father who loves us and will not leave us to bear our heavy heart alone.

When experiencing life's pain and heartache, we may not be at a place we can "thank God from a full heart." However, we need to acknowledge there is something to thank Him for every day. We can thank Him for His ever-constant Presence. We can thank Him that this is not the end of the story. We can also thank Him as we seek where He is moving in our situation.

God, we give thanks for another day. Some of us may be celebrating all the blessings You have provided. However, there are some of us that have hearts that are full of despair. But no matter what our situation, You are worthy to receive our thanks! You are moving and providing every day of our lives. Thank You for Your endless grace and mercies, Your unfailing love, and Your constant Presence. Amen.

I'm a winner either way
Philippians 1

"For to me, to live is Christ, and to die is gain." (Philippians 1:21)

As my dad was reaching the end of his journey here in this life, we would often hear him sing: "I'm a winner either way, if I go or if I stay for I still have my Jesus each passing day." (I'm a winner either way by Laura Lewis and Trina Curtis) My dad knew his final Home would be in Heaven and what awaited him over there. As Paul was writing to the Philippians, he had the same message. Paul desired to go Home. You can imagine his exhaustion and the pain he had endured. His longing to see Jesus. However, Paul recognized that by living, he would be able to continue to spread God's Word and lead more souls to Christ. There are times in life when our fragile bodies grow weak or the world as we know it comes crashing down. Sometimes we may cry out John's words: "Even so, come, Lord Jesus!" (Revelation 22:20) We must learn to trust God with our final days as well as our present days. He knows what our tomorrows hold. He will be faithful till the end. Whether we are longing for Home or longing to stay, God is there. Whether we are afraid to die or afraid to live, He will never leave us or forsake us. "Yea, though I walk through the valley of the shadow of death, I will fear no evil; for You are with me; Your rod and Your staff, they comfort me." (Psalm 23:4) God understands our thoughts and emotions during each day of our lives. He is waiting with open arms for us to run to Him with all our worries, fears, and sorrow. He will be our strength during our times of weakness. And even when we don't understand, we hold on to Hope; Hope in this life or the next. Because we know we have a Father who loves us. We have a Savior who died so we could live again. We have a Comforter who gives "the peace of God which surpasses all understanding." (Philippians 4:7)

Father, I don't know what kind of day my friends are having. I don't know which of them are facing final days or days of pain and suffering. My prayer for each of them is that they experience Your Presence and Your Peace during all their days. I pray that You become very real to them as they face each day with the confidence that You are there with them. Reveal Your love and comfort. Be their Strength, their Provider, and their Hope. "And my God ... supply all (their) needs according to (Your) riches in glory by Christ Jesus." (Philippians 4:19) Amen.

How far will you go?
Genesis 22

When God asked Abraham to sacrifice Isaac, it seems such a contrast to what we know about God. The God who gives life is asking him to take a life. The God, who promised that Abraham's descendants would be as vast as the stars, appears to be breaking that promise. Can you imagine the thoughts going through Abraham's mind as they journeyed? Abraham doesn't seem to try to put it off, he doesn't head the other way, he doesn't hide Isaac. He follows God's plan. When you are following someone, you are only willing to follow them to the degree you trust them. If you do not trust the direction they are going, you are a reluctant follower. If they have let you down before, you are a wary follower. However, the opposite is true also. If you are following someone who has not led you astray, you will almost follow them anywhere. So here stands Abraham in the position of deciding whether he should follow God. God has been faithful up to this point. Because God has proven Himself trustworthy, Abraham takes Isaac and heads out. He has plenty of time for God to move. I wonder if his steps became slower the closer he got to Moriah. Perhaps, he had thought God would have responded by now with a "good job Abraham, now you can take Isaac and go back home." However, there was no such word. Isaac even begins to question, "where is the sacrifice?" Abraham responds that God will provide. How confident do you think those words came out? I'm sure his heart was racing as he and Isaac headed for the altar. How did Abraham feel as Isaac looked up at his father? Then Abraham raises his hand to fulfill God's request. At what point in this story, would you have turned around and taken Isaac back home? Have you been following God long enough to know how faithful He is? Are you able to hold on to His promises even though you don't understand His plan? Or do you lack the faith even to start down that path? We each must determine for ourselves if God is worth following. We must decide to what degree we will follow. Are we going to turn back when the path becomes unknown? Are we going to stay where we are when it starts to become too rocky? My friend, God is God in the good times and the bad. Will you trust Him enough when difficult decisions come your way? Will you trust Him enough to follow when He leads you out of your comfort zone? Will you trust Him to follow when the path seems hopeless and frightening? Will you say: "where he leads me I will follow, I'll go with Him, with Him all the way?" ("Where He Leads Me"/Ernest Blandy)

Father, You have proven Yourself Faithful and True so many times in our lives. Yet, too often we hesitant when Your leading gets uncomfortable. Give us the courage to follow You. I will follow where You lead. Amen.

May 22
Does God have favorites?
Genesis 4

As children, we may have often felt like our parents loved a sibling more than they did us. Then find out as an adult, that your sibling thought you were the favorite. In God's family, do you ever feel like there are "favorites?" Ones that God seems to bless all the time? Cain seems to have had such thoughts when he found out Abel's offering was accepted and his was not. Can you picture him whining to God about how He loved Abel more? God's response was: "Why are you angry? . . . If you do well, will you not be accepted?" (Genesis 4:6-7) Cain, like many of us, wanted to be able to do things his own way and yet expected the approval of God. Jacob and Esau have similar stories. Esau did not place a high enough value on what God had blessed him with. Jacob, on the other hand, recognized what a blessing it was. What about King Saul and King David? King Saul grew very angry when the people acknowledged "Saul has slain his thousands, and David his ten thousands." (1 Samuel 18:7) He did not appreciate the fact that David was the "favored" one. In Acts 13:22, Paul quotes God as saying, "I have found David, the son of Jesse, a man after My own heart, who will do all My will." Jacob and David were not perfect either. Like Esau and Saul, they both had done some terrible things in their lives. However, they did submit to the Lordship of God. They acknowledged that life was not just about them and their plans and desires. What Cain, Esau, and Saul were observing was God's blessings for the obedience. God loves everyone! He loves those in prisons. He loves those from different religions. He loves those who do not even acknowledge Him. Christ shed His blood for everyone! "There is no partiality with God." (Romans 2:11) Abel, Jacob, and David did not have "perfect" lives. Abel was murdered. Jacob and David both lived with difficult family issues. Their relationship with God did not take away all their problems. Yet, they still seem "favored" because they were submitting to God's plan for their lives. Cain had the opportunity to present an acceptable offering. Esau already had the birthright. Saul had the opportunity to be a good king. However, they each chose to follow their own path and not submit to God's. When we are comparing "favorites," we are taking our eyes off our relationship with God and focusing on others. "Now therefore, if you will indeed obey My voice and keep My covenant, then you shall be a special treasure to Me above all people; for all the earth is Mine." (Ex 19:5) "I now realize how true it is that God does not show favoritism but accepts men from every nation who fear Him and do what is right." (Acts 10:34)

Lord, You want us to seek Your heart. Amen.

May 23
What are you expecting?
Philippians 4

What are you expecting to happen today? You are probably expecting to attend the appointments on your calendar. You are expecting to finish (most of) your day's to-do list. What else are you expecting: an uncomfortable conversation that may or may not happen; a phone call with news you may not want to receive; or a day where everything is going to go your way? We spend a lot of time expecting, and quite often, what we are expecting doesn't come to past the way we imagine. We are in the season of graduations and weddings. Both mark new beginnings with new expectations for the future. The grads are expecting a bright future where all their hopes and dreams come true. The bride and groom are expecting their "happily ever after." However, our expectations rarely match up with our reality. The grad is not expecting the late nights cramming for exams. The constant need to balance finances to make sure there is food on the table and money for books and tuition. And then with a degree in hand, the difficulties of finding the "perfect" job with the desired salary. The bride and groom are not expecting the struggles of learning how to live life together. The compromises that will need to be made: how to make every decision based on both perspectives or how to adapt when things don't go your way. Whether we are expecting the best or the worst, we spend a lot of energy on our expectations. Paul tells us: "be anxious for nothing." (Philippians 4:6) Most of us would probably have to admit that is not easy. Go back to your expectations for the day. Mentally examine each. Which ones do you have some control over? Which ones are entirely out of your control? Now take a moment to realize that Your Father will be with you every step of the way. How does that change your perspective, your expectation? As you examine your expectations, picture Jesus standing beside you every step of the way. Does that lighten the load? We do not need to face any appointment, any to-do list, any conversation, any expectation without Him. He is with us for the ups and downs of our journey, to our bright futures and "happily ever afters" Add to your today's expectations - what do you expect God to do for you and in you today? Life's uncertainty should lead to a greater dependence on Him. He is in control.

Father, there is not a day that goes by that You have not seen. You know and hold all our todays and tomorrows. Teach us to wake each morning with the knowledge that You are already there to guide us and provide for us through whatever our day may hold. Please help us to rein in our thoughts of all today's possible scenarios and quiet our minds to hear Your truth for the day. Amen.

Praying for victory
Psalm 20

"May He give you the desire of your heart and make all your plans succeed." (Psalm 20:4 NIV)

Who in your life today needs a victory? Do you pray scripture over them? Psalm 20 is a prayer for those in battle. Each of us is facing some battle; whether it is physical, mental, emotional or spiritual. We all need a victory today. We know that not every battle goes the way we want. However, here in Psalm 20, David is praying with all confidence that there will be a victory. When you read the verse above, you may think "I wish that were true." We wish we would all get the desires of our heart and that all our plans would succeed. But we recognize that doesn't always seem to be the case. There are times when our desires and plans do not match up with God's will. And we should desire "Your will be done" more so than ours. Can we still count it a victory when things don't go our way? Yes. If we are living for Kingdom purposes, and we can step back from the flesh, we can know there was a victory. It may not be something we see, but we trust. We trust that the battle served some Kingdom purpose that will impact a life for God somewhere else in time.

We also need to recognize that not every battle is a victory. Our enemy is very real. We know God has already won the war. However, Satan is not going down without a fight. In whatever stage of battle you are in, remember you are not alone. God is fighting for you. It is when we try to fight alone that we are most discouraged. Reread Psalm 20. See how God is fighting for us. Don't give up the fight. If you think you have lost the battle, don't surrender. Seek God, our Deliverer!

David prayed with confidence:

"We will shout for joy when you are victorious" (v5)

"Now I know that the Lord saves His anointed: (v6)

"Some trust in chariots and some in horses, but we trust in the name of the Lord our God. They are brought to their knees and fall, but we rise up and stand firm." (vs7-8)

O Lord, answer us when we call. Help us remember the battle is Yours. We trust You, Lord. May Your Kingdom come, May Your will be done on earth as it is in Heaven. Amen.

Childlike faith
Proverbs 1

As a young child, most of us probably thought the world revolved around our parents. We trusted them completely: to provide, to protect, to guide, and to always be there. We asked them a million questions to learn about life. We ran to them with our boo-boos and our heartaches. For many of us, we did not worry about what we were going to eat or sleep or wear because our parents provided what we needed. However, the older we got, the more we questioned. We questioned their authority. We questioned if they were making the right decisions for us. By those teen years, we assumed we no longer needed parental advice. We were ready to take on the world and make our own decisions. However, we quickly realized that we still needed our parents to supply the essentials - food, clothing, car. We wanted to enjoy the benefits of being the "child" without the parental nagging about the choices we made. We had life figured out. Does that sound like our Christian walk? Early in our walk, we basked in the wonders of our God. We trusted Him to take care of us and always to be there. We ran to Him with our problems and sought His Word to learn from. We relied on Him for everything. As we grew in the faith, we decided that we had learned enough and experienced enough that we were ready to be more independent in our spiritual walk. We wanted more freedom to make decisions on our own without input from our Father. We wanted the ability to make our own "rules." We had our Christian life figured out. We can never "outgrow" our dependence on our Heavenly Father. We will never experience enough or read His Word enough to be able to live successfully independent of Him. We daily need His guidance and provision. We need His Holy Spirit to speak Truth to us. There are days, more than we would like to admit, where we need His strength to carry us through. We need His wisdom for daily life decisions. We need our hope in Him when life seems hopeless. We need to return to our childlike faith where we rely on Him for everything. Where we acknowledge, and once again be amazed by, all His great works. Where we can face our tomorrows because our Father is right there with us. Yes, God wants us to grow in grace and knowledge. Yes, He desires for us to be on the "solid food" of His Word. Yes, He wants us to grow to where He can use us. However, He also wants us to acknowledge "for without Me you can do nothing." (John 15:5) *Abba Father, You are so trustworthy. You love each child unconditionally. You always have time for Your child. You desire for them to seek Your face every day. You are guiding and providing every step of our lives. You are a good, good Father. Forgive us for the many times we decide to choose our own path rather than Yours. Lead us back to Your Way. Amen!*

May 26
Bow down before Him
Matthew 2

The Wise Men traveled a far journey to meet the King. They had no expectations from the King Himself. Their only goal was to come and worship. When they found Him, they presented their gifts and bowed down before Him. During the rest of Jesus' life, few came to Him in that manner again.

After His earthly ministry began, most encounters we see with Jesus are with those who come with expectations. Those who want to see what He will do. Those who desire for Him to perform a miracle in their lives. Those who needed saving. Those who needed healing. That was the reason He came: "The Son of Man has come to seek and to save that which was lost." (Luke 19:9) But how many came just to worship Him? He had not yet fulfilled His purpose for leaving Heaven and coming down to earth. The gratitude and adoration that He did receive during His ministry were primarily based on what He was doing in the lives He encountered. Jesus did not come in the manner that they were expecting the Messiah to come. No one, at this stage of His life, realized the true gift that was being given. How often, when we approach the throne, do we come just to worship? How many of us just steal away to spend time with God? Without requests. Without our worries and fears. With just complete adoration. Don't get me wrong. God does want us to come before Him with our requests, our worries, our fears. However, there should be times when we just come to praise. When we come more for Who He is rather than for what we want from Him. My friend, no matter what you are facing today, take some time to worship.

Father, "here I am to worship, here I am to bow down, here I am to say that You're my God. You're altogether lovely, altogether worthy, altogether wonderful to me." ("Here I am to Worship"/Tim Hughes) I love You, Jesus. I lift my hands and heart to the Name above all names. Today, I bow at Your throne in awe of You, Lord.

King Jesus
Psalm 24, Revelation 5

When we picture Jesus, we often envision Him wearing a crown of thorns as our Redeemer and our Savior. How often though, do we picture Him with a golden crown and royal robes as our King? When we imagine bowing to Jesus, in our minds, it is typically at the foot of the cross as we accept His gift of love and mercy and to thank Him for all He has done. How many times do we imagine Him seated at the right hand of the Father in all His splendor as we bow before Him? How many times do we bow to the "King of Glory?" How often do we bow just to acknowledge His authority over us?

In His human form, Jesus appears to be more relatable. He is our Friend, our Provider, our Healer, our Helper. We want that type of relationship with Him. But we also need to be reminded sometimes that He is our King. We need to recognize that aspect of our relationship with Him. The freedom that comes with forgiveness does not mean that we should then do whatever we want. We need to live in the freedom of forgiveness by submitting to our King. His Word defines how we should live our lives. The Bible is not a list of recommendations but the King's Law.

In a world of "whatever I say, or think, or feel is truth," we need to acknowledge that there is a final say. There is an absolute Truth. We need to sit at the King's feet and learn from Him. We need to acknowledge to God and ourselves that we live under a Kingship. We should submit to our King's authority and power over us.

Jesus has proven Himself a King worthy to be honored. He is not a standoff, condemning King who makes decisions on a wimp or for personal gain. He is a King that loves His people. He is a King that serves His people. A King deserving of the worship of His people.

King Jesus, I bow before You today in acknowledgment of Your authority over me. You are a good King. You are a great leader who has set an example worthy to be followed. Help me follow You today in the manner worthy of a child of the King. Amen.

Sun, moon, and stars
Genesis 1

No matter what season, no matter what the weather, no matter where you are at, you know the sun, moon and stars are in place. Even if you can't see them or they seem so far away, you know they are there. We rely on their heat and light. We use them to determine our direction. The splendor of a clear night surrounded by millions of stars brightly shining is incomparable. The beauty of a full moon seemingly suspended in the dark heavens is breathtaking. The brilliant sun creeping up on the horizon revealing a new day creates a song of praise upon our lips. "When I consider Your heavens, the work of Your fingers, the moon and the stars, which You have ordained, what is man that You are mindful of him, and the son of man that You visit him?" (Psalm 8:3-4)

Have you ever tried to number the stars? Reach up to try to touch the moon when it seems so close? Man has yet to travel the vast universe that lies beyond earth's moon. Satellites have sent back pictures of what lies beyond our moon, into our solar system, and beyond. There is a satellite that has been traveling for 40 years now and still revealing more of the unknown. Again: "When I consider Your heavens, the work of Your fingers, the moon and the stars, which You have ordained, what is man that You are mindful of him, and the son of man You visit him?" (Psalm 8:3-4) Sometimes we need to let our minds soar to the vastness of God's creation or stop to examine the tiny details of a flower or bug. Take a moment to look around at the variety of the created world. Out of all His creation, we are the apple of His eye! If you read Genesis 1 slowly, pay extra attention to the "it was good and the evening and the morning" verses, you will notice that after God created man, the verse becomes "very good." Psalm 8:5-6 goes on to say: "For You have made him a little lower than the angels, and You have crowned him with glory and honor. You have made him to have dominion over the works of Your hands: you have put all things under his feet." Take time to recognize your value to God. No matter what type of day you are having, remember God loves you!

Creator God, how glorious is Your work in all the earth and the heavens! How thankful we are that You looked upon all Your creation and deemed us "very good." With all of our imperfections, You delight in us. You "demonstrated (Your) love for us in this: while we were still sinners, Christ died for us." (Romans 5:8 NIV) Thank You for Your unconditional love! Amen.

May 29
Excitement for Final Days
Matthew 24

You know how excited school-age children are at this time of the year. The closer to the last day of school, the closer to summer break they are. With a couple of months of "freedom" looming before them, it is hard to keep them focused on the here and now: the final tests and projects, finishing the year strong. It is hard to maintain rules and procedures when they know that soon, they will not have to worry about school rules.

If you watch the news, you see signs that we are closer to this world's final days. It may be tomorrow, ten or fifty years from now. But the closer to the final days, the more excited we should become. We can sense "freedom" from this fallen world is just on the horizon. However, we too should strive to finish strong. The closer we are to those final days, the harder Satan seems to fight to cause more division, more hatred, more discouragement. He distracts us from the work set before us. We should still "go therefore and make disciples of all the nations, baptizing them in the name of the Father and of the Son and of the Holy Spirit, teaching them to observe all things that I have commanded you." (Matthew 28:19-20) We should also not be slack in following His design for our lives: the "rules and procedures" He has set before us.

My friend, as we grow restless for that final Day, don't give up or give in. "Be diligent to present yourself approved to God, a worker who does not need to be ashamed, rightly dividing the word of truth." (2 Timothy 2:15) "Press toward the goal for the prize of the upward call of God in Christ Jesus." (Philippians 3:14) "Look up, and lift up your heads; for your redemption draweth nigh." (Luke 21:28 KJV)

Father, as we wait for Your coming, may You find us faithful. May You find us finishing strong. May we continue to have a heart for the unsaved around us. You are "not willing that any should perish but that all should come to repentance." (2 Peter 3:9) May we "be diligent to be found by (You) in peace, without spot and blameless." (2 Peter 3:14) "Amen. Even so, come, Lord Jesus." (Revelation 22:20)

150

In appreciation
Philippians 1

When was the last time you took the time to show appreciation for the people in your life? The ones who are always there? The ones who speak truth into your life? The ones who love you for who you are? Sometimes we are too careless with our thanks. We casually throw out a thank you without taking the time to be genuinely appreciative.

There are "big" events in life where we may pause to think about the influence of those around us. But in our day to day living, sometimes it is harder to stop and think about where we would be without those around us. In most of the epistles of Paul, even he takes the time to voice his appreciation for the people to which he was writing. He is thankful for their prayers and their gifts. He is grateful for their faithfulness to their beliefs. As a "spiritual father," he is thankful when they are holding fast and growing in their faith. How does he show his appreciation? By thanking God for them!

When was the last time you thanked God for the blessing of the people who minister to you, who love you, who serve you, who live life with you? And then how often do you let them know that you are thankful to God for putting them into your life? Don't wait for a "big" event to let people know how much you appreciate them. Take some time today to count the "people" blessings in your life.

Father, we may have people in our lives who tear us down, and too often we let those relationships define us. However, remind us of those in our lives that lift us up and encourage us. Help us see the value of those You placed in our lives to show us Your love. Father, here I sit and reflect on the many people in my life that have been blessings in so many ways, who have played different roles in who I have become, who have helped shape me and continue to encourage me to become a better person. Thank You for allowing my life to be touched by them. I pray Your blessing on their lives today. Amen!

May 31
You don't have to work for love
1 Corinthians 13

Some of us may have the misconception that the more we do for God, the more He will love us. We believe we must earn His love. However, He does not require anything from us before He gives us His love. HE IS LOVE! If you do nothing to further His kingdom today, He loves you. If you let anger or hurt cause you to sin, He loves you. If you have never acknowledged Him as Savior and Lord, He loves you. He sent Jesus to die for us while we were still sinners because He loves us!

For some of us, we would prefer if we were able to work for His love. Perhaps it is harder for us just to accept His love. All experiences in our lives may have led us to believe that no one loves without conditions or expectations. God does not love with human love. He is your Creator, your Designer, your Heavenly Father. He loves you! God wants the opportunity to show everyone how much He loves. He longs to lavish His love on all His children. Yet, there are so many who refuse to acknowledge such Love exists. Many want to put their own conditions on how He loves.

My friend, God loves YOU! God knows all about you, yet He loves you! He sees your imperfections. He knows your hidden heart. He knows all your days, all your faults and failures. And yet, no one loves you like He does! Imagine crawling up on His lap and just being held in His loving arms. He doesn't care how dirty you think you are, how messed up you think you are, how undeserving you think you are, HE LOVES YOU! We need to realize that we can do nothing to earn or lose that Love. Neither is there anything we can do to repay that Love. However, when we ponder His love for us, I hope we, in turn, offer our love back to Him. Not so He will love us more but as an acknowledgment of His love for us.

My Father, My God, the Lover of my soul, thank You for loving us. For loving us through our good days and bad days. Thank You for that unconditional Love that is not based on who I am or what I have done but on who You are. You LOVE me! I accept that You could love even me. Help me to remember that You love everyone I meet with that same Love. May I reflect Your love. May I never be a hindrance to someone's ability to see Your love. I love You, Lord! Amen.

New page
Lamentations 3

"Therefore, if anyone is in Christ, he is a new creation; old things have passed away; behold, all things have become new." (2 Corinthians 5:17)

How often do you wish you could throw the book of your life out and start all over? That book holds too many mistakes, too many heartaches, and, frankly, you know so much more now that you could definitely do a better job of rewriting it. Most of us have probably felt that way at one time or another. We can't wait until New Year's Day, so we can "begin" again. Commit more to our resolutions (the same ones we have had for years) and determine to be a better person and have a "great" year. There are other times in our lives where we also start a new page. One that will, we hope, distinguish the rest of our story from the mess in the early "chapters": graduation, wedding, first child, new job, etc. Only to live life for a few years and begin feeling the need for a new page again.

Our stories reflect sinful people living in a sinful world. People who do not always make the right choices or have the "ideal" life. Yet, we hope. We hope for that better life. We hope that we will finally get to that page in our life where everything falls into place. My friend, for those who have accepted Jesus, a time will come when there is "a new heaven and a new earth, for the first heaven and the first earth have passed away." (Revelation 21:1) Then we will have our "perfect" life.

Until then, we recognize our need for Jesus. When we first accept His forgiveness, He takes our stories with all their mistakes, failures and sin and covers them with His blood. Then we receive the Holy Spirit to help guide us in writing the rest of our story. Yes, we still make mistakes and sin, but "the steadfast love of the Lord never ceases; his mercies never come to an end; they are new every morning; great is Your faithfulness." (Lamentations 3:22-23 ESV) For the rest of our story, we have Someone who will be there every step of the way. Someone to guide us through mistakes and failures. Someone to hold us through the heartaches and disappointments.

Lord, great is Your faithfulness! You do not leave us to write our stories alone. You have provided a Plan, a Guide, and a Comforter to be with us every step of the way. May we choose to listen, trust and obey until we reach our perfect Home. Amen!

June 2
When the sun won't shine
Mark 4

There are seasons in our lives when we believe we will never see the sun again. Dark clouds of pain, anger, sadness, hopelessness surround us with no end in sight. The "weather forecast" of our lives seems grim. The storms roll in, the flood of tears rise, and there is no calm, just the endless tossing back and forth. We are trying to wait out the storms but feel like we are going under. We believe nothing will ever change and that these storms will last forever. Waves are pounding down on us; we are struggling to catch our breaths. We can't even seem to call out for help; there appears to be no one there. Where is our anchor? Where is our hope?

We know what the "right" answer is, however, we are not even sure God cares about us anymore. God, "do You not care that we are perishing?" (Mark 4:38) We may not be trusting in our Anchor for the moment. He could calm this storm. He could have even withheld this storm. We ask the question, why? Why am I going through this storm? Why isn't it stopping? But when we cry out to the Master of the winds and the waves, even out of hurt and anger, things begin to change. The storms may not be changing yet. The waves are still overwhelming. The flood of tears is still coming. But there in the midst is a glimmer of Hope, a glimpse of the Son.

Jesus faced His own storms while on this earth. He faced the garden, the cross, and the grave to be able to be your Anchor through the storms. He can speak "Peace, be still" to your troubled heart and mind. When your storms are raging, hold on to your Anchor. Even amidst, the hurt and the doubting, hold on to the Truth. God loves you and He will never leave you nor forsake you. Even when you don't feel like you have the strength, hold on to His!

Father, thank You for holding us through the endless storms in our lives. Thank You for being our Anchor even when we feel like giving up. Shine a Light into our darkness today. For there is Hope. Hope in this life that You are with us amid our storms and will carry us through. Hope that we will one day lay these storm-battered lives down and walk into our Heavenly Rest. Thank You for Your Peace in the storms. Amen!

All I need is You, Lord
Psalm 16

"You, Lord, are all I have, and you give me all I need;
my future is in your hands. How wonderful are your gifts to me;
how good they are!" (Psalm 16 5-6 GNT)

When friends let me down, all I need is You, Lord.
When things don't go my way, all I need is You, Lord.
When the enemy comes against me, all I need is You, Lord.
When my world is crashing down, all I need is You, Lord.
When I feel too weak to go on, all I need is You, Lord.
When I lost my way, all I need is You, Lord.
When I don't know what to do, all I need is You, Lord.
When my heart is heavy, all I need is You, Lord.
When all hope seems gone, all I need is You, Lord.
When I count my blessings, all I need is You, Lord.
When my joy runneth over, all I need is You, Lord.
When my future looks bright, all I need is You, Lord.
In good times and bad, all I need is You, Lord.
You are my Provider, my Protector, my Rock, my Shield, my Fortress, my
Healer, my Helper, my Strength, my Guidance, my Defender, my
Deliverer, my Friend, my Hope, my Future, my Victor, my Redeemer,
my Savior, my Lord, my King, my Abba Father. Amen!

Open my eyes
John 9

We are all born "blind." We are blind to our fault and failures, to our sinful nature. As young children, life revolves around us. We typically experience being someone's "perfect little angel." Before long, however, we begin to hear the word "no" and receive some consequence and redirection to correct our imperfect behavior. For some of us, it may take longer to understand what we are not supposed to be doing. And it takes even longer to understand the "why" of not doing it. In all reality, we are learning (or not learning) those lessons for the rest of our lives.

Some of us began learning about Truth and Love while we were still children. We learned from a parent's knee John 3:16 and heard the Christmas and Easter stories. For some of us, we were well into adulthood before we heard about the Truth. We continued to be blinded to our personal need for Truth and Love. In John 9, Jesus heals a man that had been blind since birth. His celebration is cut short by the still blind crowd. The man's eyes were open by Truth and Love, yet the crowd could not see. He was brought before several to share his story, only to be met with disbelief and dismissal. The Pharisees heard the Truth, saw proof of the Truth, but still could not see the Truth.

The Pharisees were known for their self-righteousness. They were esteemed members of society who set the rules and standards, all under God's name. Most people could not measure up to their standard of truth. However, when confronted by the embodied Truth and Love, the very Son of the God they supposedly served, they could not see that their standard could not measure up to His.

So many of us, even as Christians, live life with our own level of self-righteousness. We have our standard of truth or our interpretation of the Truth, which may change depending on our circumstance and what we are currently desiring. We adapt our standards instead of recognizing and acknowledging the sin. We seem to become blind to Truth and Love once again.

Father, open our eyes to the places in our lives where we have set the standard instead of living by Truth and Love. Where we have chosen compromise over the Truth of Your Word. We want to see the areas in our lives where You are still working so we grow into the children You want us to be. Amen.

June 5

Arise and go
Acts 9

In Acts 9, we read the supernatural conversion of Saul. However, there is another man who answered God's call even when it seemed impractical to do so. Ananias was chosen by God to go and baptize Saul. Saul was known for persecuting Christians. His initial reason for coming to Damascus was to continue the persecution, going from town to town to seek out Christians. When God called Ananias to go and minister to Saul, Ananias reminds God of Saul's purpose. However, God tells Ananias that Saul now has a new purpose. Ananias trusts and goes. Can you imagine the faith that Ananias had to walk down that road toward Straight? He could have been pondering if he was walking to his death. He could have doubted: "was that really God talking?" Maybe there was a "why me?" Yet, he had taken God at His Word and upon arrival, greeted Saul as "Brother Saul." How reaffirming to both men that God's Word was true.

Have you ever been led by God into the unknown? You don't understand the why. You don't know the how. You don't even see the whole path. You just hear the "arise and go." There may be fear and doubt, yet you trust and go.

Saul and Ananias both had their "arise and go" moments. Those moments lead to the significant impact that Saul/Paul had on the spreading of God's Word to all nations. They lead to a boldness to share the faith through whatever circumstance. Paul's messages conveyed that since God had proven Himself faithful at the start of his journey, He would continue to do so until the end.

Where will your "arise and go" moments lead?

Father, when You call us out of our comfort zones into the unknown, You know that we will need to rely on You entirely. We need to rely on Your guidance, Your provision, Your promise. Help us to boldly "arise and go" when You call. Amen.

June 6
When you don't measure up
1 Samuel 16-17

There are probably people in our lives whose standards seem so high we will never be able to measure up. They could be in our personal lives or at work. People who have an idea of who we should be and what we should be able to do. Sometimes it is exhausting and frustrating to try to meet their impossible standard. And yet we still try. Some people in our lives seem not to recognize that we are all human, we are not perfect, we make mistakes, and we can't do everything. Perhaps the person who has their standard too high for you is you.

As the youngest, David was used to not measuring up. When Samuel came to anoint the next king of Israel, David was not deemed worthy even to be invited to attend. His father and brothers had to call for him before the Lord said: "Arise, anoint him." (1 Samuel 16:12) David did not measure up to the battle standards and was left at home when the army faced the Philistines. When he brought lunch to the battleground, his brothers thought he did not even measure up to that task. When preparing for battle, David did not measure up to fit Saul's armor. However, in God's eyes, he measures up to be the one Israelite that could defeat Goliath.

Isn't it nice to know that Someone recognizes our humanness, our imperfections, and doesn't hold us to an unreasonable standard? Isn't it nice to know, in Someone's eyes, we do measure up? In fact, He sent His Son to atone for all our sins, so we could be found "spotless and blameless." (2 Peter 3:14 NIV)

Sometimes the high standards that we or others set for us are good. It gives us something to strive for and try to improve upon. However, when we measure our worth only by our ability to live up to those standards, we tend not to see our true value. Imagine if David had allowed how others viewed him define who he was. He would have stayed in the field, he would have stayed at home, and he would have missed out on what God wanted to do through him and his servant's heart.

Don't live life being defined by what you can or cannot do. You never know what giants God wants you to bring down.

Father, help us always to know how valuable we are to You. Even on those gray days when nothing seems to be going our way, remind us we are loved, not for what we do, but because of Whose we are. Amen.

June 7
Christ who strengthens me
Philippians 4

"I can do all things through Christ, who strengthens me." (Phil. 4:13)

This verse is probably one of the most quoted scriptures from the Bible. The truth, the assurance and the promise of this verse carries us through many days, both good and bad. Yes, Jesus gives us strength for those tough days: doctor visits, painful experiences, the graveside. But He is there strengthening us through the good days: starting a new job, the wedding day, the birth of a child. He is also there through the mundane days of busy schedules and endless responsibilities. How can we put into words what this verse means for each of us? Since we all have different life situations, this verse speaks to us very specifically in different ways. Why does this verse speak so much truth and assurance into our lives? We know that Jesus experienced unimaginable pain and suffering on His way to the cross. We know that He endured the cross when He could have called for the angels. We know that He died and rose again to make a way for our salvation. So, when we face our tough times, we know that Jesus knows how it feels to suffer and we remember that He did it all for us. We also experience the promise of that verse. We have a Presence with us every minute of every day. A Presence that doesn't leave us when things get hard. A Presence that will hold on to us when our world gets rocked. A Presence that will hold us when the pain becomes too much to bear. A Comforter when our days are filled with tears. With this verse, we have the freedom to admit that we can't carry it alone. We can't face another day alone. We can't suffer through "this" (whatever is currently in our lives) alone. And we know we won't! There is never a breath we take, a tear we shed, that we are alone. He is with us on the operating table, in the chair for an interview, as we are walking down the aisle on our wedding day. He is with us as we are doing the endless pile of dishes wondering about our life purpose. He is there as we take our final breath. He is Immanuel, God with us. "And He said to me, "My grace is sufficient for you, for My strength is made perfect in weakness." Therefore most gladly I will rather boast in my infirmities, that the power of Christ may rest upon me. Therefore I take pleasure in infirmities, in reproaches, in needs, in persecutions, in distresses, for Christ's sake. For when I am weak, then I am strong." (2 Corinthians 12:9-10) *Father, I am weak, but You are strong. You are my Strength for today, my Hope for tomorrow. You are my Provider, my Protector, my Comforter. May we rest in Your Presence when we are too weak to face another battle. You are our Strength. Amen.*

June 8
The Lamb has overcome
Revelation 5

When we think of what Jesus overcame during His time here on earth, we most likely think of His victory over death, hell, and the grave. However, there was so much more that Jesus overcame. He overcame stereotypes, hierarchies, and prejudices. He overcame the views that people had of themselves and others. As we read through the gospels, we see all the barriers that Jesus crossed to meet people where they were. People deemed unworthy and undesirable. People that went unnoticed by society and religious leaders. Lepers, Samaritans, tax collectors, all ignored and despised. Women and children unnoticed by the world were loved on and acknowledged by Him. Jesus came to earth to not only bring salvation to a lost and dying world but to also show us a better way to live. Yet, here we are, over 2000 years later, and we still deem certain people unworthy and undesirable. We still let people go through life unnoticed or acknowledged. Stereotypes, hierarchies, and prejudices still hinder and destroy relationships. We seem to have forgotten the example Jesus set when He was here on earth. When was the last time we read through the gospels? When was the last time we thought about Jesus' relationship with people? When was the last time we reflected on how we treat those people we encounter? Could we say that we loved more like Jesus or ignored and condemned like the Pharisees? Yes, Jesus came to bring us life and salvation. However, He also spent 3 ½ years showing us how to live. My friend, we need to stop allowing the world to dictate how we treat others and allow the Holy Spirit to guide us in loving and ministering to those around us.

Father, with such a perfect example of Love, Grace, and Mercy, why do we still allow misconceptions, fears, and hatred define our relationships? Jesus showed us the Way to compassion, understanding, and love. Father, help us identify the areas in our lives where we are not living out Jesus' example. Guide us to overcome the limitations and thought patterns that are keeping us from loving one another. You are Love and You desire for us as Your children to exhibit Your Love for everyone including the forgotten, the undeserving, the undesired. Help us to Love like You. Amen.

He will make a way
Isaiah 43

There are many times in our lives when we wonder how we are going to make it. We have looked at all our options, we have tried our best, but the way through is still unknown. When our human mind and human hands cannot make a way through, God can. However, often when we say "Here, God it's Yours," what we are really saying is "Here, God this is the way I want you to fix it." Here are the outcome and timing I want. I want it to be easy and quick. I don't want to have to struggle or suffer along the way. When we read the Bible, we gain the confidence that since God has made a way for so many, He will do the same for us. However, do we recognize that most of the time it is not an easy way? When the Israelites were in the wilderness, God was with them, protecting, guiding and providing for them. However, they were still facing the harshness of the wilderness and the fight for the Promised Land. What about Paul? He was a man on a mission for God. His passion was to share the gospel with the world. With such a noble cause, you might expect God to supernaturally raise Paul above the harshness of life. However, Paul faced beatings, shipwrecks, prisons, as he shared the gospel. Yet God was always there guiding, protecting, and providing. Maybe you are feeling like you are lost in the wilderness, fighting endless battles, or experiencing a journey of trials upon trials. You want to find a way out. God says: "I will even make a road in the wilderness and rivers in the desert." (Isa 43:19) We are serving a God who loves us. One who split the Red Sea to deliver His people. One who miraculously showed Himself to Saul (Paul) to raise up a bold man who would let nothing hinder him from spreading God's Word. When we surrender to God and His Way for us, we acknowledge that He will guide, protect and provide for us on the way. We recognize that His way may not be just a day's journey, but a lifetime of following and trusting Him. We hold on to "Your Word is a lamp to my feet and a light to my path." (Psalm 119:105)

Father, how we like to wander down our own paths of life seeking the easiest and quickest. Your Word says: "Enter by the narrow gate . . . Because narrow is the gate and difficult is the way which leads to life, and there are few who find it." (Matthew 7:13-14) We would like to be self-sufficient. However, we must acknowledge that we can do nothing without You. We can't always rely on what we think are the knowns in our lives. You have proven Yourself Faithful. Help us to trust You when we can only see a few steps in front of us. May we rely on the Light of Your Word to guide each step. May we rely on "And my God shall supply all your need according to His riches in glory by Christ Jesus." (Philippians 4:19) Be our Way-Maker, God! Amen.

Listening to advice
Numbers 22

How many of us are good at taking advice? How many of us will seek advice? How many of us seek advice, listen and then do our own thing anyway? How many of us would like to have a donkey like Baalam's? One who would steer us away from danger?

I hope that everyone has at least one person in their lives that they can turn to for good advice. Seeking advice and listening to advice is often hard to do because that means admitting we can't figure everything out on our own. Heeding good advice is sometimes harder because it may go against what we really want to do.

Several Proverbs establish the importance of seeking "wise counsel." "Without counsel, plans go awry, but in the multitude of counselors they are established." (Proverbs 15:22) "Where there is no counsel, the people fall; but in the multitude of counselors there is safety." (Proverbs 11:14) "Listen to counsel and receive instruction, that you may be wise in your latter days." (Proverbs 19:20) Balaam's "counsel" was his donkey. Balaam went on his way to see Balak expecting to receive some treasure for doing so. He was unaware of the danger of such a trip. His donkey saw the Angel of the Lord blocking Balaam's path. The donkey tried to direct his master away from the Angel but was punished for it. When the donkey was finally able to speak, he said "Am I not your own donkey, which you have always ridden, to this day? Have I been in the habit of doing this to you?" (Numbers 22:30 NIV) Balaam's eyes were then opened to see the Angel.

There are probably people in your life which you would like to be able to direct away from the danger you see in their path. The danger they can't seem to see. Perhaps there are people who see the danger in your path. Ecclesiastes 4:9 says "Two are better than one." Godly friends who will help watch each other's "paths" are a true blessing.

Father, I pray that You help each of us recognize those counselors in our lives that we can turn to when You want to use them to help guide us away from the "dangers" in our lives. I pray we will all have the ears to hear and the courage to offer, wise advice. Thank You for the counselors in our lives. Amen.

Epic fail?
John 15

Do you ever feel like a failure as a Christian? Does it seem like your ministry isn't growing or benefitting anyone? Do you feel there is no fruit for all your labor? Does your ministry feel more like a job than a service? There are times in each of our lives when we may feel this way. As a Christian, we don't always make the right choices, say the right thing, reflect Christ as we should. As ministry leaders, we see limited growth and the work seems harder than it should be. Yes, it is good to every so often "reevaluate" your Christian walk and ministry. Examine areas where there may be sin "in the camp." Examine areas where we have gotten so busy "doing" that we have lost sight of the "Who" we are doing it for. Take time daily to stay connected to the Vine.

However, there are times when we know we are where God wants us. We feel God's guidance and confirmation. And yet, we still feel like there is no growth, no blessings, no fruit. "And let us not grow weary while doing good, for in due season we shall reap if we do not lose heart." (Galatians 6:9) We cannot make the decisions for the ones our ministry is serving. We do not know what else God is doing in their life or how He is preparing them. "So then neither he who plants is anything, nor he who waters, but God who gives the increase." (1 Corinthians 3:7)

Lift your head. Do the work God has called you to do. Abide in Jesus. "For without Me you can do nothing." (John 15:5) Ask Him to send a confirmation that you are where you are supposed to be. Pray for your "fruit." Pray that God will give the increase in His timing. Pray He revives you.

Father, I lift up my brothers and sisters who may be feeling like a failure in their Christian walk or in their ministry. Stir up a renewed passion for the work You have called them to do. Help them not become discouraged. Help them realize that it is not about them but about You. Your kingdom come. Your will be done on earth as it is in heaven. (Matthew 6:10) Amen.

Hope built on Jesus
1 Corinthians 15

When we look for people or things to bring purpose to our lives, we are let down. When circumstances change, we are then left looking for a new purpose, a new reason for living. But when we build our lives on Jesus, we may be shaken but not destroyed. "We are afflicted in every way, but not crushed; perplexed, but not driven to despair; persecuted, but not forsaken; struck down, but not destroyed." (2 Corinthians 3:8-9 ESV)

Have you ever felt afflicted in every way, perplexed, persecuted, or struck down? We could probably, at least at some point in our lives, all answer yes. Some of us deal with one thing after another and don't seem to catch a break. Some of us are perplexed about the whys in life. Some of us may feel persecuted by the people around us. Some of us just feel struck down by the unexpected in life. Without Jesus, that is where we stay. But with Jesus, we are not crushed! We are not driven to despair! We are not forsaken! We are not destroyed! Because with Christ, we built our hope in Him. We built a life whose foundation is the Truth of His Word. Our foundation is not the shifting sands of feelings, emotions, and experiences. We stand firmly on God's Word. Jesus is "the author and finisher of our faith." (Hebrews 12:2) "Being confident of this very thing, that He who has begun a good work in you will complete it until the day of Jesus Christ." (Philippians 1:6) He isn't finished with us yet! Our life experiences can be used for His glory.

When life seems to have struck you down, "Be of good courage, and He will strengthen your heart, all you who hope in the Lord." (Psalm 31:24) And then one day we will hear the trumpet sound! "Death is swallowed up in victory, O Death where is your sting? O Hades, where is your victory? The sting of death is sin, and the strength of sin is the law. But thanks be to God, who gives us the victory through our Lord Jesus Christ." (1 Cor 15:54-57)

Lord Jesus, our Hope, our Peace, our Provider, to You be the Glory forever and ever. You conquered the grave so that we can live victorious both in this life and the life to come. You have promised never to leave us nor forsake us. You promised that You would give us Your strength to face each day. Thank You! Amen.

"Therefore, my beloved brothers (and sisters), be steadfast, immovable, always abounding in the work of the Lord, knowing that in the Lord your labor is not in vain." (1 Corinthians 15:58 ESV)

Vision check
Hebrew 12

"I keep my eyes always on the Lord. With Him at my right hand,
I will not be shaken." (Psalm 16:8 NIV)

Where are your eyes set? Are you continuously looking around at all
your problems in life? Do you have a hard time seeing the blessings in life?
It is so easy to fall into the habit of looking through the lenses of the flesh.
Through the flesh, we see only pain and despair. We see a fallen world
with innumerable problems. However, when we lift our eyes to Jesus, we
are better able to count our blessings. We can see the beautiful world
created by our Father. At a recent eye appointment, I learned the need for
balanced vision which is also true for our daily lives. We don't want to live
life just burdened down by the hardships we face. On the other hand,
we also cannot live life denying the troubles we or others encounter. Our
balance is when we lift up our eyes. When we look to Jesus, we look to our
Helper. "I lift up my eyes to the hills, from where does my help come? My
help comes from the Lord, who made heaven and earth." (Psalm 121:1-2)
Jesus is our example, our encouragement. Because of what He endured,
because of what He suffered, because of what He conquered, we can run
our life's race with endurance. "Therefore strengthen the hands which hang
down, and the feeble knees, and make straight paths for your feet, so that
what is lame may not be dislocated, but rather be healed."
(Hebrews 12:12-13) Run on with confidence my friend. As we struggle
with the tough things in life, look to Jesus. As we experience the joy that
life brings, look to Jesus. He is our All in All. He is our Helper through
the hard times and a Friend who rejoices with us through the good times.
With our eyes lifted to Him, we have a clearer and balanced vision of this
life. We can have an abundant life here is this world no matter what we are
facing. We also recognize that this world is not our final home. "I press
toward the goal for the prize of the upward call of God in Christ Jesus."
(Philippians 3:14) Press on brothers and sisters, "your redemption draws
near." (Luke 21:28)

*Lord Jesus, thank You for being our Helper through the good times
and bad. Thank You for the example that You set before us. Open our eyes
to what You are doing in us and through us. We are Yours. Amen.*

Giving your all to Jesus
Luke 21:1-4

How often do we go through life compartmentalizing? There is our work life, our home life, our recreation life, our church life. Most likely, we have certain people, habits, routines in each area. Typically, we change how we speak or act, even if it's just slightly, depending on where we are at and who we are with. Our conversations and attitudes may differ from one group of people to another or from one place to another. For example, we would not enjoy having to live as our "work" self all the time; we like to be able to kick back and relax as "ourselves" at home. God, however, wants to be a part of every area of your life not just your church life. He does not want you only on Sunday morning from 10-12. He wants you to allow Him into your work life, your home life, your recreation life. That does not mean He wants you sitting in a pew solemnly praying every minute of your life. What that does mean is that He wants you to open your eyes to see how He is with you everywhere you go. You do not leave Him in the church building on Sunday and reconnect with Him when you come back the next week. He is with you in the boardroom at work, in the living room with your family, on the golf course with a friend.

He does not want how we live on Sunday to differ from how we chose to live on Saturday. He wants us to be willing to serve Him on Wednesday as much as we do on Sunday. When the widow put in her two mites, she was trusting God with her life. She gave everything she had to God and then had to rely on Him to provide for the other aspects of her life. Too often, we bring our limited gifts to church and leave them there. Thereby giving God our "dutiful" offering of thanks so we can then feel free to "enjoy" the rest of the week. God wants us to live abundantly. As Christians, we should enjoy the life that God has given us. However, recognize that who we are in Christ does not change depending on who we are with or where we are at.

Father, we can't hide from You. Since You are always with us, You see the best and the worst moments of our lives. And yet You love us unconditionally. Remind us to "present (our) bodies a living sacrifice, holy, acceptable to God, which is (our) reasonable service. And do not be conformed to this world, but be transformed by the renewing of (our) mind, that (we) may prove what is that good and acceptable and perfect will of God." (Romans 12:1-2) Remind us that these verses do not just apply on Sunday morning. May we bring glory to Your name every day of our lives. Amen!

"Grace got you"
Ephesians 2

Have you heard MercyMe's song "Grace got you?" It's a fun little song that speaks a lot of truth. No matter what, "Grace got you." And we should take some time to acknowledge and live like it. "But God, who is rich in mercy, because of His great love with which He loved us, even when we were dead in trespasses, made us alive together with Christ (by grace you have been saved), and raised us up together, and made us sit together in the heavenly places in Christ Jesus." (Ephesians 2:4-6) Doesn't that excite you?! "For by grace you have been saved through faith, and that not of yourselves; it is the gift of God, not of works, lest anyone should boast." (2:8-9)

One of the lines from the song says: "Smile like you got away with something. Why? Because you just got away with something." Romans 6:14 says "For sin shall not have dominion over you, for you are not under law but under grace." When we accept God's gift of grace, we are no longer bound by sin. We are free in Christ. We are no longer walking a path to destruction and death. We are walking a path of Life. We are no longer walking a dark path lost and alone wondering how we got here and how we get out. We are walking a path full of Light and Love with a Savior who loves us guiding the Way. Doesn't that make you want to smile?! Now there are times in our lives when we face something that makes it hard to feel like singing, dancing, or laughing. But even in those times "Grace got you." My friend, take some time today to "sing" of His love for you. Take some time to "dance" to His redemption song. Smile as you think of your final Home. And know that "Grace got you." "For we are His workmanship, created in Christ Jesus for good works, which God prepared beforehand that we should walk in them." (Ephesians 2:10)

Father, we raise rejoicing voices in praise for all You have done for us. You make a way when there seems to be no way. You give us unspeakable joy and peace that passes all understanding even in our most difficult times. You are guiding us through our abundant life until we reach our eternal life with You. Thank You for loving us unconditionally. Thank You for always being there. Amen.

Inspired by "Grace Got You" by MercyMe

Faultless
Jude, Isaiah 59

"To Him who is able to keep you from falling and to present you before His glorious presence without fault and with great joy." (Jude 1:24 NIV)

Wouldn't we all like to be faultless? Never make a mistake, always make the right decisions. However, we all know that is never going to happen in this lifetime. Even as Christians, we are not perfect! However, there are times when it's not about being faultless but about being obedient. Yes, we make mistakes and bad decisions. However, there are times we are simply disobedient. We are making a choice not to take the path that God wants us to take. We want to do our own thing. Yes, God is faithful to forgive when we ask but how many times do we make conscious choices that go against His Word and then come back to "repent" afterward only to make that same choice the next day? Asking for forgiveness and repenting are two different things. Repenting for your sins means you are committing to change the sin behavior. Seeking forgiveness means you are sorry for the sin. Sometimes we get into a sin "habit." Satan knows where our weaknesses are and will use all his tricks and lies to keep us bound to that sin. He will tell you it doesn't matter, God will forgive you anyway. But there are always consequences for the sin in your life. You may not think it is hurting anyone. You may not think it's necessarily wrong, even though you know God's Word says it is. But sin does damage to you, those around you, and to the church body. In Joshua, when the Israelites had the mighty victory of Jericho, they were told not to take anything for themselves. Achan did and hide it. When the Israelites went up against Ai, a seemingly sure victory, they were defeated because there was sin in the camp. Sometimes we seem to forget "you have sinned against the Lord; and be sure your sin will find you out." (Numbers 32:23) Yes, we sin. We are not perfect. However, "what shall we say then? Shall we continue in sin that grace may abound? Certainly not! How shall we who died to sin live any longer in it?" (Romans 6:1-2) "But your iniquities have separated you from your God; and your sins have hidden His face from you." (Isaiah 59:2) Christ not only came to shed His blood to cover our sins, He also came to give us the Holy Spirit to lead and guide us. If we heed the Holy Spirit's guidance, He will lead us on the paths of righteousness. Jude 1:24 is a great promise. He can keep us from falling back into those same sin habits so one day we will be presented faultless before the throne! *Father, we come with true repentance for our sins. May we live holy, acceptable lives bringing glory to Your name. "Now to the King eternal, immortal, invisible, to God who alone is wise, be honor and glory forever and ever. Amen." (1 Timothy 1:17)*

This is my Father's world
Genesis 1

My Father created the beautiful sunrise this morning.
My Father created the birds that sing a wake-up call.
My Father created the puffy clouds that hang low.
My Father created the very air I breathe.
My Father holds the winds and the waves.
My Father holds the sun, moon, and stars in place.
My Father designed a world where everything works together for a purpose.
My Father designed a world that looks different outside my window
than in any other part of His created world.
My Father designed a universe so vast that we will never be able to uncover
all His glorious creation.
My Father created people who He loves above all else.
My Father took the time to create each person unique.
My Father provided a way so that we could be called children of God.
My Father loves unconditionally.
Do you know my Father?
Have you felt my Father's Presence?
Have you experienced my Father's grace and mercy?
Do you feel my Father's love for you?
Have you experienced my Father's peace?
My Father created you.
My Father adores you.
My Father sent His Son to die for you.
My Father is offering His gift of forgiveness.
My Father longs for you to come home, back into His open arms.
My Father can be your Father too.
Abba, Father, "how awesome are Your works!" (Psalm 66:3) You are
"a great King over all the earth." (Psalm 47:2) Thank You for the
opportunity to be Your child. "For you are all children of God through
faith in Jesus Christ." (Galatians 3:26 NLT) Thank You for Your
love for me! Amen.

Faith sight
Hebrews 11

Oh, if we could live having hindsight be our "now" sight. To live today knowing what tomorrow will bring. However, we are not God. We don't know what our future holds. "Now faith is the substance of things hoped for, the evidence of things not seen." (Hebrews 11:1) There are a lot of things we hope for our future. We have an endless list of things we hope will happen in our lives. And probably a list of things we hope won't happen in our lives. But those worries do not demonstrate our faith. Faith is trusting in a God that loves us and is active in our lives with whatever our future holds. Trusting that He will provide, guide, protect, and be there every moment of our lives.

It's a good thing that even "if you have faith as a mustard seed, you will say to this mountain, 'Move from here to there,' and it will move." (Matthew 17:20) Because most of us would probably say our faith isn't much bigger than that. We want to trust God with our future. However, we tend to spend a lot of time still worrying about it. Will our kids turn out ok? Will our bodies hold up? Will our finances hold up? There are so many unknowns in life that if we spent all our time wondering if this is going to happen or if that is going to happen, we could lose our faith sight. Yes, there are things we can do now to prepare for our future (and we should). However, the reality is that we cannot adequately prepare for all the possibilities our future self may face. As we read through Hebrews 11 and recall all the ways that God proved faithful in the lives of His people, we can trust that He will be faithful in our lives also. Rent Collective's song "Counting Every Blessing" has a line that I love. It says: "letting go and trusting when I cannot see." How much would life change for us if we were able to successfully let go and trust God with what we cannot see?

Father, we come before You as the disciples did to ask You to "increase our faith." (Luke 17:5) We acknowledge that all our tomorrows are already in Your hands. You already see the rest of our days. May we live with confident assurance that You will never leave us or forsake us. May we let go of the worry for our future and trust You with what we cannot see. Thank You for Your Word and Faithfulness. Amen.

June 19

Master plan
John 11

Most of us have had experiences where we called in an "expert" to fix something and they did not seem to know any more than we did. They may have even made things worse. Some of us may even say we had those experiences with the Master. We turned to God and our situation didn't get "fixed" the way we wanted. When their brother got sick, Mary and Martha knew to call the Master immediately. They knew they were going to lose Lazarus unless the Master came. And when He finally arrived, it appeared He was too late. Lazarus died and had already been buried for four days. But the Master had a plan that required the delay. A plan that would restore Lazarus to his sisters while revealing a greater purpose. If you have ever watched a master craftsman or artist work, you learn that sometimes while the work is in progress, it doesn't look like much. Yet, you trust that the craftsman or artist knows what they are doing. God created us. God designed our lives to fit into the rest of His Master Plan: past, present, and future. We are just a small piece of His design. However, He still takes care of us. He still molds us into what He wants us to be. We are still a valued piece of His plan. And just because we cannot see what the "final product" will look like does not mean that we should not trust the Master. There is no greater expert on something than the one who created it. They are the ones who truly know the ins and outs of the work. The ones who know the purpose of each piece and how it plays a vital role in the workings of the final product. God created us in His own image. He knows, even better than we do ourselves, how we "work." Yes, we live in a broken world where it appears the Master can't or won't fix it. However, He created us with free will so decisions that we all make affect the world we live in. Since the Garden of Eden, God has been working on His plan to restore humanity back to their perfected state and one day those that believe on Him will be welcomed into a Perfect Place. Are you trusting the Master with your life? Are you allowing Him to mold and use you for His purpose, His plan? Do you trust that He will show up right on time? When Martha heard that Jesus was coming, she went out to meet Him. Even in her grief, she acknowledged who Jesus was and what He could do. She may not have understood the why, but she knew the Truth. She trusted the Master's plan.

Father, in this life, our plans don't always go our way. But we make plans on limited information. We don't know what tomorrow holds and there is so much out of our control. But Father, You alone are the Master and have created us for a purpose to fulfill our part of Your plan. May we be found faithfully trusting and obeying Your will for our lives. Amen.

Don't believe the liar
Psalm 139

Don't you love those days when it feels like everything you do is wrong? Everything you say is wrong. Every decision you make is wrong. No one likes you. It's already too late. You will never be good enough. You rehash things you and God have already settled. Does any of this sound familiar or is it just me? Maybe you have your own list. Sometimes there is some truth to those statements. Things that you know you need to address or change. However, many times it is our enemy. The one who knows how to successfully hit us at our weakest points; making us doubt ourselves, others, and God.

Now we can spend the day buying into his lies. Easily allowing ourselves to be drawn into negative feelings about ourselves and others or we can stand on the Truth of God's Word. We are children of God. We are loved by our Father. We have the Holy Spirit to guide us. We are not perfect, but neither is anyone else. We all make mistakes. We all fall. We all fail. But we do not have to let that define us or destroy us.

Our Father wants you to hear His truth about you. He doesn't want you to listen to Satan's lies. When faced with that endless fault list, listen to God's thoughts toward you. That may involve finding a quiet spot to let His peace calm your thoughts and emotions. It may be opening the Bible and reading of His great love for you. It may be talking to a godly friend who reminds you of who you truly are.

Don't waste a day allowing Satan to make you feel like a nobody: unimportant, unlovable, unloved, unvalued, and worthless. Don't let Satan make you question your identity. Rise up and declare "I am a child of God!"

Father, "Keep me as the apple of Your eye." (Psalm 17:8). Thank You for a Love that I can be secure in, that I can count on, and that never changes. I am Yours! Amen.

All-Sufficient God
Genesis 22

Wouldn't we all like to be entirely self-sufficient; able to do everything by ourselves? Be the perfect student who excels in every subject. Be the perfect employee who can manage to successful give 110% to every task we need to accomplish. Be the perfect spouse/parent/child/friend that always handles our relationships correctly by saying the right thing, doing the right thing, and knowing what the other person needs of us. Be a person that has the perfect body, finances, and answers. However, none of us can be totally self-sufficient. But think about what all we would miss out on if we were completely self-sufficient? We would not need others in our lives. We would not need relationships that improve us, challenge us, lift us up, love us. But most of all, we would miss out on our dependence of an all-sufficient God. Think about all the ways we rely on God. Think about where you would have been if it had not been for God. First off, the reality is that we would not even exist or have breath in our bodies if it was not for God. Second, we would be living in a world without hope or a future. But even beyond all that, how would your life be without an all-sufficient God? I am sure that we have all experienced some point in our life where God made a way when there seem to be no way. He supplied the finances, the path, the answer, the person, etc., right on time. We have all experienced His mercy, grace, peace, and love at times when we felt undeserving. We have all held on to His promises and His Word when there seem to be nothing else. Even though our journey may not be easy, how has our relationship with God developed along the way? As we experience God, we change. We become aware of being unconditionally loved. We become aware of Someone who is with us every second of our lives; Someone who knows our past, present and future. We become aware of that sweet Presence that lives inside us to hold us, guide us, provide for us. We become aware of an amazing grace that looks beyond all our faults and failures and sees us for who we really are. A grace that offers us the opportunity to be clean, forgiven, and free. We each have our own journey with God. We each can testify of how God has been all-sufficient in our lives.

El Shaddai, My All-Sufficient God, You are my All in All, my Provider, my Deliverer, my Hope. You are my Strength when I am weak. When I ponder the countless ways that You have been good to me, I will never be able to thank and praise You enough. "I will praise You til I die, El Shaddai." ("El Shaddai"/Michael Card.) Amen.

Set apart
1 Peter 1-2

"But you are a chosen generation, a royal priesthood, a holy nation,
His own special people, that you may proclaim the praises of Him who
called you out of darkness into His marvelous light." (1 Peter 2:9)

If we sat down to discuss what being a Christian meant, our conversation
would probably have a lot of agreement as well as disagreement. We have
different life experiences which would influence our points of view. Do you
feel prepared for such conversations? Are you "always be prepared to give an
answer to everyone who asks you to give the reason for the hope that you
have?" (1 Peter 3:15 NIV) Some of us may not feel like we know the Bible
well enough to engage in "religion" conversations. Some of us may feel like
we don't even have the answer completely figured out for own lives. Yes, we
can explain about Jesus' death, burial and resurrection and the hope that gives.
Yes, we can share our own salvation story. However, it may get a little harder
to explain how that impacts the choices we make on how we live our life.
Non-Christians have a variety of opinions about Christians based on their
own experiences or influences. We know throughout history many things
have been done by "Christians" that did not truly reflect Christ. But are there
things in our own lives that do not reflect God's Word to those around us?
We are God's own special people. He has called us out of darkness into His
marvelous light. We are not perfect, but we are forgiven! However, are we
"obedient children, not conforming yourselves to the former lusts, as in your
ignorance; but as He who called you is holy, you also be holy in all your
conduct, because it is written, "Be holy, for I am holy.""? (1 Peter 1:14-15) Do
we "live such good lives among the pagans that, though they accuse you of
doing wrong, they may see your good deeds and glorify God on the day He
visits us."? (1 Peter 2:12 NIV) We need to remember we are not just living
life for ourselves. We are living life so that others can learn about God, to
ultimately choose to follow Him themselves. "You are the light of the world.
Let your light so shine before men, that they may see your good works and
glorify your Father in heaven." (Matthew 5:14,16) When we chose to follow
Jesus, we should then want to share His Good News with the unsaved world.
Jesus' final words to His disciples (and to us) while on earth were: "Go
therefore and make disciples of all the nations, baptizing them in the name of
the Father and of the Son and of the Holy Spirit, teaching them to observe
all things that I have commanded you." (Matt. 28:19-20) *Abba Father, I want
to live that I "may walk worthy of the Lord, fully pleasing Him, being fruitful
in every good work and increasing in the knowledge of God." (Col. 1:10)*

Truth – Part 1
John 8

"If you abide in My word, you are My disciples indeed. And you shall
know the truth, and the truth shall make you free." (John 8:31-32)

We probably all have opinions that we don't feel strong enough to
debate. We are willing to listen to multiple sides and adjust our opinion
based on what we hear. There are also opinions that we hold firm and no
one will be able to persuade us to change them. "Truth" even seems to have
multiple viewpoints and rarely do you feel like you get the "whole truth and
nothing but the truth." Unless we experience something first hand or
extensively investigate, we form our idea of the truth based on other
people's accounts. (Which may or may not be "the whole truth and nothing
but the truth.") People take strong stands for "truth" only to later have to
admit their "truth" was not completely accurate.

From generation to generation, "truth" seems to change. It becomes
"outdated" or invalid. Unfortunately, Scripture is often also viewed this
same way. We know that "All Scripture is given by inspiration of God."
(2 Timothy 3:16) Yet, people interpret it through their own lenses to
conform it to their way of thinking. We like to believe it is a subjective
Truth. And we know throughout history and from the fact that there are
so many denominations, that parts of it appear that way.

Jesus told His disciples that He would send the Spirit of Truth.
"However, when He, the Spirit of truth, has come, He will guide you into
all truth; for He will not speak on His own authority, but whatever He
hears He will speak." (John 16:13) How well do we listen to the Spirit of
Truth? He will guide us into all truth, yet with so many voices shouting out
"truth," how can we know the Truth? "There is a way that seems right to
a man, but its end is the way of death." (Proverbs 14:12) If we are not
heeding the Spirit of Truth, we can end up following such ways.

Truth – Part 2
John 8

If we are not reading God's Word for ourselves, if we are not taking time to communicate in prayer, if we are not allowing for quiet moments to listen for the Spirit's promptings, then we are opening ourselves up to being deceived. You probably know people who can quote scripture, but their lives are not reflecting the Truth. Do you ever wonder why Jesus said to the seven churches in Revelation: "He who has an ear, let him hear what the Spirit says."? He knew that we all have a listening problem. There are too many voices. The deceiver voices his lies as truths. And if we are completely honest, we just want to hear what we want to hear.

How often do we stop to listen? Listen to what God is saying to us through His Word. Listen to what that still small voice of the Spirit is gently speaking to us. Stop and listen during our prayer time instead of doing all the talking. The key to knowing the Truth is abiding in God's Word. "For the word of God is living and powerful, and sharper than any two-edged sword, piercing even to the division of soul and spirit, and of joints and marrow, and is a discerner of the thoughts and intents of the heart." (Hebrews 4:12) The word of God is "profitable for doctrine, for reproof, for correction, for instruction in righteousness that the man of God may be complete, thoroughly equipped for every good work." (2 Timothy 3:16-17)

Father, give us ears to hear Your Truth. We are wandering through life with cries of truth on all sides. Help us to hear Your Voice of Truth. Give us a hunger for Your Word. And every time that we pick it up may we hear what You are saying to us. Teach us to listen during our prayer times so that we may know Your Will. And God, for those times when we try to quiet Your Spirit's promptings by the noise of what we want to do, remind us "that the truth shall make us free." Amen.

Lost sheep
Luke 15, John 10

Have you ever felt like the lost sheep? That you somehow lost your way? That you thought you were on the right path, but now you have no clue where you are? That you did not listen to the Shepherd as carefully as you should have? Are you in a situation where you feel like if you left, no one would miss you? Do you feel invisible in the "field" with the other 99? Most of us would probably say, at least at some point in our life, yes, we have felt that way. We have felt ignored. We have felt lost, wandering around aimlessly. We have felt like no one cared. We have felt like we would never find the right path "home."

My friend, the Shepherd knows where you are always. He has come to take you back to the fold where you can again feel safe, provided for, and have clear guidance. He has always known where you were. He knows where you are when you are with the 99. He knows when you have aimlessly walked off course, following a path you will never find your way out of unless He helps. You are never out of His sight.

How long has the Shepherd been calling you? Calling you to come to Him? Calling you to step away from the ledge or trap that is unseen by you? Have you surrounded yourself by so much noise that you can't hear Him? Are you having so much "fun" you choose to ignore Him?

The Shepherd loves you so much. He will not leave you. He will not stop pursuing you. He will not stop calling. You are so important to Him that you have His undivided attention whether you are safely in the fold or on a destructive path of your choosing.

My friend, heed the voice of the Shepherd. Allow the Shepherd to rescue you, even from yourself. Allow Him to lift you up on His shoulders and carry you back home. What did the shepherd in Luke 15 do once he had found the sheep? He rejoiced. Can you imagine the rejoicing the Shepherd does when another sheep is brought back safely into the fold?

My Good Shepherd, thank You that You gave Your life for Your sheep. Thank You that You promise: "My sheep hear My voice, and I know them, and they follow Me. And I give them eternal life, and they shall never perish; neither shall anyone snatch them out of My hand." (John 10: 27-28) Thank You for pursuing Your lost sheep. Thank You for knowing each of us by name. We are Yours. Amen.

Lazarus, come forth
John 11

One of the many blessings of knowing Jesus as your Savior is the assurance that when you have to say goodbye to another believer on this side of Heaven, it's not forever. It's "I will see you on the other side." We have all lost loved ones. Their names are probably on your mind and heart right now. Those who we carry with us everywhere we go. Those who have left an empty spot in our hearts and lives. But THANK GOD, even though we had to say goodbye in this life, it is only a temporary separation.

Even though Jesus showed up "too late," Mary and Martha knew that they would be reunited with Lazarus someday. "Martha said to Him (Jesus) "I know that he will rise again in the resurrection at the last day." (John 11:24) However, Jesus had plans to reunite them that very day.

One day, we too will have our reunion day! A day when we will once again see those dear faces that we have not seen for years. When Jesus called Lazarus back from the grave, He did so to bring glory to God so that people would believe. As we hold on to the promise of a reunion day, we should be sharing our hope with those who do not believe. We need to "be prepared to give an answer to everyone who asks you to give the reason for the hope that you have." (1 Peter 3:15 NIV) Because just as you are longing to be reunited with all your loved ones someday, others are too. Your testimony may be an answer to someone else's prayer.

"When we all get to Heaven, what a day of rejoicing that will be! When we all see Jesus, we'll sing and shout the victory!"

("When we all get to Heaven"/Eliza Hewitt)

Father, we all have days where all we seem to do is long for our reunion day. The longing to see the precious faces of our loved ones is all we can think about. But Father, may we also take those days to share with others the unspeakable joy we have in the assurance of that promised day. Stir up a desire within us to continue to share the Good News of Your Salvation Plan with those who don't know You. May we boldly and urgently declare Your Truth. Again, thank You for our promised reunion day! Amen.

When doubts come
John 20

The other disciples' words were not enough. Thomas knew that Jesus had died. He could not just believe when they said Jesus was alive. He would need to see (and touch) the Resurrected Savior for himself. After all that time together, with shared experiences, why couldn't Thomas believe the others? Why was seeing not enough? Why did he have to touch Jesus? Did he not believe that God was able to raise Jesus from the grave? He had seen Lazarus so, in theory, he would have to admit it could be possible. Did Thomas think that the other disciples had been too easily deceived? Was he trying to put a belief decision off for a little while? Was he starting to figure out how to live life without Jesus and was now being asked to accept that Jesus was back? We will never know what was going through Thomas' head from the time the disciples said "Jesus is alive" until the time when Thomas saw Him. However, we can probably think of situations in life where we had our own questions and doubts. Hopefully, we all have people in our life that we can trust, those whose viewpoints and advice we value. But have there been times you doubted them? We believe God. But are there times we still doubt that He will do what He says He will do? What about self-doubt? That's a big one. How often do we question ourselves? We doubt how we interpret things. We doubt decisions we make. We doubt if we are doing the right thing or saying the right thing. When Thomas saw and touched Jesus, his doubts were gone. But Jesus told him; "Blessed are those who have not seen and yet have believed." (John 20:29) There are times that we need to believe despite the doubts. We need to choose to take someone at their word. We need to believe we made the right decision even though we still question. Most of all, we can take God at His Word. And the good thing about it, we do not just have to take someone else's word for it. We can experience it for ourselves. But sometimes that involves a step of faith. Amidst the doubts, a step that says even though I don't have the answers and I don't know how this is going to work, I still believe. What areas of your life are you allowing doubts to stop you from moving forward? Sometimes we keep ourselves from experiencing something better because of our doubts, the doubts in ourselves, the doubts in God. We don't have to live life confined by our doubts. We can ask God to help our unbelief. Ask Him to give us the courage to step out in faith. *Father, You want us to be able to take You at Your Word. You desire our trust and obedience. Forgive us for the many times we, like Thomas, choose to doubt rather than believe. Give us the wisdom to know when doubts are hindering our obedience. Amen.*

June 28
Can we mess up too much?
John 21

"If we confess our sins, He is faithful and just to forgive us our sins and to cleanse us from all unrighteousness. If we say that we have not sinned, we make Him a liar, and His word is not in us." (1 John 1:9-10)

In a letter to Timothy, Paul wrote that he was the "chiefest of sinners." I wonder if Peter disagreed. Yes, Paul had persecuted the church before his conversion. But Peter. . . Peter had spent the past three years with Jesus. He was one of Jesus' closest friends. He experienced more with Jesus than most. He was there at the Transfiguration. He walked on water. He was one of the first to acknowledge that Jesus was Christ, the Son of the living God. He felt like he would follow Jesus anywhere. Jesus tried to warn Peter what was to come. Stubborn Peter felt like he was strong enough, dedicated enough, to even die with Jesus. When it was time to make the ultimate sacrifice, he couldn't do it. And worse, he denied. Denied everything he knew was true; denied the Christ, the Son of the living God. The trial was not what he expected. This sudden change of events proved more than he was ready for, so he denied. He heads back to his life before. Before he followed Jesus. Before he denied. Before Jesus died. Do you think he spent those three days reliving the past three years or just those last few hours before Jesus died? Do you think he wondered how he could have believed Jesus or how he could have denied Him? It didn't seem to matter now. Peter had heard that Jesus had risen but may have assumed that since he had messed up so badly, he could never be forgiven. However, he soon found out how much Jesus still loved him. When Peter hears Paul say he is the "chiefest of sinners," Peter may disagree. By denying Christ, after all they had been through together, he may think because of the denial he was "chiefest." Maybe you feel like you fall under that category too. That you are one of the "chiefest of sinners." But the Good News is that Jesus took your sins to Calvary also. He died in your place for those sins. Just as Peter and Paul had to recognize their sins and seek forgiveness, we too must accept Jesus' gift of salvation and forgiveness. After receiving the gift of forgiveness, Peter and Paul never forgot where they had been and what God had done for them. By the way, Peter and Paul became bold leaders in the Early Church bringing God's Word to thousands at a time. *Father, thank You for Your Word where we learn about real people who seem to have "big" sins receiving mercy not the justice they deserve. You show Your love for us by how much love and compassion You had for them. God, ALL our sins separate us from You, but You sent Jesus to die for them ALL. Thank You for Your forgiveness and mercy.*

Don't miss the miracle
Acts 16

He almost missed it. Almost missed the miracle. Almost took his own life, afraid of facing the consequences instead of witnessing the life-changing. But a miracle had happened and his life would never be the same. He was just doing his job. He made sure the prisoners were secure. There were no escapes on his watch. The night had already proven eventful. The last prisoners delivered, Paul and Silas, were singing and talking to God right there in their cell for most of the evening. That was probably a first in all his years as a jailer. But then the earthquake hit. The prison doors opened. The jailer believed everyone had escaped, so felt his only alternative was to take his own life. Then he hears a voice, a voice he had been listening to for most of the evening. Paul assures him all the prisoners are still there, no one escaped. He goes to hear more. When the jailer learns about God's love for him from Paul, he is the one who finds the freedom that night.

Have you ever experienced something that could only have been God? Or do you dismiss things as coincidence? Sometimes we too can miss what God is doing in our lives. We would all like to see the "big" miracles in life. (And they do still happen.) But we miss the "little" miracles in our everyday life. Our every breath is a miracle. Having the Holy Spirit inside us to guide and provide is a miracle. Life beyond death is a miracle.

God works in the unseen of our lives every day. Yes, we pray for specific miracles. Yes, we have seen some of those answered the way we wanted while others were not. Yes, it involves trusting God with the bad times as well as the good times. But don't give up on God. He loves us through every day of this life into our eternal life with Him. So even on your hardest day, look around for the "miracles" God is giving you every day.

Father, You alone know what every day holds for us. You alone hold those days in Your hand. We are never outside of Your Presence. You know what we need before we ask. Open our eyes to see the miracles You work in our lives every day. Amen.

Just believe
John 3

We all have different personalities. Some of us are "feelers," while others are "thinkers." We process situations and even emotions differently. Some of us may quickly jump into something, while others need to take the time to analyze and evaluate. Some of us can easily accept Jesus' gift of salvation by accepting we have a Heavenly Father who loves us. Some of us need to try to figure out how what we have experienced was allowed by a loving Father or if the Bible is even true. We all come to a decision point bringing different emotions, experiences, and preconceived thoughts. But all must come to that point where we decide what we will do with Jesus. Some may try to put off deciding by ignoring or walking away. Some may have to think about it for a while. They need to take time to determine truth from perceived reality. They don't just blindly accept everything. Some jump in without fully understanding what following Jesus means. They jump in thinking if I accept Jesus then my life will be perfect. Some may try to find a way around Jesus. They want to pick and choose what they believe. We come to the decision point at different times in our lives. Some accept Jesus as a child. Some accept Jesus later in life after experiences reveal the need for a Savior. Some wait until their death bed to recognize that they are getting ready to spend eternity without Him. Jesus said: "I am the way, the truth, and the life. No one comes to the Father except through Me." (John 14:6) Everyone comes to that point in life when they have to make a decision. God "desires all men to be saved and to come to the knowledge of the truth." (1 Timothy 3:4) But the decision is left up to you and me. We need to choose to believe. Whether you decided to follow Jesus because you have read through the Gospels about His life here on earth and all that He has done for us or because you are at a point in life where you cannot carry your problems by yourself any longer, just believe. Don't put it off. We are not promised tomorrow. We are not promised time on our deathbeds to accept. Accept Jesus' gift now. Admit to God you are a sinner and repent. Believe that Jesus is the Son of God. Confess your faith in Jesus as your Savior and Lord. *Father, we like to think we can ignore You. We like to think life is all about us. We like to think we have it all figured out. But God, You loved us so much You sent Jesus, Your Beloved Son, to die a cruel death for us, for our sins. You have called all to repentance. You desire for all of us to accept Your gift of salvation. We don't have to work to earn it because we can't. We can never be good enough or smart enough, to deserve it. I pray for my friends who keep putting off deciding, for those who are still pondering what is Truth, I pray that today will be their day of salvation.*

Evaluation time
Philippians 1-2

For those of us who work outside of the home, most probably have an annual review or some other type of evaluation process. We are evaluated on whether we are meeting our goals, fulfilling our job description, etc. We may even be asked to do a self-evaluation. For those of us who work at home, we may be "evaluated" by other members of our family, but there is a lot of self-evaluation with the goal of becoming more efficient and a striving for perfection. Evaluation time can be stressful. We examine how many times we messed up this year, how many goals and expectations we didn't meet. We seem to forget all the goals we did meet, all the success we did have. We seem to think that we never measure up. And we dread the evaluation meeting with "the boss." Paul writes to the Philippians: "Only let your conduct be worthy of the gospel of Christ." (Philippians 1:27) God doesn't "sit us down" in a formal meeting to evaluate us. He doesn't just check in with us once a year to see how we are doing, to point out where all we failed. He is actively working in our lives to make us into what He wants us to be. Philippians 2:13 says: "For it is God who works in you both to will and to do for His good pleasure." The Easy-to-Read Version states it like this: "Yes, it is God who is working in you. He helps you want to do what pleases him, and He gives you the power to do it." Too often we try to live our Christian life in our own power. We try to live up to standards that we have set. God knows we are humans and that we have a lot of faults, He made us. But He is the one "who is able to keep you from stumbling and to present you faultless." (Jude 1:24)

When we recognize that we can do nothing on our own, when we acknowledge that we are sheep who tend to wander, we can rejoice that we have a "God who is working in us." He helps. And He gives us the power. The next time you feel like a failure as a Christian, the next time you mess up again, lift your eyes to the Shepherd. He is working on you.

Father, thank You for not leaving us alone to fend for ourselves, to figure things out by ourselves. Thank You that where we are now is not where we are going to stay. With all our imperfections, rough edges, selfish ambitions, You are still working on us. And someday we will become our "perfect" self when we get Home. Amen.

Inspired by "He's Still Working on Me" by The Hemphills.

God has given us everything we need
2 Peter 1

"His divine power has given us everything we need for life and godliness,
through the knowledge of Him who called us by His own glory
and goodness." (2 Peter 1:3 NIV)

At the end of 2 Peter 1, Peter reminds his readers that he was an
eyewitness. He did not just have to rely on the writings of the prophets. He
personally had seen Jesus perform miracles. And he had even heard the
very voice of God. "For He (Jesus) received from God the Father honor and
glory when such a voice came to Him from the Excellent Glory: "This is
My beloved Son, in whom I am well pleased." And we heard this voice
which came from heaven when we were with Him on the holy mountain."
(2 Peter 1:17-18) Peter had experienced so much with Jesus that when he
says: "His divine power has given us everything we need," we can be
confident Peter knew what he was talking about. God has given everything we
need for this earthly life as well as our Christian walk. He has equipped us to
live the way He has planned for us. Isn't it great to know that the Maker of
this world has given us everything we need? For life, He created this earth
to be life-sustaining. He gives us the air, food, water, and light we need. In our
Christian walk, we have His Word and His Holy Spirit to guide us every
step of the way. However, ultimately, we decide how we live our life. Even
after we have accepted Jesus into our lives, we decide how committed we are
to live the way He wants. In verses 5-7, Peter tells us to be diligent about
adding to our faith. The Life Application Bible commentary says: "Faith
must be more than belief in certain facts; it must result in action, growth in
Christian character, and the practice of moral discipline." Peter says we
should add to our faith: goodness, knowledge, self-control, perseverance,
godliness, brotherly kindness, and love. We seek what God has given us,
not our own ideas and plans. We don't try to live life struggling to figure out
how it all works. We go to "Him who called us by His own glory and
goodness." We seek His knowledge and goodness. The closer we get to God,
the more natural it is to have self-control, brotherly kindness, and love. We
don't just say "thanks God for saving me, now I've got it from here." We
seek Him every day to learn from Him, to discover His Will for our lives, to
love like Him. We want to follow our will for our lives. We want to love who
we want. We want to think we know it all. But when we acknowledge we
are nothing without Him, then God can use what He has given us for His
glory and purpose. *Father, we are nothing without You. Give us Your
knowledge and wisdom so that we will follow You. Amen.*

Privileged children
1 John 3

"Behold what manner of love the Father has bestowed on us, that we should be called children of God." (1 John 3:1)

There are several "children" (some of which are grown now) that are "my babies." They have a very special place in my heart and will always be my "kids." However, they do not have the same privileges that my sons do. They do not receive the same love that my sons do. As parents, my husband and I have certain responsibilities and obligations to our sons. We are responsible for taking care of them, providing for them, teaching them, disciplining them, and loving them. We support them, encourage them, and help them try to success while instructing them in how they should live. We love them unconditionally (as much as humanly possible) while training them to become honorable, godly men.

At one point in time, Abraham's descendants, through Isaac, were God's chosen people. However, Jesus gave His life for all people and His blood shed on the cross was for everyone. "Remember that at that time you were separate from Christ, excluded from citizenship in Israel and foreigners to the covenants of the promise, without hope and without God in the world. But now in Christ Jesus you who once were far away have been brought near through the blood of Christ." (Ephesians 2:12-13 NIV) Because of Jesus' sacrifice on the cross, we can now become children of God. "And if children, then heirs - heirs of God and joint heirs with Christ." (Romans 8:17) We can enjoy the privileges of being God's children. Our Father will provide for us. He will love us unconditionally. He will teach us and discipline us. We can go to our Father with every need. We can "climb up in His lap" just to be held by our Father. There is nothing that can separate us from His love. And someday, we will enjoy the treasures of Home.

Father, I am so glad that Your love is not based on what I do but on what Jesus did. I feel so unworthy to be called Your child. But by accepting Your gift, I am. And even when I mess up, Your love never changes. Thank You for being such a good Father who loves me, teaches me, is there for me every single moment of my life. Amen.

Freedom
Ephesians 2

How many of you could testify that at some point you felt like you had "no hope and without God in the world?" (Ephesians 2:12) Even if we grew up hearing about God's love, we still had to come to the place where we asked for His forgiveness and accepted His salvation gift. For some, we lived life the way we wanted, until we finally had to come to the realization that we needed a Savior. Some of us may still be in a place with no hope and without God in the world. In this life, we crave love, acceptance, and freedom. And we look everywhere to find them. We look for them in people, money, sex, the bottle. Anywhere we think we are getting the acceptance as well as an escape from life's problems. However, there is something innately in us that only reconnecting with our Creator will satisfy. That love, acceptance, and freedom we so desire is only found entirely in God. People, money, things can only satisfy temporarily and partially. Our soul longs to be with its Maker. When sin entered the world, our connection with God was broken. However, God had a plan. Back in the Old Testament, God resided with His people in the Holy of Holies in the Tabernacle and later the Temple. Only the High Priests could enter once a year after a thorough cleansing. When Moses met with God on top of the mountain, the children of Israel were not even allowed to come close or touch the mountain. But then God sends His Son to bridge the gap so that everyone once again could have access to God. Jesus became our great High Priest so that we can "come boldly to the throne of grace, that we may obtain mercy and find grace to help in time of need." (Hebrews 4:16) Jesus died on the cross carrying your sins and mine to offer up the ultimate blood sacrifice for all sins. He arose victorious over death, Hell, and the grave to give us an abundant life where we can once again experience the Love of our Father, the acceptance of our Savior and the freedom from the bondage of sin. My friend, if you are still "without hope and without God in this world," ask God to show you the way back to Him. He sent His Son to die for you. He is waiting with open arms for you to come back to Him. If you are unsatisfied with the love, acceptance, and lack of freedom you have right now, come to Him and experience what He offers.

Lord Jesus, You came to set us free from the bondage of sin, from guilt and doubt, from hopelessness and loneliness. You came to give us love and forgiveness, to deliver us from evil, to give us hope and a future. All You ask of us is to accept Your gift of salvation by admitting that we are nothing without You, repenting for the sins that separate us from You, believing and accepting that Your death on the cross paid the ransom for those sins. And that by accepting Your sacrifice, we are free. Amen.

Trust issues
Matthew 25

We like to think that we "trust in the Lord with all (our) heart." (Proverbs 3:5) But if we are honest with ourselves and with God, we sometimes have limited trust. We trust God to a certain degree with our families, our job/career, our finances, and our calling. But there are times when we feel like we are more invested than He is. He may not be moving fast enough for us. We may even think that He is moving in the wrong direction. We have responsibilities in life and we want God to meet "our" expectations and deadlines. How easy it is to get wrapped up in "our" life. How quickly we sometimes forget that He is the one who gives us life. He is the one who gives us our family. They are truly His. Our job/career is just another place for us to serve and share Him. Our money has been given by Him; everything is His. Our calling is from Him for His Kingdom purposes. Puts things in perspective, right?

We have trust issues because we like to think everything is "ours." It is our family, our job, our finances, our calling, our responsibility. The reality is that everything we have has been given to us by God. Yes, He has called us to be good stewards of what He has given us, but He is the Lord and Master. He expects us to take good care of it, but ultimately, it's all His. He has a plan and a purpose for it all.

Lord, sometimes we need to be reminded to surrender it all to You again. We need to remember that this life is not about us and what we want but about Your plan and purpose. You are so good to us God and You have given us so many blessings. Help us be the stewards You desire. Amen.

Just be you
1 Corinthians 12

Do you ever wonder why God did not make us the same? Why we each have our own personality, strengths, and weaknesses? Are there people in your life that you wish you could be more like? My sisters and I, even though we came from the same parents, all have different personalities. We have had conversations about which personality trait of each other's we wish we too possessed. Each of us could probably name one or two things about our personality or "weaknesses" that we would change if we could. God made us the way He did for a reason. Yes, life experiences also help shape us but those "character flaws" we feel we have can be used by God. Look at Peter and Paul, these men both had traits that got them into trouble, but those same traits were used by God in mighty ways. What about Mary and Martha? Again, different personalities but both used for the Kingdom. If you read through the Bible, you will discover people with a lot of different personalities, strengths, and weaknesses and the way God used them each in a specific way. God knew He needed the Peters and Pauls in this world as well as the Johns and Barnabas(es). John and Barnabas complemented Peter and Paul. They had strengths in areas that Peter and Paul did not. Peter and Paul may have been more of the "front men," but John and Barnabas created a needed balance of compassion and support. How does that apply to us? God made you the way you are for a purpose. Your purpose may not be the same as mine. Your strength may be one of my weaknesses making you better equipped to minister in that area. I may have strengths that God will use in a different way. But the point is, allow God to use you. The you with all your faults, failures and weaknesses. God uses us all together for His Kingdom purposes. You are not expected nor equipped to do everything, neither am I. But when the Church body works together, God is glorified. If you are struggling to figure out if God can even use you, He can. If you don't know where to start, ask Him for guidance. Submit yourselves to Him. "Humble yourselves in the sight of the Lord, and He will lift you up." (James 4:10)

Creator God, we sometimes question why You made us the way You did. But we need to recognize that "You created my inmost being; you knit me together in my mother's womb. I praise you because I am fearfully and wonderfully made." (Psalm 139:13-14 NIV) Use us for the purpose and plan that You created for us. Your kingdom come, Your will be done on earth as it is in heaven. (Matthew 6:10) Amen.

Where's your joy?
Psalm 30

Wouldn't we all rather live on the "mountaintops" in our lives where everything seems to be going our way? But there are times when we are in the lowest "valleys." Where our trust of the Master is truly tested. It is easy to hope and love and trust when it is obvious how God is moving in our lives. When we recognize His leading, His Presence, His Provision. But there are times that life is just too dark to be able to see any good, any Hope, any Love. Here is where trust comes from faith and not by sight. We must trust that He is near. We must trust that He cares. We must trust that He has a plan. During those times, it is hard to be joyful. We read the words of James: "count it all joy when you fall into various trials," (James 1:2) and think "how am I supposed to be joyful in a time like this?" We read Psalm 30:5: "Weeping may endure for a night, but joy comes in the morning" and think "God, I'm not even sure I'm going to make it through the night." But our joy is not based on our current situation. It is not based on how we think or feel. As Christians, our joy is found in our Redeemer. It is based on His Promises. Because when we look past all the problems in this life, we recognize that they will have an end whether in this life or the next. You may think: "But I want relieve now. I want to experience joy now." Let's take our eyes off our problems for a moment and cast them to our Father. "Gaze" into His heart for a moment. Pick up His Word to remind yourself how much you are loved. This might mean making a conscious decision to accept a Love that you currently aren't feeling. When your load seems unbearable, acknowledge "the joy of the Lord is your strength." (Neh. 8:10) Stop trying to carry it all alone. Ask the Father who loves you to be your Strength, your Light, your Hope during your darkest days. Remember the angel appeared to the shepherds and said: "I bring you good tidings of great joy which will be to all people." (Luke 2:10) Our great joy is Jesus. Remember in your darkest days; you are never alone. Your Father is your Strength, your Comforter, your Provider, your Hope, your Future. "Now may the God of hope fill you with all joy and peace in believing, that you may abound in hope by the power of the Holy Spirit." (Romans: 15:13)

God, I pray for those who are going through their darkest days. Be their Light, be their Comforter, be their Hope. Thank You for the Promise that one day You will turn their mourning into dancing. Thank You for a Promised Home where can rest in Peace and Love forever. Father, I also pray for those who are facing their darkest days without You. Open their hearts and minds to hear about Your Great Love. That they too will find You to be the Light of their world. Amen.

Is the Bible true?
2 Timothy 3

"All Scripture is given by inspiration of God, and is profitable for doctrine, for reproof, for correction, for instruction in righteousness, that the man of God may be complete, thoroughly equipped for every good work."
(2 Timothy 3:16-17)

I remember a story from when I was growing up that one of our pastors would share. It was about a man that said: "If you can prove that one thing in the Bible is true, I will believe it all." The man he was speaking with reaches over and twists the man's nose causing it to bleed. He then quotes Proverbs 30:33: "wringing the nose produces blood." The Bible is a "book" that people for centuries have had to decide what they are going to do with. Some have chosen to dismiss it as just another book. Some have been willing to die to share it with others. Some view it as just a historical document. Some chose to live their life by it. Some dismiss it as a book of fairy tales and myths. Some rejoice in the miraculous because they have experienced the power of God. Some view it as an interesting read but out-of-date and irrelevant to their lives. Some will testify of how "living and active" (Hebrews 4:12 ESV) the Bible is in their lives. It's a book everyone must decide for themselves whether they believe. It is not a book to be ignored. Is there any other book that you feel guilty if you have not picked it up for a while? Is there any other book that you see in the "bookstores" year after year after year (for decades and centuries?) Is there any other book that you can read over and over and still discover something new and profound? Is there any other book that you can open up consistently and read exactly what you need to hear for that day? The Bible, God's Holy Word, is living and active. Even though it was written over an extensive timeframe by many different authors, even though it's been almost 2000 years since the last "story" happen, it is still a book that is being published. Books are still being written about it. People still debate and argue over it. People are still willing to die for it. It still a book that gives hope and peace. It is a book that still brings comfort and joy. It is a book that still sets the standard of living. It is a book that still gives us a promise for our future. Tell me, is the Bible true?

Father, thank You for your living and active Word. The Word that we can turn to for whatever our day holds. The Word that can speak directly to our hearts and minds. The Word that brings Life, Joy, Peace, Truth, Hope, and Love to our world. May Your Word go out into all people that everyone will hear Your Love and Redemption "story." Amen.

Focal point
Psalm 91

Have you walked into a person's home and learned a lot about them? You discover their favorite sports team or band. There may be family pictures everywhere. Usually there is one piece, a focal point, that catches your eye. It may be a picture or poster, a musical instrument, a trophy case, a vase of flowers. You recognize how important whatever it represents is to the person. If someone did a quick look around the "room" of your life, what would be the focal point that draws their attention? Would it be your love for your family, loyalty to your friends, dedication to your job, passion for your favorite activity, etc.? What about your faith? Would they find that as your focal point on Sunday but nowhere else in your life's "room?" What is your focal point(s) right now? You may be under a deadline at work to finish a project and that is getting all your attention. You may be a parent of a young child who is relying on you for everything. There may be an illness in the family that is draining all your energy. We all go through times where life seems to shift our focus off God and onto whatever we are facing at that moment. After a while, we begin to feel the effects of our focal shift. We begin to feel like God is so far away, He is not answering prayers, He doesn't care anymore. We become more frustrated as time goes on. What we don't seem to realize is that those times are the exact times we need to turn our focus back on God. Yes, things happen where we can't seem to find the time to read His Word or pray. But the longer we don't take the time for Him, the more unsettling life becomes. How do we keep God as a focal point when too much is happening in life? Communicate with Him. We need to try to find those quiet times when it is just God and us daily, but sometimes we just can't seem to make that happen. The good thing about prayer is we do not need to be on our knees, in our "prayer closet," every time we pray. God hears us all the time. We can talk to God as we are driving, rocking a crying child or picking up toys for the millionth time. Place Bible verses around your home, office, car. Let God know that you want Him as your focal point. Ask Him to show you how you can do that with your current schedule, life situation, etc. "Ask, and it will be given to you; seek, and you will find; knock, and it will be opened to you. For everyone who asks receives, and he who seeks finds, and to him who knocks it will be opened." (Matthew 7:7-8) *Father, when You are the focal point of our lives, it is easy to say: "He who dwells in the secret place of the Most High shall abide under the shadow of the Almighty. I will say of the Lord, "He is my refuge and my fortress; My God, in Him I will trust." (Psalm 91:1-2) Father God, teach us to balance life with You at the center.*

July 10
"The Resurrected King is resurrecting me" ("Resurrecting"/Elevation Worship)
1 Corinthians 15

As Christians, most of us anxiously await Resurrection Day when "the trumpet will sound, and the dead will be raised incorruptible, and we shall be changed. For this corruptible must put on incorruption, and this mortal must put on immortality." (1 Corinthians 15:52-53) The Day when we lay aside these broken bodies and receive our glorious bodies! The Day we are reunited with those who have gone on before. What a day of rejoicing that will be! Even in this life, we are living under the power of the Resurrected King! Sometimes we forget that. Our problems seem too big; our valleys seem to be too deep. The situation seems too hopeless. We need to be reminded that the God who raised Jesus from the grave is living in us through the Holy Spirit. We need to be reminded that we can "cast(ing) all your cares upon Him, for He cares for you." (1 Peter 5:7) What in your life needs resurrecting? Relationships? Finances? Prayer life? Thought patterns? We do not need to wait until Resurrection Day before we see Jesus' Resurrection Power! Think about those areas in your life where you need a touch from the Master. Are there areas that we try to keep "hidden" from our Maker? Are there areas in our lives that are too "dead" that we need a miracle? Do we need delivered from our past? Do we feel too weak to keep going on? God is always working on us. He is active in our lives. He wants to release His Resurrection Power in us. He loves us enough to not give up on us. He is molding us into what He wants us to be. He refines us so we can become more like Him. He is bringing freedom from those attitudes, misconceptions, "flaws" that hinder us from becoming who we were created to be. What do you need from Him today? Cry out to your Abba Father. Cry out to your Resurrected King. When we come before Him with our broken pieces, when we come before Him with our failures and regrets, our Resurrected King can bring life to those areas we long have given up on.

Resurrected King, we are so grateful that we do not have to stay where we are. We are thankful that we do not need to rely on our own power to make needed changes. We are thankful that we do not need to have hope only in this life. "If in this life only we have hope in Christ, we are of all men the most pitiable." (1 Corinthians 15:19) We are thankful that we can be called children of God and experience Your Resurrection Power throughout our lives both in our circumstances and in who we are. For Yours is the Kingdom, the Glory, and Power forever. Amen.

July 11
Diagnosing the problem – Part 1
Genesis 3

How many of you sometimes self-diagnosed why you feel the way you do either physically or mentally? How many of you have experienced a doctor or a counselor who only treated the symptoms? We sometimes try to address our "surface symptoms" believing they are the problem. We do not allow ourselves to dig deeper because we may not want to know what is wrong with us. We go through life trying to fix the symptoms without truly dealing with the cause. However, we will never find true healing unless we determine and treat the cause.

The cause of our problems and the world's problems is sin. When sin entered the Garden of Eden, the perfect body and the perfect world became imperfect. We were no longer in complete harmony with God our Creator. There was a separation that could not be bridged through human effort. Throughout the history of the world, men and women have tried to live "perfect" lives once again. They have tried to live up to their Father's standards. But within our own strength, wisdom, and power, we are unable to measure up. And then we make excuses: "the devil made me do it." Instead of acknowledging our sin, we blame the effects of circumstance, society, and others. We try to fix the symptoms of our separation by trying to find self-help/self-healing solutions.

God designed a redemption plan to fix the problem. He sent Jesus to take on human form to become the needed sacrifice to cleanse a sinful people; making them once again worthy to be in the Holy God's Presence. However, we still wander around trying to find our own solutions to fix our symptoms. We look around at the world around us crying out for justice, love, and peace to fix the symptoms. What is needed in our lives and the world around us is to address the root problem. Address the sin in our lives, address the sin in the world around us. "If My people who are called by My name will humble themselves, and pray and seek My face, and turn from their wicked ways, then I will hear from Heaven, and will forgive their sin and heal their land." (2 Chronicles 7:14)

Diagnosing the problem – Part 2
Genesis 3

When we accept God's salvation gift, then "as far as the east is from the west, so far has He removed our transgressions from us." (Psalm 103:12) But because we still live in a sinful body and a sinful world, we will continue to struggle with sin. "For the sinful nature desires what is contrary to the Spirit, and the Spirit what is contrary to the sinful nature. They are in conflict with each other, so that you do not do what you want." (Galatians 5:17 NIV) However, we need to remember: "I have been crucified with Christ; it is no longer I who live, but Christ lives in me; and the life which I now live in the flesh I live by faith in the Son of God, who loved me and gave Himself for me." (Galatians 2:20) We need to stop addressing the symptoms and start treating the problem. Acknowledge the sin in our lives. "My dear children, I write this to you so that you will not sin. But if anybody does sin, we have one who speaks to the Father in our defense - Jesus Christ, the Righteous One. He is the atoning sacrifice for our sins, and not only for ours but also for the sins of the whole world." (1 John 2:1-2 NIV) Repent and allow Jesus to bring the healing.

Father, we have so many ideas of what is wrong with us and with our world. We blame everything and everyone instead of admitting that we and the world we live in are lost without You. We want to believe that we can be the solution. But God we are nothing without You. We acknowledge that it is the sin in us and in the world that is the true problem and only You have the answer. You sent Your Own Son into the world to bring the deliverance we need. Father, we humbly come before You and seek Your face. We turn from our wicked ways so that You will forgive us our sins and heal our land. Amen.

Just give me Jesus
Luke 19

Cries for truth, love, peace, and hope surround us every day. People are crying out for their ideas of what that looks like. Cries for what seems "right in their own eyes." More than likely you have conflicting voices in your own world. People have this view of truth, love, peace, and hope while others have almost an entirely different view. The Triumphal Entry crowd was also crying out for truth, love, peace, and hope. They expected Jesus to come in and free them from oppression, allowing them to be in charge for once. They expected Him to become their king and meet all their needs and desires. They had their ideas of what truth, love, peace, and hope were. And by the end of the week, Jesus dying on Calvary's cross did not fit into those ideals. How were they going to be freed from their oppression? How were their lives going to get better? How were they supposed to continue hoping as their "king" was being crucified? The crowd was looking for their ideal king, when in fact Jesus came to die the King of kings and Lord of lords. Jesus was the embodied Truth, Love, Peace, and Hope. "Jesus said to him, "I am the way, the truth, and the life. No one comes to the Father except through Me." (John 14:6) Jesus was fulfilling His Father's plan. The Word of God is the absolute Truth. We cannot change it to make it fit into our outlook of truth. God is Love. While here on earth, Jesus showed us how to love one another. "Let all that you do be done with love." (1 Corinthians 16:14) Sometimes I think we forget Love when we are trying to spread Truth. We would like "peace on earth," but we live in a fallen world. However, God will give us "the peace of God which surpasses all understanding." (Philippians 4:7) God's Peace is not from external factors but within us so no matter the storm, His Presence will bring peace to our troubled souls. Here in this life, we hope for a better world. Because Jesus conquered death, Hell, and the grave, we have Hope that one day we will live in a Land where all things are made new, and we can lay down all the struggles in this life and rest in His Presence. So, when the loud cries around me cause chaos and confusion, just give me Jesus. When I seek Truth, let me open my Bible and ask God to speak His Truth in my life. And pray that I, in turn, can speak His Truth in Love with those I encounter. When life is full of hate and disagreements, just give me Jesus. May I shine His Love to all those I meet. When I'm feeling bruised and battered from life's storms, just give me Jesus. May His Peace be my calm amid whatever I face. When circumstances in my life seem hopeless, just give me Jesus. Let Hope remind me of my Father's Power, Provision, and Promise. Amen. Inspired by "Just Give Me Jesus" by Unspoken

Privilege of prayer
Revelation 4

We all have a long list of personal prayer needs. We pray for prayer requests posted on Facebook or other social media. We watch the news and pray for situations around the world. Isn't it amazing to think of the number of prayers we have personally prayed? The number of prayers going up from saints around the world? Isn't it awesome to think about how God hears our every prayer? What a privilege prayer is! To be able to come boldly to God, the Creator of the universe, the Great I AM, the Alpha and the Omega with our every concern and problem. "Let us therefore come boldly to the throne of grace, that we may obtain mercy and find grace to help in time of need." (Hebrews 4:16) We can take everything to God in prayer, bring all our worries, fears, doubts, insecurities, hopelessness, sorrow, pain. We can pray in those times when there is nothing else we can do. We can give it to the One who can do something. Prayer also consists of praising. We have the privilege of joining with the angels in praising the Lover of our soul, the Prince of Peace, the Everlasting Father. "And they do not rest day or night, saying: "Holy, holy, holy, Lord God Almighty, Who was and is and is to come!" Whenever the living creatures give glory and honor and thanks to Him who sits on the throne, who lives forever and ever, the twenty-four elders fall down before Him who sits on the throne and worship Him who lives forever and ever, and cast their crowns before the throne, saying: "You are worthy, O Lord, to receive glory and honor and power; for You created all things and by Your will they exist and were created." (Revelation 4:8-11) "And every creature which is in heaven and on the earth and under the earth and such as are in the sea, and all that are in them, I heard saying: "Blessing and honor and glory and power be to Him who sits on the throne, and to the Lamb, forever and ever!" (Revelation 5:13)

We are privileged to be able to communicate with the One who holds the world in His hands. Someone who can hear and speak to us through His Word and His Holy Spirit. The same God that heard Elijah's prayer and poured fire down from Heaven is the same God we call on today.

Lord God, thank You for the privilege to be able to talk with You anytime we want. For the confidence that we have that You hear our prayers. For the reassurance that You care about what we care about. "Now to Him who is able to do exceedingly abundantly above all that we ask or think, according to the power that works in us, to Him be the glory in the church by Christ Jesus to all generations, forever and ever. Amen." (Ephesians 3:20-21)

Talk about Him
1 Chronicles 16

We give our two-cents about anything, sharing our opinions on any subject matter even, if we were honest, we don't know much about it. However, because religion is often such a controversial subject, there may be times we shy away from those conversations. Sometimes we fear the discussion may get too deep and we won't know the right answers. We may be a little afraid of people's reactions to our testimony. We may be afraid to let God down. But when we are in "religion" or faith conversations, we do not need to be profound. We can simply explain how "once I was lost, but now I'm found." When King David was bringing the Ark back to Jerusalem, he delivered a psalm. He starts out by saying: "Oh, give thanks to the Lord! Call upon His name; make known His deeds among the peoples! Sing to Him, sing psalms to Him; talk of all His wondrous works!" (1 Chronicles 16:8-9) We don't need to get into "religion" debates, we need to get into relationship conversations. God does not need us to defend Him. He is God! "Blessed be the name of God forever and ever, for wisdom and might are His. And He changes the times and the seasons; He removes kings and raises up kings; He gives wisdom to the wise and knowledge to those who have understanding. He reveals deep and secret things; He knows what is in the darkness, and light dwells with Him." (Daniel 2:20-22) What He does want us to do is tell our story.
1 Peter 3:15 (NIV) says: "always be prepared to give an answer to everyone who asks you to give the reason for the hope that you have." Testify my brothers and sisters! "For the Holy Spirit will teach you at that time what you should say." (Luke 12:12 NIV) We do not need to be prepared with two hours' worth of material to share, checking our notes to make sure we cover all the essential details. We simply share an example of how the God of the universe is very real and personal to us; how we have seen Him move, how He has brought us through. We may only be called to plant a seed. And if He does call us to water the seed and we find ourselves in that two-hour conversation, we can trust that God will use us as His instrument. He will provide the words that those listening need to hear.

Father, may we always be willing to talk about You! We sometimes are afraid to speak up, even among our brothers and sisters. But Father God, You want us to share Your love and truth in our little part of the world. "But you are a chosen generation, a royal priesthood, a holy nation, His own special people, that you may proclaim the praises of Him who called you out of darkness into His marvelous light." (1 Peter 2:9) God, give us the boldness and the words to share of Your amazing grace and love. Amen.

July 16
My Father has a place for you
John 14

There are places we probably go where we feel out of place. There are times we feel like we don't quite fit in with the people around us. Some of us may feel out of place at work, with our friends, or at home. Some of us may even say that we have yet to find our "place" in this world. There are many different reasons we may feel like we are out of place. We may be unsure of our role within our family and friends. We may not be confident enough in our abilities at work. We may be afraid of what people really think about us. Circumstances in life may have us unsettled and uprooted. Perhaps we may have never even had a place truly to call home. I have good news for all of us! God our Father has a place for us all! You and I have a place in His family that no one else can fill. And it is not based on who we are but who He is. It is not based on our abilities, talents, resources but on His amazing grace. Our "place" in life is not defined by where we are but on our relationship with Him. No matter where we find ourselves, we have Him by our side. Our sense of "home" rests in the love of our Father. His Presence is always with us providing that "place we belong" wherever we go.

Jesus is also preparing an eternal place for us. "Let not your hearts be troubled; you believe in God, believe also in Me. In My Father's house are many mansions; if it were not so, I would have told you. I go to prepare a place for you. And if I go and prepare a place for you, I will come again and receive you to Myself; that where I am, there you may be also." (John 14:1-3) My friend, if you are still seeking your "place" in this world. Come to Jesus! Come into your Father's waiting arms! And rest in the certainty of an Eternal Home with Him.

Father, thank You for being our "Home": our place of Love, Security, Peace, and Rest. We do not need to wander aimlessly around trying to find where we belong. You are our Maker and our Provider. Thank You for the promise that one day, we will go to the Place that has been prepared for us. Amen!

July 17

Jealous God
Exodus 20

"For you shall worship no other god, for the Lord, whose name is
Jealous, is a jealous God" (Exodus 34:14)

When we look at the attributes of God, we like to think about how
loving He is, how merciful, how patient, how forgiving. And all of that is
very true. However, we do not like to think about God as being the jealous
"type." We want Him to love us, forgive us, be merciful but not
necessarily be jealous for us. Almost in a way, we would like to define our
relationship with God. "God, here is the role You play in my life." "Here
are the places You are allowed in my life; these other areas are still mine."
And so forth. "Take heed to yourselves, lest you forget the covenant of the
Lord your God which He made with you, . . . For the Lord your God is a
consuming fire, a jealous God." (Deuteronomy 4:23-24) What in your life
causes God to be jealous? What have you placed as the most important
thing in your life? Where is God in your importance list? God does not
want to take second or third place in your life. "You shall have no other
gods before Me." (Exodus 20:3) What gods are before Him right now in
your life? Your family, your career, your hobbies, your possessions? When
the scribes asked Jesus what the most important commandment was, Jesus
answered: "The first of all the commandments is: 'Hear, O Israel, the Lord
our God, the Lord is one. And you shall love the Lord your God with all
your heart, with all your soul, with all your mind, and with all your strength."
(Mark 12:29-30) We don't always get this right. We want God to be first in
our lives but then distractions and obligations seem to get in the way. Even
amidst our busiest of schedules, God can still be first in our lives when we
acknowledge it is all about Him. "Or do you not know that your body is the
temple of the Holy Spirit who is in you, whom you have from God, and
you are not your own? For you were bought at a price; therefore glorify
God in your body and in your spirit, which are God's." (1 Corinth. 6:19-20)
My friend, God is jealous for us because He wants what is best for us, His
Will for our lives. That doesn't mean life will be a "bed of roses." We live in
a fallen world, but our relationship with Him sustains us through whatever
comes our way. Every so often we need to take the time to examine our
priorities.

*Lord God, You want what is best for us. How many times do
You watch us allow our enemy to lead us down the wrong path? You love
us! You are jealous for us. May we love you with all our hearts, souls,
minds, and strength! Amen.*

Calm my anxious heart
Philippians 4

"Be anxious for nothing, but in everything by prayer and supplication, with thanksgiving, let your requests be made known to God." (Phil. 4:6)

How many of you need some calm in your life today? There always seems to be something to worry about; whether it be the same old thing or something new. Life seems to be one problem after another. And if our personal life is calm, then we can watch the news and find other things to worry about. We know we are supposed to be "casting all your care upon Him, for He cares for you." (1 Peter 5:7) But if we are honest, sometimes we just want to hold on to them ourselves (for various reasons). One of the biggest problems with worry is that we tend to try to find a way we can fix or solve it. We also tend to make the problems bigger than they really are. Philippians 4:8 seems to be the answer to worry. The answer to having calm. "Finally, brethren, whatever things are true, whatever things are noble, whatever things are just, whatever things are pure, whatever things are lovely, whatever things are of good report, if there is any virtue and if there is anything praiseworthy - meditate on these things." Can we all admit to sometimes adding anxiety to our lives by blowing things out of proportion? We create scenarios in our mind that are based on our emotions and reactions to situations and not on the truth of the situation. Can we admit that we sometimes dwell on the negative aspects of our lives instead of the countless blessings we receive? Can we admit that we are more likely to discuss the "bad" report about someone instead of the good? Where is our praise? 2 Corinthians 10:5 (NIV) says: "We demolish arguments and every pretension that sets itself up against the knowledge of God, and we take captive every thought to make it obedient to Christ." When we allow our minds to wander away from what is true, noble, just, pure, lovely, of good report, our enemy can use that to pull us down in a pit where we can no longer see anything praiseworthy. Yes, we all experience things in life that cause us worry and anxiety. But when we allow that worry and anxiety to become bigger than our God, we are not holding that situation up to the light of God's Truth and Love. When we view a problem "against the knowledge of God," we are able to see how God is with us providing; how He is bigger than the problem. *Lord, we bring our anxious hearts and minds to You. We want to experience "the peace of God which surpasses all understanding," and know that it "will guard your hearts and minds through Christ Jesus." (Philippians 4:7) You are bigger than any problem. Remind us to "be of good cheer, I (Jesus) have overcome the world." (John 16:33) Amen.*

My way or God's way
Numbers 20

Throughout every day of our lives, we face numerous decisions. Most decisions do not seem to warrant a "consultation" with God before making, what to wear, what to eat, etc. Those routine everyday decisions that we make without much thought. On the other hand, when we face those "big" decisions, we do turn to God for guidance. This often defines our decision-making process. However, it is not always so easy. In Exodus 17, when the people were crying out for water, God told Moses to strike the rock for water to quench their thirst. But in Numbers 20, God tells Moses to speak to the rock. Instead, Moses strikes it. Doesn't seem like a big deal, right? That's the way God had him do it before. But God responded: "Because you did not trust in me enough to honor me as holy in the sight of the Israelites, you will not bring this community into the land I give them." (Numbers 20:12 NIV) Doesn't that seem a little extreme after all that Moses had done for God? God had a specific plan and purpose for having Moses speak to the rock that time. "Every way of a man is right in his own eyes." (Proverbs 21:2) Moses may not have even thought about how he was deciding to choose his own way instead of doing it God's way. But he experienced the consequences of that choice. Instead of just consulting God on big decisions, we need to be aware of His promptings and His Word. If we are honest with ourselves, we acknowledge that we sometimes make choices that we know go against God's Word, (even if it seems to be a "small" thing.) There may also be times where we ignore a prompting from God. (Again, doesn't seem like a big deal.) However, what would be accomplished for God if you followed His prompting? For example, even a simple lunch decision could be used by God. Perhaps God will place in your path someone who needs to hear that God loves them. God orchestrates divine appointments and wants us to be open to being where He can use us. That doesn't necessarily mean we need to pray every day before we go to lunch, "where do You want me to have lunch today?" But maybe it does mean that before you begin your day that you ask God to use you for His kingdom purposes that day. We can choose to live our lives with our own agenda, or we can choose to live with Kingdom purpose.

Father, our lives are not our own. They are Yours. How often we forget that! We go through living life for ourselves and do not seek how You want to use us for Your purposes. Lord, we surrender to You our schedules and our goals. Use us to further Your kingdom. Amen!

Our children are watching
Deuteronomy 11

"This will be written for the generation to come, that a people yet to be created may praise the Lord." (Psalm 102:18)

I'm sure you have heard and perhaps even have said something about "this generation today." And most of the time it is said negatively. However, what example has been set before them? What spiritual foundation have we laid for them? Are we laying a foundation built on the Solid Rock or sinking sand? How do our children view our faith? Do they recognize that it is what our life is built on or is it just another aspect of our life? Do we exhibit our personal relationship with Christ or do they just see the "rules" we follow because of our beliefs? Do they recognize a loving God who is active in our lives or a judging Being that is somewhere just waiting for us to mess up? Do they acknowledge that God has a plan for our lives and that He wants us to worship and serve Him only? Or do they think they can pick and choose what they do without consequences? Beginning at a young age, children watch us. They know when our actions match up with our words and when they don't. Moses charged the Israelites: "Therefore you shall lay up these words of mine in your heart and in your soul, and bind them as a sign on your hand, and they shall be as frontlets between your eyes. You shall teach them to your children, speaking of them when you sit in your house, when you walk by the way, when you lie down, and when you rise up. And you shall write them on the doorposts of your house and on your gates, that your days and the days of your children may be multiplied in the land of which the Lord swore to your fathers to give them, like the days of the heavens above the earth." (Deuteronomy 11:18-21)

Don't we want to live out our faith in such a way that our children will choose to follow Christ for themselves? We can't make the decision for them however we can live an example that they will want to follow. Share with your children about what God is doing in your life, what you learn from God, how much you love Him, how much He loves you and them. Let it be an everyday conversation. They need to see Jesus in you.

Father, You have gifted us with our children and charged us to "bring them up in the training and instruction of the Lord." (Ephesians 6:4 NIV) When they look at us, may they see You. Help us to live out our faith before them that they will want to get to know You for themselves. Guide us as we guide them. Amen.

Come to the well
John 4

Are you feeling dry and thirsty? Are you longing for a cool drink of water? Do you feel like you have been in a desert for a while? Have you been working hard and just need a refreshing break? We all experience a physical thirst at one time or another. But what about spiritual? Do you crave something to revive you? Perhaps you have been away from God for a while and just need to come home. Perhaps you have been through a rough season and just need a chance to sit at His feet and rest. Perhaps you have been so busy you have not stopped for a "drink" of His Word. Come to the Well!

When the Samaritan woman came to the well for water, she thought she would be returning to her lonely world. Her world where she never could seem to make the right decisions, a world she perhaps felt trapped in. A world where she was shunned and rejected. She probably was thirsty for something to quench her loneliness, her guilty, her shame. And then she came to the Well. When she came to the well to satisfy her physical thirst, she met Jesus who told her about the Living Water that would quench her soul.

When we experience a "dry spell," whether a time away from God, a spiritual battle, a busy season, or a seemingly hopeless situation, we can find what we need in Jesus. He will revive our weary souls. He will make us clean from sin and shame. He will bring Hope and Peace. He restores our souls. He gives us rest. Come to the Well of His love and forgiveness. Come to the Well of His mercy and grace. Come to the Well of His Word and promises. Come to the Well of peace and hope. Come to Jesus.

Lord Jesus, You can provide us with everything we need. You can heal our brokenness. You can restore our joy. When we come to You and lay it all at Your feet, You will lift us up. Father, I pray for those who need a drink from Your Living Water today. May they come to the Well to find what is missing from their life, to find rest and hope. Amen.

Hope restored
John 20

Some of us may have experienced our world crashing down. Everything we believed in, built our lives and futures on, just fell apart. Leaving us broken, lost, alone and afraid. When I read about Mary in the garden, that's the world I envision for her. So many emotions going on in her heart and mind. Grief for the loss of a dear friend. Confusion about how this could happen. Disappointment that He did not fulfill His promises. Desperation as she began to think "what now?" Loneliness as the one person who truly understood her is gone. Hopelessness as she looked to her bleak future. Then she hears her name. Can we stop for a moment to think about what she began to experience at that moment? That moment when Hope is restored. Her pain replaced by joy. The loneliness replaced by Love. The bleak future replaced by the Promise. The desperation replaced by Peace. As she hears the Master speak her name, the knowledge that her world was just made whole. Never again would she lose Hope. Never again would she feel life had no purpose. Never again would she have to question her future. Was it any wonder the early church grew at such a fast pace? These friends of Jesus who experienced a lost hope, broken dreams, a faith shaken both in God and themselves. Their world had crashed down as their Teacher and Friend died on the cross. To lose everything they had built their lives on and then to hear "Why do you seek the living among the dead? He is not here, but is risen!" (Luke 24:6) With Hope restored, the confidence, the passion, the evidence of Truth, the joy, the courage, all could not be contained. What did Jesus' friends have to fear now? What doubts could overshadow the Truth of a Risen Savior? With their Hope restored, they went around spreading the message of Hope, Love, and Life to all they met. My friend, if your world has crashed around you and you do not have Hope, let me introduce you. Jesus left the splendors of Heaven to come to earth to experience life as a human. He came to fulfill His Father's plan. "For God so loved the world that He gave His only begotten Son, that whoever believes in Him should not perish but have everlasting life. For God did not send His Son into the world to condemn the world, but that the world through Him might be saved." (John 3:16-17) Jesus suffered, bled and died for YOU, to cover your sins and mine. But that is not where the story ends. On the third day, Hope arose defeating death, Hell, and the grave. For those of us who have Hope, when our world comes crashing down, we have a Friend who never leaves or forsakes. We have a Promise of a better future. We have a Comforter and Guide.

Father, thank You that on that third day, Hope was restored. You bring us Love, Peace, Joy, Forgiveness, Hope, and one day a Home. Amen.

Church, love
John 14

"A new commandment I give to you, that you love one another; as I have loved you, that you also love one another. By this all will know that you are My disciples, if you have love for one another." (John 14:34-35)

How do we love like Jesus? We are human and offering unconditional love is something that we struggle with all the time. We like to have stipulations to love. They need to be worthy. They need to live life the way we think they should. They have limited times they can "mess up." That is not the way Jesus loved. Jesus broke down the "rules" of love. The Pharisees had their own rules of who was worthy of love thereby eliminating the poor, the diseased, women, children, "sinners" - the very ones who needed love extended to them. What expectations have you placed on the people in your life that need to be met before you love them? Is that how Jesus loved? When Jesus went to wash His disciples' feet, He knew one would betray Him, one would deny Him, one would doubt Him, and none would stand with Him at the trial. And He still showed His love for them. He knew what He was about to face yet He spent some of His final hours making sure they knew how much He loved them. If we step back and look at the people in our lives, community, world, how do they need to be loved? It is not about how we are willing to love; it is about how they need to be loved. "But if you love those who love you, what credit is that to you? For even sinners love those who love them. And if you do good to those who do good to you, what credit is that to you? For even sinners do the same. And if you lend to those from whom you hope to receive back, what credit is that to you? For even sinners lend to sinners to receive as much back. But love your enemies, do good, and lend, hoping for nothing in return; and your reward will be great, and you will be sons of the Most High. For He is kind to the unthankful and evil. Therefore be merciful, just as your Father is merciful." (Luke 6:32-36) Think about how much God loves you. It is unfathomable. As messed up and imperfect as we are, as vast as His universe is, He loves you and He loves me. He also loves that person you are struggling to love. If we look at everyone we meet as being so loved by God, no matter who they are or what they have done, does is change how we view them? "I can see Your heart eight billion different ways, every precious one a child You died to save. If You gave Your life to love them, so will I." ("So Will I"/Hillsong Worship)

Lord Jesus, You died to show Your love for every single person that would ever live. Father, teach us to love more like You. Amen.

He holds my tomorrows
Matthew 6

We all face those times when we don't know what tomorrow will bring. Times of uncertainty are a part of life. We would all like just a quick peek ahead, so we can begin to "prepare." But life doesn't happen that way. When tomorrow comes with the unexpected, we are not sure what to do.

Jesus knew that we would face those unknown tomorrows. In Matthew 6, as part of the Sermon on the Mount, He states: "Therefore do not worry about tomorrow, for tomorrow will worry about its own things. Sufficient for the day is its own trouble." (v34) If we are honest with ourselves, we have enough to "worry" about today without worrying about what tomorrow holds. Sure, hindsight is 20/20, and from there we can see where we may have been able to prevent a problem. But we can live life the best way we know how and still end up with unexpected problems. There are too many factors outside of our control.

But isn't it good to know Who holds our tomorrows? No matter what comes our way, He is not caught off guard. He knows what each day of our lives looks like. He is there to love us, hold us, guide us, carry us, fight for us. He is there to give Peace amidst our storms. To give Hope to our hopeless situation. And then one day, He will lead us to a Land with no uncertain tomorrows. A time when our enemy has no more power. That the effects of sin will no longer bring sorrow, shame, death, disease. "Because He lives, I can face tomorrow, because He lives, all fear is gone; because I know He holds the future, and life is worth the living, just because He lives!" ("Because He Lives"/Bill Gaither)

Jesus' answer for our uncertain tomorrows? "But seek first the kingdom of God and His righteousness, and all these things shall be added to you." (Matthew 6:33) Keep your eyes fixed on Him. When the darkness seems to overshadow you, keep your eyes on the Light of the world.

Father, we never know for sure what our tomorrows hold. We are so thankful that You are already there. Father, speak Peace to our troubled minds. Father, we trust You to guide and provide for all the days of our lives. "Your Kingdom come, Your Will be done, on earth as it is in heaven." (Matthew 6:10) "For Yours is the Kingdom and the Power and the Glory forever. Amen." (Matthew 6:13)

The Way, the Truth and the Life
Ecclesiastes 1-3

"Jesus said to him, "I am the way, the truth, and the life. No one comes to the Father except through me." (John 14:6)

Navigating through life is not always easy. Decisions are hard to make when you consider the ramifications they will have on the rest of your life. Unexpected obstacles create roadblocks and force detours along the way. No matter how hard you prepare, situations come out of nowhere and change your plans. King Solomon in all his wisdom recognized that "Vanity of vanities, all is vanity." (Ecclesiastes 1:2) He also acknowledged "that which has been is what will be, that which is done is what will be done, and there is nothing new under the sun." (Ecclesiastes 1:9) In Ecclesiastes 3, he states "to everything there is a season, a time for every purpose under heaven." (v1) Even with all the riches he possessed and all the wisdom that God bestowed on him, Solomon still could not procure his "perfect" life.

If our life is lived solely for this world, then it may be hard to find purpose and perspective. 1 Corinthians 15:19 (KJV) says: "If in this life only we have hope in Christ, we are of all men most miserable." If we live life only to see how far we can get, we are living in vain.

Jesus says: "I am the Way, the Truth, and the Life." Jesus gives us the purpose and perspective we need to make life worth living. Solomon concludes Ecclesiastes with these words: "Let us hear the conclusion of the whole matter: Fear God, and keep His commandments: for this is the whole duty of man. For God shall bring every work into judgment, with every secret thing, whether it be good, or whether it be evil. (Ecclesiastes 12:13-14 KJV)

A life lived for Christ has more direction. When the unexpected comes, it may knock us off course some, but our Anchor holds. Decisions can be with Kingdom purpose in mind. When we feel like we have lost our way, the Good Shepherd is searching for us. Life is worth living when He is the Way, the Truth, and the Life.

Father, thank You for giving life meaning and purpose. Thank You for the direction You provide as we navigate life. May we keep our eyes on You. Amen.

Inspired by "The Way" by Pat Barrett

Fear the Lord
Psalm 112, Proverbs 31

"Her children rise up and call her blessed; her husband also, and he praises her. "Many daughters have done well, but you excel them all." Charm is deceitful and beauty is passing, but a woman who fears the Lord, she shall be praised." (Proverbs 31:28-30)

"The older we become, the more we appreciate how we were raised." While that statement is true for some, it isn't for everyone. For some of us, we are thankful for the solid foundation our parents set for us. While others may have to acknowledge they had no foundation whatsoever. We can all look back and recognize the mistakes our parents made. Many without too many ramifications, while others greatly impact decisions we make as adults. Perhaps as our parents get older (and so do we), we can let go of some of the "mistakes" that we have held against them. As parents, do you ever wonder what your children, as adults, will look back and recall about how they were raised? Do you wonder what memories they will hold most dear? What mistakes do they swear they will never make with their own children? Because children do not come with an instruction manual, parents don't always get it right. However, what foundation do you want to set for your children? What are those core values, beliefs, traditions, truths that you want your adult children to have? That answer will look different from household to household. In Proverbs 31, we see the "qualifications" of an "ideal" woman. Most of us may read through them and wonder how that woman got any sleep? How did she accomplish so much in so little time? Did her children behave perfectly? Did her husband listen to everything she said? However, as awesome as a businesswoman she was, as kind as she was, as clean as her house always seem to be, how prepared she was, her key to being a virtuous woman was that she was "a woman who fears the Lord."

The greatest thing we can pass on to our children is to fear the Lord. "The fear of the Lord is the beginning of wisdom; a good understanding have all those who do His commandments." (Psalm 111:10) What faith example are we to our children? Do we exhibit that not only is God's Word important to read, it is also essential to live by? Do our children see us reflecting God's love to everyone? Are they witnessing the results of our personal relationship with Him? Don't we want to be known as someone who fears the Lord?

Lord, there is no greater gift we can give our children than the knowledge of You. Help us to live in such a way that they see You in us. That they will want to establish their own relationship with You. We pray that our children will choose to "fear the Lord." Amen.

God of all our days
Psalm 139

He holds every one of our days. For those days when everything is going just right, He is God. For those days when the world seems to be falling apart, He is God. For those days when we make all the right choices, He is God. For those days when we can't seem to get it together, He is God. For those days when we are rejoicing, He is God. For those days when we face the heartache, He is God.

The God who spoke this universe into being is the God of all our days. He is there when we are trying to outrun our past. He is already there for those unknown tomorrows. And He is here with us today. If we stop to look around us and our circumstances, we can see how He is actively working in our lives. He pursues us when we have lost our way. He is waiting with outstretched loving arms to welcome us home. "But You, O Lord, are a shield for me, my Glory and the One who lifts up my head." (Psalm 3:3) He is our Provider and Protector. In our weakness, He is our Strength. In our troubles, He is our Deliverer.

What do you need the God of all your days to do for you today? What concerns do you need to surrender? What sins do you need to confess? What part of His plan do you need to accept? The God of your yesterdays, today, and tomorrows never changes. Cry to Him for help. He loves you. He is All-Powerful and All-Knowing. You can trust Him with all your days.

Lord, no matter how scary, how painful, how lonely our days may be, You are there. You love us so much and faithfully care for us. There is nothing beyond Your control and nothing that You don't already know. Father, may we relinquish all our days to You. Guide us into the life You have designed for us. Use us in the way that is pleasing to You.

Inspired by "God of All My Days" by Casting Crowns

Sufficient Grace
2 Corinthians 12

"My grace is sufficient for you, for My strength is made
perfect in weakness." (2 Corinthians 12:9)

When we read about all that Paul said and did, we could almost imagine
Paul as a "superman." He was hard-working, bold, not intimidated, spoke up
for what he believed in, did not let circumstances keep him from doing what
he needed to do, and on and on and on. He wrote 13 books in the New
Testament and took three mission trips to spread God's Word to the Gentiles.
He was imprisoned, beaten, stoned, and shipwrecked. His message stayed the
same; his passion never faltered, his courage was unwavering. But in
2 Corinthians, Paul shares that he had a "thorn in the flesh." Paul asks God
to remove this "thorn" three times, but God responds: "My grace is sufficient
for you." With everything Paul was doing for God, we would think God
would remove the thorn so Paul could do more. We are not even sure what
the thorn was. However, from the rest of that verse, we read God's reason
for not removing the thorn: "for My strength is made perfect in weakness."
Maybe the reason Paul was so bold and courageous was due to the thorn.
Because Paul was not relying on his own strength and power, but on God's.
Often we feel too weak, for whatever reason, to do much good. We feel
unequipped to do anything for God. We have our own "thorn in the flesh"
to contend with thereby making us think we are unable to accomplish much.
But Paul says to that: "Therefore I take pleasure in infirmities, in reproaches,
in needs, in persecutions, in distresses, for Christ's sake. For when I am
weak, then I am strong." (2 Corinthians 12:10) Oh, if only we could learn
that lesson like Paul. We do not like to admit that we are weak. We pursue our
strengths, those areas where we can be self-sufficient, and hide our
weaknesses. However, when we become too self-sufficient, we miss out on
understanding what God's sufficient grace really means. When we think we
don't need God in whatever aspect of our lives, we are missing out on what
He wants to do with that aspect through His greater strength. Let us, like
Paul, say: "Therefore I will boast all the more gladly about my weaknesses, so
that God's power may rest on me." (2 Corinthians 12:9 NIV)

Lord, we are so weak. Take all our weaknesses and use them for Your
Glory that Your Power will be revealed through them. Father, take all of our
strengths and show us how we can use them for You. Thank You for
sufficient grace because we are nothing without You. Amen!

July 29
What is the unknown in your life?
Acts 17

The people of Athens were very religious. Just walking through town, Paul was disturbed by the number of idols he saw there. The people of Athens also had an altar "to the unknown God." (Acts 17:23) Paul preached a message to them on Mars Hill (named after the Greek god, Ares), to introduce them to this "unknown God." This was the God he knew. This was the God he served. This was the God he worshipped. He explained to them that their "unknown God" was the very Creator of the world. This "unknown God" was the very One who gives us all life and breath. "For in Him we live and move and have our being." (v28)

Is there something unknown in your life? Are you looking for something to satisfy? Are you trying to "cover all your bases" so you don't want to commit to something yet? What idols are you serving? Do you recognize something is missing in your life? Are you trying to fill that lonely place, that deep longing space inside, with people or things? Do you walk through life passing that "altar to the unknown God" daily? Do you recognize that at some point in your life, you will need to address that "unknown God?" God is not Someone you can ignore completely. You MUST decide what you believe about this God. You can ignore Him for a while, but He never completely goes away. You can say the timing isn't right, only to be reminded again a little later. My God pursues us. He "is longsuffering toward us, not willing that any should perish but that all should come to repentance." (2 Peter 3:9) He is the very Creator of the world. He gives us our very life and breath. "For in Him we live and move and have our being." (Acts 17:28) He loves you. He wants you to accept His gift of salvation. He wants you to experience His forgiveness. He wants you to live in His freedom. He wants to bring you Peace and Hope. He wants you to recognize that you have a Father that loves you, a Savior who gave His life for you, and a Friend that will be with you wherever you go. He wants you to know how it feels to be clean. He wants you to find rest. He wants you to lay it all down at His feet and allow Him to carry your loads. God wants a personal relationship with you.

Lord God, I pray today for those who still have not experienced You. Those who need Your gift of forgiveness and Love. Who need Peace and Hope. Who needs freedom. Draw them to You. Thank You for never giving up on us. Thank You for pursuing us. Jesus, thank You for dying so we could have life. Amen.

Thank You, Jesus
John 19

Thank You, Jesus, for your salvation gift. Now:
   I am free.
   I am worthy.
   I am loved.
   I am forgiven.
   My past does not define my present and future.
   My sin and shame are covered by Your precious blood.
When God looks at me, He does not see my failures; He sees His child.
   I can talk to God whenever I want.
   I never have to face anything alone.
   I know You can calm my storms.
   I can cast my cares on You for You care for me.
   You are always with me.
   You know me better than I know myself.
   I do not have to rely on my own strength and wisdom.
   I can call on You at any time.
   Your guidance and protection comfort me.
   I do not need to fear for You are with me.
   Greater is He that is in me than he that is in the world.
   My Hope is in You.
   I don't have to believe the lies because of Your Voice of Truth.
   I can have Peace and Joy no matter the circumstance.
   Victory is Yours!
   I have the promise of my Heavenly Home
   One day, I will live in a Home without evil and hate.
   One day, You will wipe away every tear.
One day, I will be reunited with those who have already gone on.
One day, I will bow at Your feet to thank and praise You for all eternity!
Thank You!

Where could I go but to the Lord?
Psalm 139

"But Simon Peter answered Him, "Lord, to whom shall we go? You have the words of eternal life." (John 6:68)

We need other people. We need friends and family as we walk through life. But there are times when those closest to us, let us down. They can't understand how we are feeling. They mislead us unintentionally. They judge us too harshly and too quickly. They become too self-centered. We are human and we all fail each other. There are also times when our friends and family, as much as they want, are not able to help us. There are situations out of our control and there is nothing anyone can do to "fix" it. Thank God, "but there is a friend who sticks closer than a brother." (Proverbs 18:24) In Psalm 139, it says: "O Lord, You have searched me and known me. You know my sitting down and my rising up; You understand my thought afar off. You comprehend my path and my lying down, and are acquainted with all my ways." (v.1-3) If we are honest with ourselves, we will admit that there are times we just don't understand ourselves. We don't know why we are thinking or feeling the way we are. We do or say something that seems so out of character for us. Sometimes we can't even put into words how we are feeling. But our Creator knows us. He understands us. He doesn't need our words; He knows our heart. When so much in life seems out of control, where could I go but to the Lord? When friends forsake, where could I go but to the Lord? When my heart is heavy, where could I go but to the Lord? When my health is failing, where could I go but to the Lord? "Where can I go from Your Spirit? Or where can I flee from Your presence?" (Psalm 139:7) We need our Friend, our Savior, our Lord with us every step of life's journey. There are too many obstacles, too many traps, too many heartaches, too many distractions, too many disappointments to face life without Him.

Lord, in the words of Peter: "to whom shall we go? You have the words of eternal life. Also we have come to believe and know that You are the Christ, the Son of the living God." (John 6:68-69) With all our thoughts and feelings, God, there is only You who can completely understand. There is no one else that can be with us all the time. There is no one else that can supply our every need. Lord, where can I go but to You for all my problems, my failures, my Hope, my dreams? Amen.

Inspired by "Where Could I Go" by Gaither Vocal Band

Fervent prayers
Ephesians 6

"The effective, fervent prayer of a righteous man avails much." (James 5:16)

I don't know about you, but everywhere I turn, I seem to see our "adversary the devil walk(ing) about like a roaring lion, seeking whom he may devour." (1 Peter 5:8) I see him trying to devour our homes, churches, cities, country, world. And unfortunately, I see him being successful. I also notice that we, as God's children, as His hands and feet, are often on the sidelines. Paul wrote to the Ephesians and to all of us: "For we do not wrestle against flesh and blood, but against principalities, against powers, against the rulers of the darkness of this age, against spiritual hosts of wickedness in the heavenly places." (Ephesians 6:12) We like the grace, the peace, the love, the hope that we get from accepting Jesus as our Savior and Lord. However, most of us like to ignore the fact that we then gain an enemy. An enemy who has, from the beginning of time, tried to destroy man and his relationship with God. Most of us do not consider ourselves warriors; we would rather avoid battles than engage in them. That, my friend, is what our enemy counts on.

My friend, we need righteous men and women to raise up effective, fervent prayers to our Father. We need to "Put on the whole armor of God, that (we) may be able to stand against the wiles of the devil." (Ephesians 6:11) We need to be "praying always with all prayer and supplication in the Spirit, being watchful to this end with all perseverance and supplication for all the saints." (Ephesians 6:18) We need to pray for one another.

Father, forgive us for laying down our swords and shields. Forgive us for not standing. Forgive us for not resisting our enemy. Forgive us for not submitting to You. Forgive us for not praying for one another. Lord God, we pray right now for those who are in the heat of the battle. We pray that you give them Your strength, Your courage, Your words, Your victory. Place on our hearts and minds right now those who need our prayers. Those we need to stand in the gap for. Those who the enemy is seeking to destroy. Father, teach us how to pray effective, fervent prayers. Amen.

Inspired by the final scene of "War Room". Raise us up, Lord.

August 2
Don't stop praying
Daniel 6

We all wish we could have a life of smooth sailing. Our world looks bright, not a cloud in the sky. But the reality is those days are few and far between. Daniel's life was full of unsettling waves and dark clouds. As a young man, he was taken from his home and his family to become a member of the king's household. Right from the start, they try to change Daniel. They tried to force Daniel to conform to their beliefs and customs. But even though he was still young, he had been instilled with the truth about God. Daniel chose to cling to God amid his circumstances. As Daniel arose among the ranks there in Babylon, he relied on his God every step of the way. He did not allow his situation, his homesickness, his loneliness, his pride, his position to stop him from following and obeying the God of his youth. In Daniel 6, all the other governors and satraps tried to find fault with Daniel. The only accusation they could bring against him? He faithfully prayed. Daniel was living a life of unknowns. He was surrounded by a new home, expectations, responsibilities, and customs. The one consistency in his life was God. Daniel did not just say a quick prayer in the morning and before he went to bed. He did not just say a quick grace at meal times. Daniel took the time to pray. "Now when Daniel knew that the writing was signed, he went home. And in his upper room, with his window open toward Jerusalem, he knelt down on his knees three times that day, and gave thanks before his God, as was his custom since early days." (Daniel 6:10) Even when he realized he could be signing his death warrant, he prayed. "Daniel distinguished himself above the governors and satraps, because an excellent spirit was in him." (v3) "They could find no charge or fault, because he was faithful; nor was there any error or fault found in him." (v4) Daniel prayed. Daniel knew he had nothing else that he could ultimately depend on except God. Too often, we assume there are areas where we can be a little self-sufficient. The reality is we can't even take a breath without Him. During our busy schedules and responsibilities, let us pray. My friend, the relationship we have with God is the most important thing in life. We need to take the time to talk with Him, to listen to Him, to worship Him, to rest in Him. The result of Daniel's constant communication with his God? Even the king recognized: "Your God, whom you serve continually, He will deliver you." (v16) So if your prayer life has been a little neglected lately, take some time with your Father. There is nothing more important in your schedule than Him. *Father, too often we allow life's distractions to keep us from taking the time to sit at Your feet. Lord Jesus, You paid the ultimate price so we could have this privilege of prayer. Thank You!*

Childlike trust
1 Samuel 17, Psalm 121

When did we "outgrow' taking God at His Word? When did we begin to think that we're adults now, so we have to take care of ourselves? When did life begin obscuring our view of God? As grown children, how often do we return to our family home? We walk in and help ourselves to food. Ask mom or dad for help with something or seek their advice. We still rely on them. And if we are in a place where we can no longer go to them for help, we truly miss running home to mommy and daddy. Then, why do we seem to stop trusting our Heavenly Father? Why do we stop running to Him when we need something? When the Israelite army faced Goliath, they thought they knew the consequences. They had been in too many battles to recognize that this was one they did not want to engage in. They had already acknowledged that the moment they stepped onto the battlefield, they would become the Philistines slaves. Then here comes David, the young shepherd boy. Perhaps David wasn't old enough to understand the ramifications of this battle. However, David was the only one who seems to recognize it for what it truly was. This battle was not about the soldiers' strength and fighting ability. It was about the power of their God. For whatever reason, they seem to have forgotten Who they were fighting for and Who was fighting for them. Little David walks in recalling how God had given him the victory in his own battles. He recognized that His God was bigger than the lion and the bear. His God was bigger than Goliath. The Israelite army had had their own victories. They too had witnessed the power of their God. But how quickly they seem to forget. Don't we do the same thing? Don't we look at the problems in our lives and forget to trust? Forget that our Father wants us to come to Him for help? David later writes: "I will lift up my eyes to the hills- from whence comes my help? My help comes from the Lord, who made heaven and earth." (Psalm 121:1-2) Do you imagine that as he is writing this, his mind is going back to that battlefield with Goliath? My friend, don't allow your problems to become bigger than your God. Don't stop trusting the Miracle Worker from the Bible. "Be strong and of good courage; do not be afraid, nor be dismayed, for the Lord your God is with you wherever you go." (Joshua 1:9) Don't lose your childlike trust. *Abba Father, forgive us those times when we seem to forget Whose we are. We know that You can do all things, that nothing is impossible for You. But too often we become self-sufficient, distracted by our problems, or battle worn. Remind us, Father, that You are near. That we do not have to fight alone. Father, for my friends who need a victory in their lives right now, I pray You fight for them. I pray that You open their eyes to see that their God is bigger than their Goliath. Lord, give them the victory.*

August 4
Oh, won't it be wonderful there?
Revelation 21

One of the many blessings of summer is spending more time with family and friends. Neighbors sit out on the porch talking with one another, friends come together for a cookout. Reunions bring fond memories and laughter as families get to spend time with one another. Kids riding their bikes around the neighborhood. We find the time and take the time to spend with one another. But summer ends all too quickly. The weather turns cooler. Days shorten. We once again go back to living in our little world. Then only seem to find time on special occasions to be with one another. We need each other. We need those we can laugh with, cry with, enjoy a good argument with. We watch each other's kids grow up and form their own special bonds. There are days we wish we could be in multiple places at the same time, so we can spend time with one another more often. One of the blessings of Heaven will be those we are at Home with. We will be able to stroll on those streets of gold with our loved ones. Stand side by side with our brothers and sisters around the world singing praises to our Father. Sit at the feet of the saints of old as they share their redemption stories. We will never have to say "well, it's time for me to go now." We long for the Day when: "For the Lord Himself will descend from Heaven with a shout, with the voice of an archangel, and with the trumpet of God. And the dead in Christ will rise first. Then we who are alive and remain shall be caught up together with them in the clouds to meet the Lord in the air. And thus we shall always be with the Lord." (1 Thess 4:16-17) My friend, as much as we may enjoy our friends and family on this earth. There will come a day when we will trade these worn bodies for glorified bodies. Bodies that will never know sickness, pain, sorrow, sin. We will enter our eternal Home where Love reigns. We will get to join those throughout the ages singing "Worthy are You, Lord." Time will be no more. Separation will be no more. We will have all eternity with our Lord and Savior Jesus Christ. We will have all eternity with our loved ones who have gone on and all believers around the world. Oh, won't it be wonderful there? *Father God, how we long for Home. How we long for that Day when we don't have to rush away from family and friends. How we long for that Day when we can all come together around Your throne to thank You for all You have done for us. Thank You that one day: "Behold, the tabernacle of God is with men, and He will dwell with them, and they shall be His people. God Himself will be with them and be their God. And God will wipe away every tear from their eyes; there shall be no more death, nor sorrow, nor crying. There shall be no more pain, for the former things have passed away." (Revelation 21:3-4)*

August 5
He who began a good work
Philippians 1

"Being confident of this very thing, that He who has begun a good work in you will complete it until the day of Jesus Christ." (Philippians 1:6)

We often get frustrated when we can't find a solution or are unable to finish something. It can be a small thing such as something for school or a project we are working on. Sometimes it's a bigger issue, such as a life situation, that we can't seem to figure out or fix. Most of the time, when those circumstances arise, we just don't have all the information we need, or we have some misinformation. When the situation involves other people, we may just be waiting for them to "get themselves together." We may often feel like giving up. But aren't you thankful that God never gives up on us? How many of you hold on to Philippians 1:6? Your circumstances may feel hopeless. You may not like who you are right now. Life seems out of control. You feel like you have messed up one too many times. This verse promises that God is still working on you and me. And He will be faithful to complete the work He has started.

Sometimes in our own situations, we don't know what to do. But God has a plan for our life. In our situations, we may not be able to see the outcome. But God is present yesterday, today, and forever. In our situations, we may feel powerless. But God is All-Powerful. In our situations, everything may seem out of control. But God is in control. In our situations, we may not be able to identify the truth. But God is Truth. Our situation may seem hopeless. But when God looks at us, He never sees a hopeless case. We do not need to figure out our lives all by ourselves. We do not need to fix life situations by ourselves. Our Father in His infinite wisdom does a good work in us and through us. Trust Him with the work He is doing in your life. Allow Him to guide you in the way you should go. We often wish we had an instruction manual for life. However, we have the actual Creator of the universe, the Designer of all our days, to turn to for direction and guidance. And we can hold on to His promise that He will complete it.

Father, thank You for the promise that You are working on us, for us, and through us. Thank You that You do not expect us to blindly try to navigate this dark life without Your Light. Great is Your faithfulness! And Father, You love us enough that we can bring the "small" things in life to You as well as the "big" things. You care for us. Amen!

Love them
1 Corinthians 13

Would you all agree that some people are easier to love than others? You love your family and friends (at least most of them.) But when you meet a total stranger, your first instinct probably isn't "here is someone else for me to love." Jesus said: "But if you love those who love you, what credit is that to you? For even sinners love those who love them." (Luke 6:32) John writes: "Beloved, let us love one another, for love is of God; and everyone who loves is born of God and knows God. He who does not love does not know God, for God is love. ... Beloved, if God so loved us, we also ought to love one another" (1 John 4:7-8,11) If we treated everyone we met with God's love, how much different would our part of the world be? When we read through 1 Corinthians 13, we must admit, it is sometimes hard to love like that (even for the people we easily love.) Sometimes we feel justified in being selfish, in giving up, in lashing out in anger. But we can still reflect God's love by how we respond in those situations. Love "always protects, always trusts, always hopes, always perseveres." (1 Corinthians 13:7)

Don't you wish every love was like this? We are human, so our love does not always protect, trusts, hopes or perseveres. Our human love fails. But when we allow God's love to shine through us, the way we treat people is different. We can be more patient with them. We can forgive more easily. God's love is not based on emotion or feelings but on a decision. God loves us all, and He desires for us to love each other. Who in your life needs you to love them as God does?

Father, thank You for Your unconditional love. Help us to love others like You. "Show me how to love the unlovable." ("Forgiveness"/ Matthew West) Guide us to the ones You want us to share Your love with. Amen.

Inspired by "The Proof of Your Love" by King and Country

Speak life
James 3

"The tongue is so set among our members that it defiles the whole body, and sets on fire the course of nature; and it is set on fire by hell." (James 3:6)

When I look back on my life, a lot of my regrets seem to come from words I have spoken. People I judged too harshly without having all the facts. Words of advice I gave without really knowing what I was talking about. Snide remarks to make others feel bad. Words spoken in anger or condemnation. "Truths" shared without verifying the source. And I would say that I'm not alone. Our mouths get us into a lot of trouble. When Jesus was speaking to the Pharisees one day, He said: "For out of the abundance of the heart the mouth speaks. A good man out of the good treasure of his heart brings forth good things, and an evil man out of the evil treasure brings forth evil things. But I say to you that for every idle word men may speak, they will give an account of it in the day of judgment. For by your words you will be justified, and by your words you will be condemned." (Matthew 12:34-37)

What are our words reflecting about our hearts right now? Are we speaking words from a bitter, angry heart? Are we speaking words from our own prejudices and preconceived judgments? Are those around us hearing words of hate, dissatisfaction, disappointment? Or are they hearing words of love, affirmation, hope? We all go through seasons where our loads are heavy, and words of encouragement do not come easy. We all go through times when we recognize that we are blessed beyond all measure and spread excitement everywhere we go. What season are you in right now? We need to stop to reflect our words no matter what season we are in. We need to acknowledge when our words may not reflect our Father's love. The world needs our words of love and hope and peace. They need to know our Father's heart. James says: "Out of the same mouth proceed blessing and cursing. My brethren, these things ought not to be so." (3:10) Take a day to reflect on your words. How are you speaking life to those around you? In what ways are you not? Does everyone receive the same words, or do you pick and choose who receive the "life words" and who does not? To truly reflect our Father's heart, everyone needs to hear the life words, the love words, the hope words.

Father, may our words reflect You. May we speak life words to those who need to hear Your love and hope today. Teach us to "speak life" to everyone we meet. Amen.

Inspired by "Speak Life" by TobyMac

August 8
The God of OUR universe
Isaiah 55

How many of you have ever said a prayer and thought "I'll go ahead and pray but I don't know what good it will do?" How many of you have expectations when you pray of how they should be answered? Too often when we pray, we are praying to the God of OUR universe. The God we think we know. The reality is our God is so much bigger than we can even imagine. "For My thoughts are not your thoughts, nor are your ways My ways," says the Lord. "For as the heavens are higher than the earth, so are My ways higher than your ways, and My thoughts than your thoughts." (Isaiah 55:8-9) We read this verse but because we can't fathom what that looks like, we put God back into our "box." The box where we can understand Him. Often, we only pray the prayers we know how God can answer. We also expect prayers answered on our timetable. "But, beloved, do not forget this one thing, that with the Lord one day is as a thousand years, and a thousand years as one day." (2 Peter 3:8) When God does not answer in our desired way or in our timeframe, we start to believe He doesn't care, He isn't listening, etc. "The Lord is not slack concerning His promise." (2 Peter 3:9) God promises: "So shall My word be that goes forth from My mouth; it shall not return to Me void, but it shall accomplish what I please, and it shall prosper in the thing for which I sent it." (Isaiah 55:11) We would like it to accomplish what we please, and to prosper in the way we want. But God is not just the God of OUR universe. He is the God of everyone's universe past, present, and future. We can only see and understand our small part of the universe. We cannot see how our part plays into the Master's plan. That's when we acknowledge that we are the ones limited and offer ourselves up to be used for His higher purposes. Instead of trying to get God to stay in our universe box, we should make ourselves available to come out of the box. Open ourselves up to what God wants to do in our lives that is higher than what we can even imagine.

God, when we see pictures of the discovered universe, it is already so vast and unfathomable. We don't even know what has yet to be discovered. You have been from the beginning of time. We have read of wonders and miracles in Your Word but do not know what You are currently doing in the lives of those all around the world. It's amazing to think how You are working in my life and in the lives of my brothers and sisters all around the world all at the same time and for the same ultimate purpose. May we open our hearts and minds, our hands and feet, to be used for Your Higher Purpose in our lives. Amen.

August 9
God of wonders
Psalm 89

The clouds once again reflected how amazing our Creator God is. The sun was setting, peeking behind the clouds. There were layers and layers of different size and color clouds that created a breathtaking trip home. What an awesome God we serve! As we read through scripture and the endless accounts of His grace and mercy, how often do we pause to say "Wow, God!" The mighty ways He moved to rescue His people. The many different methods He chose to bring that deliverance, that redemption.

As Creator, He has the whole universe at His disposal to use for His purposes. For those of us who have been reading scripture for years, sometimes I think we miss the wow factor when we read some of those familiar "stories" such as the Creation or the Flood. We know these "stories" by heart, so often we just do a quick read through without stopping to acknowledge how breathtaking those events were. Our mind's eye envisions pictures we may have seen as children. We picture Earth with its green grass and trees, animals that we all recognize, the sun, moon, and a few stars, and of course, Adam and Eve. However, when God spoke, a universe was created that we have not even completely discovered yet. (Look up images from the Hubble Telescope!)

Imagine as the animals are lining up to go into the ark. We envision lions and elephants and zebras and giraffes. But there are countless other animals from all around the world that we have never heard of or seen. Who but God could bring them all to one place, for one purpose? The Master called, and they all responded. God is not just a God of Wonder but a God of details. Have you ever stopped to examine a bug closely? Even the smallest among His creation exhibits the care of His design. Everything created with intentional purpose. How awesome is our God! And we don't read about God's wonders in just the first few chapters of Genesis. Evidence of His wonder is found on every page of His Word. And it is found in every day of our lives. "God of wonders, beyond our galaxy. You are holy, holy. The universe declares Your majesty. You are holy, holy." ("God of Wonders"/Third Day)

Lord God, how awesome is Your name! The work of Your hands is incomparable! "I will sing of the Lord's great love forever." (Psalm 89 NIV) Thank You for the beauty You surround us with. Thank You for creating us in Your image. How awesome is Your name!

Stand strong
Exodus 14

"Having done all, to stand. Stand therefore." (Ephesians 6:13-14)

During a time in my life when everything seemed to be pressing in, the scripture above was what God gave me to hold on to. Sometimes life feels like it is completely out of our control. We don't know what to expect; we don't know how to respond, we don't know what to do. But at times, that is the exact place God needs us, so we can: "Do not be afraid. Stand still, and see the salvation of the Lord, which He will accomplish for you today." (Exodus 14:13) If we can't figure out a solution or if we are unable to fix it, we often think it is an impossible situation. Even when we have seen God do other miraculous things in our lives, we seem to forget to look to Him. The Israelites had just witnessed the miraculous but are now facing the impossible. Pharaoh's army is behind them; the Red Sea in front. But God tells Moses to say: "Stand still." That is often our problem. We are so busy looking for the answer or fretting about what's going to happen, that we are not looking for God in the situation. God has promised countless times that He will be with us. He has promised to supply our every need. He has promised to fight for us. He has promised that He will never leave us. He has promised. What He hasn't promised is that things will work out the way we want. We need to stand on His promises when all else seems like chaos around us. "Watch, stand fast in the faith, be brave, be strong." (1 Corinthians 16:13) We need to stand on His Word even when compromise seems like the better alternative. We need to stand on Who He is and Whose we are. "Being confident of this very thing, that He who has begun a good work in you will complete it until the day of Jesus Christ." (Philippians 1:6) We need to stand on His Love and our Hope.

When you have done all that you know to do. When you know you are where God wants you. Stand. Stand on the truth of His Word. Stand on Who you know He is. When we are standing, we are not doing anything. We are not moving in the situation. We are not the one striving for the answer. But when we are standing, we are not sleeping. When we are standing on Him, we are not distracted. When we are standing, we are on alert. So, when God says move, we are ready to move.

"Now to Him who is able to keep you from stumbling and to present you faultless before the presence of His glory with exceeding joy, to God our Savior who alone is wise be glory and majesty dominion and power, both now and forever. Amen." (Jude 1:24-25)

August 11
Give them Jesus
Acts 3

When those around you are hurting, there is typically not much you can do for them. You can be there, you can listen, you can hold their hand, and you can take care of some of the little details for them. It doesn't feel like much. But the best thing you can do for them is give them Jesus. Cover them with your prayers, be His hands and feet to them, love them as He does. What about those friends who seem to have lost their way or who are aimlessly wandering through life? We try to offer words of human wisdom or encouragement. What they need is for us to give them Jesus.

Again, taking them to our Father who can do infinitely more than we can ask or imagine. We need to ask Him to open their ears and hearts to hear His direction and see His purpose for their lives. What about those who are lonely or afraid? Jesus is the only One who can be with them always. He is the only One who can calm their storms. He's the only One who can give them hope and peace.

When the lame man approached Peter and John for money, they had something better to give him. They gave him Jesus. "Then Peter said, "Silver and gold I do not have, but what I do have I give you: in the name of Jesus Christ of Nazareth, rise up and walk." (Acts 3:6) Often when we see those who need help, we do one of two things. We may see a need and just pray for that person, or we jump in to try to help with good intentions but without the needed resources or wisdom. For some, God may only expect our prayers. For others, He may also have a specific way for us to be an instrument He can use in their lives. Be open to how God wants us to "give them Jesus." He can give us the words to say. He can show us how to best love them.

Lord, in this world of hurting people, we know they need Jesus. Guide us to demonstrate Your Light and Love to those who need it. Give us the wisdom and resources to help those You have placed in our paths to help. Thank You that You are personally involved in every life. Amen.

A parent's prayers
Luke 2

A friend texted this week to share that her young son had gotten saved. An elderly man yesterday talked about how his most heartfelt prayer was for his lost son. As Christian parents, we spend a lot of time praying for our kids. When they are young, we pray that they will follow God's direction, for their safety, their futures, their salvation. As they grow up, we pray that they will follow God's direction, for their safety, their futures, their salvation/relationship with God. The prayers are the same just more specific depending on their stage in life. Do you think Joseph and Mary prayed for Jesus over the years? Can you imagine what those prayers may have sounded like? Do you think they talked with Jesus' Father on how they were to raise Him? Do you think they prayed that Jesus would have the strength to follow His Father's plan? At the beginning of Luke 2, Joseph and Mary were facing His birth. By the end of the chapter, they began watching Him grow into the Teacher He would later become.

Joseph and Mary were raising the very Son of God. Could you even contemplate what that would look like? Luke 2:51 says: "Then He went down with them and came to Nazareth, and was subject to them, but His mother kept all these things in her heart." The Son of God was "subjected" to them. Envision how often Joseph and Mary were on their knees, praying for wisdom and guidance as they raised the Son of God, their Savior and Redeemer.

We don't know what the future holds for our children. As we pray for them, we also pray for ourselves that we will be the parents they need us to be. We pray that we will guide them and prepare them for whatever that future holds. But just as Joseph and Mary were not raising Jesus alone, we are not raising our children alone either. We will make mistakes. I sure Joseph and Mary did as well. We are all human. But we need to entrust our children to the Father, who knows the plan He has for them.

Lord, we hold our children dear to our hearts, but Father, we know they are also dear to You. We have limited control over our children and even less as they grow older. Father, remind us, that even though we cannot be with them everywhere they go, and that we can't make all their decisions for them, You are always with them. You are there to guide and protect. Lord, have Your way in the lives of our children as well as our lives as parents. Amen.

All things new
Revelation 21

If you have been in a store lately, you have probably seen children with their families walking the aisles of school supplies, looking at the latest fashions, and trying on new shoes. It's that time of the year again. A new school year. A chance to reconnect with friends and make new ones. Learn new routines and schedules. Starting a new beginning filled with expectations, doubts, and worry. Will I get the teacher I want? Will Suzy or Billy still be my friend? Will the math be easier this year? Can I avoid Bobby pick on me this year? Etc. A lot of new but also a lot of the same.

We too face "new" times in our lives that too quickly just become more of the same. The same routine, the same problems, the same life. When one of life's problems finally gets resolved, it is not long before we face another one. We figure out this aspect of life, only to be hit with another one and must start making life adjustments. But there will come a day when "the former things have passed away." (Revelation 21:4) Life as we know it will pass away and our new life will begin. Gone are sin, hate, shame, anger, and death. We, who know Christ as our Savior, will live a new life of peace, harmony, love. Those things that bring heartache, gone. Those things that frustrate and upsets, gone. Those things that destroy and devastate, gone. We will live life the way God intended. So hold on my friend, someday all things will become new. Those heavy loads you carry now will be no more. Those hopeless situations disappear when the Hope of nations comes. These earthly bodies will pass away; we will receive glorified bodies that will never know sin, pain, disease or death. One day all things will be new. And these lives that face a world of sorrow and suffering every day will be exchanged for "a new heaven and a new earth." (Revelation 21:1)

Lord, thank You that this life that we struggle with now is only temporary. Thank You that You have created a new heaven and a new earth for us. Thank You that Eternity has been paid for by the blood of the Lamb and we will one day enter in our Eternal Home. A new Home where the cares of this present world are no more. Amen.

August 14
Thanksgiving song
Psalm 136

In this Psalm, the repetition line says: "For His mercy endures forever." The Psalmist goes through Creation events as well as times of deliverance. After each line, comes "For His mercy endures forever." One of the definitions of mercy from Merriam-Webster Online is: "compassionate treatment of those in distress." How many of you are in a season where all around you is distress? All through the Bible and the history books, we read of distressing times. Moments of peace are quickly quenched by the latest crisis. But thank God His mercy endures forever.

If God's mercy was limited, it would have run out a long time ago. The countless lives that have come before us who needed the mercies of a loving God. The sin-filled world where hate and war destroy families, cities, countries all around the world throughout every generation. Thank God, His mercy endures forever.

If you were the Psalmist, what would this Psalm look like in your life? In what ways have you seen God move? In what ways has He delivered you? In what ways has He been with you in your distress? "Oh, give thanks to the Lord, for He is good! For His mercy endures forever. Oh, gives thanks to the God of gods! For His mercy endures forever. Oh, give thanks to the Lord of lords! For His mercy endures forever." (Psalm 136:1-3)

Thank Him for the mercy He has given to you. Thank Him for the mercy He is reaching out to your unsaved family and friends. Thank Him that "mercy triumphs over judgment." (James 2:13) Thank Him that He gives "beauty for ashes, the oil of joy for mourning, the garment of praise for the spirit of heaviness." (Isaiah 61:3) Thank Him that "For You, Lord, are good, and ready to forgive, and abundant in mercy to all those who call upon You." (Psalm 86:5)

"Teach me Your way, O Lord; I will walk in Your truth; unite my heart to fear Your name. I will praise You, O Lord my God, with all my heart, I will glorify Your name forevermore. For great is Your mercy toward me, and You have delivered my soul from the depths of Sheol (the grave)." (Psalm 86:11-13) Amen.

New horizon
Psalm 121

How long have you been looking at the current problem in your life? Are you tired of seeing the same situations and emotions? How long have you been striving for an answer or solution? Perhaps it's time to change your perspective. Psalm 121:1-2 says: "I will lift up my eyes to the hills - from whence comes my help? My help comes from the Lord, who made heaven and earth." Maybe it's time to gaze upon a "new horizon," even through life's toughest days. Time to take our eyes off the problem and on to our Helper. "The Lord is your keeper; the Lord is your shade at your right hand." (Psalm 121:5)

Can we all admit that sometimes we need a keeper? We tend to get ourselves in trouble often. We get lost. We make mistakes. Frankly, sometimes we are a mess! But that is not the only kind of keeper we need. The NIV says: "The Lord watches over you." The Message reads it as: "God's your Guardian, right at your side to protect you." Envision being sheltered in His arms. Not only is He our Helper, but He is also our Deliverer. He is our Protector. He is our Provider. He is our Problem-Solver. He is our Comforter and Friend. He is the God of all Wisdom. There is no Goliath-size problem that He cannot overcome. Even when problems are not resolved in our timeframe or in the way we want, He is trustworthy. My friend, take some time every day to look to the "new horizon." Thank Him for His Presence amid your problem.

Lord God, You "will watch over (our) coming and going both now and forevermore." (Psalm 121:8 NIV) Thank You! What a blessing to realize we do not need to walk our life's journey alone. We don't have to have all the answers. We don't always have to get it right. You are a God of mercy and grace. You are a God of hope and peace. You are a God who protects, provides and directs. Thank You! Amen.

August 16
Who is holding you up?
Exodus 17

My friend, we all need prayer. We each have our own prayer list.
Those people we faithful pray for such as family and friends. Those that
God lays on our hearts. We know the power of prayer and how it changes
things. Aren't you glad that just as you are praying for others, others are
praying for you? Sometimes we get neglectful in our prayer life. We don't
take the time to pray as we should. Sometimes our prayers get selfish, and
we just pray for our small world. Has anyone else had to ask God for
forgiveness in the area of prayer? When you have recognized that there
were some things that the enemy has more easily come in and stolen or
destroyed because you were not "being watchful to this end with all
perseverance and supplication for all the saints?" (Ephesians 6:18)

Now think about how many times God has laid someone on your
heart. How many unseen victories due to those on their knees. Aren't you
thankful that we do not live life alone? That we don't have to pray for those
things heavy on our hearts by ourselves? That even when we don't know
how to pray specifically, God knows? "Likewise the Spirit also helps in our
weaknesses. For we do not know what we should pray for as we ought,
but the Spirit Himself makes intercession for us with groanings which
cannot be uttered. Now He who searches the hearts knows what the mind
of the Spirit is, because He makes intercession for the saints according to
the will of God." (Romans 8:26-27) In Exodus 17, God gives us the perfect
example of the need for us to hold each other up. Joshua was leading the
battle, but Moses was "directing" the battle. When his hands were raised,
Israel was winning. But when his arms grew tired and weak, when he would
let them drop, the battle turned in favor of the Amalekites. Along comes
Aaron and Hur who helped hold up Moses' hands, and the battle is won.
There are times we all face when we get weak from the battle. When we
think we can't take another step. When we can't survive another day.
But thank God in His mercy He surrounds us with brothers and sisters who
will lift up our "hands" in prayer. So be thankful for those who are lifting
you up in prayer. And ask God who needs to be lifted up by your prayers.

Father God, how awesome is Your great power. To think that our
prayers can touch anyone all around the world. That You orchestrate
prayer so that those who are fighting the battles have a prayer army
behind them. We need the prayers from our brothers and sisters. We are
not equipped to fight alone. Thank You for those who are praying for
me. Guide our hearts to those You need us to pray for today. Amen.

August 17
Putting others before yourself
1 Samuel 20, 2 Samuel 9

Have you ever thought about the complexity of David and Jonathan's friendship? Jonathan had every reason to dislike David. Their relationship caused a rift with his father. David would become the next king of Israel, which by birthright should have been Jonathan. In return, David, as king, would later bless Jonathan's lame son, Mephibosheth. David could have justifiably killed Mephibosheth when he learned of his presence. Instead, David created a place at his own table for him.

Have you ever thought about how much Jonathan's friendship with David cost him? He lost his father's respect. He lost the throne. And ultimately, he had to lose David to spare David's life. It is so easy to make life all about us. To not let anything deter our schedule and agenda. To adapt our relationships to our routine. How much more satisfying would our lives be if we shifted our priorities? If we put people before plans? When was the last time you changed your plans to go hang out with friends? When was the last time you turned off devices to sit and talk with your family? Living life with others makes us better people. "Two are better than one." (Ecclesiastes 4:9) Spending time with others often provides the rest and the reenergizing we need in life. Talking and laughing with others is like providing water to a thirsty soul.

Father, thank You for our friends and family who seek to spend time with us. Who are always ready with a listening ear and a heartfelt hug. Thank You for those who bring fun and the gift of laughter into our lives. Thank You for those who provide us with wisdom and good advice. Help us be good friends to those around us. Amen.

Lies from our enemy
John 8

We want to think that all our thoughts and emotions are based on truth. Some of us seem to try to live by the motto: "If I think it, it is true." Hopefully, we all recognize the reality that we cannot always trust our perspective. We may not know the backstory or enough of the details in a situation to deem our initial reaction to it as true. We have all made judgment calls based on emotion rather than fact. The enemy is good about twisting and distorting the truth. He typically weaves enough of the truth into the lie that it takes you a while to sort out the difference. Satan also like to keep repeating the same lies in our lives, perhaps hoping that if we hear it enough times, we will eventually believe it. Especially for those lies that "trip" us up occasionally. We listen to that "voice in our head" that tries to drown out the truth, stir up emotions, and make things appear larger than they are. How do we combat the lies of our enemy? With the Truth of God's Word! Jesus said: "If you abide in My word, you are My disciples indeed. And you shall know the truth, and the truth shall make you free." (John 8:31-32) Dissect the enemy's lies and shine the light of God's Word on them. Satan likes to lie to you about others, about your circumstances, and mostly about you. That is when we need to remind Satan of the Truth. When combating the lies, it is best to be specific in the Truth. Use God's Word against him. For example, when Satan tells you that you are worthless and helpless, you remind him that you are a Child of the King. If he tells you your world is falling apart, remind him that God is with you. "Fear not, for I am with you; be not dismayed, for I am your God. I will strengthen you, yes, I will help you, I will uphold you with My righteous right hand." (Isaiah 41:10) Again, it is easy to fall into the trap of lies especially when we are tired and "weak." When we don't seem to have the strength or the will to fight back. (Those may also be the times when we have not been in God's Word for a while.) See the pattern. If we are daily allowing God to speak Truth into our lives through His Word, we will more likely be able to recognize the lies of the enemy. The enemy's lies are trying to destroy our homes, churches, cities, nations and world. We need those who will stand on and up for the Truth and who will actively combat the lies of our enemy with God's Word of Truth.

God, You have promised: "if the Son makes you free, you shall be free indeed." (John 8:36) But You find us living like we are still in bondage. Teach us to stop, reflect, and compare what we hear to Your Truth. "Let the words of my mouth and the meditation of my heart be acceptable in Your sight, O Lord, my strength and my Redeemer." (Psalm 19:14)

August 19
Questioning times
Job 38, John 3

"For who has known the mind of the Lord? Or who has become His counselor?" (Romans 11:34)

Do you think God welcomes our questioning times? Those times when we don't understand why life is going the way it is? We are not the first, nor will we be the last, to question God. The Bible is full of people who questioned God; from Abraham to Moses to Job to Nicodemus. "How can this thing be?" "Why is this happening?" "When are You going to move?" These questions or ones very similar were asked by our Bible "heroes" and are the same ones we ask today. We often try to "advise" God. "God, it would appear to work better this way." "God, You need to fix it this way." Abraham said, "Bless Ishmael." Moses said, "Send someone else." In our limited human view, we only see the impossibility. We only see the current situation. We only see part of the story. God's response to all our questions? "I AM." We need to recognize that He is God and we are not. We do not have to understand. Even though we don't like the not knowing, we need to simply trust. We need to trust a God who has proven Himself faithful. We need to trust a Father who sent His Son to die for us. We need to trust the Almighty who can part the waters, calm the seas and conquer the grave. We need to trust the One who loves us even when we don't deserve it. "But God demonstrated His own love toward us, in that while we were still sinners, Christ died for us." (Romans 5:8) We need to trust the All-Powerful. "And Jesus came and spake unto them, saying, All power is given unto me in heaven and in earth." (Matthew 28:18 KJV) Our questioning times with God are a part of our communication with Him. Just as children question those around them to learn, we question God that we may learn more about Him. However, as we question, we remember that "For my thoughts are not your thoughts, nor are your ways My ways," says the Lord. "For as the heavens are higher than the earth, so are My ways higher than your ways, and My thoughts than your thoughts." (Isaiah 55:8-9) Our finite minds cannot comprehend what God is doing in the world around us. "In my search for wisdom and in my observation of people's burdens here on earth, I discovered that there is ceaseless activity, day and night. I realized that no one can discover everything God is doing under the sun. Not even the wisest people discover everything, no matter what they claim." (Ecc. 8:16-17 NLT) So as we approach our Holy God, Maker of Heaven and Earth, we lay our questions at His feet and with His infinite wisdom provides the answers. *All-Knowing Father, may we trust You more with our lives. Amen.*

August 20
Where would I be without God?
Psalm 124

"If it had not been the Lord who was on my side" (Psalm 124:1)

If you wrote this Psalm today, what would it look like in your life? We like to look at all the blessings that God has given us, but have you ever looked back at the "what ifs" in life? God is so good to us. We live in His Word, in His Promises, in His Love. We sing: "count your blessings, name them one by one; count your blessings, see what God hath done." ("Count Your Blessings"/Johnson Oatman) We sing of His Amazing Grace. But what would your life look like had you not accepted His forgiveness and mercy?

If it had not been the Lord who was on my side, fear would control.
If it had not been the Lord who was on my side, life would be hopeless and in vain.
If it had not been the Lord who was on my side, final goodbyes would be final.
If it had not been the Lord who was on my side, I would have to figure life out by myself.
If it had not been the Lord who was on my side, I would be living in the "pigpen" of despair.
If it had not been the Lord who was on my side, I would have no direction.
If it had not been the Lord who was on my side, my enemies could easily defeat me.
If it had not been the Lord who was on my side, I would be alone.

But thank God, in His mercy, is on my side. I do not need to be afraid. I have Hope. My life has purpose. I will never be alone. I will not be forsaken. He will fight for me. I will see my loved ones again.
Thank You, Jesus, for dying for me. Thank You for loving me. Thank You for always being there. Amen!

Inspired by "If It Had Not Been" by Lynda Randle, Andrae Crouch

August 21
Where is your rest?
Psalm 20, 62

"Some trust in chariots and some in horses, but we trust in the name of the Lord our God." (Psalm 20:7 NIV)

When most of us think of the idea of "home," we think acceptance, security, peace, rest, love. But for many, that is just not the case. Their home is full of chaos, anger, bitterness. So, they search elsewhere for that place of belonging, that place of rest. People may spend a lifetime trying to find that "perfect" place of love and acceptance. Because people change, circumstances change, and we lose our sense of "home."

When we set all our hope and trust in the people and things around us, we will inevitably be let down. People are human and make mistakes and bad choices. Things fall apart. People and things cannot be our only security, they cannot meet our deepest need. That need is only met when we reconnect with our Creator, our Father. "My soul finds rest in God alone; my salvation comes from Him. He alone is my rock and my salvation; He is my fortress, I will never be shaken." (Psalm 62:1-2 NIV)

Isn't it great to know that we serve a God who is active in our lives? "Trust in Him at all times, O people; pour out your hearts to Him, for God is our refuge." (Psalm 62:8 NIV) He is where we can go to find rest. He is where we can go to find peace. He is where we can go to find Love. He is where we can go to find acceptance. He is our refuge. "May He give You the desire of your heart and make all your plans succeed." (Psalm 20:4 NIV)

"You, O God, are strong, and that You, O Lord, are loving." (Psalm 62:11-12 NIV) Thank You for giving us rest. "Come to Me, all you who are weary and burdened, and I will give you rest." (Matthew 11:28 NIV) Father, we lay our tired bodies and anxious minds at Your feet. Amen.

August 22
About the Father's business – Part 1
Titus 3

"And He (Jesus) said to them: "Why did you seek Me? Did you not know that I must be about My Father's business?" (Luke 2:49)

Jesus was only 12 when He responded this way to His earthly parents. They had been searching for Him for three days. It almost appears that He is surprised that they didn't seek Him in the temple first. We are never too young nor too old to be about our Father's business. We are never too weak nor too unequipped to be about our Father's business.

What is our Father's business? Paul tells Titus: "Remind them to be subject to rulers and authorities, to obey, to be ready for every good work, to speak evil of no one, to be peaceable, gentle, and showing all humility to all men." (Titus 3:1-2)

We need to be ready "for every good work." We need to be sharing the GOOD news of our Father. In a world of bad news, bad things happening, bad people disrupting lives, we need people who are spreading the GOOD. Paul continues to write: "Once we, too, were foolish and disobedient. We were misled and became slaves to many lusts and pleasures. Our lives were full of evil and envy, and we hated each other. But - when God our Savior revealed His kindness and love, He saved us, not because of righteous things we had done, but because of His mercy. He washed away our sins, giving us a new birth and new life through the Holy Spirit. He generously poured out the Spirit upon us through Jesus Christ our Savior. Because of His grace He made us right in His sight and gave us confidence that we will inherit eternal life." (Titus 3:3-7 NLT) In an age where events are played out minute by minute on our devices, bad news travels fast. We, as believers, stand around the "water cooler" and participate in conversations wondering how people could make such bad choices. The verses above remind us that we too were once misled and hated each other. But we heard the GOOD news and accepted God's kindness and love.

August 23
About the Father's business – Part 2
Titus 3

How did you learn the GOOD news? Did you have a family that took you to church when you were young? Did you have friends later in life invite you to church? Did you have someone in your life that lived such a life that you knew they possess something you didn't and recognized that you needed that in your own life? In all those instances, someone was doing "good work." We need to remember that the best thing we can do for others is to be about our Father's business. God is "not willing that any should perish but that all should come to repentance." (2 Peter 3:9)

We need to be sharing the Truth of God's Word and Love to everyone we meet. That does not mean that we need to carry our Bibles around and walk up to everyone we meet and try to lead them to God. What that does mean is that we should be doing "good" everywhere we go. Yes, sometimes that will involve a conversation about what God is doing in our lives. However, most of the time it means that our daily actions should reflect God's kindness and love. Our conversations, our decisions, our schedules, our lives should be different. They should reflect a peace during chaos, joy amidst trouble, love among hatefulness. Paul concludes the passage of scripture with: "This is a trustworthy saying, and I want you to insist on these teachings so that all who trust in God will devote themselves to doing good. These teachings are good and beneficial for everyone." (Titus 3:8 NLT) Go forth and live a GOOD life that reflects that there is a Creator who loves us, a Savior who died for us, and a Friend who will never leave us. That there is purpose to life, there is an eternal future where peace and love reign, there is Hope.

Father, in Your loving kindness, You want Your family to be complete. You want all Your created people to be able to sit down around Your throne. But because sin separates people from You, that will not be everyone's destination. As Your children, You want us to show this dying world the hope that is within us. You desire our actions to demonstrate Your love, grace, and mercy to those around us. Forgive us when we look more like the world and less like You. Open our eyes that we may see how others see You by our words and actions. May we always be about our Father's business. Amen.

236

I know Whom I have believed
2 Timothy 1

"Nevertheless I am not ashamed, for I know whom I have believed and am persuaded that He is able to keep what I have committed to Him until that Day." (2 Timothy 1:12)

What a statement of faith and trust! Paul had complete confidence in His Lord and Savior. Why? Because Paul had experienced God's love and forgiveness. Because God had proven Himself to be Faithful and True. Paul spent time with His Father. He learned His Father's heart. He listened to His Father's voice. He watched His Father move. Paul went "all in." He was fully committed to following God. Could you make the same statement as Paul: "I know whom I have believed and am persuaded that He is able to keep what I have committed to Him?" Have you experienced God's love and forgiveness? Have you found God to be Faithful? The more we experience God, the more our trust level grows. However, there are times when doubts surface. Those are the times we need to examine where we are looking. We experience God both internally and externally. If we only trust God when we can see His work externally, we are missing the deeper level of trust that comes from the work He does inside of us. Life circumstances do not always seem to reflect an actively loving God. Bad things happen, and sometimes it's hard to see how God can bring good out of those situations. External factors change. But as we develop our relationship with God, internally is where our confidence in Him grows. Yes, battles rage within the mind as we try to reconcile the external with the Truth. But if we will "Be still, and know that I am God," (Psalm 46:10) but if we will be quiet and willing to listen, we will come to better know the God who we believe in. We will come to the place where we can say: "I am persuaded that He is able to keep what I have committed to Him." When the world looks on believers, what they can't see is the Holy Spirit that resides in us. But hopefully, they can see the effects that His Presence has on our lives. What have you committed to Him? Are you still trusting Him with it? What haven't you committed? Why? We are "persuaded that He is able to keep" based on our relationship with Him. Based on the work He is doing inside of us. That's why people cannot understand when we exhibit peace when our world is falling apart. That's why they cannot understand when we hope when the situation appears hopeless. We have the Holy Spirit working inside of us to teach us, to mold us, to correct us.

Father, You are trustworthy. You can do all things. Who better deserves our faith? There is no one else who we can trust to keep our families, our present and our future. You are God alone. Amen.

Trials of "joy"
James 1

"My brethren, count it all joy when you fall into various trials, knowing that the testing of your faith produces patience. But let patience have its perfect work, that you may be perfect and complete, lacking nothing." (James 1:2-3)

From a natural perspective, these verses don't make sense. Trials often are too painful and fresh to count them as joy. Too difficult to be worth the lesson learned. But how we experience God during those trials is something that can eventually lead to thankfulness. When we go through different types of trials, we begin to see the different ways God loves us, provides for us and protects us. Even though we may not be able to "count it all joy" as we are encountering trials, His constant Presence is there to comfort and carry through those times. However, once we can look back at how God worked during that time, we often find the "joy." God can use our trials for His glory both in the work that He does in our lives and the lives of others. Peter wrote: "Though now for a little while, if need be, you have been grieved by various trials, that the genuineness of your faith, being much more precious than gold that perishes, though it is tested by fire, may be found to praise, honor, and glory at the revelation of Jesus Christ." (1 Peter 1:6-7) When no human answer can be found, when no human can comfort, when no human can provide, the recognition of our need for a Savior takes on a new meaning. When we get to the point where our "faith actions" need to match our "faith words," that's when we find the Almighty One, the Faithful One, the God of all our days. It is easy to say all the "right" words when life is wonderful, however, the true test of our faith comes when life is not so easy. When we are unequipped to handle the trial without God. We learn the true meaning of "For He Himself has said, "I will never leave you nor forsake you." (Hebrews 13:5) We experience "I can do all things through Christ who strengthens me"(Philippians 4:13) at a deeper level. And we grasp just how much "My God shall supply all your need according to His riches in glory by Christ Jesus." (Philippians 4:19) Part of the process is holding on to that mustard seed faith when we can't "see" God moving, when we can't hear His voice, when we can't sense that He is near. That's when we trust and obey, when we hold on to the Truth of His Word. "Now faith is the substance of things hoped for, the evidence of things not see." (Hebrews 11:1) When trials come, keep hoping, trusting, reading His Word, and praying even when you think He isn't listening or doesn't care. He is there.

Father, thank You that when trials come our way, You are near. We are never out of Your hand. You are faithful to complete the work You began in us. You want us to experience the faith that can move mountains. We love You, Lord! Amen.

August 26
In His Presence
Matthew 17

"I was glad when they said to me, "Let us go into the house
of the Lord." (Psalm 122:1)

When we spend time with Jesus, we often envision the human Jesus.
The aspects of Jesus that we can understand. We feel like He is more
relatable in His human likeness. "For in that He Himself has suffered,
being tempted, He is able to aid those who are tempted." (Hebrews 2:18)
This Jesus is our Friend and our Teacher. But take a moment to imagine
being on the mountain with Peter, James, and John, to get a glimpse
of the transfigured King Jesus. On Sunday mornings, we look around at
the faces we do church with. They are our brothers and sisters in Christ and
we can almost picture Jesus among them as we serve together for Him. But
when we enter into worship, whether in the sanctuary or in our personal
time, our view of Jesus changes into one of majesty. Jesus seated on the
throne in robes of white. "His face shone like the sun, and His clothes
became as white as the light." (Matthew 17:2) When we come to worship,
we are worshipping our King Jesus. Several writers of the Bible had visions
of the glorified Jesus, the Jesus of Heaven. However, as eloquent as their
words are, human words are inadequate to describe our Great God. During
worship time, do you envision yourself around His throne singing praises
to our Resurrected Savior, the Lord of lords? Do you picture yourself on
your knees in humble adoration or on a mountaintop declaring the glory
of our Almighty God? Sometimes our worship time may take us back to
the cross where, from our knees, we can offer our deep appreciation
for His precious gift of amazing grace and love. When our hearts come to
worship, things of this world fade away. Jesus becomes the focus of
everything within us. Whether hands are raised high or heads bowed low,
we enter a time where we try to convey our adoration, our thanks, our love
to our Immanuel alone.

*Lord Jesus, we join the angels declaring: "Holy, Holy, Holy is the Lord
of hosts; the whole earth is full of His glory." (Isaiah 6:3) "Blessing and
glory and wisdom, thanksgiving and honor and power and might, be to
our God forever and ever. Amen." (Revelations 7:12)*

August 27
It is finished, it is done
Ephesians 2

"He said, "It is finished!" And bowed His head, He gave up
His spirit." (John 19:30)

Why do we work so hard trying to be worthy of salvation? We think we
need to get "cleaned up" before we approach God. And even after we accept
God's salvation gift, we may still work to be good enough. When Jesus said,
"It is finished," the salvation plan was complete. Jesus' sacrifice on the cross
met the atonement requirements. Nothing else needed to be done. "For by
grace you have been saved through faith, and that not of yourselves; it is the
gift of God, not of works, lest anyone should boast." (Ephesians 2:8-9) And
yet, we still try to earn the right to be called children of God. Don't get me
wrong. It is an awesome privilege to be called a child of God, and we should
"walk worthy of the Lord, fully pleasing Him, being fruitful in every good
work and increasing in the knowledge of God." (Colossians 1:10) But there
is a difference between walking to please God and working to try to earn your
place in the family. If we are continually striving to be "good enough," we will
become frustrated with our inability to do so. We are imperfect people living
in this imperfect world. Paul writes: "And I know that nothing good lives in
me, that is, in my sinful nature. I want to do what is right, but I can't. I want
to do what is good, but I don't. I don't want to do what is wrong, but I do it
anyway. But if I do what I don't want to do, I am not really the one doing
wrong; it is sin living in me that does it." (Romans 7:18-20 NLT) But thanks
be to God: "But God demonstrated His own love toward us, in that while we
were still sinners, Christ died for us. Much more then, having now been
justified by His blood, we shall be saved from wrath through Him."
(Romans 5:8-9) There is nothing we can do to deserve His grace and mercy.
That's why we: "present your bodies a living sacrifice, holy, acceptable to
God, which is your reasonable service. And do not be conformed to this
world, but be transformed by the renewing of your mind, that you may prove
what is that good and acceptable and perfect will of God." (Romans 12:1-2)
It is finished, it is done. The only thing we need to do is accept. My friend,
have you accepted the gift Jesus is offering you? The gift that restores you to
your Father, the One True God? You may think "I'm not good enough. I'm
not strong enough." But my friend: "For God so loved (insert YOUR name)
that He gave His only begotten Son, that (YOU) believes in Him should not
perish but have everlasting life. For God did not send His Son into the world
to condemn (YOU), but that (YOU) through Him might be saved."
(John 3:16 edited) *Abba Father, thank You for redeeming us. Amen.*

August 28
I know my Redeemer lives
Job 19

"For I know that my Redeemer lives, and that in the end He will stand
upon the earth. And after my skin has been destroyed, yet in my flesh
I will see God; I myself will see Him - I, and not another. How my
heart yearns within me!" (Job 19:25-27 NIV)

As you read Job 19, you may find yourself a little surprised when you
reach these verses. The story of Job addresses questions we still have today.
Questions we still can't answer. Yes, to a certain degree we understand why
bad things happen, we live in a fallen, sinful world. However, what we don't
understand is why God seems to move in some situations but appears to
not be there in others. We grasp "For who has known the mind of the
Lord? Or who has become His counselor?" (Romans 11:34) We know
"For My thoughts are not your thoughts, nor are your ways My ways,"
says the Lord." (Isaiah 55:8) But what is harder to comprehend is when life
doesn't seem fair. Amidst his questions, amidst his loss, amidst his pain, Job
could still say "I know that my Redeemer lives!" We could spend our lives,
like Job's friends, coming up with various reasons why a good God lets bad
things happen, but at the end of the day, it comes down to a level of trust.
Do you trust your Father enough to be satisfied not knowing the answers
that only He knows? How much frustration, anger, disappointment will we
spend on trying to "state our case" before God? Yes, some of that
frustration, anger, disappointment is a natural response as we experience
life and God understands that. He is big enough to handle our questions,
our emotions, our thoughts. But when we lose trust because of those
questions, when we can't move forward in our relationship with God
because of those emotions, we are trying to bring God down to our size.
Job and his friends learned that doesn't work. Whatever you are going
through, can you still say: "I know my Redeemer lives?" Can you look past
your problems to see your Provider? Can you look past your pain to see
your Comforter? Can you look past the hopeless to see your Hope? Can
you look past your present to see your Future? Job says: "I myself will see
Him - I, and not another. How my heart yearns within me." Does your
heart yearn to see Your Father? *God, thank You that there will be a Day
when the things of this earth will pass away, and we will see You face to
face. That the pain of this world will be forgotten, and we will forever be
in Your Presence, our Creator, the Lover of our Soul, our Redeemer. Your
kingdom come, Your will be done on earth as it is in heaven. Amen.*
Inspired by "My Redeemer Lives" by Nicole C Mullen

241

August 29

Facing your fears
Numbers 13

There are times in our lives when we cannot see past our fears. These fears can be external in nature or internal. They seem like insurmountable obstacles. They hinder our lives in various ways. Sometimes the fear seems justified; while other times we acknowledge it seems "all in our heads." Fear can be paralyzing. In Numbers 13, Moses charges 12 spies to go into the Promised Land, the land promised to them by God Himself, and evaluate the situation. They went in probably with high expectations. During their 40 days journey, all that ten of the spies could see were the frightening obstacles in their way. It was not going to be easy to claim their inheritance. Joshua and Caleb, on the other hand, looked around at all the blessings awaiting them. From the human view, those ten spies were justified in their fears. People were living throughout the land, some who were giants. Israel was not a warrior nation, but they would have to fight for their land. Upon hearing the report, all Israel could see was the impossibility of the situation. In their minds, they were going in under their own might and strength and realized that was not enough. They seem to forget that God was with them. We too view our fears as impossible. We do not have the wisdom, the courage, the strength to get past them. But thanks be to God, we do not have to face our fears alone. We need Joshuas and Calebs in our lives to remind us what God can do. God wants us to live in freedom. "And you shall know the truth, and the truth shall make you free." (John 8:32) "I sought the Lord, and He heard me, and delivered me from all my fears." (Psalm 34:4) "Peace I leave with you, My peace I give to you; not as the world gives do I give to you. Let not your heart be troubled, neither let it be afraid." (John 14:27) Facing our fears is never a comfortable thing to do. Too many life experiences may have made that fear a reality. There may be too many lies that we have allowed to become truth in our lives. But we serve a mighty God! "Be anxious for nothing, but in everything by prayer and supplication, with thanksgiving, let your requests be made known to God; and the peace of God which surpasses all understanding, will guard your hearts and minds through Christ Jesus." (Philippians 4:6-7) Ask Him for help! Ask Him to shine the Light of His truth and love on the fear in your life. Ask Him to send a Joshua or Caleb to walk beside you as you face your fears. *Father, we thank you that: "Yet in all these things we are more than conquerors through Him who loved us." (Romans 8:37) Thank You that the same Power that raised Jesus from the grave is living in us. Abba Father, I pray for my brothers and sisters who are facing fears that are preventing them from living the life You intended for them. Surround them with Your love and truth. Amen.*

August 30
Heaven bound
Revelation 21

We like to know which direction our life is heading. We make plans and set goals of what our life will look like five, ten years from now. At work, we often pursue the course that leads to the greatest success. In our personal lives, we make significant decisions based on our goals for the future. But, as we all know, sometimes we are blown off these courses when the unexpected happens. If we are honest, life rarely follows our "ideal" path. Too many obstacles and detours happen that cause us to lose sight of our original course. And most of us never seem to find it again. We redefine our goals and adapt our plans each time we face a change. But isn't it great to know, that no matter how many times our plans or goals fall apart, we know our final destination? And nothing can keep us from that! For believers, we know we are Heaven bound! All life's twists and turns cannot change that truth. We may go through times when it's so dark; we seem to lose sight. But we hold on to His promises. "For I am persuaded that neither death nor life, nor angels nor principalities nor powers, nor things present nor things to come, nor height nor depth, nor any other created thing, shall be able to separate us from the love of God which is in Christ Jesus our Lord." (Romans 8:38-39) In those last few hours before His trial and crucifixion, Jesus told His disciples: "Let not your heart be troubled; you believe in God, believe also in Me. In My Father's house are many mansions; if it were not so, I would have told you. I go to prepare a place for you. And if I go and prepare a place for you, I will come again and receive you to Myself; that where I am, there you may be also." (John 14: 1-3) In Revelation, John writes: "Then I, John, saw the holy city, New Jerusalem, coming down out of heaven from God, prepared as a bride adorned for her husband. And I heard a loud voice from heaven saying, "Behold, the tabernacle of God is with men, and He will dwell with them, and they shall be His people. God Himself will be with them and be their God." (Revelation 21: 2-3) As the years roll by, Home sounds sweeter. When we are tired of all the heartache, all the destroyed dreams, all the evil in this world, we just want to say: "Even so, come, Lord Jesus!" (Revelation 22:20) Come and take us Home. And one day, that will be our reality. We will see Jesus face to face! So, my friend, when life is not going the way you want, "look up and lift up your heads, because your redemption draws near." (Luke 21:28) *Father, thank You that even when we don't understand what is happening in our world, we are anchored to the promise of our Heavenly Home. On our darkest days, we can still glimpse the Hope of our Eternity with You. Father, thank You that we are Heaven Bound!*

Our Amazing God
Psalm 145

"Stand still, and see the salvation of the Lord, which He will
accomplish for you today." (Exodus 14:13)

How often do we "stand still" and take the time to really focus on our
Amazing God? To look around at all He is doing in our lives? Probably
not often enough. Our busy lives seem to only allow quick "stand still"
moments. And if we have been a Christian for a while, we almost start to
take for granted how amazing our God is. But when we do stop to count our
blessings, we again recognize how great is our God.

Even just taking a simple breath should cause us to pause and
acknowledge that without Him, we could do nothing. Watching the clouds
should remind us how big and mighty and still active our Creator God is.
But what should really amaze is when we reflect about our individual lives.
To think that our One God is engaged in each of the lives of the almost eight
billion people on this planet. That He cares for each one of us. That He
knows exactly what we need. And He does not relate to us in a
"cookie cutter" way but treats us as individuals by moving in the way we
personally need at any given time. Even in our darkest days, if we really stop
to look for the ways He is working in our lives, we find Him there with us.
If it has been a while since you have taken the time to "stand still" or if you
are looking around thinking I'm not seeing anything amazing, choose to
spend some time with Him. Come and be reminded: "Great is the Lord, and
greatly to be praised; and His greatness is unsearchable." (Psalm 145:3)

*Amazing God, "My mouth shall speak the praise of the Lord, and all
flesh shall bless (Your) holy name forever and ever." (Psalm 145:21) Open our
eyes to see how You are moving in our lives. Thank You, that You know me
by name. That you know the inmost parts of me. You understand me and love
me just the same. You care for me. You make a way when there seems to be
no way. You are my Hope. You are my Anchor. You are my Peace. Amen.*

September 1
What shape is your vessel in?
Jeremiah 18

"But now, O Lord, You are our Father, we are the clay, and You
our Potter; and all of us are the work of Your hand."
(Isaiah 64:8 NASB)

Do you feel like you are just a lump of clay without form or purpose?
Do you feel like you are too broken and chipped to be useful? Do you look
good on the "outside," but inside finds you full of cracks and missing
pieces? Do you feel like since you can't hold anything, you can't give
anything back? The good news, my friend, is we can always go to the
Potter. We may feel like our vessel is falling apart and worthless.
However, in the Potter's hands, He remolds us into His design. But too
often, we refuse to go to the Potter. We try to "glue" ourselves back
together. We try to look to others to find our "missing pieces." We try
to keep moving so no one can see what we are lacking. We shine up the
outside, so no one can see how deep the cracks are on the inside. But
our Potter knows. Our Potter sees us. Our Potter still sees His
masterpiece. He is able to mend the broken pieces, transform our defects,
and build us back up again.

So, bring your broken pieces to Your Creator. Ask Him to complete
the work He has started in you. It might not be easy. The refining fire never
is. But we trust our Potter and place ourselves in His capable, loving hands.

*Father God, we lay our crumbling vessels into Your hands. Mold us
and make us into what You would have us be that all may see Your
glory and Your goodness. Amen.*

September 2
Swift or beautiful feet
Romans 10

Let's be honest with ourselves for a minute. Let's ask ourselves: are we quicker at sharing bad news (and since we are being honest here) whether we know it is true or not? Or quicker at sharing good news and truth? Sometimes all we seem to hear is bad news, especially in the news media industry. We often want to feast off and continue to feed the drama. Are we as quick to share the Good News of Jesus Christ?

Proverbs 6 states: "These six things the Lord hates, yes, seven are an abomination to Him: a proud look, a lying tongue, hands that shed innocent blood, a heart that devises wicked plans, feet that are swift in running to evil, a false witness who speaks lies, and one who sows discord among brethren." (vs. 16-19) Does that list make anyone else pause for a moment?

Do we ever just stop and think before we pass on "news?" Examine our motivation? Evaluate to decide if it is something that honestly needs to be shared? Or are we just trying to get a reaction? Yes, there are times we need to pass along what is going on in our lives or the lives of others. But sometimes, we don't.

Romans 10 says: "How beautiful are the feet of those who preach the gospel of peace, who brings glad tidings of good things." (v. 15) Too often we think it is just the preacher's job to share the good news. But shouldn't we all be sharing Christ with others? "Always be prepared to give an answer to everyone who asks you to give the reason for the hope that you have. But do this with gentleness and respect." (1 Peter 3:15 NIV)

Pass on your hope and joy amidst your troubles and trials. Pass on your peace in the midst of your pain. Pass on God's love in a world of hate and evil. Pass on the Truth of God's Word instead of the lies.

Father, we need to speak more of Your Hope, Your Love, Your Peace, Your Truth. We need to speak life to those around us. Help us to live, so the world sees the difference You make in our lives. Amen.

Waiting times
Isaiah 40

"Have you not known? Have you not heard? The Everlasting God, the Lord, the Creator of the ends of the earth, neither faints nor is weary. His understanding is unsearchable. He gives power to the weak, and to those who have no might He increases strength. Even the youths shall faint and be weary, and the young men shall utterly fall, but those who wait on the Lord shall renew their strength; they shall mount up with wings like eagles, they shall run and not be weary, they shall walk and not faint."
(Isaiah 40:28-31)

Anyone else face times when all you had to hold on to was Scripture? Those times when there was nothing else you could do. Those times when there were no other answers. There was no other peace. There was no other hope. We have all been there. Those are the times when all we can do is wait on the Lord. Reread the verses above slowly. Allow them to speak Truth and Hope and Strength into your life today. "Those who have no might He increases strength." How many of you need to hear that today? You have no might to get past the pain. You have no might to face what today, tomorrow, next week holds. You have no might to find your answers. You have no might to keep fighting the good fight. You have no might to stay committed to your vows. You have no might to say "no" to the things of this world. My friend, "He gives power to the weak." Hold on to that promise. You do not have to have the answers. You do not have to have the strength. You do not have to have the wisdom. All you need is to "Be still, and know that I am God." (Psalm 46:10) He is the "Everlasting God, the Lord, the Creator of the ends of the earth." There is nothing too big, too impossible, too small, too insignificant for Him to care about and to carry you through. Don't give up! May I recommend writing the verses above down on cards. Place one on your mirror, your fridge door, your car, your work. Have the words written down so that you can literally hold on to them. When you are at your weakest, read them. Memorize them. Hold on to them. (And not just these verses, any verses that speak the truth you need to hear.) When He is all we have to hold on to, He is all we need!

Father, thank You for providing the Power and the Strength. Thank You that when we are at our weakest, You are there. You will renew our strength. You will renew our hope. You will renew our peace. Thank You that You are an All-Sufficient God. Amen.

Inspired by "While I'm Waiting" by John Waller

When we don't get our way
Philippians 4

What is our reaction when we don't get our way? It may depend on the situation itself or on how long it has been going on. It may depend on our emotional and physical condition. It also may depend on how much we have been reading God's Word and the status of our prayer life. We may notice that the more difficult the situation and the more time-consuming it is, the less time we are spending with God. When that happens, it becomes easier to think God doesn't care about us or our circumstances. It is also easier to "put words in God's mouth." We think or speak what we think is God's response without stopping to listen to what He is actually saying. No matter how many times we have seen God move or how much faith we think we have, we still run into times when we get distracted by our feelings and doubts. We still end up trying to stumble through situations on our own. We still face discontentment. Paul writes, "For I have learned in whatever state I am, to be content." (Philippians 4:11) Most of us would like to figure out how to do that. How much time do we spend wishing things were different? Even when we recognize that a situation is not going to change, we still live life with the "what ifs." Part of the problem may be what we are seeking. Jesus told his disciples: "But seek first the kingdom of God and His righteousness, and all these things shall be added to you." (Matthew 6:33) If we are completely honest, too often we seek first the "kingdom of self." We want our needs met. We want people to understand and agree with our perspective. We want things done our way. Our response when it does not happen our way can cause hurt and disappointment. We are all humans, those are natural reactions and we all experience them in some form or fashion. It becomes a problem when we allow that to become our normal state in life. Proverbs 3 says, "Trust in the Lord with all your heart, and lean not on your own understanding; in all your ways acknowledge Him, and He shall direct your paths." (vs. 5-6) Are we able to trust when we are not getting our way? When we are disappointed or discontent? Some of us can say, "Yes, even in the midst of my problems, still I trust." However, some of us can't find the ability to do so. No matter the reason, no matter how long we have been there, no matter our lack of trust, God loves. God understands. God can help. Thank God, He does not give up on us. Seek Him through it all. When we are not getting our way talk to Him. Ask Him to reveal Himself to you amidst your discontentment and disappointments. Ask Him to guide you to the path of contentment. Lord, You bring peace among our storms and provide strength in our weakness. *Father, in those areas where we are experiencing discontentment, show us Your way to know You are all we need.*

Living in a lion's den
Daniel 6

Do you ever feel like you are in a den with hungry, roaring lions? Maybe at work where everyone seems out to get each other as they all strive for the next promotion or the boss' favor. Perhaps it is in your family life where angry shouts tend to be the only form of communication. News reports seem to reveal every day that our world is full of roaring lions. There may even be "lions" living in your head roaring words like "worthless, powerless, ugly, hopeless." Do you dread waking up to the "lion's den" in your world? Well, I have good news, the God we serve can "shut the lions' mouths." How often do we pray for God to move in situations where the "lions" are roaring? Do we pray for our co-workers who are not getting along, that God will bring some harmony in the workplace? Instead of arguing with the angry lions in our family, do we steal away and pray for them? For the lions in our mind, do we claim God's Word? You and I are His children, and the thoughts and emotions we have about ourselves need to be filtered through that Truth. What about the evil that seems to abound in our neighborhoods, in our cities, in our country, in our world? Do we pray specifically when we learn of situations that need the Master's touch? Daniel had no fear of the lions. Even knowing the consequence, he chose to obey God. I don't imagine that Daniel's enemies had to pull him kicking and screaming into the den. Daniel knew in Whom he believed in. He had found Him to be Faithful and True. He knew the Creator of the lions, the One who gave them life. Daniel knew he would be delivered, ultimately the lions couldn't touch him. They may roar, but they had no power over him. I hope that you too have experienced times when God has "shut the lion's mouths." Times when you have seen Him move in ways that seemed impossible. The same God who delivered Daniel is your Deliverer too. As you face your daily lions, remember to step out in obedience and confidence. Your God is in control!

Lord, sometimes the world we live in is a scary place with our enemy who "walks about like a roaring lion, seeking whom he may devour." (1 Peter 5:8) But You have called us to "Submit to God. Resist the devil and he will flee from you. Draw near to God and He will draw near to you." (James 4:7-8) Give us the boldness of Daniel to stand on Your Truth and do not fear the "lions" that try to steal our peace and joy. Remind us "You are of God, little children, and have overcome them, because He who is in you is greater than he who is in the world." (1 John 4:4) Amen.

No matter what
Psalm 51

"For I am persuaded that neither death nor life, nor angels nor principalities nor powers, nor things present nor things to come, nor height nor depth, nor any other created thing, shall be able to separate us from the love of God which is in Christ Jesus our Lord." (Romans 8:38-39)

Let's be honest. We all mess up. We all make mistakes. We can't seem to beat the addiction. We made choices that have caused us to lose our family. We are living with all the consequences of our actions. Which may lead to brokenness and loneliness. If that is where you are today, my friend, do you know that you are still loved? Our limited human mind cannot comprehend how God could love us. We are a people full of faults and failures. How can we still be loved? My friend, God's love for us is not based on what you or I have done. When you are at your lowest point, when all you see is dark despair, please understand that is the very reason Jesus came to die for you. He wants to pull you out of that darkness and into His Light. He loves you even when He sees everything about you! He sees your hopeless condition. He came into this world to offer you Hope, Abundant Life, Peace. He died to show you His Love. Maybe you have heard all this before or perhaps this is the first you have heard of a God who loves. We all make a mess of things when we try to live life on our own without direction or purpose. "For all have sinned and fall short of the glory of God." (Romans 3:23) But my Father waits with open arms to welcome you home. What do you need to do? Accept His gift of amazing grace. Come to Him and seek forgiveness. Tell Him what a mess you have made of your life and you need Him to come and give you a new life. Accept His gift of Love and Mercy. "Have mercy on me, O God, because of Your unfailing love. Because of Your great compassion, blot out the stain of my sins. Wash me clean from my guilt. Purify me from sin." (Psalm 51:1-2) Surrender control of your life to Him. He wants You to come to Him no matter what you have done, no matter where you are. By doing so, "though your sins are like scarlet, they shall be white as snow; though they are red like crimson, they shall be as wool." (Isaiah 1:18) Come experience a Love like you have never known. Maybe you are a believer who chose to follow your own path again and find yourself in a mess of your own making. God still loves you. He doesn't give up on you. Allow Him to be Lord of your life again.

Father God, we come to you a broken people. On our own, we are a people who seem to mess up everything we touch. We need YOU! We need to know that You love us no matter what. We need to know that You can take our brokenness and use it for Your glory. Amen.

Inspired by "No Matter What" by Ryan Stevenson

September 7
Change your world
Matthew 5

"You are the light of the world. A city that is set on a hill cannot be hidden." (Matthew 5:14)

I don't know about you but sometimes I feel like giving up on this world. There is so much unimaginable evil. Hate seems to win every time. Is it the worst time in history? Probably not, but it sure feels that way sometimes. Children killing children. Families being destroyed. Senseless loss of life. Human trafficking and slavery. These things have been going on since the Fall of Man and we still haven't learned our lessons. We live in a lost world in need of a Savior. And thank God He provided One. What can we do to bring change? Each of us is only one person; we can't seem to do much to "fix" the world. But are there things we can do to change our part of the world? Are there ways we can share God's love? Are there ways we can bring Hope and Peace? Are there ways we can let everyone we meet know that they are precious in His sight? We have the Light. We need to shine in our dark world. "Blessed are the merciful, for they shall obtain mercy. Blessed are the pure in heart, for they shall see God. Blessed are the peacemakers, for they shall be called sons of God." (Matthew 5:7-9) In our own actions every day, are we being merciful to those around us, are we being peacemakers? Do our actions and reactions to people and events around us give pause to those watching? Do they notice something different about us? I don't know about you, but I desire to be different. I don't want to respond to situations with a human mindset, I want to respond with the attitude of "what would Jesus do?" How would God want me to view this circumstance? How can I bring the Light? Most of the time, hopefully, we automatically respond in Love. Jesus says, "For out of the abundance of the heart the mouth speaks. A good man out of the good treasure of his heart brings forth good things, and an evil man out of the evil treasure brings forth evil things." (Matthew 12:34-35) Paul writes, "Set your mind on things above, not on things on the earth." (Colossians 3:2) If we are living our lives for Him and not ourselves, we will "let your light so shine before men, that they may see your good works and glorify your Father in heaven." (Matthew 5:16) Shine forth, my friends. "Watch, stand fast in the faith, be brave, be strong. Let all you that you do be done with love." (1 Corinthians 16: 13-14)

Father, thank You for not giving up on this sinful world. You "desire all men to be saved and to come to the knowledge of the truth." (1 Timothy 2:4) Father, help us to shine Your light into this dark world. Amen.

September 8
Is God jealous for you?
Exodus 20

"I am the Lord your God, who brought you out of the land of Egypt, out of the house of bondage. You shall have no other gods before Me." (Exodus 20:2-3)

What in our lives have we placed before our Creator God? Is it our work, our family, our hobbies, our schedules, our possessions? Just living life sometimes throws our priorities off when schedules become too full, when stresses become our focus, when we allow our thoughts to control our emotions. We all experience those times. Times when we seem to tell God, "wait, I'll get back to you soon." Oh, if only we could recognize that I AM wants to walk life with us! Our enemy likes when we are distracted. Because when we are not paying attention, he sows seeds of discontentment, anger, and disappointment into our relationships, including our relationship with God. He likes to get us to turn our eyes off God and onto what is going on around us. And often we are unaware that it is even happening. When God is jealous for us, it is not a matter of not giving Him the attention He so richly deserves. God is jealous for us because He is our Redeemer, our Savior, our Deliverer, our Helper. He knows how difficult life can be. He wants us to recognize that "He is able to keep what I have committed to Him until that Day." (2 Timothy 1:12) He wants us to figure out He is all we need. There is no area of our life that He wants us to try to hide from Him. He made you. He knows you better than you know yourself. He understands you. My friend, if your life is too busy for God, you need to adjust your priorities. Time spent with Him is the most important thing we can do for ourselves. When our eyes are fixed on our Savior and our Helper, things come back into proper perspective. God has blessed us with the people in our lives. He has given us everything we have. He wants us to experience abundant life and to do so we need to acknowledge "Christ is all and in all." (Colossians 3:11)

Lord God, forgive us for allowing things of this world to come before You. You are our Everything. Thank You for the many blessings You have bestowed on us. Thank You for making us worthy of Your goodness and kindness. Help us to live a life that shows that love, that goodness, that kindness to all we meet. Amen.

Your choice
Joshua 6

"Choose for yourselves this day whom you will serve, whether the gods which your fathers served that were on the other side of the River, or the gods of the Amorites, in whose land you dwell. But as for me and my house, we will serve the Lord." (Joshua 24:15)

How many of you have/had a praying momma, papa, grandma or grandpa? Could you name those who are praying for you right now? Ultimately though, those prayers are not enough to get you into Heaven. God does not force us to accept His salvation gift. You make that choice. However, you also receive the reward or consequence of that choice. Adam and Eve made a choice which ended up bringing sin and death into the world. God did not create us to be robots with the only controller in His hand. He gave us free will to choose what we believe. The decision to serve Him cannot be made for you. You are the only one who can decide who Jesus is in your life. Thank God for that privilege! Please understand God "desires all men to be saved and to come to the knowledge of the truth." (1 Timothy 2:4) Never think "God doesn't want me." or "I have gone too far, He won't be able to rescue me." God made you. He knows you. Yet He loves you. He sent His Son to die for you. May I ask a question, if you died today, would you be satisfied with the choice you have made? While you think you are putting off deciding, you are still making a choice. And someday, that "not today" choice will become your final decision. Choose you this day! Most of you know the choice you need to make but have a variety of reasons why you are not "ready" to choose God. Friend, my God is bigger than all your reasons and excuses. This is between you and God alone. Relying on the "faith of our fathers" is not going to be enough when you are approaching the throne of God. The Bible says, "Therefore God also has highly exalted Him and given Him the name which is above every name, that at the name of Jesus every knee should bow, of those in heaven, and of those on earth, and of those under the earth, and that every tongue should confess that Jesus Christ is Lord, to the glory of God the Father." (Philippians 2:9-11) My friend, when will you bow?

Father God, I pray that today will be the day that all who hear Your Word will choose "but for me and my house, we will serve the Lord." Thank You for not giving up on us. Thank You for pursuing us. Thank You for those praying mommas and papas, those prayer warriors all around the world who are bringing the name of their unbelieving loved ones to Your throne room. You said, "the effective, fervent prayer of a righteous man avails much." Encourage my brothers and sisters to not give up praying for their unsaved. Amen.

September 10
Be a blessing
Proverbs 11

"Therefore encourage one another and build each other up, just as in fact you are doing." (1 Thessalonians 5:11 NIV)

Let's be honest, how many of us woke up this morning thinking "how can I encourage or build someone up today?" Probably not our first thought of the day and perhaps not even on our radar. Think back over yesterday, did you receive a blessing or had the opportunity to be a blessing to someone else? When we purposefully look for life's blessings or consciously seek ways to be a blessing, life takes on new meaning.

Blessings come in all shapes and sizes. Perhaps there are even times we don't recognize the blessing because we are looking for something bigger and better. Blessings don't necessarily cost anything. They may take the form of a listening ear, a kind word, a hug. Even a small blessing can change a person's day. "The one who blesses others is abundantly blessed; those who help others are helped." (Proverbs 11:25 MSG) When we chose to bless someone, to "love one another," we bring light to their world and ours.

Often, we think we can't afford to be a blessing. We don't have the funds or the time to touch someone else's life. The truth of the matter is when we allow others to interrupt our agendas and schedules, when we allow ourselves to take our eyes off self, we become more satisfied with life. If life has you down, bless someone. Send an encouraging text or email. Bake some cookies. Look outside of "your" world for those to bless. God can open doors for willing hearts to find ways to bless those in your community, those in need, those who are lonely. And you will find it true that you become more blessed.

Father, too often we are so busy and self-absorbed to "love one another." We go through life seeking ways to get what we think we deserve. All the while, not recognizing that one of the greatest things we can do for ourselves is to take time for others. As we live life with others, our lives become richer. Lord, help me be a blessing to someone today. Amen.

What is the enemy trying to destroy in your life?
Jude

For some of us, today brings back vivid memories of the attacks on American soil. For some, it is just another history lesson. We, as the American people, never thought that the enemy would be able to come in and destroy our sense of security. We lived in America, "the greatest country in the world." We had the "best" technology and military defense. We were prepared for battle, protected against our enemies and undefeatable. But as those towers began to fall, all that false security came crashing down. Now we live in a country where trust is hard to find. Are you experiencing some "towers falling" in your life? Has the unexpected destroyed parts of your world? There are natural causes that sometimes seem to destroy our world. However, there are times when the destruction is due to an attack from the enemy. Some of us live life without even being aware of how "your adversary the devil walks about like a roaring lion, seeking whom he may devour." (1 Peter 5:8) We think "I read my Bible; I pray" but we stay blinded to the small ways our enemy plants fear and doubts into our "secure" world. How he twists "truth" to make "all a man's ways seem right to him." (Proverbs 21:2 NIV) We accept his lies about ourselves, others, and our God. Why do you think the Bible is full of "be sober, be vigilant . . . Resist him" (1 Peter 5:8-9) "Be strong in the Lord and in the power of His might. Put on the whole armor of God, that you may be able to stand against the wiles of the devil." (Ephesians 6:10-11)? How have we allowed the enemy to infiltrate our "secure" world? My friend, what areas in your life do you need to better secure? "For though we walk in flesh, we do not war according to the flesh. For the weapons of our warfare are not carnal but mighty in God for pulling down strongholds, casting down arguments and every high thing that exalts itself against the knowledge of God, bringing every thought into captivity to the obedience of Christ." (2 Corinthians 10:3-5) In what areas do you need to tear down the strongholds of lies and again be grounded in the Truth of God's Word? Rise up, my brothers and sisters, and be courageous. Take up the armor of God and stand.

Father, forgive us for "leaving our post." For not being watchful and vigilant. For allowing the enemy to "creep in unnoticed." (v 4) Strengthen us to stand on Your Word. Please give us the courage to resist. Open our eyes to the attacks in our lives. Thank You that we are not in this battle alone. Amen.

Inspired by "Courageous" by Casting Crowns

September 12
What are we listening to?
James 1

"Let every man be swift to hear, slow to speak, slow to wrath."
(James 1:19)

We have both internal and external voices surrounding us almost every single moment of the day. We hear the voice inside our heads pointing out our every flaw. While, too often, the voices around us are doing the same thing. We are bombarded with negative words that demand to be heard, while the voices of kindness and goodness seem to be drowned out. With all those loud negative voices around us, words of encouragement are hard to hear. But oh, how we need them!

Don't you sometimes wish that the voices of encouragement were louder than the endless negative voices that seem to shout for all to hear? Don't you wish that God's Voice of Truth would roar more often, rather than remain that still small voice asking us to simply trust? God calls to us throughout the Bible to "Be still, and know that I am God." (Psalm 46:10) But we find ourselves too busy to stop and listen. Those loud voices in our world demand our attention and a reaction. However, "as cold water to a weary soul, so is good news from a far country." (Proverbs 25:25) Doesn't your day appear a little brighter with just a kind word? How many of you, in your noisy world, are thirsty for encouraging words?

And where is your voice? Do you find it among the surrounding noise or is it a steady, calm, quiet presence to those you encounter? How is your voice impacting others? Are you providing those much-needed words of kindness and goodness? Are you spreading God's Word of Truth, Love, and Peace? My friend, we need to find those moments to "Be still." We need to encourage others to do the same.

Father God, "He who has ears to hear, let him hear!" (Matthew 11:15) Please remind us to be encouraging voices in our world. Voices that spread kindness and goodness as well as Your Truth and Love. May we have an ear to hear You among all the other voices in our world. May we choose to use our voice to lift each other up. It's in Your Precious Name we pray, Amen.

September 13
Looking for an escape
Psalm 55

"My heart is severely pained within me, and the terrors of death have fallen on me. Fearfulness and trembling have come upon me, and horror has overwhelmed me. So I said, "Oh, that I had wings like a dove! I would fly away and be at rest. Indeed, I would wander far off, and remain in the wilderness, I would hasten my escape from the windy storm and tempest."
(Psalm 55:4-8)

Can we all agree that we would like to escape life's storms? Could evacuate? To take wing and fly somewhere calmer and more peaceful? Some place where we don't have to experience the upheaval or witness the destruction? However, most storms hit without warning, leaving us unprepared and seemingly defenseless, leaving us barely holding on. And after we have weathered the storm, (by the grace of God), we still find ourselves amid the destruction left behind. David knew all about life's storm. Rarely do we read through David's life story and find peaceful times. From his brother issues to running from Saul to the destruction generated within his own family, storms raged around him. Even though David was a man after God's own heart, he still experienced storms' destruction. David was a warrior. We see him in battles early in his life. He battled out of obligation, as he was protecting the sheep. He battled in righteous indignation as he faced Goliath. He was forced to defend himself from his father-in-law, King Saul and later, his own son, Absalom. Many of David's psalms cry out for deliverance. Having experienced all that, he could still say, "Cast your burden on the Lord, and He shall sustain you; He shall never permit the righteous to be moved." (Psalm 55:22) There are times we may feel like giving in and giving up, but isn't it great to know, that God will sustain you! Some days when we feel like we are unable to continue holding on to hope, He sustains us. My friend, your anchor is holding. He will not permit you to move. When your soul yearns for rest, when you are weary from the struggle, what is your responsibility? "Cast your burden on the Lord." You do not need to face the dark alone. You do not need to figure out how to pick up the pieces alone. "He will sustain you."

Thank You, God, that when life's storms leave us without direction and peace, You will sustain us. You don't remove the storms from our lives, yet You ground us in Your love and hope. Father, we cast our weary souls on You, for You care for us. (1 Peter 5:7) Thank You for Your sustaining grace. Amen.

257

September 14
Beautiful sunset
1 Corinthians 15

"Precious in the sight of the Lord is the death of His saints." (Psalm 116:15)

Death is not something we like to talk about. It's not something we want to think about. It is something we would like to put off for as long as we can. However, it is not something we can avoid. The Bible says, "it is appointed unto men once to die, and after this the judgment." (Hebrews 9:27 KJV) The death of a loved one is devastating to those left behind. However, have you ever been at the bedside of a believer as they were taking their final breath here in this life? Have you ever imagined what it would be like for them as they take their next breath in Heaven? The pain that they had been living with for so long, gone forever. Their suffering and heartbreak are forgotten as they open their eyes to their beautiful new Home. And as their welcoming committee of family and friends run to greet them, in the midst stands their Savior. Too often, we view death from the human perspective with our fear of the unknown. However, death is basically what we live for; it is the doorway to our eternal life. When our "appointed time" comes and our Father says, "It's time to come Home," on this side of Eternity there may be regrets and a longing for more time, but on the other side of Eternity, we will be reunited with our Creator, our Savior! Paul writes, "For to me, to live is Christ, and to die is gain… For I am hard-pressed between the two, having a desire to depart and be with Christ, which is far better." (Philippians 1:21-22) Yes, we want to enjoy living this life as long as we can, but we have the assurance, that when it's our time to go, the God we serve is more than enough to walk with us on our journey Home. David wrote in Psalm 23, "Yea, though I walk through the valley of the shadow of death, I will fear no evil, for You are with me." (v. 4) Oh, what waits for us on the other side! Can you see God, just like the father in the parable about the prodigal son, waiting to welcome you Home with open arms? Can you see Him rejoicing that He is no longer separated from you? You are safely Home!

Father, thank You for the promise of Heaven. That as we leave behind these bodies, we will be reunited with You. "Then, when our dying bodies have been transformed into bodies that will never die, this scripture will be fulfilled: Death is swallowed up in victory. O death, where is your victory? O death, where is your sting?" (1 Corinthians 15:54-55 NLT) Amen!

September 15
What's on your plate?
Ecclesiastes 3

"He has made everything beautiful in its time." (Ecclesiastes 3:11)

Have you ever wrote down everything "on your plate?" I think it's something we should all do at different times in our lives. We all know how things "fall between the cracks" when we are trying to do too much at one time. If asked, we would probably state that it is all important. And most of the time it probably is. However, what does life begin to look like when our plate is too full for an extended period of time? Sometimes, the most important are the things that start falling between the cracks - your family and your relationship with God. We are good at staying busy. We fill up our plates for many reasons. From pursuing a passion to trying to find our self-worth, we feel that if it doesn't happen now, it may never happen. And sometimes that true. But how often do we find ourselves running our children to their events, but not taking the time to talk with them and find out what is going on in their world? How often do couples have so much on their plates that they are passing each other to run to the next thing on their agenda and not getting to spend precious time together? How often do we spend so much time doing God's work that we neglect our personal time with Him? Do you allow time for taking care of yourself? If we are too busy to enjoy time with our family, if we are too busy to enjoy time with our God, we are too busy. We get in a such a rush to get everything done that we don't recognize what is not getting done. David wrote, "All the days ordained for me were written in your book before one of them came to be." (Psalm 139:16 NIV) We acknowledge God created us. However, sometimes we go through life acting like He did His job by creating us and now it's up to us to figure the rest out. God cares about every aspect of our lives, which includes our too busy schedules. He can direct our days. "Trust in the Lord with all your heart, and lean not on your own understanding; in all your ways acknowledge Him, and He shall direct your path." (Proverbs 3:5-6) Ask Him to reveal to you what areas of your life need to be reprioritized. What aspects have been neglected for way too long? Trust Him to direct your path. Surrender your days to Him.

"Now may the God of peace who brought up our Lord Jesus from the dead, that great Shepherd of the sheep, through the blood of the everlasting covenant, make you complete in every good work to do His will, working in you what is well pleasing in His sight, through Jesus Christ, to whom be glory forever and ever. Amen." (Hebrews 13:20-21)

September 16

Trust song
Isaiah 12

"Behold, God is my salvation, I will trust and not be afraid; for YAH, the Lord, is my strength and song; He also has become my salvation." (Isaiah 12:2)

As you sing your trust song to the Lord, what are those things that come easily to mind? Recent blessings, areas in your life where everything is running smoothly? What about the standards: "I trust You with my family, my finances, my life?" There are areas where we can easily say those words with all honesty. However, how does the trust song sound when things are not as easy? When your "perfect" little world isn't perfect? When family is not what it seems? When finances are starting to get tighter? When we can't see the answer or the way out of a situation? How loudly do you sing the trust song then? How often do we trust only as far as we can see? If we are honest, probably too often. I saw a church sign that said something like: "We do not practice trust until our faith is put to the test." Dictionary.com defines trust as: "firm belief in the reliability, truth, ability, or strength of someone or something." In what areas is your belief in God's reliability, truth, ability or strength not quite firm?

Most often it's those areas where we need to trust Him the most. Those areas that we are powerless in. Those areas that are most painful. Those areas where it is harder to say, "I will trust and not be afraid." Sometimes we forget what faith really is. "Now faith is the substance of things hoped for, the evidence of things not seen. For by it the elders obtained a good testimony." (Hebrews 11:1-2) When we trust God with those things that are going well or those things we can "jump in and fix," that's limited trust. When your trust song has "lyrics" of "I trust You in this storm even though I don't know how long it will last or what the outcome will be." That's firm belief that God is reliable, that He is truthful, that He is all-powerful, that He is good even during the storm.

Father, it seems in our nature to try to "help" You with our life. We often think we know better than You or that You are unaware of some of the things going on in our lives. How foolish we are! But Abba Father, when we get to those places where You are all we have, help us to recognize that You are all we need. Let our trust song rise forth in both the good and the bad times. Amen.

September 17
Imitate God
Ephesians 5

"Therefore, be imitators of God as dear children." (Ephesians 5:1)

Have you ever heard your words come out of the mouth of your child? Do you see them trying to do things the way you do? Your children are learning by example and what an awesome responsibility you are the one they choose to imitate. As God's children, can we say the same about us? Are our Father's words coming out of our mouths? Are our actions imitating His? You probably remember words your parents used to say that you promised yourself you would never say. But now find yourself speaking the same words to your own children. You can probably look back to see how some of your parents' actions have impacted how you choose to live your life. What about your Heavenly Father? Can you see the impact His example makes on your actions? "For you were once darkness, but now you are light in the Lord. Walk as children of light (for the fruit of the Spirit is in all goodness, righteousness, and truth), finding out what is acceptable to the Lord." (Ephesians 5:8-10) There were mistakes your parents made that you learned from. And you hope your children learn from your mistakes. Our Heavenly Father is perfect. He is always good. He is always right. And even when we don't understand, we still trust "He who has begun a good work in you will complete it until the day of Jesus Christ." (Philippians 1:6) You may think why bother trying to "imitate God." He is perfect; I am not. He is always right; I rarely get it right. Jesus says, "Take My yoke upon you and learn from Me, for I am gentle and lowly in heart, and you will find rest for your souls." (Matthew 11:24) There are some things your children must work at to be like you. However, there are other things that simply because they are in your presence they pick up almost as second nature. When we spend time with our Father, there are areas we will naturally start imitating. However, there may be areas where we need to "learn from Him." Do you consciously try to imitate Christ? Do you choose to love? Do you choose forgiveness? Do you choose to turn away from evil? Do you choose to follow your Father's example?

Lord, help us to walk as children of the Light that we will pursue what is acceptable in Your sight. Give us a desire to be in Your Word and in Your Presence so we can learn how to imitate You. You are "the way, the truth, and the life." (John 14:6) Amen.

A sinner's prayer
Romans 7

This prayer is from a sinner saved by grace. Father, I messed up again today. I wasn't very loving to some people. I was too judgmental and harsh. I made some decisions based on what I thought was right without asking what Your will was in the situation. Here lately, I have been tempted to walk down paths that You have already delivered me from. Again, I realize how I allowed my flesh to have its way when I should wait on the Spirit's guidance. Forgive me! My guess is that you could probably say a similar prayer yourself today. Paul writes, "For if I know the law but still can't keep it, and if the power of sin within me keeps sabotaging my best intentions, I obviously need help! I realize that I don't have what it takes. I can will it, but I can't do it. I decide to do good, but I don't really do it; I decide not to do bad but then I do it anyway. My decisions, such as they are, don't result in actions. Something has gone wrong deep within me and gets the better of me every time. I've tried everything and nothing helps, I'm at the end of my rope. Is there no one who can do anything for me? Isn't that the real question? The answer, thank God, is that Jesus Christ can and does." (Romans 7: 14-25 MSG) John writes, "My dear children, I write this to you so that you will not sin. But if anyone does sin, we have One who speaks to the Father in our defense - Jesus Christ, the Righteous One. He is the atoning sacrifice for our sins, and not only ours but also for the sins of the whole world." (1 John 2:1-2 NIV) Thank God, when I accepted Jesus as my Savior, it did not come with the expectation that I would never make another mistake, that I would never commit another sin, that I would be loving to everyone all the time. God made us and He realizes just how imperfect we are! Even when we are trying to be a "good Christian," we fall short. Isaiah writes, "All we like sheep have gone astray; we have turned, every one, to his own way; and the Lord has laid on Him the iniquity of us all." (Isaiah 53:6) That's why we so desperately need a Savior! So, when my priorities take precedence over His, when my words do not reflect my Father's heart, when I follow my own wisdom and not His, He is faithful to forgive. He loves me enough to gently remind me to follow Him, to seek Him in all my ways. *God, who can separate us from Your love? "For I am convinced that neither death nor life, neither angels nor demons, neither the present nor the future, nor any powers, neither height nor depth, nor anything else in all creation, will be able to separate us from the love of God that is in Christ Jesus our Lord." (Romans 8:38-39 NIV) Thank You for loving us like that, Lord. Help us to "walk worthy" and when we fall, thank You for picking us back up, and reminding us that we are not on our own. Thank You for Your Holy Spirit's guidance and Presence. Amen.*

September 19
He does all things well
Mark 7

"And they were astonished beyond measure, saying, "He has done all things well. He makes both the deaf to hear and the mute to speak." (Mark 7:37)

In today's world, where the expectation is that we can multitask successfully, how many of us do anything really well? We typically have so many balls in the air that we never seem to be able to give a hundred percent to just one thing. Most things we do are not done to the degree they would be if we could focus solely on them. How many times have you had to redo something because you didn't seem to have the time to do it right the first time? Aren't we thankful that God does all things well?

When we share with one another what God is doing in our lives, we often are astonished at how God is working. There are times we may look around at our "broken" world and think "is God even doing anything?" But when we stop to reflect on how He is moving, we stand amazed. God does not do anything halfway. He is never too busy to do it right the first time. He is "able to do exceedingly abundantly above all that we ask or think, according to the power that works in us." (Ephesians 3:20) If only we would stop to realize. If only we would stop to ask.

How often are we "astonished beyond measure" when God answers prayer? Do we set our expectations too low thinking that then we won't be disappointed if it doesn't get answered? When the people brought the deaf, mute man to Jesus in Mark 7, "they begged Him to put His hand on him." (v. 32) We understand when we pray that we pray "Thou will be done." However, how often do we say a quick prayer of "bless (insert name here)" without being specific in how we would like to see God move. God does all things well including how He answers our prayers. Take a moment to "Stand still, and see the salvation of the Lord, which He will accomplish for you today." (Exodus 14:13)

Lord, we stand astonished beyond measure of how You accomplish Your plan. You do all things "well," "exceedingly abundantly above all we ask or think." I am reminded of the children's song "My God is so big, so strong and so mighty, there's nothing my God cannot do - for you." ("My God is so big"/ Ruth Harms Calkin) Oh, if only we lived like we believed those words. Amen.

Kingdom heirs
Hebrews 11

"The Spirit Himself bears witness with our spirit that we are children of God, and if children, then heirs - heirs of God and joint heirs with Christ." (Romans 8:16-17)

What are you heirs to in this life? For some of you, you have received or will receive an inheritance from your parents. For others, there is no inheritance to be had. For some of you, you could do without the "inheritance" left you. But thank God, we, like Abraham, "wait(ed) for the city, which has foundations, whose builder and maker is God." (v. 10) Inheritances don't always have to be money or property, sometimes we receive an inheritance of greater worth, such as a strong faith. As you read through Hebrews 11, you recognize that those listed were awaiting their eternal inheritance. "But now they desire a better, that is, a heavenly country. Therefore God is not ashamed to be called their God, for He has prepared a city for them." (Hebrews 11:16) We may feel poor in this world, but one day we will receive our rich reward. As children of God, we are joint-heirs with Jesus. Our Father God made everything; He owns everything. I don't know about you, but those riches are not what I am looking forward to the most. I am looking forward to a land of rest and peace. I'm looking forward to a land where there will be no more tears, no more pain, no more separation. I am looking forward to hearing my Father say, "Well done, good and faithful servant; you have been faithful over a few things, I will make you ruler over many things. Enter into the joy of your Lord." (Matthew 25:23)

That's an inheritance we can count on. One that will not depreciate, one that will not be destroyed, one that will not be fought over. One Jesus has promised, "In My Father's house are many mansions; if it were not so, I would have told you. I go to prepare a place for you. And if I go and prepare a place for you, I will come again and receive you to Myself; that where I am, there you may be also." (John 14:2-3) That's our greatest inheritance - to be with Christ for all eternity! To be able to worship at His feet offering up endless praise and thanking Him for His salvation gift.

O Holy God, what a privilege to be able to call you Abba, Father. To recognize that we are children of the one True God. And since we are children, heirs! Thank You for the promise that one day we will step from this world into our eternal inheritance. Amen and Amen!

September 21
For those what-ifs
Genesis 19

"But his (Lot's) wife looked back behind him and became a pillar of salt."
(Genesis 19:26)

How much time do we spend on the what-ifs in life? What if we had made a better decision way back when? What if we had pursued our dreams? What if we hadn't given up? We all have those what-if moments. And most likely those moments come when we feel like nothing is going right in our life. Would our world be a little more "perfect" if . . .? We could all finish that question differently.

Do you imagine there were "what-ifs" running through Lot's wife's head as she looked back? "What if we had been a little more persistent, would the rest of our family had been saved?" "What if we had made a better decision about where we chose to live?" Because Lot's wife decided to look back instead to the place God was leading them, she became a pillar of salt.

How is living in your "what-ifs" affecting your life today? If we live too much in the "what-ifs" of our past, we could miss out on the life we have now. What about those "what-ifs" of the future? What if something goes wrong? What if I never amount to anything? What if this is all there is to life? What if we took our eyes off how our life could be different and focused on what God is doing with the life we are living now? He has a plan for our life. We may not always understand that plan, but we can trust Him with it. What if God is using our past mistakes, our poor decisions for His glory? What if He is using our life for a higher purpose? What if we "practiced what we preached" and trusted God with our actions and not just our words?

Father, we could live our whole life in a world of what ifs. How much would we miss out on? Father, Your Word tells us to "Trust in the Lord with all your heart, and lean not on your own understanding; in all your ways acknowledge Him, and He will direct your paths." (Proverbs 3:5-6) How much different would our life be if instead of asking "what if," we asked, "what is God doing in my life?" You are there for every moment of our lives. May we choose to trust You with all those moments. Amen.

Inspired by "What If" by Blanca

What do your brothers and sisters look like?
1 Samuel 16

As I stood in the checkout lane admiring the beauty of the sunset, I listened as those around me also stopped to behold the breathtaking view. It almost felt like we had all paused for a moment to join in worship of our Creator God. I didn't know these people. They did not all look like me. But as I listen to them exclaim their pleasure, I pondered how many were thanking God for such a wonderful sight. It made me wonder how many of them were my brothers and sisters. How often do we make a judgment call on whether a person is a fellow believer? If we are in a room full of strangers, do we ever stop to think about how many of them may be our brothers and sisters? Would it impact how we spoke with them or how we acted around them? Would we go up to certain ones based on their appearance and actions and assume they were Christians? And bypass others who did not fit our "ideal" image of what a Christian should look or act like? How quickly we judge! Can we honestly say that we look or act like an "ideal" believer all the time? Aren't you glad God doesn't expect that of you? Shouldn't we recognize that about others too? When the prophet Samuel went to Jesse's house to anoint the future king of Israel, he had his ideal image in mind of what that king should look like. King Saul had looked the part, so perhaps Samuel was looking for similar physical characteristics. As the older sons were introduced, Samuel assumed it would be one of them. However, God dismissed them all in favor of the youngest son, David. David was young; he didn't look much like a king. But God had reminded Samuel, "For the Lord does not see as man sees; for man looks at the outward appearance, but the Lord looks at the heart." (I Samuel 16:7) Have you ever experienced a time when you meet someone that you thought didn't look like a Christian, but once you got to know them and heard their story, you began to see their heart for God? God made us all differently. We all look different. We all have different personalities. God uses our differences to reach people everywhere. Let's try to be more aware of those times we quickly make assumptions about others. They may prove to be a beloved brother or sister who is loving and serving God with all their heart, soul, mind and strength.

Lord, one of the things I love the most about Your creation is the variety. There is so much unique beauty that surrounds us every day. Everything serves its own purpose. That is how You made us humans also. You made us in Your image, and we are all uniquely beautiful in our own ways. May we all join in unity and appreciation of one another as we serve You together. Amen.

September 23
Our Compassionate God
Psalm 145

"The Lord is gracious and full of compassion, slow to anger and great
in mercy. The Lord is good to all, and His tender mercies are
over all His works." (Psalm 145:8-9)

When I read through these verses, I envision a newborn baby in their
Father's arms. How gentle and tender God is with us as He looks on us
with love and admiration. But did you notice where my image has us? We
were innocent newborn babies. But in the reality of these verses, we could
be stubborn toddlers or rebellious teenagers, and our Father would still look
on us with such love and compassion. We often think God's love for us is
based on how we are living or acting at that moment. In our minds, He
should love the Billy Grahams in life more than the prisoners on
death-row. However, that is not how God's love works. We, as humans,
find it "easier" to love those who are making the right decisions rather than
the ones who are struggling with their life choices. But verse 9 above says,
"the Lord is good to ALL, and His tender mercies are over ALL His
works." He loves us during those battles with addictions, those times we
walk in the flesh, those times we turn our backs on Him. Sometimes I
think we need to be reminded of that. We feel that to deserve someone's
love, we always need to measure up to their expectations. And we transfer
that mindset to how God should love us. My friend, God loves you. There
are no additional qualifications. Our current image of God may depend on
if we are being "good or bad." When we are being "good," we imagine the
tender proud look of our Father. And then when we are "bad," we may
envision an angry frightening judge. Those are the times we need to
remember, "the Lord is gracious and full of compassion, slow to anger and
great in mercy." Because when we imagine that God is disappointed or
angry with us, we tend to want to hide from Him. However, if we
imagine that tender look of love on our Father's face, we long to run to
Him and just be held. Does God want us to choose to live life the way
He has planned for us? Yes! But when we fail, we don't lose His love. It
doesn't diminish. Nothing we do takes God off guard. He knows all our
days. If you find yourself having one of your "bad" days, remind yourself
that you are still loved. *Father God, sometimes we seem to need reminding
just how much You love us. We often transfer our own emotions and
feeling onto You and think that is how You view us. Thank You, Father,
that nothing can separate us from Your love. You know all our faults and
failures, our thoughts and emotions, yet You love us anyway. May we obey
Your command to love one another as You have loved us. Amen.*

September 24
Running the race
Hebrew 12

"Let us run with endurance the race that is set before us." (Hebrews 12:1)

Have you ever been to a track or cross-country meet and watched the long-distance runners throughout the race? There are times you see a runner that seems to be just floating as they run, a born runner. Then, there are those who strain with everything that is in them to cross that finish line. Runners seem to go through times when they feel like giving up, thinking they do not have the endurance to finish the race. Yet they press on! Some must overcome obstacles along the way but are still determined to finish the race. But no matter the struggle to get to that point, when the finish line is in sight, the runners pick up the pace. They dig deep and recognize they are almost there. They can do it! Our life journey often feels like a never-ending race. There are times we may want to quit or at least stop and walk for a while. There are times we think we have almost pushed ourselves to the limit. But all along the way, we have those cheering us on. And eventually that finish line will be in sight! How many times do you think you don't have what it takes? You watch as the other "runners" go by and think I will never catch up. You may even begin wondering what's the point. Then you hear the crowd calling your name reminding you that you can do it. "Blessed is the man who perseveres under trial, because when he has stood the test, he will receive the crown of life that God has promised to those who love him." (James 1:12 NIV) Sometimes we need to be reminded that the race is worth running. We need to complete our own race and not worry about how the other runners are doing. But the good news in all of this, is that we don't run alone. God is right there every step of the race. He knows how much further it is to the finish line. He puts those around us to cheer us on. When it is hard to catch our breath and our bodies feel weak and we don't think we can take another step, He strengthens us. He provides the strength that we need for that next step, then the next and the next. Keep running, my friend. You can do it! One day you will be able to say, "I have fought the good fight, I have finished the race, I have kept the faith. Finally, there is laid up for me the crown of righteousness." (2 Timothy 4:7-8) *Lord Jesus, we can endure because You endured. "Looking unto Jesus, the author and finisher of our faith, who for the joy that was set before Him endured the cross, despising the shame, and has sat down at the right hand of the throne of God." (Hebrews 12:2) And You provide the endurance we need when we need it. We may struggle along the journey, but one day we will cross that "finish line" into eternity. We will hear You say, "Well done, good and faithful servant." (Matt. 25:21)*

September 25
When Love broke thru
1 John 4

Do you remember that moment when Love broke thru? When you acknowledged there was a God in Heaven that loved you? That it wasn't based on who you were or what you did but on who He is? We believers all have that story. Some stories start when we were young and still "innocent," while others start with us hitting bottom with nowhere else to go. No matter what our story, we are thankful that Love broke thru. However, as we look at the world around us, we realize how many still need to hear that they have a God who loves them. How many need Love to break through in their lives?

Again, think back to your story. Who helped reveal Love to you? What circumstances led to the realization that you needed a God who loves? You may have had a praying family that was lifting you up to the Father. You may have had someone in your life that recognized what a mess you had made of your life. Someone was praying for you. Who are you pray for? When Love breaks thru in our lives, we want everyone to experience it. Everyone needs to know they are loved. Everyone needs to know, "This is how God showed His love among us; He sent His one and only Son into the world that we might live through Him. This is love; not that we loved God, but that He loved us and sent His Son as an atoning sacrifice for our sins." (1 John 4: 9-10 NIV) Share your Love story with others.

Thank You, Father, that someone prayed for me. Someone shared Your great love for me. Father, lay on my heart those who need my prayers. Those who need to experience Your Love for themselves. Help me to "always be prepared to give an answer to everyone who asks you to give the reason for the hope that you have." (1 Peter 3:15 NIV) Amen.

Habit of complaining
Psalm 150

"Do all things without complaining and disputing." (Philippians 2:14)

Is it fair to say we seem to like to complain? That it is almost an instinct especially when things don't go our way or something is an inconvenience? We complain about the weather (almost every day). It's too hot; it's too cold; it's too rainy. We complain about the traffic. We complain about other people. We seem to find something to complain about faster than finding a reason to give thanks. As I reflected on yesterday, I came up with several examples where I or someone I was with complained about something.
And as I pondered this, I acknowledged how easy it would have been to turn that complaint into a thanksgiving.

Complaining is not something new. We read a lot of complaining throughout the Bible. The Children of Israel were especially known for it. Adam and Eve complained. Even Jesus' disciples complained. Most of the time, we think complaining is harmless. But have you ever been around someone that all they did was complain? You don't want to be around them very long. When our words of dissatisfaction outnumber our words of encouragement and thanksgivings, we become known as a negative person. And how does that impact our witness?

In Psalm 150, we are reminded "Let everything that has breath praise the Lord." (Psalm 150:6) Again, as I reflected on yesterday, it was a little harder to identify those moments of praise. Praise time is not limited to those few moments during your alone time with God. Sitting in traffic can be praise time. Waiting at a doctor's office can be praise time. As you go through your day and those frequent opportunities for complaining arise, "praise ye the Lord." Purposefully turn your complaint into a moment of praise.

Father, You said, "But I say to you that for every idle word men may speak, they will give account of it in the day of judgment." (Matthew 12:36) Father, forgive us for those complaints that may stand in the way of our praise. May we recognize them as the idle words they are which sometimes interferes with our thanksgiving and praise. I pray that "His praise will always be on my lips." (Psalm 34:1 NIV) Amen.

September 27
Waiting on the Lord
Genesis 6

Waiting is not something any of us like to do. We want all the answers now. We want to be doing something to fix our situation rather than just waiting for God to move. We think we are ready for whatever is coming our way, so let it come. However, God knows us. He knows what a mess we make of things when we jump in unprepared. He knows how many times we settle for something "less" so that we, at least, feel like we are doing something. And He also knows the path before us.

We often think every open door is from God, every idea that pops into our heads. Many times, that is just our impatience showing. When we "present your bodies a living sacrifice, holy, acceptable to God, which is your reasonable service" (Romans 12:1), we are also submitting to God's timeframe. When we must wait a week or a month on God, we think perhaps He's forgotten us; perhaps we missed what He wanted us to do. But think about all those that waited in the Bible: Noah, Abraham, Jacob, David, and the list goes on. Did these people just have to wait a week or two until their answers came? They waited years and years for God to fulfill His promise for their lives. The advantage we have as we read His Word is that we get a glimpse of what God was doing in their lives while they waited. We saw how He was preparing them, how He was preparing others, how He was removing obstacles. Don't you wish we could see that in our own lives? As we read the "end" of their stories, we see how it all came together for God's glory and to further His kingdom.

God is working in our lives every day too. We may not see how He is preparing us. We may not understand how He is already using us. But He is moving. We think the eventual outcome of our situation is when God will move, however, we don't realize that God is working in the "process" as well. While we wait, God is not expecting us to sit around twiddling our thumbs. Noah didn't wait for the ark to build itself. Abraham didn't wait for the Promised Land to come to him. Just as God was teaching them, preparing them, moving mountains, He is doing that for us as well.

Father, as we wait on You, may we see Your hand in our lives every day. As we wait for the answer to come, for the situation to be resolved, for the outcome, may we acknowledge You in all our ways. Thank You for guiding us, providing for us, protecting us. Have Your way in our lives. Your kingdom come, Your will be done. Amen.

September 28
Wanting more
Psalm 84

We never seem to have enough: enough time, enough money, enough energy, enough willpower. We always seem to desire more. We devise ways to rework our schedule to find more time. We try to hit all the sales to give us a little extra cash. We have 3 or 4 cups of coffee (or sneak some chocolate) to give us that extra boost to get us through the day. We stay strong for a few days to try to accomplish our goals only to have a bad day that throws it all out the window. Do you ever find yourself wanting more of God? More time to spend with Him, to get into His Word and pray more? Do you just want to get to know Him more? The Psalmist writes "My soul longs, yes, even faints for the courts of the Lord; my heart and my flesh cry out for the living God." (Psalm 84:2) Does your heart ever have that cry?

When chaos surrounds, when life pressures get too heavy, when we don't know where to turn, our hearts seem to cry out for more time with the Father. More time with our Father to put things back into perspective. More time with our Father to remind us we are loved. More time with our Father to remember there will be a better day. More time with our Father just to be held. More time with our Father to rest in His strength.

My Lord, "Better is one day in your courts than a thousand elsewhere; I would rather be a doorkeeper in the house of my God than dwell in the tents of the wicked." (Psalm 84:10 NIV) I come before You to acknowledge that I can't live life without You. There are too many voices calling "truth, truth," too many expectations and demands, too many hopeless moments, too many unanswered questions. But when I come into Your Presence, all that fades away. You calm my troubled heart, wipe away my tears, and remind me of all Your promises! I need more of You and less of me. Thank You for always being there. Amen.

September 29
Spiritual birth
Luke 18

Happy (spiritual) birthday to me. When I was 15 years old, I accepted Jesus into my life. I had been raised in church my whole life. I sang with my family almost every Sunday. I read my Bible. I enjoyed listening to people talk about God. But until I repented of my sins and accepted His gift of forgiveness, what I knew about God was head knowledge, not heart knowledge. I could correctly answer all the questions in Sunday School. I knew the words to all the hymns we sang and could even tell you what page number they were on in the hymnal. I also had several verses memorized. But all of that was not enough to get me into heaven. I had to experience God. I had to ask Him to forgive me so that I could truly begin a relationship with Him.

In Luke 18, the rich young ruler came to Jesus wanting to know what he needed to do to get to heaven. This young man at first seems relieved. He knew and had obeyed the Law. His head was in the right place. However, his heart wasn't. Jesus recognized that this man hadn't let his head knowledge affect his heart knowledge. He knew the right things to say and do, however, he did not recognize that there needed to be a change. A change to his priorities, a change to his goals, a change to his life. There are, unfortunately, people still today who go through life just knowing of God. They read the Bible and perhaps can even quote it. They may have a general idea of how to "obey" but have never sought God's forgiveness nor experienced a personal relationship with Him. Oh, what they are missing out on! My friend, do you know of God or do you know God? Are you just a hearer of the Word or a doer as well? You may be a Bible scholar who has read the Bible cover to cover, but until you ask Jesus to become your Savior and Lord, you will never truly experience the freedom that comes from having your sins forgiven. You will never truly appreciate the love that God has for us. "Oh, taste and see that the Lord is good; Blessed is the man who trusts in Him!" (Psalm 34:8)

Father, I pray that everyone that opens your Word will find You. "And you will seek Me and find Me, when you search for Me with all your heart." (Jeremiah 29:13) That they will choose to follow You. That they will experience Your forgiveness. That as they read Your Word, that both their head and their hearts will be open to You. Amen.

September 30
It will never lose its power
1 Peter 1

Kingdoms rise and fall. Records get broken. Fads come and go. But God's Word stays the same. No one stays in power forever. Sports' superstars are eventually replaced by someone younger, faster, stronger. No one rules a kingdom forever; the royal crown ultimately gets past down to the next generation. The healthiest person ages and begins to lose their strength. Circumstances change and there comes a time when everyone loses their power, their prestige, their fame. But thank God we serve a God who "is the same yesterday, today, and forever." (Hebrews 13:8)

We serve a God who is ageless. He will never grow too old or weak to fulfill His promises. We serve a God who stands the test of time. Many great people have walked this land, but not a one could live forever and continue to amaze the world with their strength, their wisdom, their power. Jesus Christ is the only One who has conquered death, Hell, and the grave.

People build themselves up to display how wonderful they are, wanting all to acknowledge their accomplishments. But ultimately their name is replaced by someone more current who has proven to be better. But the God I serve will never lose His power. No one is going to show up to knock God off His throne. No one is going to disprove His Word. God is never going to wear Himself out as He helps us day by day. The same power that raised Jesus from the grave is living in us today. It will sustain us day by day until we reach that Promised Land. We can rely on the strength that it provides. We can rest in the comfort it gives. And we can know that Resurrection Power will lead us safely Home. My God is King of Kings and Lord of Lords. He is Everlasting. He is from Age to Age. He is the Alpha and the Omega, the First and the Last. His dominion will have no end. Heaven and earth declare His Majesty. What a mighty God we serve!!!!! And one day, we will join all our fellow believers past, present, and future to worship the same God who created the heavens and the earth and who created the new heaven and the new earth. What a glorious time awaits us around His throne where we will worship for all eternity! Praise to our Father, the giver of life.

Lord, no one will ever measure up to You. None can compare. And even with how great and powerful and awesome You are, yet You choose to call us Yours. You desire to spend time with us. You adore us and You are there when we call. We are so undeserving of Your great mercy, but You love us anyways. Thank You for the gift of Your Son. Amen.

October 1
Stop fighting
Luke 15

When my boys were younger, the thing that would upset me the most was when they would be mean to one another. Play fighting and wrestling was one thing, but when they would say or do something that would hurt the other, that's when mama stepped in. It happened a lot when one thought they were right and the other was wrong. They did not always understand each other nor were willing to accept that they may both be right (or wrong). Christian brothers and sisters sometimes act the same way. We often make assumptions and don't try to understand. If they are not "acting" like we are, then they are doing it wrong. Do you ever think our Father looks down on us in sadness as He watches how we treat one another? How we judge one another? How we place having to be right above the feelings of others?

In the story of the Prodigal Son, the oldest son was more worried about being acknowledged for doing what was right than about his brother. A brother that had made a lot of mistakes and had dealt with the consequences of them. A brother who needed love and forgiveness. When our brothers and sisters are hurting, they do not need us judging them. They need us to love them. We ALL make mistakes and need to recognize that none of us is perfect. In the Sermon on the Mount, Jesus says "Why do you look at the speck in your brother's eye, but do not consider the plank in your own eye?" (Matthew 7:3) We like to think that every Christian should agree on everything; so, therefore, everyone should agree with us. But we should also recognize that agreeing on everything rarely happens in any relationship. Paul writes to the Ephesians, "Always be humble and gentle. Be patient with each other, making allowance for each other's faults because of your love." (Ephesians 4:2 NLT) Consider your actions or words recently about your brothers and sisters. Were they loving and understanding? Or condemning and hurtful? "Bear one another's burdens, and so fulfill the law of Christ." (Galatians 6:2)

Our Father, forgive us when we are tearing each other down instead of lifting up. Open our eyes to see what our brothers and sisters need from us. Yes, sometimes it may be a word of correction spoken in love but most of the time, it should be a word of encouragement and support. "Let us love one another, for love is of God." (1 John 4:7) Father, may we love one another as You love us. Amen.

October 2
Am I enough?
Ephesians 2

How many of you have ever had to apply for college or a job? How many have ever asked or been asked the question, will you marry me? How many have held a newborn in your arms? Those are just a few of the times in life when we wonder am I enough? Am I smart enough? Am I good enough? Am I strong enough? As we face those life changes, we wonder if we are enough for what will be expected of us. We often look at others and imagine how well they are doing with life. They appear to be the perfect college student, the perfect employee, the perfect spouse, the perfect parent. We think we will never be able to measure up. We may think we are not worthy or that we will surely fail. We each experience "job performance" reviews in some form or fashion in life and wonder how we "rate" in life. We will fail sometimes. We will make mistakes. We will get it wrong. There are times we don't have the knowledge or skill set needed for the "job." Sometimes the expectations are too high and unattainable. Sometimes our self-expectations are higher than reality. Sometimes we are misunderstood. But when I come to my Father, I never need to wonder am I enough!

My Father adores me. My Father can look past my faults and failures to see my heart. My Father understands that I trip and fall. He knows what all I am capable of even more than I do. When doubts pop up about my worth, God's Word reveals the Truth. "There is none righteous, no, not one." (Romans 3:10) "For by grace you have been saved through faith, and that not of yourselves; it is the gift of God, not of works, lest anyone should boast." (Ephesians 2:8-9) When I ask "Am I enough?", my Father answers, "Yes, I have loved you with an everlasting love." (Jeremiah 31:3) "Fear not, for I have redeemed you; I have called you by your name; you are Mine." (Isaiah 43:1)

Father, when I get passed up for that job promotion, when family doesn't seem to understand or appreciate me, You remind me that I am enough for the Great I AM. My worth is not based on my knowledge, on my performance, on my strength. I am worthy because I am Your child. I am enough because of Your Son's precious gift. Thank You! Amen.

October 3
Still learning
1 Samuel 3

Eli was priest when God sent Samuel to come live and work at the temple. Eli was tired and began letting things go. He did not even try to correct his sons anymore. God used young Samuel to teach Eli. One would have thought Eli knew it all. Instead, God used Samuel's willing heart to speak truth into Eli's life.

I have been a Christian for over 30 years. I have read my Bible. I've taught Sunday School. Sat under many a sermon. Attended conferences where the Word of God was taught. And yet I'm still learning.

God never looks at us and thinks ok they know everything now. (That was the point of Adam and Eve leaving the garden.) He still is teaching us and molding us into what He wants us to be. He uses His Word. "For the word of God is living and powerful, and sharper than any two-edged sword, piercing even to the division of soul and spirit, and of joints and marrow, and is a discerner of the thoughts and intents of the heart." (Hebrews 4:12) God also uses those around us. And it doesn't have to be an "older" Christian, sometimes "a little child shall lead them." (Isaiah 11:6) The innocent observation or question from a young believer can also be used to teach.

However, sometimes we do believe we know-it-all. We can quote the books of the Bible. We can quote scripture left and right. We have experienced God in a lot of different ways. Only to come across a new experience and learn a new lesson from God. Paul says, "Not that I have already attained, or am already perfected" (Philippians 3:12) Paul recognized that he still had things to learn. If we can recognize that truth about ourselves, that we don't know it all, it can free us from trying to live "perfect" lives. Accept the fact that you forever will be learning and know that God provides the teaching you need.

Father, thank You for the reminder that You are still working on us. We learn from Your living Word. We learn from those examples set before us. Teach us Your way so that we may walk therein. Amen.

My God
Psalm 23

I stand amazed that the Creator of the Universe is the lover of my soul.
The One who holds all wisdom calls me by name.
The One who hung the stars hears my every word and my every thought.
The One who spoke everything into being, speaks to me.
The One who gave me life, resides in me.
In all His beautiful creation, I am the apple of His eye.
Amid the billions of people on this planet, He knows my name.
With all the cares of this world, He sees each of my tears that fall.
The One who owns everything says I am His.

And what is truly amazing is that every one of us can say that.
We all can have a personal relationship with the Maker of the heavens
and the earth.
We all can experience His working in our lives every day.
We all can bask in His great love.
We all can stand on His promises.
The Almighty is our Father who wants to spend time with us.

Can you say that the King of kings and the Lord of lords is MY God?
Do you know Him as a Friend that sticks closer than a brother?
You can. He wants a personal relationship with all His created people.
Will you answer His call?

October 5
Favorite Scripture
Psalm 119

"But his delight is in the law of the Lord, and in His law he meditates day and night." (Psalm 1:2)

Where does your Bible seem to open to automatically? That scripture that you always seem to turn to? If asked to quote our "life verse," every one of us would probably offer different responses with different reasons for those responses. Perhaps your "life verse" changes depending on the seasons in your life. Do you have verses that you speak over your family? The ones that bring peace and comfort and serve as a reminder. God's Word can become an active part of our day. When we read God's Word, we need to let it minister to our weary souls. Let it guide us into the way we should go. Encourage us for the next steps along our path.

We can be meditating on God's Word throughout the day no matter where we are. We can hold fast to the promises in His Word as we struggle with life's uncertainties. Scripture serves to remind us we are never alone. The words we need were spoken before we were even born. God's Word is not meant just to be kept to ourselves. We need to share His Word with everyone who needs to hear it. What practical ways are you finding for sharing it?

Lord, "let the words of my mouth and the meditation of my heart, be acceptable in Your sight, O Lord, my strength and my Redeemer." (Psalm 19:14)

October 6
True friendships
Proverbs 27

"As iron sharpens iron, so a man sharpens the countenance of his friend." (Proverbs 27:17)

Tis Homecoming season! We watch as parents post pictures of how well their child looks all dressed up. For the teenagers, they are looking for the most creative way to ask someone to homecoming. They are looking for the perfect outfit. They may perhaps be secretly trying out their dance moves. But mostly they are going expecting a fun time with their friends.

For the adults in these teens' lives, this time brings back memories of their own homecoming and forgotten friends. When in high school, we can't imagine life without our friends. And for those tight friendships, we can't imagine not continuing that friendship after school. Some do last a lifetime, but most are buried under new friendships, new experiences, new responsibilities. You all can probably recall those friendships that have been neglected. Those friends left behind when we moved, got a new job, started a family. Those friends that life has seemingly gotten in the way of us spending time with.

However, friends are an important part of our lives. We all need those friends in our lives that are honest with us and have our best interest in mind. "The pleasantness of one's friend springs from his earnest counsel." (Proverbs 27:9 NIV) "Wounds from a friend can be trusted." (Proverbs 27:6 NIV) We need those friends who "force" us to stop and have fun. We need those friends we can laugh with, cry with, and share our thoughts with. We need friends who take care of us. And we need to be that kind of friend. "A friend loves at all times." (Proverbs 17:17)

Father, You have called us to love one another. Thank You for the gift of friendship. Thank You for those close friends You have placed in my life. May we "sharpen" each other as we live life together. Amen.

October 7
Forgotten sermons
James 1

If you have been in a church environment, you have probably heard something along the lines, "the preacher really stepped on my toes this morning." This saying means that the sermon held truth that hit too close to home. How often do we go to church on Sunday only to leave the church grounds and forget what we heard and experienced? Especially those times when the Word revealed something that we needed to address in our lives? James reminds us, "But be doers of the word, and not hearers only, deceiving yourselves. For if anyone is a hearer of the word and not a doer, he is like a man who looks intently at his natural face in a mirror. For he looks at himself and goes away and at once forgets what he was like. But the one who looks into the perfect law, the law of liberty, and perseveres, being no hearer who forgets but a doer who acts, he will be blessed in his doing." (James 1:22-25 ESV) If we never apply the Word we read or hear, it will never bring the change we need to see in our lives. We want to hold on to our attitudes, our anger, our hurt, our pride. We don't want to be the one to have to change. We want our situation to change. We want others to change. We want the truth to change. In our minds, we are right, and we are justified in how we feel. Perhaps we feel like God is asking too much of us. So, we figuratively stomp our feet and cross our arms and think we are not backing down. But thank God, He pursues us even when we are saying "leave me alone." It is in times like that we may not feel like God loves us. But there needs to come a time when we need to recognize He is God and we are not. He wants to do a work in our lives, but we are too busy holding on to our hurt to be open to the work He has for us. We are here on this earth to bring glory to His name. My friend, we do not go to church just to feel good. We go to receive a Word from God. And that involves hearing truth that we need to apply to our lives. "For the word of God is living and powerful and sharper than any two-edged sword, piercing even to the division of soul and spirit, and of joints and marrow, and is a discerner of the thoughts and intents of the heart. And there is no creature hidden from His sight, but all things are naked and open to the eyes of Him to whom we must give account." (Hebrews 4:12-13) So what sermons have you "forgotten?" What truth do you need to begin applying to your life? "If we confess our sins, He is faithful and just to forgive us our sins and to cleanse us from all unrighteousness. If we say that we have not sinned, we make Him a liar, and His word is not in us." (1 John 1:9-10)

Father, thank You for Your Word of Truth. May we be doers of Your Word and not hearers only Amen.

The Artist
Genesis 1

Like many others, fall is my favorite season. It seems to be a season where God puts on an art show. The brilliant colors of the sunrise and sunset are breathtaking. The dynamics of watching the leaves change color never ceases to amaze. The sounds and smells of fall enhance the art show as all of creation boasts of the Artist touch. It serves as a reminder of how awesome our God is! But what about the seasons in our lives? Are there seasons where we can stand amazed at what God is doing in our life? How is the Artist working on us to make us His masterpiece? My friend, as we enjoy the beauty of creation, may we remember that we too are a part of that Great Design. We are part of His art show. "For we are His workmanship, created in Christ Jesus for good works, which God prepared beforehand that we should walk in them." (Ephesians 2:10)

Too often, when we view ourselves, all we see are the faults and failures. But the Artist has made us in His image; we are beautiful! As we appreciate what our natural eye can see, let us take a moment to appreciate the beauty that God has created in us. We may not like how we look, but our Father does. When we think we have nothing to offer, remember that God made us with a plan and a purpose. When we look at the mess our life is in, God sees our future. "I waited patiently for the Lord; and He inclined to me and heard my cry, He also brought me up out of a horrible pit, out of the miry clay, and set my feet upon a rock, and established my steps, He has put a new song in my mouth - Praise to our God!" (Psalm 40: 1-3) The Artist is always at work in our lives, may we always find reassurance in that promise.

Lord, how majestic is Your name in all the earth. May we always recognize that You create each new day. May we acknowledge the work You are doing in us. You are faithful to complete what You have started. Give us the eyes to see the beauty You see when You look at us. May we choose to live our lives for Your Kingdom purpose and for Your glory. Amen.

October 9
My God is Awesome
Psalm 34

Are there times in our lives when it is hard to say, "My God is awesome?" Those times when He has not yet delivered, has not yet provided, has not yet protected? At least not the way we have expected or desired? Hindsight is 20/20 and it is easier to praise God on the other side of the battle or trial. But is it possible to sing "My God is awesome" during our pain, disappointment and questions? As we read through the Bible, we see time and again when people praised God despite their circumstance.

Look at Abraham as he thinks he is walking Isaac to his death. He is prepared to follow God's command but is expecting God to provide the sacrifice. Look at Paul and Silas in the jail cell facing an uncertain tomorrow. But they lifted their voices to fill the jailhouse with praise for a God they knew could deliver. The three Hebrews boys as they refused to bow to anyone but God. "If we are thrown into the blazing furnace, the God we serve is able to save us from it, and He will rescue us from your hand, O king. But even if He does not, we want you to know, O king, that we will not serve your gods or worship the image of gold you have set up." (Daniel 3:17-18) Jesus, as He was facing an agonizing death, prays, "Father, if it is Your will, take this cup away from Me; nevertheless not My will, but Yours be done." (Luke 22:42)

"I will bless the Lord at all times; His praise shall continually be in my mouth, my soul shall make its boast in the Lord; the humble shall hear of it and be glad. Oh, magnify the Lord with me, and let us exalt His name together. I sought the Lord, and He heard me, and delivered me from all my fears." (Psalm 34:1-4) Even if God never did another thing for us, He is worthy of our continual praise. "For God so loved the world that He gave His only begotten Son, that whoever believes in Him should not perish but have everlasting life." (John 3:16) God is still working in and through our lives. He didn't just send Jesus to die for us and then leave us alone to "figure" life out. He is with us every step of our journey. Thanks be to God! Psalm 34 goes on to say, "Oh, taste and see that the Lord is good; blessed is the man who trusts in Him!" (v.8) Our God is trustworthy even when we don't understand. Our God is awesome for never leaving us to face battles or trials alone.

Lord God, I raise my hands in praise to Your faithfulness, Your love, Your care. Thank You for being my strength when I am weak. Thank You for the promises that I stand on as I face each day. My God, You are awesome! Amen and Amen.

Inspired by "My God is Awesome" by Charles Jenkins

Lay it down
Hebrews 12

"Let us lay aside every weight." (Hebrews 12:1)

My friend, what do you need to lay down today: guilt, fear, shame, worry, a specific sin? Is it time to take a trip back to the feet of Jesus and lay it down? Perhaps, you have done that before, only to pick the weight back up. Sometimes the weight doesn't seem too heavy as you start your race with ease. But the longer you run, the harder it is to carry. Do you continue to add weight as you run: those habits you can't seem to break, those failures that discourage? Sometimes we may even find ourselves carrying weight that is not our own. Sometimes we try to "play God" and find ourselves trying to control situations that we have no control over. Sometimes we try to take on the weight of our friends and family, weight that is not ours to carry. Sometimes we allow the weight of uncertainty to slow us down. Our self-doubts hinder our journey as we ponder if we are on the right track. How do we lay the weight down? We may need to first identify the weight. We may be running without even recognize all the weight we are carrying. There may be weight we acknowledge, while others we may have forgotten. Our enemy may have been adding "small" weights along the way that go unnoticed at first until they start to add up. Some of our weight may feel too overwhelming to the point we are barely crawling. We can't seem to find a way to let it go all at once, we need to release it bit by bit thereby gaining the strength to relinquish bigger and bigger parts. As we turn the weight over to God, our enemy likes to try to convince us to pick it back up seeming to say, "are you sure you want to leave this here?" It may be one of your "favorites", that constant worry you have been carrying for years. Why does the enemy try so hard to weigh us down? Because he knows if we run unhindered, we will cover more ground. He knows if we run in freedom, we will be able to breathe easier, have more endurance; and more passion for seeing others run in freedom. Lord, "I will lift up my eyes to the hills - from whence comes my help? My help comes from the Lord, who made heaven and earth." (Psalm 121:1-2) Jesus carried the cross to Calvary to give us the power to "lay aside EVERY weight, and the sin which so easily ensnares us, and let us run with endurance the race that is set before us." (Hebrews 12:1)

Loving God, open our eyes to see where we are weighted down. Give us the strength and the wisdom to lay it at Your feet and let You have control over it. You love us, Lord. Amen.

October 11
Covering up
Genesis 3

"He who covers his sins will not prosper, but whoever confesses and
forsakes them will have mercy." (Proverbs 28:13)

We like to try to cover up our flaws. We like to try to cover up our
mistakes. We like to try to cover up our insecurities. And we have many
ways we do this. We may try to cover something up by making it look
prettier than it is. We may try to ignore it. We may like to try to convince
ourselves that God is not paying that close of attention to us.

We are not the first, nor will we be the last, to try to cover up. Since the
fall of man, throughout all generations, men, women, and children have
tried to hide. Adam and Eve hid even though there was literally no one else
to blame but each other. Achan buried his stolen treasures and brought
defeat to Israel's army. David murdered to hide his sin with Bathsheba
thereby compounding the sin in his life. Anania and Sapphira tried to cover
up the fact they withheld some of their profit back from God and as a
result, both lost their lives.

As we read through the "cover-up" stories in the Bible, we recognize
that we serve a God who sees all and knows all. But still, we hide. We try to
divert God's attention to the good we are doing over here to try to pretend
that the hidden sin over there does not exist or is too small to care about.
We don't want to have to address our failures in life. But Jesus' blood is
enough to cover ALL our sins. God wants to shine His Light into those
dark places in our lives so that we are no longer bound by them. He wants
to replace that guilt and shame with His peace and joy. What if others
found out? What if we have to deal with the consequences? My friend that
is where your story turns into a picture of God's grace. Forgiveness is yours
for the asking.

Father, You call us to "walk as children of light." (Ephesians 5:8)
You have proven to be trustworthy and faithful. We need to trust You with
all our hidden parts. Shine Your light of truth and love into our lives for
Your glory and Your kingdom purpose. Amen.

My steps
Psalm 119

"Direct my steps by Your word, and let no iniquity have dominion over me."(Psalm 119:133)

Sometimes I am prone to make foolish choices. Other times I seem to wander around aimlessly. Occasionally, I hasten down a path God may not be leading me. In other words, there are times I try to direct my own steps. It is probably safe to say that we all experience those times.

God has provided many promises regarding our steps. "The steps of a good man are ordered by the Lord, and He delights in his way. Though he fall, he shall not be utterly cast down; for the Lord upholds him with His hand." (Psalm 37:23) Anyone else need to be reminded that the Lord upholds us? "A man's heart plans his way, but the Lord directs his steps." (Proverbs 16:9) I like to make plans and I want things to go the way I plan. However, I am constantly being reminded that my plans are not always made with the right intentions or with wisdom. My plans can be self-serving. My plans may not be God's plans.

But thank God, he directs my paths. "Trust in the Lord with all your heart, and lean not on your own understanding; in all your ways acknowledge Him, and He shall direct your paths." (Proverbs 3:5-6) Do you know how often I cling to those verses? If left to our own wisdom and desires, how quickly we can get off course. "There is a way that seems right to man, but its end is the way of death." (Proverbs 14:12) Thank God, for the Holy Spirit living in us to direct our steps. "Then you will walk safely in your way, and your foot will not stumble." (Proverbs 3:23) "For the Lord will be your confidence, and will keep your foot from being caught. (Proverbs 3:26) I don't know about you, but I need that confidence. I need to know that I am not walking alone. I need to know that He has a path for me. I need to know that He is holding on to me. I need to know that I am not living this life alone.

Abba Father, thank You for directing my steps. Thank You for always being there. Thank You for not allowing me to wander aimlessly around. Thank You for having a plan and a purpose for my life. May I be found faithfully following Your will for my life. Amen.

October 13
Friend Jesus
John 15

"You are My friends if you do whatever I command you." (John 15:14)

When we worship Jesus, we could worship Him forever for just one of the roles He has in our lives. When we take the time to think about who He is, we realize that we could use every word we speak, every breath we take and still not be able to thank and praise Him enough. He is our Savior. He is our Lord. He is our King. He is our Provider. He is our Protector. He is our Deliverer. He is our Rescuer. He is our Hope. He is our Peace. He is our Friend. He is everything we need when we need it.

When I think about Jesus as my Friend, I envision a constant companion who knows everything about me. One I can share everything with. One understands me yet loves me anyways. He is a Friend that wants the best for my life. He is a Friend that always listens. He is with me no matter what I face. I feel secure in His Presence. He is there to give me courage when I am afraid. He is there to offer hope when I am discouraged. He is there to offer peace when the storms are raging. He is there to hold me when I need comfort. He is my best Friend.

However, He is also Lord of my life. I need to acknowledge that He is Holy. I need to acknowledge that He has a say in how I live my life. I need to acknowledge I am His. I was bought with a price. "For you were bought with a price; therefore glorify God in your body and in your spirit, which are God's." (1 Corinthians 6:20) I need to trust and obey His will for my life.

Lord Jesus, as I thank You for being such a Faithful Friend, I also humbly bow to You as Lord of my life. You are my Savior and Redeemer. You paid my sin debt. I can never praise You enough for that precious gift. I pray that I will "be diligent to present yourself approved to God, a worker who does not need to be ashamed, rightly dividing the word of truth." (2 Timothy 2:15) Amen.

October 14
Our Forever God
John 14

How many of you have been searching for your "forever" home? Perhaps your childhood was spent moving from place to place. Perhaps your "family" dynamics seem always to be changing. Perhaps you have searched for a love that will last only to be disappointed time after time. Perhaps you are well into adulthood and are still searching. Maybe from your experiences, you no longer believe in a lasting love. Maybe you no longer believe in unconditional love. Maybe you believe that a forever home is just a myth. My friend, let me introduce you to a Love that is Faithful and True. Life doesn't always end up with a fairy tale ending. Dreams do not always come true. Promises are made to be broken. If this is the only way you have experienced life, let me introduce you to the Giver of Life. When we accept Jesus as our Lord and Savior, we are entering into an eternal relationship. He will never stop loving you. He loved you before you even acknowledged Him. "But God demonstrated His own love toward us, in that while we were still sinners, Christ died for us." (Romans 5:8) He already knows everything about you, so you don't have to worry about what will happen when He finds out the truth about you. He knows you better than you know yourself and yet He still offers you His grace, His peace, His joy, His love. He promises, "for He Himself has said, "I will never leave you nor forsake you." (Hebrews 13:5) He is offering you rest and security. "Come to Me, all you who labor and are heavy laden, and I will give you rest." (Matthew 11:28) He has promised you a heavenly home. "Let not your heart be troubled; you believe in God, believe also in Me. In My Father's house are many mansions; if it were not so, I would have told you. I go to prepare a place for you. And if I go and prepare a place for you, I will come again and receive you to Myself; that where I am, there you may be also" (John 14:1-3) "When I think of all this, I fall to my knees and pray to the Father, the Creator of everything in heaven and on earth. I pray that from His glorious, unlimited resources He will empower you with inner strength through His Spirit. Then Christ will make His home in your hearts as you trust in Him. Your roots will grow down into God's love and keep you strong. And may you have the power to understand, as all God's people should, how wide, how long, how high, and how deep His love is. May you experience the love of Christ, though it is too great to understand fully. Then you will be made complete with all the fullness of life and power that comes from God. Now all glory to God, who is able, through his mighty power at work within us, to accomplish infinitely more than we might ask or think. Glory to Him in the church and in Christ Jesus through all generations forever and ever! Amen." (Ephesians 3:14-21 NLT)

October 15

Wait for it
Habakkuk 2

"Though it tarries, wait for it; because it will surely come." (Habakkuk 2:3)

How many times have you found yourself in a place where you had almost given up right before the answer came? We want answers and solutions immediately. Waiting days, months, years feeds the doubts already in our mind that nothing will ever change. We want God to move in our situation NOW to prove to ourselves and to the world around us that He is God. We are not a patient people. We live on a schedule with deadlines to meet. Being still is not something we do well. And yet God commands us to "Be still and know that I am God. I will be exalted among the nations. I will be exalted in the earth!" (Psalm 46:10) How we long for the Day when God will be exalted in all the earth! Until then, we often ask God, "Why do You delay?" "Can't You see how bad the world is?" "Can't You see how desperate my situation is?" And yet the first answer we typically get is "be still" and "wait for it; because it will surely come." Do you wonder if we are called to "be still" because we are always trying to fix our situation ourselves? We rely on our own wisdom and knowledge to try to find a solution to a problem we may not even understand. Perhaps we are called to "be still" so we can pay attention to when God is moving. We get so busy that we miss out on some of the "little" ways God is already moving in our situation. Sometimes, we are simply too busy to be where God needs us to be. God is not ignoring us or our situation. He isn't thinking "I'm going to pretend I didn't hear that prayer." In fact, He knows even better than we do what we need. "Now to Him who is able to do exceedingly abundantly above all that we ask or think, according to the power that works in us." (Ephesians 3:20) Sometimes the answer is no. Sometimes we do not like the answer. But even then, there is a "wait for it" because "we know that all things work together for good to those who love God, to those who are the called according to His purpose." (Romans 8:28) We may never know, on this side of eternity, what good came out of our situation, but we trust God that there is some. While we wait, let's hold on to the last part "because it will surely come." I don't know what you are waiting "to come" in your life. I don't know how long you have been waiting. I don't know how God is currently moving in your life and in your situation. What I do know is that "it will surely come." I don't know what that will look like for you. I don't know if you will have the answer on this side of eternity. But I trust God to be faithful to His promises for you. *My Father, I pray for all my brothers and sisters who are in the "wait for it" stage of life. A stage we all face at some point in our life. I pray that You strengthen and encourage them to hold on until "it will surely come." You are good and You love us.*

October 16
Not my will
Luke 22

"Not my will." Sometimes those are tough words to utter. Frankly, there are times we would prefer to speak "my will be done." We want instant satisfaction. We want life to run smoothly. Uttering the words "not my will" requires a surrender and a deeper trust in God. There may be some aspects of our situation where it is easier to say, "Thy will be done." But there may also be some aspects that we would prefer to (or at least think we can) maintain some control in the process and outcome.

What thoughts race through your head when you pray "Thy will be done?" In the back of your mind, do you ever wonder what He is going to ask you to give up or do? What troubles will you have to go through to get to the place He wants you to be? Sometimes we seem to forget that we are speaking to our good and loving Father. We may feel safer holding onto "our will." It is more familiar ground. But we need to trust our Father's will. When we surrender "not my will" to "Thy will be done", we are releasing those desires, those plans, those dreams that may not be coinciding with His plans and purpose for our lives. We are acknowledging His Lordship over us. We are recognizing that there is much more to life than just our small world. Will God ask us to give up everything to follow His will? We often envision, "Thy will be done" involving a mission trip, a sacrifice, some "big" change. However, God can also use you right where you are. He may have a bigger plan and purpose for you right where you are. Your desires and dreams may be fulfilled far above what you ever imagined.

Where in your life do you need to say, "not my will, but Thy will be done?" Is it with your family? Is it at your job? Are you able to identify why you are unable to speak those words in certain areas of your life? Or are you at a place where you recognize that you have made a mess of things and need to surrender to "Thy will be done"? The more we are able to surrender to His will, the more we will learn He is worthy of our trust.

Father, "Your kingdom come, Your will be done on earth as it is in heaven." (Matthew 6:10)

October 17
In context
Jeremiah 29

How often do we pull scripture out of context and end up missing out on the rest of the story? We like to quote Jeremiah 29:11. However, how many of us recognize the rest of the passage? "This is what the Lord says: "When seventy years are completed for Babylon, I will come to you and fulfill my gracious promise to bring you back to this place. For I know the plans I have for you," declares the Lord, "plans to prosper you and not to harm you, plans to give you hope and a future. Then you will call upon me and come and pray to me, and I will listen to you. You will seek me and find me when you seek me with all your heart. I will be found by you," declares the Lord, "and will bring you back from captivity. I will gather you from all the nations and places where I have banished you," declares the Lord, "and will bring you back to the place from which I carried you into exile." (Jeremiah 29: 10-14 NIV) Adds more perspective to verse 11, doesn't it? God had plans to prosper them and not to harm them, to give them a hope and a future. But this was after they spent 70 years in captivity. This was after they called on Him and sought Him with all their heart. Verse 11 was a promise amidst their discipline, amidst their heartache. A promise to give them hope. How often do we hold on to the same promise? However, we do not know what context that verse is spoken into our lives. What does our "70 years of captivity" looks like? We know we have the hope of an eternal future in Heaven. This life is not the end of the story, it's only the beginning. What about the promise in verses 13-14, "You will seek me and find me when you seek me with all your heart."? To find the God of the universe, the Maker of heaven and earth and maintain a close relationship with Him so that we are not walking this "captivity time" alone, that is a blessing beyond measure. God did not stick the Israelites off in Babylon alone and say you must face these 70 years alone. He was with them in Babylon. He was there in the fiery furnace. He was there in the lion's den. Later, He was there to give provisions and protection to those who rebuilt Jerusalem's walls. He was there to protect His people from Haman. God did not leave His people alone. And eventually He sent His Son to offer the Atonement for all mankind. My friend, you may not be in a "prosperous" season in your life right now. You may feel like a captive to any number of things. But God's plans provide hope and promise a future. Remember that you are not alone. Your loving Father can give you courage and strength during this "captivity" time. He can provide and protect. And eventually lead you out of your captivity. *Father, thank You for having a plan for our lives. Thank You for our hope and our future.*

October 18
He fills us with skill
Exodus 35

"He has filled them with skill to do all manner of work." (Exodus 35:35)

How many of you know someone who can do something you wish you could do? Perhaps it is someone who can fix anything on a car. Perhaps they can talk to anyone. Perhaps they seem to have all the "right" answers. Perhaps they can create beautiful masterpieces. Perhaps they are a natural athlete. These may be things that we can work on improving in our lives, but in all honesty, we probably will not have them come as naturally as someone else. But can we recognize our own skills?

When we remember that God made us the way we are, we can acknowledge that we don't have to be good at everything. We don't have to know how to do everything. God "filled us each with skill to do all manner of work." If we all had the same skill set, we would not get much done. Ephesian 4 tells us, even within the body of Christ, "He Himself gave some to be apostles, some prophets, some evangelists, and some pastors and teachers." (v.11) When we realize that God made us the way we are for a reason, for a specific purpose, we can refocus on what He wants us to be. He is the One who has filled us with the skills that we do have. He has given them to us to be used by Him for His Kingdom. In Exodus 35, for example, God had specific people set apart to provide the artistic design for the tabernacle.

Yes, we can seek to improve our skills in other areas. But don't lose sight of what skills you already have. If you do not see how God is using your skill set, ask Him to show you. Perhaps you feel like you have no skill set. Again, ask God to reveal how He wants to use your life for His glory. Because it's all about Him. We are here for His purpose. We are here for His glory.

Father, sometimes we lose sight that You are the one who created us. You told Jeremiah, "Before I formed you in the womb I knew you, before you were born I set you apart." (Jeremiah 1:5 NIV) You created us all for a purpose. We are willing vessels to be used for that kingdom purpose. When You ask, "Whom shall I send, and who will go for Us?", our response is, "Then I said, "Here am I! Send me." (Isaiah 6:8) Amen.

October 19
Keep singing
Psalm 96

Keep singing when your dreams are fading.
Keep singing when life is not going the way you want it to.
Keep singing when there seems nothing to look forward to.
Keep singing when hope seems lost.
Keep singing when all you feel is heartache and pain.
Keep singing when you can't seem to lift your head.
Keep singing even when you don't feel like it.
Keep singing even when you don't want.
Because.
"Oh, sing to the Lord a new song! Sing to the Lord, all the earth. Sing to the Lord, bless His name; Proclaim the good news of His salvation from day to day. Declare His glory among the nations, His wonders among all peoples. For the Lord is great and greatly to be praised!" (Psalm 96:1-4)
Our singing is not based on how we feel; it is based on who He is.
When we stop to think about our salvation.
When we stop to think about all of life's blessings.
When we stop to think we got up this morning.
When we stop to think this is just our temporary home.
When we stop to think about His Presence.
When we stop to think about His Love.
When we stop to acknowledge He is coming again.
"How can I keep from singing Your praise. How can I ever say enough how amazing is Your love? How can I keep from shouting Your name? I know I am loved by the King and it makes my heart want to sing."
("How can I keep from singing"/Chris Tomlin)
Oh my loving Father, I sing a new song of love and thanksgiving to You. You are wonderful to me. You have blessed me more than I ever could deserve. You sent Your precious Son to die to buy my pardon. Thank You for Your Presence. Thank You for being so trustworthy. Thank You for loving me. "O Lord, our Lord, how majestic is your name in all the earth!" (Psalm 8:9 NIV) "I will praise you, O Lord, with all my heart; I will tell of all your wonders. I will be glad and rejoice in you; I will sing praise to your name, O most High." (Psalm 9:1-2 NIV)
My friend, join me with your own new song.

Inspired by "How can I keep from singing?" by Chris Tomlin

October 20
Just to hear our Father's "Voice"
John 10

"Moreover He said to me, "Son of man, receive into your heart all My words that I speak to you, and hear with your ears." (Ezekiel 3:10)

Let us pray. When you hear those words, what images pop into your head? Do you imagine a bowed head at the dinner table? Do you picture yourself on bended knee in a church? Are your hands raised up toward heaven? Are you at the foot of the cross or before the throne? Are you in your Father's lap with His arms surrounding you?

During our prayer journey, we experience our prayer life in different ways. Some days, we can't even utter a single word. Some days, our heavy hearts cry out for relief. Some days, our hearts of overwhelming joy sing out in praise and thanksgiving. In almost every prayer time, what we truly long for is to hear our Father's "voice." The Voice that reminds us we are not alone. The Voice that reminds us we are loved. The Voice that reminds us we are forgiven. The Voice that reminds us He is still in control. The Voice that comforts us. The Voice that calls us to give Him our cares. The Voice that offers direction. The Voice that calms the storms (or calms the child).

Jesus said "My sheep hear My voice, and I know them, and they follow Me. And I give them eternal life, and they shall never perish; neither shall anyone snatch them out of My hand." (John 10:27-28)

There are times we seem too busy to stop and listen to our Father, to heed His call and direction for our lives. There are times we think we have life well in hand and only choose occasionally to "chat" with our Father. But for those who recognize that we are nothing without our Father, we long to hang on His every word.

My friend, if you are only experiencing prayer time while you are in church, you are missing out on the day to day privilege of talking to our Father. Our Father is never too busy to listen and talk with you.

Father, life is so much better when we are spending time with You. To seek Your direction. To experience Your peace and hope. Thank You for the privilege of calling You, Abba Father, my Daddy! Amen.

Enjoy the view
Psalm 121

There are times when we get so focused on our heavenly Home that we miss out on the view along the way. Life gets hard and we long for our Eternal rest. There may be times when it is hard to look past the hurt, pain, and despair. But even in desperation, we can still catch a glimmer of hope. Even in the anguish, we can still find beauty amidst the ashes.

Think about the view of love around you. Enjoy your time spent with family and friends. Enjoy their laughter, their accomplishments, their strengths, those times when you just sit to chat. Remember the precious memories made with those who are waiting on the other side.

Think about your blessings. Enjoy those things we sometimes take for granted. Sometimes we lose sight of what we have been blessed with because our view is on "better" things. But when we stop to count our blessings, our hearts are filled with thanksgiving.

Enjoy the view of yourselves. Sometimes we only look at our faults and failures, our imperfections. But when we are reminded that God created us in His image, that we are the apple of His eye, that He loves us unconditional, we can acknowledge that we are something special.

Take in the breathtaking view of creation. Stop and smell the roses. Enjoy some cloud watching. Breathe in the fresh air. What a beautiful world we live in. You may be in a place right now where your view is not so great. There are times in our lives when all we seem to have is God. "I will lift up my eyes to the hills - from whence comes my help? My help comes from the Lord, who made heaven and earth." (Psalm 121:1-2) When your earthly view seems to have nothing to offer, lift your eyes.

The God of the universe, the Maker of heaven and earth has made a way where we can have a personal relationship with Him. His Spirit lives inside us. His Son died for us. We have the privilege of entering His throne room whenever we want. He invites us to lay our cares on Him. He has promised to never leave or forsake. He is there in the good times. He is there in the bad times. He is the Comforter, the Prince of Peace. He's our Provider. He's our Protector. What an amazing view when we recognize that we are never alone in this world! He is always there.

Father God, thank You for all that You have gifted us with. We are truly a people that have been blessed beyond measure. Thank You for walking our life's journey with us. You are our Provider, our Deliverer. You fight for us. You love us more than we can ever imagine. May our lives bring glory to Your name. Amen.

October 22
Walking in Truth and Love
3 John

"I have no greater joy than to hear that my children walk in truth."
(3 John 1:4)

As we travel our life's journey, can we say that we always walk in truth and love? Is that also the perspective of others? Do we reflect "But you are a chosen generation, a royal priesthood, a holy nation, His own special people, that you may proclaim the praises of Him who called you out of darkness into His marvelous light; who once were not a people but are now the people of God, who had not obtained mercy but now have obtained mercy."? (1 Peter 2:9) Perhaps we are known as one that walks in truth but we don't love as we should. Perhaps we love well but don't always walk in truth. We probably have all been in situations where the truth was shared almost defensively, maybe even a little angrily. People sometimes "pull out" the scripture to prove how "right" they are. In times like that, the truth is not necessarily being shared in love. At other times, because we are trying to love everyone, we may compromise the truth in "little" ways so we don't hurt anyone's feelings. We don't need to be harsh in sharing the truth but neither do we need to allow others to believe non-truths because we don't want to offend them. Jesus always shared His truth in love.

At one point or another, we probably have shared truth without love, Loved without truth or both. And will probably do so again. But in a world where everyone has their own "truth," in a world where hate and fear seem to reign, we, as God's chosen people, need to do a better job of walking in truth AND love. We may sometimes need to be reminded that every person we meet is loved by God, that God wants them to accept His gift of salvation so that they can be reconciled with their Father. "Therefore, as God's chosen people, holy and dearly loved, clothe yourselves with compassion, kindness, humility, gentleness and patience. . . Let the word of Christ dwell in you richly as you teach and admonish one another with all wisdom, and as you sing psalms, hymns and spiritual songs with gratitude in your hearts to God. And whatever you do whether in word or deed, do it all in the name of the Lord Jesus, giving thanks to God the Father through Him." (Colossians 3:12, 16-17 NIV)

"Teach me Your way, O Lord, and I will walk in Your truth; give me an undivided heart, that I may fear Your name." (Psalm 86:11 NIV) Teach me to love like You. Teach me to walk in truth and love. Amen.

October 23
Taking care of one another
Galatians 5

"And let our people also learn to maintain good works, to meet urgent needs, that they may not be unfruitful." (Titus 3:14)

How well do we take care of those around us? Not just those who live in the same household. Not just those we live life with. But our neighbor in need. Our brother or sister in another part of the world. We were placed on this earth to love one another. How well are we loving?

In our busy lives, we sometimes are so focused on our agenda that we lose sight of our true purpose in life. We are to be the hands and feet of Jesus. Often, we are so busy trying to fulfill our plan, we forget about His. There are seasons in life that we are the receivers. We are in the place where we need to be loved on and cared for. But there are also seasons when we need to be the givers of love and hope. In Genesis 1:28, it appears the first words God spoke to man are "Be fruitful and multiply."

In John 15, Jesus talks with his disciples about bearing fruit. "I am the vine, you are the branches. He who abides in Me, and I in him, bears much fruit; for without Me you can do nothing." (v. 5) Then in Galatians 5, we receive the "list" of the Fruit of the Spirit: "love, joy, peace, longsuffering, kindness, goodness, faithfulness, gentleness, self-control." (v. 22-23) Wouldn't we all appreciate a world where there was more love, joy, peace, longsuffering, kindness, goodness, faithfulness, gentleness, and self-control?

Jesus said, "for without Me you can do nothing." We need to open our eyes, our hearts, our minds to what God wants to do through our lives, who He wants us to take care of, who we need to love. Who in our world has an urgent need that we can meet? Yes, we are still to take care of those in our household. Yes, we are to take care of ourselves. But who else has God placed in your path for you to care for?

Father, sometimes we don't do a very good job of loving one another. Sometimes we miss opportunities that You have placed in our path. Sometimes we ignore Your promptings. Forgive us. Father, I want to abide with You. I want to bear much fruit. And I know I can do nothing without You. Father, help me to do a better job of being Your hands and feet. Direct me in the way I should go. Amen.

Walking with God
Genesis 3

"He has shown you, O man, what is good; and what does the Lord require of you but to do justly, to love mercy, and to walk humbly with your God?" (Micah 6:8)

"And they heard the sound of the Lord God walking in the garden in the cool of the day." (Genesis 3:8) How many times before had God came to walk in the garden, to visit with Adam and Eve? But this time, instead of waiting with anticipation, Adam and Eve hid. This time they recognized the state they were in, and they were afraid. Sin had entered the world.

Disobedience now separated them from their Maker. But hope was not lost, for just a few short chapters later, we read "And Enoch walked with God; and he was not, for God took him." (Genesis 5:23) The writer of Hebrews explains "By faith Enoch was taken away so that he did not see death, "and was not found, because God had taken him"; for before he was taken he had this testimony, that he pleased God." (Hebrews 11:5) In Genesis 6:9, we are told: "Noah walked with God." He was a just man and had "found grace in the eyes of the Lord." (Genesis 6:8) Even before Jesus came to earth, before He paid the ultimate sacrifice to redeem us, we find the words, "What does the Lord require of you but to do justly, to love mercy, and to walk humbly with your God?" We are living on the post-Resurrection side of this verse where the Holy Spirit is with us to guide us. We are living on the other side of "It is finished" where we have a clearer picture of God's salvation plan and rest assured in Jesus' victory. We are living with the Word of God that shows Jesus' example of how to live out this verse. Yet, this verse was written around 700 years before Jesus was even born. Those saints of old decided to walk humbly with God even though they did not fully understand how the promise would be fulfilled and when.

God still wants to walk with us today. Don't you love that imagery? That we are not walking our life's path alone, the Creator of everything is right there with us. We are to walk humbly with God, meaning we need to be the follower. Even though we don't know when the promise of His return will be fulfilled, we continue to walk with Him through the good times and the bad times. Because He has proven Himself to be faithful. He was faithful to Enoch, Noah, and Abraham. He will also be faithful in our lives.

Father, thank You for walking with us. Thank You for making a way to redeem us. Thank You for always being the same. Amen.

Let's be real
Romans 8

We like to pretend we have everything together. That's the image we try to display in our social media. It is the image we try to paint on our faces as we walk out the door. If only, we could present the "real" us to everyone we meet. Most of us shudder at the thought. We can't let anyone know our imperfections, our struggles, our failures, our mistakes. Especially if we are a Christian, because "good" Christians never have any problems, never mess up. What a misconception! Reading through the Bible should easily dispel that delusion. However, we still find ourselves trying to portray an example of perfection. We seem afraid that our failures will reflect poorly on God. But when we allow others to see God's amazing grace and love toward us despite all our mistakes, we are a living testimony of what God wants to do in the lives of everyone. People need to see the transforming power of the cross and its impact on our daily lives. People need to see how brokenness can be restored through God's love and forgiveness. They need to witness how God is our Strength when we are weak. They need to see how God lovingly pursues us and picks us up when we fall and fail. He doesn't just deem us unworthy and throws us away. People need to see our battle scars and fatigue so that they can see God's sustaining power through it all. Let's be real with people. Let's make God real to people. There are a lot of different mindsets when it comes to who God is. Many may see Him as a harsh judge. Others may see Him as an angry taskmaster ready to strike at the first mistake. We need to reflect a Holy God who is merciful and loving. We need to exhibit the unconditional love of our good Father. We need to display a trust amidst our circumstances that He is always with us.

Father, remind us that You are still working on us. We will not achieve perfection while we are still in these natural bodies or this sinful world, but we are covered by Your Son's precious cleansing blood. Thank You for Jesus "who pleads our case before the Father. He is Jesus Christ, the one who is truly righteous. He Himself is the sacrifice that atones for our sins — and not only our sins but the sins of all the world." (1 John 2:1-2 NLT) Thank You for loving us no matter what shape we are in. No matter how many times we have messed up. No matter how many times we ignored Your truth. You don't expect a perfect person. We don't have to come to You all cleaned up (we couldn't if we tried). We come as we are and place our mess into Your hands and allow You to mold us into Your masterpiece. Amen.

October 26
Keep fighting the good fight
2 Kings 6

"I have fought the good fight, I have finished the race, I have kept the faith. Finally, there is laid up for me the crown of righteousness, which, the Lord, the righteous Judge, will give to me on that Day, and not to me only but also to all who have loved His appearing." (2 Timothy 2:7-8)

Don't give up. Don't quit. Get back up. Get back in the fight. You may feel like you are in the last few moments of the battle. You can barely stand. You don't know how many more punches you can take. You have seen the enemy take out those around you. You are not even sure if you called, that the King of Glory would come. "Who is this King of glory? The Lord strong and mighty, the Lord mighty in battle." (Psalm 24:8) Fall to your knees before Him. Lift your weary hands. And pray. "For the battle is not yours, but God's." (2 Chronicles 20:15) Then raise your sword, the Word of God, and give the battle to Him. For those of you who have been knockout and feel like you have already lost the war, get back in the fight. Reconnect with your loving Father who will fight for you. Fighting is never easy. Sometimes we lose sight of the prize. Sometimes we forget why we are fighting. Sometimes we wonder if the battle is worth it. The closer we are to victory, the tougher the battles. Our enemy knows his outcome; however, he wants to mislead as many as he can along the way. He relentlessly attacks. He distorts the Truth. He distracts from the Promise. He tries to place distance between us and the Almighty. But our prayers and our praise put him back in his place. The battleground may not change, but our perspective of the battle will. Remember when Elisha's servant saw the vast army that surrounded them. He said, "Alas,my master! What shall we do?" So he (Elisha) answered, "Do not fear, for those who are with us are more than those who are with them." And Elisha prayed and said, "Lord, I pray, open his eyes that he may see." (2 Kings 6:15-17) When the servant lifted his eyes above the threat, he could then see God's plan and provision.

Father, I surrender to You. I can't fight this battle on my own. I don't have the answers, but I know the Answer. Jesus has already won the war. My battle scars may be many. I may have lost many a battle. But my victory has already been fought and paid for. My victory is assured! Lord, I put my trust and faith in Your Truth. Help me to stand. "Yours is the kingdom and the power and the glory forever." Amen

Inspired by "Surrounded (Fight My Battles)" by Michael W. Smith

October 27
We are all in this together
1 Peter 5

All around the world, we have brothers and sisters in the faith. People we will never meet this side of Heaven. Those we spiritually come alongside as we lift praises to God, our Father. But even with this truth, the reality is that too often we feel alone. We feel like we are the only one who is facing challenges. We are the only one who cares. We are the only one who is doing something for God. We each face our own struggles. For some, their faith is all they have to get them through each day. For others, they must live out their faith in hiding. Many are called to boldly share their faith, only to experience persecution, some even unto death. Many have been ostracized by family and friends because of their beliefs. Many may be on the verge of giving up because the path has gotten too long and hard. We sometimes feel like Elijah in 1 Kings 19: "I alone am left." (v 14) Just as He did for Elijah, sometimes God needs to remind us, "Yet I have reserved seven thousand in Israel, all whose knees have not bowed to Baal." (v 18) Would you all agree that it is easier to face any situation when you know someone has your back? When you know you have support, encouragement, when you know you are not alone? Ecclesiastes 4:12 says, "Though one may be overpowered by another, two can withstand him, and a threefold cord is not quickly broken." My friend, remember that you have brothers and sisters that you can turn to. You have a Father who can lay on the heart of one of your siblings halfway around the world to pray for you (even though you have never met and they don't even know your name or situation). This is also a call to remember to pray for them. We sometimes get so overwhelmed by our own problems that we can't see our brothers and sisters around us who are also facing difficult situations. We sometimes feel like our brothers and sisters have it all together and wonder why we can't. My friend, we are all in this together. We are called to be beacons of light and hope to a lost world. Sometimes, we look around and feel like there is not a lot of light but lift your head and imagine those little lights that are shining all around the world. My friend, you are not alone. "Be sober-minded; be watchful. Your adversary the devil prowls around like a roaring lion, seeking someone to devour. Resist him, firm in your faith, knowing that the same kinds of suffering are being experienced by your brotherhood throughout the world. And after you have suffered for a little while, the God of all grace, who has called you to His eternal glory in Christ; will Himself restore, confirm, strengthen, and establish you. To Him be the dominion forever and ever. Amen." (1 Peter 5:8-10 ESV)

JOY
John 15

"These things I have spoken to you, that My joy may remain in you, and that your joy may be full." (John 15:11)

Are you a joyful person? Are you surrounded by other joyful people? Overall, it seems like joy is something that is hard to find. With personal and world events that devastate, we look around wondering what there is to be joyful about. Too often, we assume that we must be happy to be joyful. But they are two very different things. Jesus says the way to be joyful is to remember "As the Father loved Me, I also have loved you; abide in My love. If you keep My commandments, you will abide in My love, just as I have kept My Father's commandments and abide in His love. These things I have spoken to you, that My joy may remain in you, and that your joy may be full." (John 15:9-11) Jesus kept God's commandments and abided in His love all the way to the cross. As Jesus was in the garden praying, "Father, if it is Your will, take this cup away from Me; nevertheless not My will, but Yours, be done." (Luke 22:42) As He was breathing His last breath and uttered: "Father, into Your hands I commit My spirit." (Luke 23:46) As He spoke Mary's name after He arose from the grave, He was abiding in His Father's love.

During the apprehension in the garden, during the agony on the cross, during the rejoicing after the Resurrection, Jesus abided in God's love. He relied on a Love that would sustain Him. He relinquished to a Love that carried Him through His death. He relished in a Love that would give Him the victory. So "that My joy may remain in you, and that your joy may be full." We don't have to be happy with all that is going on in this world. We don't have to be happy in our present circumstance. But we can still be joyful because Jesus kept His Father's commandments and abided in His love. What do we need to do to be joyful? "Abide in My love. If you keep My commandments, you will abide in My love."

Father, thank You that Your love is enough! Thank You that we can be joyful no matter how devastating the situation because of Jesus. I pray for all those who are facing heartbreak and despair today. I pray that even through all of that, your Love will sustain and bring hope. "Joyful, joyful we adore thee... Giver of immortal gladness." Amen.

Heavy but thankful hearts
Isaiah 35

The news and Facebook feeds have held many heartbreaking stories lately. It saddens my heart as I read through what so many people are facing. But as I prayed for them, I found myself also thanking God. I was thanking Him for the fact that this is not the way that it will always be. Thanking Him that there will be a day when death will be no more. Thanking Him that Love wins and hate will be defeated. Thanking Him that while we are still on this earth, He is always there to carry us through. Amidst the heartbreaking stories, there are those that bring rejoicing because they testify of the fact that God is still on His throne. He is still working in lives. He is still performing miracles. I wish every story I read could cause rejoicing. I wish that love and peace reigned in our world today. I wish that no one would face pain or loss. But this world is not our final Home. This world with all its evil and hate. This world that provides "answers" of drugs, suicide, murder. This world that tries to redefine love, peace, and joy. Only God can bring peace amidst this chaos. Only God can provide joy in the midst of sadness. Only God can take a heart of hate and evil and transform it with His love, forgiveness, and hope. Only God can promise us a forever Home without tears, heartache, and pain. Only God provides the Answer. "For God so loved the world that He gave His only begotten Son, that whoever believes in Him should not perish but have everlasting life. For God did not send His Son into the world to condemn the world, but that the world through Him might be saved." (John 3:16-17) So as my heart longs to comfort all those who are facing their darkest days, it also rejoices in the fact that this is all temporary. As my arms long to hug all those crying out today, I am thankful that the God who spoke heaven and earth into being, my loving Father, is able to be right there with them.

My loving Father, when our hearts are heavy and broken by all the cares of this world, thank You. Thank You that You never leave us to carry them alone. Thank You that You made a way that one day we will never again face the problems of this life. Thank You that someday we will be reunited with all the saints. Thank You that we will one day live in our Eternal Home. "But only the redeemed will walk there, and the ransomed of the Lord will return. They will enter Zion with singing; everlasting joy will crown their heads. Gladness and joy will overtake them, and sorrow and sighing will flee away." (Isaiah 35:9-10) Amen and Amen.

God is in control
Daniel 2

"And He changes the times and the seasons; He removes kings and raises up kings." (Daniel 2:21)

We enjoy reading through Daniel 3 about the deliverance from the fiery furnace. We love to read through Daniel 6 about the rescue from the lion's den. The later prophetic chapters in Daniel bring hope for our future. But how often do we focus on what God was doing in the lives of the kings in Daniel? Reading through Daniel, we meet several different kings and the mighty way God moved in their lives. These men were feared. They commanded respect. They were obeyed. Yet when the God who made them demanded their attention, these men ended up recognizing they were not as all-powerful as they seem. Proverbs 21:1 says "The king's heart is in the hand of the Lord, like the rivers of water; He turns it wherever He wishes." Think about the king in Nehemiah. Not only did he allow Nehemiah to go back and build up Jerusalem's walls, he also sent supplies and protection. Kings and kingdoms rise and fall. But our God is always on His throne. King Nebuchadnezzar acknowledged "Truly your God is the God of gods, the Lord of kings, and a revealer of secrets, since you could reveal this secret." (Daniel 2:47) Philippians 2 says "Therefore God also has highly exalted Him (Jesus) and given Him the name which is above every name, that at the name of Jesus every knee should bow, of those in heaven, and of those on earth, and of those under the earth, and that every tongue should confess that Jesus Christ is Lord, to the glory of God the Father." (v 9-11)

My friend, as we watch all the politics play out in our nation and around the world, let us remember that God is the One ultimately in charge. Someday all His prophecies will be fulfilled. Someday His plan will be complete. When that Day comes, only His Kingdom will remain. "Which He will manifest in His own time, He who is the blessed and only Potentate, the King of kings and the Lord of lords, who alone has immortality, dwelling in unapproachable light, whom no man has seen or can see, to whom be honor and everlasting power. Amen." (1 Timothy 6:15-16)

Father God, You alone are worthy of praise. You alone are worthy of our devotion. You have all power in heaven and on earth. "Your Kingdom come, Your will be done on earth as it is in heaven." (Matthew 6:10) May we walk worthy of Your calling and fulfill Your purpose for our lives. Amen.

Taking chances
Luke 12

"And I'll sit back and say to myself, "My friend, you have enough stored away for years to come. Now take it easy! Eat, drink, and be merry!" (Luke 12:19 NLT)

My friends, how many of you are living life the way you want with no thoughts of God? How many of you think you have plenty of time to do what you want to do? How many of you have decided you will wait to serve God when you are older or after you have your fun? My friend, you are not promised tomorrow. How would you live your life if you knew tomorrow "your soul will be required of you?" (Luke 12:20)

Your Father loves you. Your Father does not want to be separated from you. Your Father longs to have a relationship with you here on earth. He wants to bring hope to your life. He wants to give you peace. He longs to bring you joy. Don't take chances on spending eternity absent from His Presence.

Father, I am so blessed by having You in my life. I am thankful that I am never alone. I am thankful that I know I am loved unconditionally. Your Spirit lives within me bringing me comfort, peace, hope, and joy no matter the circumstance. I can come to You at any time with any problem or concern and know You are there. Father, for those who have yet to experience that relationship with You, I pray that today will be the day of their salvation. I pray they accept Your precious gift. I pray that today will be the day they will decide to make Heaven their eternal destination. Thank You for pursuing us. Thank You for loving us no matter what. Thank You that You do not expect us to get "all cleaned up" before we come, but that You want us to come just as we are! Amen.

Rest
Matthew 11

How often do we really allow ourselves time to rest? Time to not only rest our bodies but our minds as well. Are you one of those people that seems to have a million things going through your mind all the time? Thinking through what needs to be done. Worrying about situations you or loved ones are facing. Trying to figure out answers to all life's problems. Even in our alone time with God sometimes it is hard to lay down all our cares (even though that is what we are called to do) and just spend time resting in His Presence. How often, as we pray, do we have to bring our thoughts under control because they start to wander off? How many times does Jesus have to remind us, "Come to Me, all you who labor and are heavy laden, and I will give you rest."? (Matthew 11:28) Yes, there are times when our load is very heavy, and our hearts are breaking, and there seems to be no rest. Even then, we need to be reminded "Come to Me." He is there to carry us as we go through life's storms, heartaches, and disappointments.

But even in life's "calmer" moments, we still have a hard time resting. There is always something to do. There is always someone we worry about. How long do we wrestle with our cares and schedules, before we come to Jesus? How often do we wait until we are completely exhausted, physically and mentally, before we come to Jesus and say, "I can't do this anymore on my own."?

Father, may we choose to come to You for rest daily. May we lay each day's worries and agenda at Your feet and find the rest You have for us that day. Amen.

Mighty in God
2 Corinthians 10

> "For the weapons of our warfare are not carnal but mighty in God for pulling down strongholds." (2 Corinthians 10:4)

Too often we allow ourselves to live defeated lives. We say we have hope, but the hope we mostly seem to rely on is our future hope, not necessarily our present hope. Sometimes it seems we roll over and allow the evil one to declare victory in our lives. What we need to do is reflect that we serve a Mighty God that is here with us in the present not just waiting for us in the future! "For though we walk in the flesh, we do not war according to the flesh. For the weapons of our warfare are not carnal but mighty in God for pulling down strongholds, casting down arguments and every high thing that exalts itself against the knowledge of God, bringing every thought into captivity to the obedience of Christ, and being ready to punish all disobedience when your obedience is fulfilled." (2 Corinthians 10:3-6) Those are some strong words from Paul. The weapons that we have in our arsenal are MIGHTY IN GOD to pull down strongholds. They are MIGHTY IN GOD to cast down EVERY high thing that exalts itself against the knowledge of God. Our weapons are MIGHTY IN GOD to bring EVERY thought into captivity to the obedience of Christ.

According to Ephesians 6, our weapons are truth, righteousness, peace, faith, salvation, the Word of God and then "praying always." Too often, we go into battle and try to pull down the strongholds in our lives under our own strength and power. We don't prepare for the battle by spending time putting on the whole armor of God, by spending time in His Word and on our knees. Time after time, we say a quick "Help me" prayer and jump into battle. Our weapons are MIGHTY IN GOD. There are times we need to get self out of the way. We need to stop trying to figure out the battle plan on our own and give the battle back to God. We serve a Mighty God and we need to live like we believe that!

Our Mighty God, Yours is the victory! You know the strongholds in each of our lives that need to be pulled down. You know the thoughts that need to be taken captive. You know the things that are exalting themselves against Your knowledge which need to be cast down in our lives. Father, the battle is Yours. Fight our battle for us. Lord, "And do not lead us into temptation, but deliver us from the evil one. For Yours is the kingdom and the power and the glory forever. Amen." (Matthew 6:13)

When we don't have the answer
Genesis 3

Throughout history, people have had to face senseless tragedies and heartaches. During those times, we find ourselves crying out, "Why?" I'm sure we have all heard unhelpful and sometimes (unintentional) hurtful advice being offered. Reasons that did not bring comfort. Answers that did not restore. We just don't know what to say when life isn't fair. One of our first instincts as Christians is to respond, "God has a purpose." We want to defend God in those situations. Sometimes we seem to forget that death and disease were never God's intent. He had created a perfect world where love and peace reign. A world where everything was "good." When sin entered the world, that's when death and destruction came to be. Then God watched as His "good" world began to fill with evil and hate. Brother fought against brother. People chose their way over His. His world had gotten so "bad," that He decided to "start over." Among everyone on the earth, Noah was the only one who "found grace in the eyes of the Lord." (Genesis 6:8) So God sent the Flood. But then promised that a flood would never again destroy the earth. "I will never again curse the ground because of the human race, even though everything they think or imagine is bent toward evil from childhood. I will never again destroy all living things." (Genesis 8:21 NLT) But even after the Flood, God's "good" world again began to be filled with evil men. And ultimately, God's own Son had to become the sacrifice that would bring salvation and hope down to humanity. When we are faced with those "why" circumstances that don't seem to have an answer, we don't have to try to find that answer. We don't need to try to figure why God would let something like that happen. We don't need to defend God. Because sin entered the world, everyone must live with the effects and consequences in this life. But thank God, because of Jesus' death on the cross and victory over death and the grave, we will not always live in a sin-filled world. One day, we will get to live in a "new heaven and new earth."

Father, how we long for that day when "the devil, who deceived them, was cast into the lake of fire and brimstone" (Revelation 20:10) Thank You for creating the "new heaven and the new earth" where "And God will wipe away every tear from their eyes; there shall be no more death, nor sorrow, nor crying. There shall be no more pain, for the former things have passed away." (Revelation 21:4) And thank You that as we face those seemingly senseless circumstances in our lives, that You are there. We are thankful that You are big enough for our hurts, our anger, our questions, our pain. Thank You that You are there to hold us, to comfort us, to bring us peace. Because You paid the price that sin demanded of this world. Oh, how You love us! Amen.

November 4
Tell the devil not today
1 Corinthians 15

Don't you love it when scripture or lyrics to a song seem to jump out at you? I have heard "Not Today" by Hillsong several times and love singing along. But this time when I heard it, several lines seem to jump out at me. In the first verse, the statement is made "fear must have thought I was faithless when it came for my heart." How often does fear seem to attack, especially when we are in a weakened condition? But thank God that even when we are weak, we still can hold on to our faith. And even if our faith is mustard seed size, that is enough to carry us through. For we have experienced God. We know He is faithful. We know that He is there. We know He is our Strength. We never need to be "faithless" because He has proven Himself Faithful and True.

The second verse of that song asks "Tell me did the enemy panic as You took up that cross? Tell me did the darkness cry mercy as You rolled back that rock?" We often envision Satan standing in the background of the cross, gloating over his victory. But to think that at some point, he recognized that "victory" actually sealed his fate. Because on the third day, nothing in Satan's power could keep Jesus from coming out of that tomb! And the good news doesn't stop there. That same Resurrection Power is living in us today. Satan may come at us thinking he has the upper hand, that victory is his. But thanks be to God, that is not the case. Once we accept Jesus into our lives, Satan will not have the ultimate victory in our lives. He may win some battles. He may knock us down. He may try to convince us that Jesus is ready to give up on us. He may try to trick us into believing that he is the true victor. But we have read the back of the book. The devil is headed to the lake of fire; while every knee will bow and every tongue will confess that Jesus is Lord. (Philippians 2:10-11) Our God reigns!

Our Victor! Thank You for the cross and the resurrection. Because of those two events in history, we have hope. We do not have to succumb to Satan's lies. We don't have to fall into his traps. And even if we do, we don't have to stay there. For we are Your children. "But thanks be to God, who gives us the victory through our Lord Jesus Christ." (1 Corinthians 15:57) Tell the devil, not today. Amen.

Inspired by "Not Today" by Hillsong United

Be who you were created to be
Genesis 1

"Then God said, "Let Us make man in Our image, according to Our likeness; ... So God created man in His own image "(Genesis 1:26-27)

There are many times in our society when we try to change something about ourselves to fit in. We are under the assumption that there is something wrong with us, that we are not "good" enough. It could be our appearance. It could be our beliefs. We always seem to be measuring ourselves by other people's expectations. When we are constantly faced with a negative perspective of who we are, it leads to low self-esteem, depression, making poor choices to fit in. And once we make changes, there are always other ways we need to "improve." Why do we find ourselves in that place? We have lost our identity. God made us in His image. What more could we want? There may be areas where we need to improve ourselves. However, instead of comparing ourselves to others' expectation, we should look to our Maker. Sadly, this too is an area where we are made to feel we don't measure up. I am sure that at some point in your Christian life, you were made to feel like you were not good enough by others. There are times when the Spirit speaks to you through the Word of God, a sermon, Godly counsel. Those are times when God is molding you into what He wants you to be. But there are times when we are made to feel like we miss the mark based solely on someone else's opinion not from God Himself. The best way to counteract those who make us feel like we will never measure up is to find those who will allow us to be ourselves. Those who love us through our mistakes. Most of all, we need to spend time with our Maker. As we spend time with God, we recognize that He is the Potter, we are the clay. We are sure of our identity as His child. We don't need others' affirmation as much because we are confident in who we are in our Maker's eyes. Learning to seek God first in this area takes time. Our natural inclination is to seek the approval of others. And when that is hard to find, it makes us question who we are. But those are the times, we need to find scripture verses that confirm for us who we are in Christ. "The Spirit Himself bears witness with our spirit that we are children of God, and if children, then heirs - heirs of God and joint heirs with Christ." (Romans 8:16-17) So, before we begin making change after change to try to fit in, let's go back to the Maker. Let's allow Him to remind us who He made us to be. Then we can face others' expectations with a secure identity. You are a child of the one true King. One who loves you unconditionally.

Father, remind us that our identity is found in You, not in this world.

310

Love them - Part 1
Ezekiel 33

"Son of man, I have made you a watchman for the house of Israel;
therefore hear a word from My mouth, and give them warning
from Me." (Ezekiel 3:17)

We all have those people in our lives that we just don't know what to
do with. It seems they will never learn. They do not take advice. They
continue down their self-destructing path making choices that
compound their problems. It hurts as you try to encourage them to turn
around and go a better way, only to once again be ignored. At times, they
seem to stop and recognize what is going on. They apologize and promise
to do better, then start that downward path again. Part of you wants to
give up and walk away. But they are too important; they are too loved.
There are times (maybe too many times) that they come wanting you to
"bail" them out of the mess of their own making. And we often want to
"fix" their problems hoping that it will be the last time and make
everything better. However, the cycle continues.

Can you imagine the prophets of old passing on God's message of
love and forgiveness, of hope and mercy? Then watching as the children
of Israel continue down the same destructive path? Many of the
prophets spend their lives sharing God's Word to a people that would not
heed the warning. How many times did they want to cry out "why bother?"
How many times did they just want to walk away thinking "that's enough,
I am through talking to those who will never listen and will never learn?"
However, God had other plans. He loved His people. He loved them
enough to rescue them at times; while other times allowing them to
experience the consequences of following the path they chose over Him.

Love them – Part 2
Ezekiel 33

Aren't you thankful that God never gives up on us? As God watched the children of Israel spiraling down that destructive path, He never once stopped loving them. He sent those to try to steer them back to His way but continued to promise He would be with them as they experienced the captivity and destruction of Jerusalem. Even after His prophets were ignored and treated poorly, God still offered love, mercy, and hope amidst the judgment. He promised a remnant would be saved. He promised Jerusalem would be restored. He promised a Savior.

For those in your life who continue down a destructive path, keep loving and praying. Don't give up your watch post. Sometimes loving them means offering a helping hand. At times, it may involve crying out the warning. At other heartbreaking times, it may be allowing them to experience the full consequences of their decisions. But through it all, keep loving, keep hoping, keep praying.

Father, we are a stubborn people. A people who likes to try to do things our own way. Many of us have learned that we can't live this life on our own. We need Your guidance, Your purpose, Your plan. However, there are still those who are not heeding the watchman's call — those who are breaking the hearts of those who love them. Father God, thank You for Your example of love, mercy, grace, hope, even during judgment times. Help us to love like You. Loving God, we bring before You today those who are on a destructive path. Place those watchmen in their lives who will not cease to call out the warning. And we pray, that they will recognize "For He is our God, and we are the people of His pasture, and the sheep of His hand. Today, if you hear His voice: "Do not harden your hearts, as in the rebellion." (Psalm 95:7-8) May we all remember "if My people who are called by My name will humble themselves, and pray and seek My face, and turn from their wicked ways, then I will hear from heaven, and will forgive their sin and heal their land." (2 Chronicles 7:14) We pray that Your redemption and Your healing become real in their lives. Amen.

November 8
Surprise us, Lord
Ephesians 3

"Now to Him who is able to do immeasurably more than all we ask
or imagine, according to His power that is at work within us."
(Ephesians 3:20 NIV)

"For who has known the mind of the Lord that he may instruct
Him?" (1 Corinthians 2:16) Sometimes when we pray, we seem to forget
this verse. Sometimes when we pray, we are "instructing" God on how to
answer a specific prayer. It is the only answer our human minds can figure
out that will "fix" or "solve" the problem. Perhaps we think we only need
"this," but God knows we may also need "that." We think this answer will
make us happy. However, God is aware of the true impact it will have on
our lives. In Ephesians 3:20, we read that He "is able to do immeasurably
more than all we ask or imagine." I don't know about you, but I would
like the immeasurably more. The more that brings more people to love.
The more that provides what we need AND what can be used to meet the
needs of others. The more increasing my knowledge of Him. The more that
has me standing in amazement of His goodness, love, and grace. The
more exhibiting His great power and purpose. I want the "immeasurably
more" of His purpose and plan to have its way in my life. Would you
agree? We make plans for our lives. We set and strive to attain goals. We
look at those in our group of family and friends and think this is all the
people I need in my life. What immeasurably more does God want to bring
to our lives? Not just as a blessing to us (although that is part of it), but as a
blessing to others - to accomplish immeasurably more for His kingdom? As
we pray for His kingdom to come, His will to be done, let us also pray
"Now to Him who is able to do immeasurably more than all we ask or
imagine, according to His power that is at work within us, to Him be glory
in the church and in Christ Jesus throughout all generations, for ever and
ever! Amen." (Ephesians 3:20-21 NIV)

*Father God, You are so good to us even at those times in our lives when it
may be hard to see. You are always at work within us and through us. You can
do more than we can ask or imagine in our lives. Help us to be those willing
vessels to accomplish Your plan and purpose for our lives even amidst our
uncertainties and fears. Open our eyes to see where You are already working.
"Your kingdom come. Your will be done on earth as in heaven." (Matthew 6:10)
Do immeasurably more than our limited minds can ask or imagine. You are the
Creator of this vast universe. You have all power. May Your glory be
revealed to us and through us. Amen.*

November 9
Appreciate those you do life with
1 Thessalonians 5

As we read through the New Testament, we find the apostle Paul ministering around the known world. We see him with faithful friends who help him along his journey. Friends that he worked with, ministered with, suffered with. With everything he went through, it is evident, from his writings, how much those relationships meant to Paul throughout his travels. God placed people in Paul's life to encourage him, strengthen him, protect him, and teach him.

When we first meet Saul/Paul, he appears to be a man that doesn't need much. He has respect, ambition, drive, a true sense of self. He has plans to try, almost single-handedly, to wipe out the new Christian religion. But God has other plans. After his conversion, Paul begins to learn the vital role fellow believers have in supporting one another on the Christian walk.

My friend, we need each other. Perhaps you feel like you can't do much for anyone. But maybe God has placed you in the life of someone to encourage, to pray for, and to offer a listening ear. Perhaps you have been let down one too many times by those around you. Maybe God is saying "open your eyes to see those who are trustworthy that I placed around you." When we are facing life storms, it is those who can stand with us and pray for us that helps carry us through those dark days.

Recognize the value you offer to those around you. Recognize the value others offer to your life. "So encourage each other and build each other up, just as you are already doing." (1 Thessalonians 5:11 NLT) God has created us as a family. Take care of your family and let them take care of you.

Father, thank You for those You place in our lives that encourage and support us, who pray for and with us, those that love us despite our faults and failures, those who show You in all they do. Father, may we too encourage and love on those You placed in our lives. Amen.

Maze of life
John 15

Do you ever feel like your life is like a maze? And you are never going to find your way out? Every turn you make seems to take you away from where you need to go? You find yourself going in circles? It appears you are just aimlessly wandering around? There may be times in our lives we find ourselves making bad decision after bad decision. Perhaps something takes on the appearance of what we need in our lives. Only we find out too late it was a choice that again leads us away from where we should be going. It could be that we feel like we have no clear direction for our lives, we don't know where we should be headed. Work dynamics or family dynamics have changed thereby leaving us in a maze of confusion as to what our next steps should be. At times, we may decide we just want to stay where we are because it has become familiar. Jesus is your answer and mine. He says "I am the vine, you are the branches. He who abides in Me, and I in him, bears much fruit; for without Me you can do nothing." (John 15:5) What does it mean to abide? We "stay" with Jesus and allow Him to "stay" with us. If we are in tune with the Creator of life, He will direct us in the ways we should go. Have you learned yet that without Him you can do nothing? When we become too self-sufficient, we often find ourselves even further in the maze of confusion. But what about those times when we don't sense any direction from Him? When we haven't heard from Him? There may be times when we are to wait. However, there may be times when we have already received the answer but haven't chosen to follow it yet. There may be times when God is still teaching/preparing us for the next steps. There may be times we are dealing with the consequences of choices we made. But even in those times, we hold on to His promises. "Trust in the Lord with all your heart, and lean not on your own understanding; in all your ways acknowledge Him, and He shall direct your paths." (Proverbs 3:5-6) Perhaps you know that you have walked away from His path for you and decided to follow your own. He still loves you. He is still there ready for you to seek His direction for your life again. He will accept you just as you are. Come abide with Him again.

Father, when the "maze" of our life has us going in circles filled with frustration and disappointment, we will choose to trust in You. We will choose to acknowledge You and seek Your direction for our lives. Forgive us when we choose to follow our own path. Light the way back to Your path for our lives. Thank You for loving us no matter how long it takes us to figure out that You are "the way, the truth, and the life. No one comes to the Father except through (You)." (John 14:6) Amen.

315

November 11
You are not an accident
Psalm 139

My friend, no matter how messed up your life is right now. No matter how many mistakes you have made. No matter how unlovable you feel. God wants you to know that you are not an accident. The Creator of the heavens and earth loves YOU with an unconditional, everlasting love. He sacrificed His one and only begotten Son for YOU. He wants to remind you that YOU are His. "How precious also are Your thoughts to me, O God! How great is the sum of them!" (Psalm 139:17) This verse is not only for David but for each of us. "I will praise You, for I am fearfully and wonderfully made." (Psalm 139:14) When we recognize that we are not here just by chance, when we recognize that we have a Maker, it gives us meaning and purpose.

Do you know that you are the apple of God's eye? Zechariah 2:8 says "for he who touches you touches the apple of His eye." My friend, God wants you to find your worth in His love for you. He knows no one is perfect. "There is none righteous, no, not one." (Romans 3:10) But He seeks a heart willing to submit to Him. Our sins separate us from God. But when we accept what Jesus did for us on the cross, when we tell Him we are sorry for those sins, that we want Him to have control of our lives, He will forgive us.

Isaiah 1:18 says "Come now, and let us reason together," says the Lord, "though your sins are like scarlet, they shall be as white as snow. Though they are red like crimson, they shall be as wool." God wants you to relinquish your mess to Him. You may be thinking "see I knew God wanted something from me." God doesn't withhold His love from you until you repent. "But God demonstrates His own love toward us, in that while we were still sinners, Christ died for us." (Romans 5:8) He loves you. There are not qualifications that you need to meet for you to receive that love. However, He wants you to do life His way for your benefit. "Come to Me, all you who labor and are heavy laden, and I will give you rest. Take My yoke upon you and learn from Me, for I am gentle and lowly in heart, and you will find rest for your souls. For My yoke is easy and My burden is light." (Matthew 11: 28-30) Are you seeking rest today? Are you seeking peace? Allow your Creator, your loving Father to love on you. Allow Him to guide you.

Loving Father, I pray for my friends today who are struggling to find Purpose to their life. For those who are trying to find a way out of the mess and chaos that surrounds them. Father, I pray that they recognize Your love for them today. I pray they will decide to lay that mess at Your feet and surrender their life to You. Help them find their worth in You today, O God.

November 12
Perfect Love
1 John 4

We are imperfect people. Therefore, we don't always love well. Sometimes we are too judgmental, too harsh, and too selfish. Sometimes we misunderstand. Sometimes we are easily angered. Sometimes we are vengeful. Sometimes we allow fear and doubt to cause us to believe lies. Sometimes we don't feel loved or loving. But in those relationships where there is true love, there is an understanding that we are loving and being loved by imperfect people, so forgiveness and grace should always be available.

Oh, if we could base every decision on our love for God and His love for us. If we would choose to see everyone around us through God's eyes, choose to love them as He does. But we can't, and we don't. Our thoughts and emotions often cloud our view. Our selfish nature demands more, to receive more than give. What about our love for ourselves? Do we allow others to define how we view ourselves? Or do we choose to see ourselves through God's eyes? We wish that we could love and be loved with the 1 Corinthians 13 love. Love that is longsuffering, that is kind, that is not selfish - perfect love. Only God can completely love like that. However, the closer we walk with Him, the more we will more naturally love like Him. "God is love, and he who abides in love abides in God, and God in him." (1 John 4:16) "We love Him because He first loved us." (v.19)

Take some time to reflect on how you are loving those around you, including yourself. Do you find yourself frustrated over the little things? Do you find that you are not quite as patient as you should be? Is it easier to see their imperfections than their strengths? Ask your Father to help you love as He does. Ask Him to open your eyes to see the blessing of the relationship instead of the problems. Pray for an understanding heart, one that is not quick to condemn but one that is patient and kind.

Father, in a world where "love" seems to be based more on conditions than dedication, teach us to love. Help us to recognize that we need to focus on how we are loving and not take it for granted. Remind us that love is not only about our current emotion but on a commitment. Right now, bring to our hearts those that we need to love better. Show us how they need us to love them. Amen.

He set me free
Acts 12

Do you ever think about the what-ifs or maybes of your life? The "if it had not been for God" situations? Do you recall the "prisons" or "chains" that had you enslaved? Do you recall that day when God set you free? In some situations, there may not be one specific day but a journey that you recall when you think about how God brought you through. How many of you feel like you are living in freedom today? Too often we seem to be freed from one thing, only to find ourselves bound by something else. Our enemy, the devil, is always seeking ways to entrap us. However, life itself, with all its ups and downs, can also create situations that leave us longing for freedom. For some of us, the prison doors may even be opened, but we are too afraid, too busy, too distracted, to notice. For others of us, we may be "banging" on the prison bars to be set free. In Acts 12, Peter did not realize he was being led out of the prison. He believed the angel was a vision. "So he went out and followed him, and did not know that what was done by the angel was real, but thought he was seeing a vision." (Acts 12:9) When Peter finally realized what was going on, he went to the house of Mary, John Mark's mother. The people were gathered there specifically to pray for him. However, they did not believe when the servant told them Peter was at the door. How often do we continue to act like we are still bound even when we have received our freedom?

If you are in a time in your life when you feel like you have not yet received your freedom perhaps from a home or work situation, a physical or mental health issue, an addiction, etc., please be encouraged that your ultimate freedom has already been won. These chains and prisons are only temporary (even though they may feel permanent.) Because of Christ's sacrifice on the cross, that freedom is guaranteed when we accept Him as our Savior and Lord. We can still live in this freedom even when our current circumstance seems to say otherwise. Jesus' love gift on the cross opened sin's prison door. We no longer have to be bound to our failures, our mistakes, our habits, our sins. We can allow Jesus to cleanse us from all unrighteousness. "If we confess our sins, He is faithful and just to forgive us our sins and to cleanse us from all unrighteousness." (1 John 1:9)

Father, thank You for our freedom! Lord, break every chain especially in those areas where we still feel bound. Open our eyes to see the freedom that we have been given. Guide us to our freedom in those areas where we see no way out. You are the Waymaker! Remind us that no matter the situation we can still experience Your freedom. Amen.

Inspired by "He set me free" by Bill and Gloria Gaither

What are you feeding your soul?
Isaiah 55

"Why do you spend money for what is not bread, and your wages for what does not satisfy? Listen carefully to Me and eat what is good, and let your soul delight itself in abundance." (Isaiah 55:2)

How many of you have promised yourself you would eat better? Old habits can be hard to break. But we should not give up trying. Our success or failure to hold to our goals often depends on what we are surrounding ourselves with. If we still go to the store and purchase sweets and soda/pop along with the veggies and water, we are most likely setting ourselves up to fail. If we still walk past our favorite bakery every day, we are probably setting ourselves up to fail. As important as it is to watch what we put into our physical bodies, it is more important to watch what we are putting into our heart and mind. If we are surrounding ourselves with a lot of negative – people, the news, unhealthy situations, we will find ourselves living with a negative mindset. But the opposite is also true. If we surround ourselves with positive people, things that make us happy, etc., we will find ourselves being able to see the positive side of life. The most important thing to watch is how you are feeding your relationship with God. If you only occasionally read your Bible, if you only occasionally remember to pray, then you will find yourself having a harder time hearing what God is saying to you. Your relationship with God needs to be the most important thing. God doesn't demand how often you read His Word or stop to talk with Him. Since He created us with a free will, He leaves the decision up to us on how close we want to walk with Him. But the more time You spend with Him, the more time you want to spend with Him. Perhaps it has been a while since you last spend some quality time with God. Perhaps you have made some big mistakes and are afraid He no longer wants to talk to you. Perhaps life priorities have shifted, and you have placed Him further down the list. My friend, it is never too late. It is never one too many times. He always pursues us. He is always ready to "pick up" where you left off. "Oh, taste and see that the Lord is good; blessed is the man who trusts in Him!" (Psalm 34:8) As you constantly seek ways to improve yourself, don't neglect your most important relationship. Make reading your Bible a priority. Make spending time with the Father a priority. If you do not already have a church home, find one. Find fellow believers who you can worship with, pray with, who encourage. *Father, may our relationship grow through the upcoming holiday season. May we learn more about Your love and mercy. May we seek Your will for our lives. Amen.*

November 15
Whosoever
John 8

"And the Spirit and the bride say, Come. And let him that heareth say,
Come. And let him that is athirst come. And whosoever will,
let him take the water of life freely." (Revelation 22:17 KJV)

You must be in church to find God. You must get cleaned up before you
become a Christian. You have messed up way too much to deserve God.
Those misconceptions exist in our world today. And unfortunately, we as
Christians have helped create them. When on earth, Jesus did not just hang
out at the temple. He went to where the people were. He didn't look at the
sinners and say, "get cleaned up and then we will talk," He just had dinner
with them. What most rocked the Pharisee's world about Jesus was that He
did not "play" by their religious rules. He didn't look down or condemn the
poor, the sick, the needy. Instead, He loved them. Instead, He made them
feel valued and worthy. Time after time in the New Testament, when we see
Jesus, He is with those forgotten, broken, and ashamed. We witness these
people who were ignored become amazed that Jesus would stop for them.
Blind men, tax collecting thieves, Samaritans, lepers, demon-possessed, and
the list goes on. People that society had written off as hopeless, Jesus came to
give them hope. People that felt unlovable He came to love. We today are not
any better than the Pharisees. We too deem those unworthy who have messed
up too much, who are broken, who are too different. If they can't clean
themselves up and come to church, then they don't deserve mercy and love.
However, it is not our mercy and love that we are to be showing; it's God's.
And those people are the exact people He came to save. "For the Son of Man
has come to seek and to save that which was lost." (Luke 19:10) Thank You,
Jesus! Because if we are honest, there are ways that we too live among the
helpless and hopeless. We may do a good job of covering it up, but we all
have things in our lives that we need to be saved from. "Hypocrite! First
remove the plank from your own eye, and then you will see clearly to remove
the speck from your brother's eye." (Matthew 7:5) Do you get that verse?
Sometimes our "issue" is bigger than those we look down on. If "whosoever"
have accepted Jesus as their Savior and Lord, then they are our brothers and
sisters. Whether they are the homeless laying on the park bench or the king in
his palace, whether they are in prisons or sing in the church choir, we are all
brothers and sisters in Christ. We will be spending eternity with the
whosoever. Let's not wait until then, let's start spending time with our family
now. *Father, how great is Your love, kindness, goodness. Father, help us to
love "the least of these." May we show Your love to those who need it most.*

320

November 16
Reading God's Word
Psalm 119

"How sweet are Your words to my taste, sweeter than honey
to my mouth!" (Psalm 119:103)

How many of you still get excited when it is time to open the Word of
God? How many would say confusion was more of your response? How
many have read it with desperation for answers or comfort? How many
have opened the Holy Bible almost with dread because you knew it would
bring light to some things hidden in the darkness? Each time we sit down
and partake of God's Word, we experience something different. "For the
word of God is alive and active. Sharper than any double-edged sword, it
penetrates even to dividing soul and spirit, joints and marrow; it judges the
thoughts and attitudes of the heart. Nothing in all creation is hidden from
God's sight. Everything is uncovered and laid bare before the eyes of Him
to whom we must give account." (Hebrews 4:12-13 NIV) God's Word
changes and challenges us. It encourages and confronts us. Isn't it amazing
that words written over 2000 years ago are still relevant today? Think about
how hopeless we would be without the promises in this Book. How
miserable we would be without God's Love Story. We don't just read God's
Word for ourselves. We read it for those we do life with. We read it so that
we can share with a lost and dying world. When God's Word becomes alive
and active in our personal lives, it impacts the way we live, love, and share.
For those who are confused by what the Bible says, ask God to reveal the
meaning. For those of you who feel like the Bible is outdated and irrelevant,
it holds the Truth we need today. For those of you who read daily, pass
those Precious Words on. "Therefore you shall lay up these words of mine
in your heart and in your soul, and bind them as a sign on your hand, and
they shall be as frontlets between your eyes. You shall teach them to your
children, speaking of them when you sit in your house, when you walk by
the way, when you lie down, and when you rise up. And you shall write
them on the doorposts of your house and on your gates." (Deuteronomy
11:18-20) God's Word needs to be a part of everything we do. God's Word
brings life, hope, promise.

*Almighty God, thank You for Your life-giving Word. "With my whole heart I
have sought You; oh, let me not wander from Your commandments! Your word I have
hidden in my heart, that I might not sin against You. Blessed are You, O Lord!
Teach me Your statutes. With my lips I have declared all the judgments of Your
mouth. I have rejoiced in the way of Your testimonies, as much as in all riches. I
will mediate on Your precepts, and contemplate Your ways. I will delight
myself in Your statutes; I will not forget Your word." (Psalm 119:10-16)*

November 17
Be strong and of good courage
Joshua 1

"Have I not commanded you? Be strong and of good courage; do
not be afraid, nor be dismayed, for the Lord your God
is with you wherever you go." (Joshua 1:9)

It's a verse we like to quote but listen to the words. "Have I not
commanded you?" "Be strong and of good courage" "Do not be afraid"
"Nor be dismayed" "For the Lord Your God is with you wherever you go"
Does that verse convict anyone else? How often are we afraid or dismayed?
With so much going on in our own lives, with so much going on in the world
around us, it is easy to be afraid and dismayed. It is easy to want to give up.
But we are called to "be strong and of good courage." Often when we quote
this verse, these are the words we start with. However, the verse starts with
"Have I not commanded you?" People are afraid and dismayed today. They
feel helpless and hopeless. They want to know that there is more to life than
just what we can see. We, as God's hands and feet, need to show them what a
difference it makes when "the Lord your God is with you wherever you go."
That's why we need to be strong and of good courage. Why we should not be
afraid or dismayed. We know the end of the story. We know that we have a
Friend with us always - a Friend who is the Maker of the universe, the Great
I AM, the Almighty! "The Lord of Heaven's Armies has spoken— who can
change his plans? When his hand is raised, who can stop him?" (Isaiah 14:27
NLT) Sometimes we get so caught up with the here and now that we forget
this is only a moment in God's time. We assume what we can see for the
foreseeable future is all there is. But my friend, God is working in hearts and
minds all around the world. He is working to fulfill His plans. "The Lord is
not slack concerning His promise, as some count slackness, but is
longsuffering toward us, not willing that any should perish but that all should
come to repentance." (2 Peter 3:9) Yes, life can be scary - when you are
awaiting test results, are suddenly facing life alone, don't know where the
next meal is coming from. But "do not be dismayed for the Lord your God is
with you wherever you go." Our human hearts and mind have a hard time
with that. Because sometimes we just want to allow ourselves to be dismayed
and afraid. The problem is when that becomes our only reality; we take God
out of the equation so to speak. But the reality is that we have a Father who
loves us. We have a Father who spoke this very world into being. We have a
Father who is active in our lives. We have a Father that can calm a storm,
defeat a giant, shut the lion's mouths, part the sea, deliver from fire, and
praise God Almighty so much more! So, when you find yourself afraid and
dismayed, pray for strength and courage for "the Lord your God is with you."

November 18
Try Me and see
Malachi 3

"Bring the whole tithe into the storehouse, that there may be food in my house. Test me in this," says the Lord Almighty, "and see if I will not throw open the floodgates of heaven and pour out so much blessing that there will not be room enough to store it." (Malachi 3:10 NIV)

How often do we give God only a certain portion of our time, talents, resources? We seem to say "God, here's Your hour for this week" as we head into the church building. "Lord, I'll commit to this one act of service occasionally." "God, here is what I can afford to give you this week." Do you recognize any of those thought patterns? God is not asking us to quit our jobs, sell our houses and move into the church. He is not asking us to give Him every cent we have thereby leaving our family out in the street and hungry. He is not saying that we must spend all our free time in some service for Him. What God is asking is that we give Him what He asks for. If He asks you to give that $20 in your pocket to the homeless man on the street, He will bless you. If He lays on your heart to start serving at a mission center once a month, He will bless you. If He ask you to go into full time ministry, He will bless you. Sometimes we are "afraid" to try because we are afraid God will ask "too much" of us. He may ask us to do something we don't want or feel too unequip to do. He may ask us to shift our priorities. (Which is often the case.) When we commit to doing what He asks us to do, then we can watch how He blesses in ways we don't expect. We can trust Him to provide and guide in all that He asks. God knows our reasons for not bringing the "whole" - time, talent, resources. We don't have the time or energy. We have other things we would like to accomplish before we "settle down" to doing things God's way. We don't trust "ourselves" to not fail, to not quit, to not mess up. God wants us to step out on faith and trust Him. "And try Me now in this," says the Lord of hosts, "If I will not open for you the windows of heaven and pour out for you such a blessing that there will not be room enough to receive it." (NKJV) Did you catch the reasoning for bringing the whole? "That there may be food in my house." God wants us taking care of each other. He wants us loving on one another. He wants us to be His witnesses to the lost. It takes us working together – combining our time, our talents, our resources for His Kingdom purposes. He wants to use us to bless other people, He wants to use other people to bless us. God knows what He is doing - He made the whole universe out of nothing. Trust that He knows what He is doing with your life too.

Lord, You are trustworthy and good! Amen.

November 19
Who but God?
Job 38

Do you ever think we have gotten "too smart" for our own good? We live in a society where we can easily communicate with people all around the world. We send satellites into deep space to try to learn all the secrets of the universe. We dive into the depths of the oceans to discover its hidden treasures. We are finding ways to manipulate and fabricate to bring improvements to our own bodies. We have adopted the "If I think it, thereby it must be true" mantra. We ignore God's Truth to replace it with our own. "Every way of a man is right in his own eyes." (Proverbs 21:2) We have become gods in our own eyes. Sometimes we, and the world around us, need to be reminded that we are nothing without God. "When I consider Your heavens, the work of Your fingers, the moon and the stars, which You have obtained, what is man that You are mindful of him, and the son of man that You visit him?" (Psalm 8:3-4) God has given men and women the wisdom to create modern technology - medical, communication, transportation advancements, all of which have improved our standards of living today. But somewhere along the way, we have taken God out of the picture. Somewhere along the way, we have lost sight of our Creator, our Ever-Present Father. Somewhere along the way, we decided we no longer needed Him. When we read Job 38 - 41, we are reminded just how small we truly are. Yes, there are so many things that we can do now that was not thought possible a hundred years ago or even twenty. But when we stop to realize that it is His air that gives breath to our bodies. It is His designs that enable us to live on this earth. When we realize there is so much more He is doing than we can even think or imagine. Then we can see how tiny we really are in God's vast world. But as tiny as we are, we are still precious in His sight. He knows each of us by name. We are here by His design. He has a plan for our lives. He has given us the free will to choose whether we will follow His plan or "do what is right in our own eyes." As we reap the benefits of today's society, let's not forget to acknowledge and thank our Creator Father who makes all things possible.

Father, we are nothing without You. Our wisdom and strength are limited. But Yours is not. May we always remember, "Among the gods there is none like You, O Lord; nor are there any works like Your works. All nations whom You have made shall come and worship before You, O Lord, and shall glorify Your name. For You are great, and do wondrous things; You alone are God." (Psalm 86:8-10) Amen.

November 20
God knows
John 14

When we face troubles in our lives, we may feel even worse when we feel like no one else understands, no one cares, no one is there to lean on. We may receive unwanted and unhelpful advice. We may receive judgment instead of kindness. We may just want to scream, "you don't know how I feel, you don't know the whole situation, you just don't know!" We may feel alone in the world. We may feel condemned by the world. We may feel lost and afraid. But my friend, God knows. God knows everything about you. God knows how you truly feel. God knows what you have experienced. God knows the hurt, the shame, the pain. God knows your heart. He knows your deepest desires. Even our closest friends may not be able to fully understand what we are going through. They too may offer well-meaning, but hurtful advice. They may try to understand but you know they never will. But my friend, God knows. God knows exactly what we need. Have you ever had someone call or show up at your door when you felt most alone and afraid? Have you ever read or heard something that was what you needed most to be spoken into your life? God knows. "For your Father knows the things you have need of before you ask Him." (Matthew 6:8) God knows you. He knows your past, your present, your future. He knows your successes and your failures. He knows your motivations and your hidden secrets. He knows your hopes and dreams and your deepest fears. He knows your name. He knows the number of hairs on your head. He knew you before you were born. He knows you. So, when you feel like no one understands you, no one cares, no one is there, remember He knows.

Father, thank You for being Someone we can turn to in any situation. Someone who does not misunderstands us. Someone who can hear our heart even when we can't speak the words. Someone who cares. Someone who can supply everything we need. Thank You for being Someone who is always there. Amen.

Living in the "New Me"
2 Corinthians 5

"Therefore, if anyone is in Christ, he is a new creation; old things have passed away; behold, all things have become new." (2 Corinthians 5:17)

When we first get saved, (and sometimes even after we have been a Christian for 20 years), one of the things we often struggle with is our old habits and thought patterns. We go around acting like we are still bound in chains even after we have been set free. We feel bound to our mistakes, our sins, our past, our old identity. We cannot seem to reconcile the "old" us with the redeemed us. Our human minds cannot grasp "As far as the east is from the west, so far has He removed our transgressions from us." (Psalm 103:12) We carry the guilt and shame a lot longer than we must. We feel like we are worthless and have nothing to offer. We just don't understand how the Almighty God can love someone like us, how He has a plan and a purpose for us. But a look at the cross reminds us. It reminds us that Jesus suffered and died in our place. He died so we can be clean. Our past, our sin habit, our failures will be cast "into the depths of the sea." (Micah 7:19) God knows what a sinner we are. He knows how much we fail. Yet, Christ came to die for us, even knowing our condition, so that we can be reconciled back to God. When we repent from our sins and accept Jesus into our hearts, we can be clean. The good news is that He doesn't just clean us up. He doesn't just cover our sins with the blood of Christ. He is with us to help us overcome, so that habit, that addiction can be defeated. He can teach us who we are in Him. We no longer have to live as if we are worthless but as children of the King. Sometimes it is a miraculous transformation where we no longer desire the things of our past. Sometimes it is a process as God loves and teaches us through the ups and downs. Sometimes we fall back into those old habits, but God is there to gently remind us, we no longer need to stay there. God is patient. He understands us better than we do ourselves. He doesn't give up on us as we learn more about His grace and mercy, more about His power. My friend, accept the "new" you, the one forgiven and clean, the one adored by the Father, the one who does not have to allow your failures and mistakes to define you. God loves you. God does not add anything to that statement – such as when you are perfect, when you are loving, when you are doing what you are supposed to. He loves you. Ask Him each day to help you live free.

Father, You are our Potter. You can take the mess our lives are in and make something beautiful from it. And even in those times, when we forget that You are still working on us and we still feel like a lump of clay, remind us that we are precious in Your sight. And that we are children of the King of kings.

Mercy
Isaiah 59

Thank God for His mercy. Do you ever stop to think about where you would be if it were not for God's mercy? Would your sin account be so high, you could never repay? All of ours would. Would you be lost and afraid? All of us would. There would be no hope. There would be nowhere to turn. If we were all to face God's judgment without His mercy, the verdict would be guilty. When we think about God, we like to think about how much He loves everyone. And He does. However, that seems to be all people want to hear about God. We no longer want to discuss His holiness and righteousness. We don't want to discuss His judgment. But sin separates us from God. "But your iniquities have separated you from your God; and your sins have hidden His face from you." (Isaiah 59:1-2) Think about all those lost in the Genesis 7 Flood, those lost in Sodom and Gomorrah. God loved those people. His call for righteousness had been rejected, and He sent His judgment. Proverbs 6:16-19 states "These six things the Lord hates, yes, seven are an abomination to Him: a proud look, a lying tongue, hands that shed innocent blood, a heart that devises wicked plans, feet that are swift in running to evil, a false witness who speaks lies, and one who sows discord among brethren." Just from this list, we would all be condemned. But for Mercy. The first verse of Isaiah 59 says: "Behold, the Lord's hand is not shortened, that it cannot save; nor His ear heavy, that it cannot hear." There is no one too guilty that God cannot save. But we cannot, and should not, think for one moment that because God loves us, He won't bring judgment on us. There will be a Judgment Day for all of us. One that we have no defense for. But for Mercy. "For God so loved the world that He gave His only begotten Son, that whoever believes in Him should not perish but have everlasting life." (John 3:16) Because of God's great mercy, He sent His Son to pay the price. And for those who believe in Him, who accept that precious gift, when we stand before God, we stand there with Jesus, our Defender, our Redeemer, God's Mercy. My friend, don't just rely on God's love getting you into Heaven. You must be willing to accept Jesus as your Savior and Lord. You need to confess and turn away from your sins. "If we confess our sins, He is faithful and just to forgive us our sins and to cleanse us from all unrighteousness." (1 John 1:9) That's mercy, my friend. *Father, thank You for Your love and Your mercy. Thank You that one day the evil and hatred in this world will be destroyed. Thank You that You have made a way that our sins may be forgiven and we can be found among those who are counted worthy, not by anything we have done, but because of Jesus' sacrifice, to make Heaven our home.*

November 23
Under construction
2 Corinthians 12

"Being confident of this very thing, that He who has begun a good work in you will complete it until the day of Jesus Christ." (Philippians 1:6)

Sometimes I forget that I am still "under construction." I have lived long enough, have had enough experiences, that I should not mess up, I should not fall, I should not fail. But I do. Yes, there are areas where I feel like I have it somewhat together, but then there are other areas I just can't seem to figure out, or something new comes along that I need to learn to navigate. I'm just unfinished. Do you have your own "under construction" sign? Those areas where you just can't seem to get it right? Those areas where you feel like you are constantly failing? We are a people that do not like to fail. We are a people that like to think we have it all together. But we don't and we won't until we are no longer a part of this world. We need to wear our "under construction" signs proudly. Because by admitting we can't do life alone is exactly where we should be. We need a Savior, we need a Guide, we need a Provider, we need Help. Paul says, "And He (Jesus) said to me, "My grace is sufficient for you, for My strength is made perfect in weakness." Therefore most gladly I will rather boast in my infirmities, that the power of Christ may rest upon me. I take pleasure in infirmities, in reproaches, in needs, in persecutions, in distresses, for Christ's sake. For when I am weak, then I am strong."
(2 Corinthians 12: 9-10) We need to admit that we need God. Instead of going through life wishing we had it "all together," we should be thankful to admit that we need God. We should be thankful that we don't have to have all the answers. We should be thankful that we are not expected to never make a mistake. We should be thankful that God understands everything about us. We should be thankful that we have a loving God "who is able to do exceedingly abundantly above all that we ask or think, according to the power that WORKS IN US." (Ephesians 3:20) We don't have to do life alone; God is there with us every step of the way.

Father, I am so thankful that I don't have to figure everything out on my own. I am so thankful that You are there to guide, provide, love. I am thankful that You are there to pick me back up. Father, thank You for never leaving my side. You are in the deserts of my life, in the valleys, on the mountaintops. Thank You that when I am weak, then I am strong through Your power in me. Use me for Your kingdom purposes. Amen.

November 24
Thanking God amidst the chaos
Psalm 107

As we are just days away from celebrating Thanksgiving, we sometimes get so wrapped up in preparing for the day that we miss the reason we celebrate. We seem to fret about travel plans. How will the traffic be? Will there be any delays? We scrabble to clean the house and prepare to host family and friends. We plan out the menu and decide who brings what. We have to "fight" other shoppers for the best-looking turkey or ham. We are anxious about how our favorite football team will do. And somewhere in the mix is a quick prayer before we eat. Sound familiar? As we spend time this week getting ready for Thanksgiving, we don't have to wait until Thursday to spend time giving thanks. As we prepare for the holiday, we can thank God for all the "chaos." We can be thankful for those we have in our lives to celebrate with. We can thank Him for the resources He has provided to meet our needs. We can thank Him for the memories we share, the laughter, the traditions, the love. But perhaps this has been a chaotic year that it is hard to be thankful for. Perhaps it has been a year of separation and loss. Perhaps a year where the resources have been thin. A year where too much pain and heartache make it hard to look up. My friend, God is still there every step of your way. He is providing the strength to make it through each day. He is offering hope for a Day when the cares of this life will all fade away. He loves you with an everlasting love. Thank God that we don't have to face the tough days alone.

Lord God, thank You for "every good and every perfect gift." (James 1:17) Too often we don't take the time to discover and appreciate those gifts. Thank You for your understanding and loving patience. Thank You for being a constant Light when darkness seems to surround. Thanks for being our Hope and our Future. We give thanks with a grateful heart. Amen.

Thank You letter to Jesus
Colossians 3

"Let the message about Christ, in all its richness, fill your lives. Teach and counsel each other with all the wisdom He gives. Sing psalms and hymns and spiritual songs to God with thankful hearts. And whatever you do or say, do it as a representative of the Lord Jesus, giving thanks through Him to God the Father." (Colossians 3:16-17 NLT)

Lord Jesus, how can I ever begin to thank You for all You have done for me? For who You are in my life?

My Light - You are there no matter how dark it seems to be.

My Rock - I can stand on Your promises and truth when everything else seems unreliable and fragile.

My Hope - I know the best is yet to come.

My Friend - I am never alone.

My Peace - When chaos surrounds, I can "be still and know."

My Joy - When life gets too heavy, You are still my unspeakable joy.

My Comfort - When my heart is breaking, You wrap me in Your loving arms and wipe away my tears.

My Protector - I am never out of Your hand.

My Provider - You meet my every need.

My Defender - You fight for me.

My Righteousness - Because of Your gift on the cross, I don't have to try to be perfect.

My Redeemer - You set me free from the bondage of sin and death!

My King - I live to serve only You.

My Love - You love me unconditionally even when I don't deserve it.

You give me life, every breath I take.

You give me a song that the world can't take away.

You have blessed me beyond measure.

Where would I be without You? Lost. Wandering aimlessly around. Living a life without purpose and meaning. Struggling to distinguish truth from the lies. Trying to figure out who I am.

But through You, I have been forgiven! I know who I am, I am Yours. I know I am here for Your purpose and Your glory. I can rest in Your love. Thank You, My Savior and Lord, Jesus Christ.

Thanksgiving
Romans 5

"But God demonstrated His own love toward us, in that while we were
still sinners, Christ died for us." (Romans 5:8)

As we come together to prepare and consume Thanksgiving dinner, we
like to reminisce. And because we are family, we love to bring up those
"remember when you did that" memories: those mistakes, those times of
disobedience, those times mom or dad "don't" know about. Most of the
time it brings laughter, but at times it may bring regret. We often wish we
could go back and undo some of those mistakes. But let's face it, we still
make mistakes. Ten or twenty years from now, our current mistakes may
be the memories flowing around the dinner table. How many of us wish we
could be perfect? Never sin again? Make no mistakes? Get it right every
time? We are human and unequipped to do so. Thank God, He recognizes
that "there is none righteous, no, not one." (Romans 3:10) That's the
reason He had to come. "For when we were still without strength, in due
time Christ died for the ungodly." (Romans 5:6) We can't save ourselves.
We can't clean ourselves up. We can't rewind and undo when we mess
up. But thank God we have a Savior! "That if you confess with your mouth
the Lord Jesus and believe in your heart that God has raised Him from the
dead, you will be saved. For with the heart one believes unto righteousness,
and with the mouth confession is made unto salvation. For the Scripture
says, "Whoever believes on Him will not be put to shame." For there is no
distinction between Jew and Greek, for the same Lord over all is rich to all
who call upon Him. For "whoever calls on the name of the Lord shall be
saved." (Romans 10:9-13) When we lay our "filthy rags" of unrighteousness
at His feet. When we recognize that we can do nothing on our own. When
we "confess our sins, He is faithful and just to forgive us our sins and to
cleanse us from all unrighteousness." (1 John 1:9) When we experience His
forgiveness and grace. When we recognize that "as far as the east is from
the west, so far has He removed our transgressions from us."
(Psalm 103:12) Then we experience the greatest reason for Thanksgiving.

*Father, we give thanks for a Savior that paid the death price, not only
for us but for everyone. We give thanks "For He made Him who knew no
sin to be sin for us, that we might become the righteousness of God in
Him." (2 Corinthian 5:21) Because of Jesus, we can be reconciled back to
You. We give thanks that our sins are gone. We give thanks that You are
with us all the time. We give thanks that we have a promised eternal Home
with You. Amen.*

See you later
John 11

During the holidays, we find so much to be thankful for and to celebrate, especially to be with family and friends. But it often turns bittersweet when it is time to say goodbye. The holidays may be the only time when all the family is together. And when it is time to go, we realize that it may be a while before we are all together again. Don't you wish that life allowed more time to connect with family and friends on a regular basis? Where schedules aligned and distance was not a factor? Our precious time together seems to go by too quickly and we are soon parting with a hug and a "see you later." The holidays also bring a remembrance of those no longer around the table — those who are waiting for us on the other side. As we look around the table, we may realize that there may be even more missing faces the next time we are all together. But there will be a Day when there will be no more goodbyes or see you laters. We will be reunited with those who have gone on before. We can sit down with our family and friends for all eternity. That final reunion day is for all those who know Jesus as their Savior and Lord. Will you be at that Reunion? Do your family and friends have the confidence that when it is time to say goodbye, they can say "see you on the other side?" My friend, please accept Jesus' gift of salvation. Repent of your sins. Acknowledge Jesus as your Savior and Lord. So that you can have the assurance that Heaven will be your home. And your goodbyes will be just "see you later."

Father, thank You for the Resurrection. Thank You for our family and friends. Thank You that someday we will have all eternity to be with those who know You as their Savior and Lord. Father, as I think about the Reunion Day and those in my life right now who have not yet made their "calling and election sure." (2 Peter 1:10 NIV) I pray that before the next time we are all gathered at the table together again, they will have accepted Your forgiveness, grace, and mercy. Amen.

Scars
Isaiah 53

We all have scars. Either physically, emotionally, spiritually. Some we wear proudly. Others we hide in shame. Some represent victory while others defeat. Some were self-made, while others are the evidence of how we have been wronged. Scars linger. They may not be as raw and tender as they once were, but they are still there as a reminder. How have your scars impacted your life? Do you live in fear and hurt from the scars you sustained? Is it hard for you to be open to those around you? Do you feel unworthy and unlovable because of the cause of the scars? My friend, may I offer some hope? "Surely He has borne our griefs and carried our sorrows; yet we esteemed Him stricken, smitten by God, and afflicted. But He was wounded for our transgressions, He was bruised for our iniquities; the chastisement for our peace was upon Him, and by His stripes we are healed." (Isaiah 53:4-5) The NLT reads "Yet it was our weaknesses He carried; it was our sorrows that weighed Him down. And we thought His troubles were a punishment from God, a punishment for His own sins! But He was pierced for our rebellion, crushed for our sins. He was beaten so we could be whole. He was whipped so we could be healed." In what ways do you need healing? In what ways do you need to be made whole? My friend, it a journey that starts out with a "Help me, Jesus." Jesus understands suffering. Jesus understands pain. Jesus understands rejection. Jesus understands. Isn't that all we need sometimes? Someone who truly understands what we are going through. Jesus knows. Jesus loves. Jesus is there. My friend, those healing journeys are usually long. Because Jesus is not satisfied with the surface scars, He wants all your scars. Those you have buried deep inside. Those you refuse to even look at. Those so painful they take your breath away. But He shines the Light of His Love into all those dark places and gently says "Look at My hands and feet, look at the stripes on My back. I endured it all to bring healing to you, to bring you peace." My friend, trust Him with your scars. He is the only One who can fully understand and heal.

Father God, I pray today for those who need Your healing touch. Who need to be reminded that You sent Your Only Begotten Son to die for them. Shine Your healing Light into their dark world. Teach them to trust You. Teach them that You are Faithful and True and that You will never leave them. Amen.

In His Hands
Hebrews 11

Why do we always assume our timing is God's timing? This hurtful thing is happening, remove it now. This inconvenient thing is happening, fix it now. This I don't want to deal with at all thing, so make it go away now. Resembles our prayer life a little, right? We never understand, nor appreciate, when we are going through something "bad." Things going on that we look to the heavens and think, "aren't you seeing this God, aren't You going to do something about it?" We know He loves us and we know He cares, so we assume that He will "swoop" in and make it right. We assume, if we can't see anything happening, that He isn't doing anything at all yet. We forget we are all in His hands. We assume He will fix it the way we want, when we want. We forget that there is a bigger purpose to life than just the here and now. It's not easy when life gets hard. We get discouraged, angry, afraid, hurt, that our loving Father seems not to care what we are going through. We may be so focused on the reason for our problems, that we miss out on what God is doing around us. How He is still providing. How He is still moving. How He is still right there. How we are never out of His hands. Kingdom purpose living recognizes that there is more going on than what we can see in our little part of the world. Kingdom purpose living recognizes that we are not here to live carefree lives. Kingdom purpose living recognizes others around us and acknowledge their struggles. Kingdom purpose living recognizes that our problems may be serving a purpose in God's timeline.

My friend, don't lose faith in the God that loves you when His answer to your prayers may be "No" or "Wait." He sees your pain and hurt. He understands your frustration and anger. He knows your disappointment when you don't get the answer you want now. If we could only see the bigger picture, to see the outcome, to see how our experience impacts the Kingdom purpose, then it may be easier to accept our current situation. But that's where faith comes in. We need to maintain faith that God will be with us. We need to maintain faith that our struggles may be serving a purpose. We need to have faith in God. Hebrews 11:1 says "Now faith is the substance of things hoped for, the evidence of things not seen." My friend, don't lose faith. Remember He is always there.

Father, we so long for our heavenly Home where there will be no more struggles and pain and heartache. But we are not Home yet. Thank You for being with us through everything we face. Thank You for not leaving us to face life alone. Open our eyes to the work You are doing around us. Your kingdom come, Your will be done. Amen.

November 30
Don't grow weary
Galatians 6

"And let us not grow weary while doing good, for in due season we shall reap if we do not lose heart." (Galatians 6:9)

As we approach the final month of the year, we may look back with discouragement as we realize not much has changed. We are still living the same routine with the same responsibilities and problems. We may regret that we did not get more marked off our to-do or bucket list. We did not make as much progress toward our goals as we wanted. We did not take more time to build up our relationships. Our bank account has not grown. We may be feeling under appreciated. Perhaps we had expected God to move in our situation by now. Sometimes it is easy to grow weary when we don't feel like we are ever going to reach our goals or when we are not receiving enough benefits or accolades along the way. Most often, if we would admit it, we grow weary when we take our eyes off God and look around at our circumstances and ourselves. When life becomes just about us, we lose focus of what God is doing around and through us. Yes, we can sometimes get weary when we are "working" for God. But again, if we take a close enough look, we will find that perhaps we took on more than He asked of us. There may still be areas where we are trying to do it both His way and ours. We are not fully listening to and waiting for Him. At times, we grow weary of being "good." Trying to do everything right. Trying to follow all the "rules." Trying to meet others' expectations. Perhaps we are weary of always being the giver without receiving much in return. We may grow weary of doing good. There always seems to be a need that requires our time, energy and resources. We often long just to spend all of that on ourselves. However, again the weariness grows most often when we take our eyes off God. We need to allow ourselves to take Sabbath rest. Because we can grow weary if we are always moving, always giving, always trying to be perfect. We need to lay aside all our responsibilities and obligations, our appointment book and to-do list and spend time resting with our Father. "The Lord is my Shepherd; I shall not want. He makes me to lie down in green pastures; He leads me beside still waters. He restores my soul." (Psalm 23:1-3) "We shall reap if we do not lose heart." (Galatians 6:9) When we are becoming discouraged, disappointed, frustrated, we need to place all that at God's feet. Allowing Him to restore hope, a renewed passion, and rest (physically, mentally, and spiritually).

Abba Father, we come to You with all the weariness that we are facing right now. Revive us, O Lord. Renew our minds. Restore our strength.

335

Unfailing Love
John 3:16

God, thank You that when life seems almost too much to bear, Your love is unfailing. Thank You that when we feel broken and ashamed, Your love is unfailing. Thank You that when we don't know what to do, Your love is unfailing. Thank You that when all hope seems lost, Your love is unfailing. Thank You, God, for a love that is not dependent on what we do nor on our circumstance. Your unfailing love is constant and reliable. Your amazing love knows exactly what we need. Your faithful love doesn't require us to earn it by doing everything right. Your beautiful love displays itself in so many ways.

"For God so loved the world." What beautiful words! God, no matter how many times we fail, Your love is still unfailing. You created us for Your unfailing love. You made a way for our salvation through Your unfailing love. You are with us every day because of Your unfailing love.

God, we feel so undeserving of that unfailing love, but You say we are. We fail in how we love You, but Your response is always with Your perfect love. Even when we can't see or feel Your love, You still love us with Your amazing love. You want everyone to learn and accept Your unfailing, sacrificial love. My heavenly Father, no one loves me like You do. No one understands me like You do. Thank You for the many ways I can see and feel Your love. But also for the many ways that I don't even realize You are loving me. Thank You for Your unfailing love. Amen.

Inspired by "Nobody loves me like You" by Chris Tomlin

December 2
Light my path
Psalm 119

"Your word is a lamp to my feet and a light to my path." (Psalm 119:105)

So often my path grows dark. I don't know what is around the next bend. I don't know exactly where the path leads. I sometimes stumble. I may not know which way to go. Sometimes I feel like I have lost my way. I don't like walking into the unknown. Sound familiar? Traveling the paths of our lives seems tricky. There doesn't seem to be enough signs to say, "go this way, don't go that way." There may be too many obstacles. There may be too many different paths to choose from. We are frustrated when we can only see a few feet in front of us. When we try to look too far ahead, all we see is darkness. Or we may like where we are currently at and decide to stay there. Those are only some of the reasons we need the light of God's truth, His Word to guide us. There may be times we feel we have this path figured out, that we know which way to go. We are confidently heading down our path, only to stumble and fall. Looking back, we realize it had been a while since we waited on God to light the way. It had been a while since we followed. We were so busy and so self-assured that this was the right path, this was the right way to go. We may have missed out on "stops" along the way. Those people who God may have wanted us to acknowledge and love. No matter where we are in our life's path, we need God to light the way. Psalm 37 says, "The Lord makes firm the steps of the one who delights in Him; though he may stumble, he will not fall, for the Lord upholds him with His hand." (v 23-24 NIV) We need God every day of our lives not just during the bad days or the uncertain days. We need the light of His Truth to guide us, to sustain us, to provide for us. If you are at a place where God's Word is not a lamp to your feet or a light to your path, come back to the Light. Come back to the place where you seek His face. Our paths are too uncertain and too filled with the enemy's snares, to rely on our own limited sight and knowledge. We need God to light the way. Jesus says, "I am the light of the world. He who follows Me shall not walk in darkness, but have the light of life" (John 8:12)

Father, we need Your Light every day of our lives. We need the Truth of Your Word every day. We need to follow You every day. "Let my cry come before You, O Lord; give me understanding according to Your Word! Let my plea come before You; deliver me according to Your Word. My lips will pour forth praise, for You teach me Your statutes. My tongue will sing of Your Word, for all Your commandments are right. Let Your hand be ready to help me, for I have chosen Your precepts. I long for Your salvation, O Lord, and Your law is my delight. Let my soul live and praise You, and let Your rules help me." (Psalm 119:169-175 ESV)

December 3
Honest prayers
Psalm 13

Do you ever have times when you don't know how to pray for certain people or circumstances? Do you know how you would like to pray but are unsure that is how you should pray? When, if you are honest, praying "thy will be done" is a little scary. Sometimes when we pray, we almost act like we are speaking to a genie who will grant all our wishes. At other times, we may approach God as if He is an angry father, so we don't want to ask for too much. Sometimes, we want our desired answer and refuse to acknowledge that may not be the answer that is God's will. When we read through the Psalms, we see David pouring out honest prayers to God. He doesn't follow a set format for prayer. He just cries out what is on his heart. "How long, O Lord? Will You forget me forever? How long will You hide Your face from me?" (Psalm 13:1) How many times is that the cry of our heart; especially, as we wait for our prayers to be answered? Sometimes we don't know how to pray because we don't know what the answer should be, right? Those prayers where there is an obvious solution are easier to pray. We know, or at least think we know, how the prayer should be answered. But those times, when we can't picture how the problem is going to be resolved, how the person will get out of the situation, those are the tough prayers. Those are the prayers where we can't offer our opinion or advice to God. Those are the prayers where we recognize there is more going on than we know. Those are the prayers where the work God wants to do is more important than the surface issues that are being faced. Those are the prayers where we get honest with God. But there is good news. "And the Holy Spirit helps us in our weakness. For example, we don't know what God wants us to pray for. But the Holy Spirit prays for us with groanings that cannot be expressed in words. And the Father who knows all hearts knows what the Spirit is saying, for the Spirit pleads for us believers in harmony with God's own will." (Romans 8:26-27 NLT) "For your Father knows the things you have need of before you ask Him." (Matthew 6:8) God wants our honest prayers, even those we have no words for. And He knows what we need. David ends Psalm 13 with this: "But I have trusted in Your mercy; my heart shall rejoice in Your salvation. I will sing to the Lord, because He has dealt bountifully with me." (v 5-6) He trusted God amid his questions, amid his frustrations, amid his fears. *Father, we bring our heavy hearts to You. We bring those prayers that we can't find the words, we can't find the hope, we can't find the peace, and we lay them at Your feet. We trust in Your mercy, Your goodness, Your love. We praise You that we don't have to carry them alone. Your kingdom come, Your will be done on earth as it is in heaven.*

You are my King
Psalm 24

In a world where it seems to be encouraged to choose a side, my loyalties are to my King.

When everyone wants to validate their own truth, my truth comes from my King.

When people are treated differently based on who they are, my view is directed by my King.

When things seem to be falling apart, I turn my eyes to my King.

When turmoil surrounds, my peace is from my King.

When circumstances seem desperate, my hope is in my King.

When there never seems to be enough, my provisions are made by my King.

When darkness tries to overshadow, my joy is in my King.

When the path is unclear, my direction comes from my King.

When sorrow abounds, my comfort is found in my King.

When I feel defeated, my victory is through my King.

When I am afraid, my assurance is my King.

When I feel alone, my King is there.

When I feel unlovable, I am loved by my King.

Lord God, I proudly acknowledge You as my King. You alone are worthy of all praise and devotion. You are All-Powerful, All-Loving, Everlasting. You are my Creator, my Redeemer, my Savior, my Provider, my King. I submit to You my King. I love You, my King. Amen.

Inspired by "That's My King" by Dr. S. M. Lockridge

December 5
Who are you?
Psalm 139

Do you ever feel like other people put identifying labels on you? They seem to make judgments about you from what they see. They make assumptions about who you are based on their own criteria. In their mind, you fit in this "box," and that is the only way they will ever see you. Perhaps it is based on how you look. Perhaps it is based on your past. Perhaps it is based on what you do or don't do. There may be family members or close friends who do a good job of understanding you. They can look past your mistakes, your "defense mechanisms," your imperfections to see you. However, you find yourself thinking that they still don't know the real you. They may still misunderstand your words or actions. You may still feel some judgment when you don't make the choices they think you should make. They may still offer too much advice and opinions on how to "fix" you. You may even have a distorted view of yourself. All you can see is your failures, your faults, the ways you don't "measure up." You look around thinking "everyone else seems to have this figured out, why can't I?" Sometimes, you don't even understand yourself.

Do you ever feel like no one sees the real you? My friend, God does. "Before I formed you in the womb I knew you." (Jeremiah 1:5) With God, you don't need to explain yourself. With God, you don't have to put on a "front." With God, you don't have to try to do everything right. With God, you don't have to try to earn His love. With God, you don't always have to pretend to be happy. "O Lord, You have searched me and known me. You know my sitting down and my rising up; You understand my thought afar off. You comprehend my path and my lying down, and are acquainted with all my ways." (Psalm 139:1-3) Thank God! If we could just sit in His presence without hiding behind our facades (even though we too often still try). If we could just take our honest thoughts and emotions and lay them at His feet. If we could allow Him to love us just as we are. Even those who have been Christians for a while still struggle with this. Why? Because we don't like to look that closely at ourselves. We don't want to admit just how weak we truly are. But when we recognize the reality, God made us; there is nothing hidden from His sight; His love is unconditional, all our reasons for still trying to hide become void.

Father, thank You for seeing (and still loving) the real us. The one we don't even fully understand. Remind us to look at ourselves and others the way You do. Amen.

December 6
I've been changed
Galatians 5

Like everything else, we learn more about God the more time we spend with Him. However, like any relationship, we experience different levels of closeness with Him. There may be times when we seem to be in a routine relationship with Him. Then there are other times when, based on experiences we face, we draw closer to Him. There may also be times when we seemingly lose ground. Our relationship with God requires our time, our energy, our focus. It requires us to invite God into every aspect of our lives. The more we do that, the more the relationship flourishes; the less we do that, the more we feel dissatisfied and alone. When we accept Jesus as our Savior and Lord, we are blessed to have our sins covered by the blood of Jesus. We are forgiven! We are no longer bound by those chains. We have been changed! We should continue to change throughout our relationship with God. As we draw closer to Him, our perspective and actions should become more like Him. No matter how long we have been a Christian, we are still changing. Our experiences change and we learn who God is to us in that stage of our lives. Changes may affect how we see ourselves and/or how we see others, but those changes will also impact how we see God. During times of change, times of learning, God may reveal another aspect of Himself, He may clarify more of who He is and how He works. Will we ever truly grasp "the love of Christ which passes all knowledge?" (Eph. 3:19) No, our human, finite minds will never fully comprehend why God chooses to move the way He does or how much He loves. Yet, we get different glimpses of Him as we go through life. And those glimpses bring opportunities for change. Life, with all its ups and downs, allows us to experience God's faithfulness, His love, His peace, in different ways. And the more we learn, the more we should want to be more like Him. The more we experience, the more we realize just how dependent we are on Him. The closer we are to Him, the more the fruit of the Spirit grows in our lives. "But the fruit of the Spirit is love, joy, peace, longsuffering, kindness, goodness, faithfulness, gentleness, self-control." (Gal. 5:22-23) We love differently. We respond to circumstances differently. Thank God, I've been changed! "If we live in the Spirit, let us also walk in the Spirit." (Galatians 5:25) I don't have to try to do life by myself. I don't have to try to figure it all out. I learn more along the way. "Not that I have already attained, or am already perfected; but I press on, that I may lay hold of that for which Christ Jesus has also laid hold of me." (Philippians 3:12) *Father, thank You for changing me. Thank You that You continue to teach me how to be more like You. I desire to love more like You, to see others as You do.*

341

You are God alone
Psalm 97

Where else could I go? The world seems to have different solutions for dealing with life. They hit the bottle or the drugs to make them forget or to "feel" better. Their actions are motivated by hate and anger as they seek, often destructive, ways to fix their problems. They use and misuse other people to get what they want. They make idols out of themselves or their "heroes." But in the end, most are still unsatisfied with the results. The problems are still there. The answers still seem unattainable. They still feel hopeless, alone, and afraid. If not for God, you and I would probably be in a similar situation. If not for our loving Father, you and I would wander aimlessly seeking direction and purpose. You and I would struggle to find something or someone to fill that deep loneliness. You and I would go around seeking advice from anyone willing to listen. You and I would grasp for something to grab hold of when we feel like we are drowning in life's fiercest storms. If not for God, we would be lost with no hope, no future, no peace. But thank God, He is who He says He is! "For You, Lord, are most high above all the earth; You are exalted far above all gods." (Psalm 97:9) We have a God who hears every prayer we utter and even knows those we don't. We have an Ever-Present God who is always with us who reassures us of His Presence. We have an All-Knowing God who knows what our tomorrows hold but who also holds our tomorrows. We have a God who can speak "Peace, be still" that will either calm the storms or calm His child. We have a Living All-Powerful God who can make a way when there seems to be no way. My friend, we serve the Almighty God! "Therefore know this day, and consider it in your heart, that the Lord Himself is God in heaven above and on the earth beneath; there is no other." (Deut. 4:39)

Our loving Father, we bow before You to thank You for being Faithful and True. Thank You for always being there when we call. Thank You for loving us even when we are in a place where we seem unworthy of that love. Thank You for that peace that passes understanding and for that unspeakable joy. Thank You for our promised future. Thank You for guiding our way. "Now to the King eternal, immortal, invisible, to God who alone is wise, be honor and glory forever and ever. Amen." (1 Timothy 1:17)

December 8
Go, follow
Ruth

Sometimes when we fall, we stay there longer than we should. We give many reasons why: it's too hard to get up, we don't deserve to get up, we will just fall again, we are afraid. We accept defeat. God never intends for us to stay down. He is there to help us to get back up. There is another place God never intends for us to stay. It is a place of complacency. Too often when we get in a good routine in life, we want to stay there. It feels safe and secure. It's a familiar place where there is no challenge, no risk, no unknowns. A place where we may not feel like we need to depend on God very much. We have things under control. How many people in the Bible changed the world for God by being complacent? Most of the Bible "heroes" received a "Go" or "Follow" command by God. God needed them to expand His kingdom here on earth. How often are we willing to change our plans for His? Again, we have reasons for staying where it is safe. We are too busy, too unequipped, too unworthy, or too afraid to Go or Follow when He calls. The Go or Follow path isn't easy. It isn't comfortable. It can be scary. For most of us, walking into the unknown and stepping outside of our comfort zones is unnatural. It requires a decision, a determination, a level of trust. When told to go back to her own homeland, Ruth responded to Naomi "For wherever you go, I will go." (Ruth 1:16) Ruth had a kingdom purpose to fulfill and could not do so by staying in her homeland. God does not always require us to leave our homeland. He does not always require us to do something "big." Sometimes it is just a mind shift, an attitude shift, an emotional shift that He requires. We have all received a Go command. The Great Commission in Matthew 28 says "Go therefore and make disciples of all the nations baptizing them in the name of the Father and of the Son and of the Holy Spirit teaching them to observe all things that I have commanded you." (vs 19-20) Your "nation" may be your neighborhood, your workplace, your shopping place. It may be your local rec center, your local bar, your local prison. It may be a mission trip halfway around the world. God has us working together to fulfill His kingdom purpose. He has us working together to spread His Good News. That is why we are here! We are created for a purpose. We are to live life beyond ourselves. The rest of Matthew 28:20 says "and lo, I am with you always, even to the end of the age." That's the promise we hold onto. *Father, when You tell us to Go or to Follow, thank You for equipping us for that calling, for being with us wherever You send us, for guiding and providing. Father, we desire to impact our world for You. May we Go where You send us. May we Follow where You lead. Amen.*

December 9
Broken places
Isaiah 53

"He heals the brokenhearted and binds up their wounds." (Psalm 147:3)

We all have them. Those places in our lives where we bear the scars of a time of brokenness in our lives. Some of those areas may have healed over nicely, while others are still very tender. Some are fresh. Some have been broken, and repaired, several times. Are you envisioning those places in your own life when you felt completely shattered? Are you in such a state right now? As we reflect on those broken areas in our lives, it may cause us to remember not only the situation but also the emotions: the fear, frustration, hurt, pain, sorrow. But as we reflect, can we see how God was there? Can we see how He provided strength, a level of healing, a hope? Do we recall how the following verses held true in our situation? "Fear not, for I am with you; be not dismayed, for I am your God. I will strengthen you, yes, I will help you, I will uphold you with My righteous right hand." (Isaiah 41:10) "And He said to me, "My grace is sufficient for you, for My strength is made perfect in weakness." Therefore most gladly I will rather boast in my infirmities, that the power of Christ may rest upon me." (2 Corinthians 12:9) We are not truly equipped to "fix" our brokenness. We may try to cover it up or make it "go away." We may try to pull out the "duct tape" and repair it ourselves. But in the end, we find ourselves still broken and weak. However, we can cry out for help. He doesn't wave a "magic wand" to make the brokenness go away, but He tenderly provides what His child needs throughout the healing process. He provides the strength, comfort, guidance, hope, peace and love. My friend, let me offer you Hope, whose name is Jesus. Jesus did not come into this world to die for just the "good" people. As you read through the Gospels, you will notice that Jesus spent most of His time with the broken. Those who needed healing, hope, and love. Read Isaiah 53, He went through all that for you. And did you catch verse 5? "But He was wounded for OUR transgressions, He was bruised for OUR iniquities; the chastisement for OUR peace was upon Him, and by His stripes WE are healed." Again, He does not provide that magic wand to make it all go away. However, He will be with you. He will not leave you when things get hard. He will not give up when you fall again. Allow yourself the opportunity to experience the love He already has for you. "God is our refuge and strength, a very present help in trouble." (Psalm 46:1) Cry out for His help today. *Father God, O how You love us! O how You want to be our help, our strength, our peace through life's brokenness. I come before You now for those who feel like their brokenness can never be healed. Help them to feel Your Presence. Amen.*

344

December 10
Who can stop the Lord Almighty?
Romans 8

"If God is for us, who can be against us?" (Romans 8:31)

Since the beginning of time, the enemy has tried to use anything and everything to stop God, to "dethrone" Him. Even when the devil thinks he is gaining ground and tries to impact the lives of God's people, he is still unable to stop the Lord Almighty. God is All-Knowing and All-Powerful. We cannot fathom His great love for us. And because of that great love, He is preparing an eternal Home where the problems of this world will be no more, a place where the enemy will never be able to enter. There will be a day when the devil is defeated once and for all. Throughout time, hate and evil seem to reign. But God's Word still stands. Testimonies of His love and mercy are still shared. When the evil one's lies try to destroy the Truth, God's Presence still brings hope and peace. Why? Because the devil has already been defeated, Jesus death, burial, and resurrection proved once and for all, He is the King of kings and Lord of lords. Knowing his future destination, our enemy wants to take as many people with him, away from God, as he can. Our human minds say, "just go ahead and destroy him, God." But God in His great wisdom, grace, and mercy is waiting. Why? 2 Peter 3:9 says, "The Lord is not slack concerning His promise, as some count slackness, but is longsuffering toward us, not willing that any should perish but that all should come to repentance." But as He is waiting, He is moving. As we read the Bible, we see the countless times God made a way when there seem to be no way. As we reflect on our lives, there are countless answered prayers, countless times His Presence comforted and calmed. In our most hopeless state, He's promises still brought hope. In the darkest of nights, the light of His love shone through. Our circumstances, attitudes, rebellion, cannot quench God's love for us. "Who shall separate us from the love of Christ? Shall tribulation, or distress, or persecution, or famine, or nakedness, or peril, or sword? . . . Yet in all these things we are more than conquerors through Him who loved us. For I am persuaded that neither death nor life, nor angels nor principalities nor powers, nor things present nor things to come, nor height nor depth, nor any other created thing, shall be able to separate us from the love of God which is in Christ Jesus our Lord." (Romans 8:35-39) The lies, the hate, the evil of the enemy cannot stop God from showing His love for us. They try to distract from the Truth of God's word, but God's promises still stand. Our limited view may at times prevent us from seeing and hearing the Truth, but the Spirit living within us rings out the declaration that our God reigns!

December 11
Everybody welcome
John 3:16

We all have places or people that make us feel unwelcome based on who we are, that make us feel like we don't measure up. Those places where we first need to "get it right" before we can enter. Those people we need to impress before we are accepted. Aren't you thankful that God is not like that? He wants us where we are. He wants us as we are. He does not expect us to get ourselves cleaned up and "fixed" before we approach His throne. He says "Come." We can come with our brokenness, pain, addiction, habits, "ugliness" because God loves us even through all that. God loves us when we don't know what to do. God loves us when we are too prideful to acknowledge we need Him. We cannot be too big of a mess that God doesn't want any part of us. We are adored by the Maker of the universe. We are held by the Hand that formed man out of dust. Our very breath is from the Giver of Life. He knows us. He knows our name. He knows our days. He knows how fragile we are. "For He knows our frame; He remembers that we are dust." (Psalm 103:14) And yet He loves us. The whosoever in John 3:16 includes you, it includes me. It includes everyone that has ever walked or will walk on this earth. We are all welcomed into His arms to find rest. "Come to Me, all you who labor and are heavy, and I will give you rest. Take My yoke upon you and learn from Me, for I am gentle and lowly in heart, and you will find rest for your souls. For My yoke is easy and My burden is light." (Matthew 11:28-29) Who in your life needs to be reminded of or has never heard that? My friend, maybe it is you who feels so out of place in your family, at work or school. Maybe you feel like you have fallen so hard that no one could love you, that no one wants you. God loves you. He wants you just as you are.

Father, You so loved this world that You sent Jesus, Your own Son, that everyone, the whosoever, that believes on Him would be saved and have everlasting life. We all need to be saved. Saved from our past, saved from our habits, saved from ourselves, saved from sin. And You are waiting with open arms for us to come home to You. Forgive those of us that are called by Your name when we hinder, instead of help, others to know Your unconditional love. Help us to do a better job of loving like You, to see others as You do. Amen. My friend, if you don't know God on a personal level, just begin a conversation with Him. You do not need to be on your knees or in a church building. Begin telling Him what is on your heart because He cares for you. Ask Him to show you and to teach you more about who He is. Allow Him to love you.

December 12
Be watchful
1, 2 and 3 John, Jude

We know we are on the winning side, so why in the last few books before Revelation (which addresses the end of times) are the authors repeatedly writing for us be watchful of deceivers? Satan tries to steal our joy, our truth, and our identities. When Satan successfully puts doubts in our minds, discontentment in our hearts, and distractions in our way, he can get our eyes off God and His truth. When we lose focus, Satan is ready to deceive us. Jesus tells Peter: "Simon, Simon! Indeed, Satan has asked for you, that he may sift you as wheat." (Luke 22:31) God's truth stays the same. His love and power stay the same. So why do we fall for the lies? The very same reason that Adam and Eve sinned so long ago. Satan is a deceiver. He twisted God's words, made them sound "sweeter," and offered something they thought was better. He hasn't had to change his tactics because they still work today. He is still deceiving. He distorts God's Word. He places "life would be better if . . ." thoughts. And he uses us against one another to make us jealous, make us angry, make us self-righteous. When Satan is able to weaken our faith, we become less of a threat to him. Jesus finished His message to Peter: "But I have prayed for you, that your faith should not fail." (Luke 22:32) Paul writes to the Ephesians: "till we all come to the unity of the faith and of the knowledge of the Son of God, to a perfect man, to the measure of the stature of the fullness of Christ; that we should no longer be children, tossed to and fro and carried about with every wind of doctrine, by the trickery of men, in the cunning craftiness of deceitful plotting, but speaking the truth in love, may grow up in all things into Him who is the head - Christ." (Ephesians 4:13-15) We cannot withstand Satan's lies alone. We must stand on God's Word and the truth we know about Him. We have the Holy Spirit inside us. He is there for a reason. He is a constant Companion. He is not to be kept in the background until the need arises. He is there to intercede for us. He is there to guide us. He recognizes the lies of the evil one. If you heed His voice, He will speak the Truth into your life. Our current relationship with God often factors into how easily we are deceived. If we have been in His Word consistently, we will recognize when Satan is trying to distort it. If we know who we are in Christ, we won't be pondering how our lives could be better, we are simply trusting God with our lives. Our relationship with God is one that we need to nurture. We need to spend time in His Word and His Presence. The closer we are to the Truth, the harder it will be to be deceived. *Father, as Jesus prayed for Peter, we pray that our faith will not fail. Open our ears and hearts to Your Truth.*

December 13
Just move
Exodus 14, Joshua 3

What Red Sea or Jordan River are you facing in your life? How long have you been on the riverbank? What are you waiting for? I often think about those Israelites who had to take the first steps into the Red Sea with a wall of water on each side. Or the priests that had to step into the rushing waters of the Jordan River. Even if you are a great swimmer and love the water, those experiences could be very frightening. Because if God failed or He did not keep His word, it would most certainly mean death. But after that first step, just imagine how your confidence in Him would grow with each new step. How long do we stay on the riverbanks in our lives? Are we like the Israelites at the Red Sea contemplating returning to Egypt? Are we like those standing at the Jordan River who may be deciding if it is worth it? How long before we decide to move? There had to be a first step. To step out in faith, you must come to the point where you decide if God is who He said He is and will do what He has promised to do. Unfortunately, we cannot bypass that first step of action on our part. Maybe it's your first step of salvation by admitting you are a sinner and need a Savior. Maybe it's your first step into committing to what God has called you to do. Maybe it's a call to completely come out of your Egypt and wholly surrender to Him. Whatever it is, you must move. Move out in faith, move out in hope, move out in trust. It is true that we like to be comfortable. We like to stay in the known. We may grumble and complain at our circumstance one moment but in the next, when asked to move, decide it's not so bad and stay.

At some point or even several times in your life, you will face your own Red Sea or Jordan River. What will you decide to do? Will you find the courage to take the first trust step, so you can witness what God wants to do in your life?

God, You are so faithful. Still, we doubt. Still, we fear. God, You want each of us to step out on faith into a place where we are uncomfortable, where we need to wholly rely on You. Into a place where we can experience Your power! Where we can experience all You intended for us. You are trustworthy! Grant us the courage to take that first faith step. Amen.

December 14
The important things
Luke 17

As the ten lepers call out to Jesus to have mercy on them, what do you think was going through their minds? We don't know how long they had been leprous. We don't know when the last time was they had seen their families. We don't know when they last talked with someone other than a fellow leper. We don't know to what degree leprosy had impacted their physical bodies. What we do know is they recognized they needed the Master's touch. All that Jesus tells them to do is: "Go, show yourselves to the priests." (Luke 17:14) This statement was usually made AFTER they were cured. There has been no healing yet.

The lepers could have stood there until the healing happened and then decide to go. However, they moved. They started out toward the priest with the faith that by the time they got there, they would be healed. Can you picture the moment the lepers realized they were healed? I imagine them running and leaping hurrying to the priest and their restored life. Perhaps as they journeyed, they began to talk about what they were going to do after they saw the priest. Hug their families, get a decent meal, sleep in a real bed. And perhaps as they approached the priest, it suddenly dawns on them; now there were only 9 of them. What became of the tenth? Do the others begin to wonder - was he not healed? Surely, he did not go ahead to see his family.

The lepers thought that the most important thing was to get to the priest. However, if they could have seen the tenth leper, they may have been reminded of the truly most important thing, time at the Healer's feet. The tenth leper returns to Jesus to thank Him for the healing. How often, we too, get so excited about what God is doing in our lives, that we forget to go back and spend some time at His feet thanking Him for all He has done. We get so wrapped up in our blessings; we forget the One who blesses.

Father, we cannot thank You enough for all You do for us: for all that You have done, are doing now, and for the day when all Your promises will be fulfilled. As we enjoy Your many blessings, as we share what You are doing in our lives, may we remember to come and sit at Your feet in thanksgiving. Amen!

December 15
Measure of time
Revelation 10

Our life seems to revolve around time. We are either wanting it to speed up or slow down. We wish we could jump forward or go back. Sometimes we would like for it just to stop. And all for different reasons. We feel the constraints of time in our home and work lives. We sometimes feel like we live from appointment to appointment. Time seems almost to dominate how we live our lives. We go on vacation to get away from time restraints all the while still living under them. (We are on vacation for only a week or two.) We look forward to days when our schedule is free, and we may get to sit on the porch and do nothing for a while but even recognizing then that we have limited time to do so.

But there will come a day when we live in eternity. There will be a day when "there should be time no longer." (Revelation 10:6 KJV) We will have eternity with our loved ones. We will have eternity to sit down and talk to the saints of old. We will have eternity to just worship our Savior without distractions and interruptions. We will have eternity of peace, joy, and love. We will have eternity to bow to God our Creator. We will have eternity to share our redemption story and listen to those from every tribe and every nation. We will have eternity without. We will have eternity without tears and sadness. We will have eternity without war and disease. How we long for eternity!

Lord God, You have promised an eternity in Heaven for those who have accepted Jesus as their Savior. An eternity where we walk on streets of gold. An eternity to sit at Your feet. An eternity to worship with everyone who made Heaven their Home. An eternity without tears, death, sorrow, crying or pain. (Revelation 21:4) Father, how we long for eternity! But until that day comes, help us to live our time here on earth for You. Amen.

December 16
Stand in grace, rejoice in hope
Romans 5

"We have peace with God through our Lord Jesus Christ, through
whom also we have access by faith into this grace in which we
stand, and rejoice in hope of the glory of God." (Romans 5:1-2)

We like when we know what to expect. However, we all face seasons of
change that leave us feeling uncertain of our steps. But thank God: "From
the end of the earth I will cry to You, when my heart is overwhelmed; lead
me to the Rock that is higher than I." (Psalm 61:2) When life feels like
sinking sand, "He only is my rock and my salvation; He is my defense; I
shall not be moved." (Psalm 62:6) When nothing else in life seems to be
making sense, we can stand on God. We can stand on the Truth of His
Word. We can stand on His Love. We can stand on His forgiveness
through the sacrifice of His Precious Son. We are His, and because of that
we now have the privilege of being called a child of God. And as a child of
the King, we receive His instruction, direction, protection, provision, and
promise of our eternal Home. Thereby giving us a reason to rejoice in hope.
We do not need to be "happy" to rejoice. Even when our life seems to be
falling apart, we can rejoice in hope. Since we recognize that this life is only
temporary, we can rejoice in the hope of our eternal life. When friends and
family forsake, we can rejoice in the everlasting love of our Father. When
circumstances arise that frustrates and worries, we can rejoice that our
Father in Heaven is right there with us. "We also glory in tribulations,
knowing that tribulations produces perseverance; and perseverance,
character; and character, hope. Now hope does not disappoint, because
the love of God has been poured out in our hearts by the Holy Spirit who
was given to us." (Romans 5:3-5) Thank God for Hope that does not
disappoint. When we place our hope in people and things of this earth, we
will be disappointed. When we hope that God will do things the way we
want, we will be disappointed. But when we trust Him to be who He says
He is and accomplish His will for our lives, we will not be disappointed.
"Now to Him who is able to do exceedingly abundantly above all that we
ask or think, according to the power that works in us, to Him be glory in
the church by Christ Jesus to all generations, forever and ever. Amen."
(Ephesians 3:20-21)

Thank You, Father, for being our Rock during life. Thank You that
"Jesus Christ is the same yesterday, today and forever." (Hebrews 13:8)
Thank You for Your faithfulness.

December 17

I Am Yours
Luke 10

During busy times in our lives, we find ourselves torn in many directions. We have obligations here, responsibilities there. There are people we need to spend more time with. Most of the time, determining our priorities for the day becomes a balancing act. With so many responsibilities and obligations, how can we please everyone who needs us? There is just not enough of our time and energy to go around. When faced with those times, it is helpful to remember we are God's. Since we are His, He has the right to prioritize our lives for His greater purpose. What does your day look like when You give Him control of it? He will make sure you are where you need to be. He will prompt you to reach out to those who need a word from Him. He will give you the time and energy to accomplish His plan. And when we don't relinquish our plans for His? We may miss opportunities to share His love. We become frustrated when we can't get everything done in our time frame. Life, too often, becomes more about us and not about others. Most of us can probably relate to Martha in Luke 10. We are "running" around trying to get everything done. How many of us tend to want to take Martha's "side?" All these people have shown up and someone has to feed them, make sure they are comfortable, etc. We, like Martha, learn from Jesus that "but seek first the kingdom of God and His righteousness, and all these things shall be added to you." (Matthew 6:33) He tells Martha "Martha, Martha, you are worried and troubled about many things. But one thing is needed, and Mary has chosen that good part, which will not be taken away from her." (Luke 10:41-42) How many of us need to hear the part "you are worried and troubled about many things, but one thing is needed?" Most of us would probably have to admit to being worried and troubled about many things. But we should realize that one thing is needed - our time spent with God! We need to recognize that everything we have - our time, our agenda, our resources, is His. If every day we acknowledge that, if we allow Him to be in control of it all, then we don't need to be worried and troubled about many things. *Lord, thank You for Your Word. Thank You for the reminder that You are the one thing that is needed. When our schedules become too demanding, when we are spread too thin, when we are exhausted both physically and mentally, when the work never seems to get done, may we remember that You are first. Time with You should be our priority for the day. Our agenda should coincide with Your plan and purpose for our day. When we are worried and troubled about many things, may we remember to come and rest at Your feet. May we always seek Your kingdom first. Amen.*

December 18
Be who you were created to be
Luke 1

Mary probably thought she had her life figured out. She was engaged to Joseph. They would be married and live happily ever after. But then the announcement came. "Rejoice, highly favored one, the Lord is with you; blessed are you among women." (Luke 1:28) And her life would never be the same. At this time of year, the pressure is on to find just the right present, host the perfect Christmas party, have the perfect tree. It seems like we are always living our lives trying to measure up. We look around thinking "why does everyone else seem to have it together?" We compare ourselves in almost every area of life: how we dress, how much do we make, how we raise our kids. We may even change our beliefs, values, traditions to try to better fit in with the crowd. Are we ever content just being ourselves? Imagine if Mary had, upon hearing the announcement, looked around and thought that "Rachel" was more religious than she was. Or that "Martha" would make a better mother. Or that the other "Mary's" family had more resources. Mary accepted the call on her life because she recognized that this was the purpose God had designed for her. We often envision a very humble, submissive Mary and she was. However, we may miss out on some of Mary's other qualities. Mary was a strong, determined young lady. She did not seek counsel from others when the angel appeared. She did not respond, "let me pray about it." She didn't say "wait until I go ask my father, mother and Joseph." She answered the call for herself. God made you, you. If we live life always trying to measure up to someone else's life or their expectations, we may be missing out on what God wants to do in our lives. The unique you can be used by God in ways that He may not be able to use me and vice versa. Our stories and personalities are different. Our field of influence is different. If we are discontent with our lives because we are always viewing ourselves as not measuring up, we may miss out on what God designed us to be. God may not have designed us to change the world. But He did design us to change our world. "Go therefore and make disciples of all the nations, baptizing them in the name of the Father and of the Son and of the Holy Spirit, teaching them to observe all things that I have commanded you; and lo, I am with you always, even to the end of the age." (Matthew 28:19-20) Instead of looking around to see how we are measuring up, perhaps we should be looking up. Our Creator, our Father, knows better than anyone else who we should be. So instead of setting unrealistic expectations and wishing we could be someone else, let's allow God to convey our worth, purpose, hope. Read His words for yourself. And then pass the message on. *Father, may we choose to live life as You designed.*

December 19
Trusting God's timing
Matthew 2

Would they ever see their friends and family again? Would they ever get to live as a family in the home that Joseph had gotten ready for them? Their required trip into Bethlehem had taken an unexpected turn. The Babe was born and even after it was safe to travel again, they felt compelled to stay. Which of their friends are married now with children of their own? Who may have gone on to be with the Maker? Even after the arrival of the Wise Men, Mary and Joseph still found they were unable to return home, instead found themselves going even further away. Can you imagine the thoughts going through Joseph's mind as he waited for the next steps to be revealed? He understood that life would never be the same now that the Messiah had arrived. However, he was still unsure of how to navigate raising the Christ Child. One thing he did know was that he needed to wait on His Father, the Child's Father, to guide him along the way. We too find ourselves waiting on God. We wait for an answered prayer, direction, or deliverance and often, in our mind, we find ourselves waiting "too long." The answer is months "overdue." The decision needs to be made NOW. We can't take much more. For most of us, waiting is not often a quiet time. We may feel weak, unsettled, frightened. Isaiah 41, however, seems to indicate that it can also be a strength building time. "But those who wait on the Lord shall renew their strength; they shall mount up with wings like eagles, they shall run and not be weary, they shall walk and not faint." (vs. 31) Mary and Joseph would have probably appreciated having family and friends surrounding them during the birth and those first few years of Jesus' life. To be able to seek a mother's advice, a father's guidance, to have a "baby" sitter. Instead, they find themselves escaping to a foreign country. There they wait for God's timing to return to their homeland. Too often as we wait, we begin to think God has forgotten us. That maybe we are not important enough or perhaps not good enough. Mary and Joseph were chosen by God Himself to raise the Messiah, and yet they went through times of waiting. Times they may have preferred an angel show up to explain or say it is time to move. They trusted the Father enough to answer His call to be the earthly parents of the Messiah. They would trust Him with the rest. As we wait for God to move, let's spend time with Him. Time in His Word, on our knees, serving, resting, trusting, praising.

Father, waiting times are times when we are called to put our trust in action. Do we trust You enough to wait? Or does our own sense of urgency lead us to take steps that have not been directed by You? May we learn from Mary and Joseph, to draw strength from the knowledge that You are faithful.

December 20
Quiet times
Matthew 1

Each time I ponder the Christmas story, one of the aspects I always take some time to try to process is what it would have been like during the time period between Malachi and Matthew. A time span of 400 years with no new word from God. No daily reminder of what God was doing. No prophet declaring His hope. No sign of the Promise. For 400 years, the people had to stand on the Word being passed down from generation to generation. For 400 years, they waited. They waited for the Messiah's deliverance.

We get frustrated when we "haven't" heard from God in a few days. When it's been a week, and our prayers still aren't answered. When a month has gone by, and we are still in the same situation. In our society of instant gratification, if we had to wait 400 years for Him to "speak," would we keep spreading His Word and hope? Could it be that during those 400 years, the Israelites had exactly what they needed to sustain them as they waited? Could it be that when we face our "brief" time of quiet that we have what we need to carry us through? In Matthew 6:8, Jesus says "For Your Father knows the things you have need of before you ask Him." Could it be that our quiet times are preparation times? Could those quiet times be faith-building times? Could those times be a call to trust?

We live in a time when we know "the rest of the story." And yet, we too, may sometimes feel like giving up on ever seeing God move. And sometimes we, like the Israelites, don't recognize the answer when it comes. We have such high expectations. We have a specific answer in mind. We seem to expect fanfare announcing the movement of God. Just remember how silently the Messiah came into the world.

Father, even after all these years, we still try to put You into a box of our expectations. We expect You to move in our timetable and within our human desires. During those 400 quiet years, You still loved. You still protected. You still sustained. And Father, You do the same for us during our quiet times. May we stand on Your Word. May we stand on Your hope. May we stand on Your promises. Amen.

December 21
Awaiting a miracle
Luke 1

If you are a parent, you remember those days as you awaited the arrival of your child. Whether you were waiting for the adoption to go through or for the child to be delivered, you probably experienced a wide range of thoughts and emotions. From fear to excitement, from "what are we going to do" to "I can't wait to hold this child," to everything in between. But not all miracles are awaited with eager anticipation. Some needed miracles are coming from a place of desperation and hopelessness. Zacharias and Elizabeth had probably given up on their miracle. Perhaps they had prayed for years, even decades, for Elizabeth to conceive. As they approached and then past the childbearing age, they may have felt that they had lost their chance for a miracle. They gave up on a son, a little Zacharias to follow in his father's footsteps. But God had other plans for their son. He would have a significant purpose. He was needed at a specific time. So, Zacharias and Elizabeth had to wait for their miracle to occur in God's timing. Sometimes we seem to watch as our desired miracles pass us by. The child never comes, the marriage dissolves, we lose those we love. Sometimes we seem to hold the miracle in our hands only to watch it slip away. We may cry out about the unfairness of watching others receive their miracles and we never receive ours. But that is why the miracle of Christmas is so important. When God came down, when His perfect gift was given, He provided Hope and Comfort. He knows we live in a fallen world where bad things happen, where life isn't perfect, and all our dreams do not always come true. He sent Jesus to come and live among us, to die for us so that we can be redeemed and one day join the angels around the throne of God. He sent the Holy Spirit into our lives to guide us, to be with us always, to remind us how much we are loved. "To give light to those who sit in darkness and the shadow of death, to guide our feet into the way of peace." (Luke 1:79) If your world is dark right now, if you are in the shadow of death, if the storms surround, turn to the manger, turn to the cross. Because we no longer live in a hopeless world. We recognize our Hope is in the world to come. We realize that we are never alone. Our loving Father is with us to hold us, to weep with us, to love us. And someday, if we accept Jesus as our Savior, we will receive a miracle of eternal life in a world with no mores. No more pain, no more longing, no more heartache, no more loss, no more tears. My friend, if this season is just a reminder of the miracles you never received, you are loved, you are not alone. May your loving Father be your hope, your peace, your comfort, and light during your darkest days.

December 22
Follow the Star
Matthew 2

The trip was not a quick one. Once they started, they were committed to a couple years of travel. The trip, just one way, would take more than a year. And yet, the Wise Men decided that every step of the journey would be worth it for the opportunity to worship the King of the universe. Thank God, Jesus came to earth! Thank God, He meets us where we are! However, how many of us are willing to "follow the star" when God is calling us into a deeper relationship with Him? When He ask us to step out of our comfort zone and truly experience the life He has for us.

The Wise Men knew that this would not be an easy journey. They were leaving the comforts of their homeland to travel a great distance. There were no comfortable train seats to sit back and relax. No five-star hotels to stop at along the way. They endured the journey to experience worshipping the Christ Child. And here we are unwilling to change.

We like our comfort zones. We want to keep our relationship with God in a familiar place. But are there times God is asking us to step out of that comfort zone, of that life of ease, and come to a place where we will experience Him at a deeper level? A place where He can teach us more about Himself. A place where our trust is tested. A place that we truly must rely on Him. For some it may mean a move. For some it may mean a change of mind and heart. It may mean sacrifice. But knowing our Father loves us, knowing He has a plan for our life, isn't it worth it to "follow that star" to where He leads us? "Where He leads me, I will follow. I'll go with Him, with Him all the way." ("Where He Leads Me"/Blandy)

Father, here I sit imagining the Wise Men's journey. What reactions did their friends and family have when they started on their way? Did they fully know how far they would have to go? And yet, they recognized that by following the star they would find their heart's desire, worshipping at the very feet of Your Son, the Messiah. Father, I pray that we too may realize that by following where You lead, we can learn more of You. May that be our heart's desire. Amen.

December 23
Go tell it on the mountain
Luke 2

"And all those who heard it marveled at those things which were told them by the shepherds." (Luke 2:18)

Who would listen to a shepherd? Usually, the only ones who ever listen to them were fellow shepherds and the sheep. Herding sheep was a position that did not earn much respect. Perhaps most people felt that shepherds did not know enough to bother conversing with them. Maybe the shepherds knew their place and kept to themselves. But not this time! Did they wake people as they began sharing the Good News? Was it the first sight people saw as daylight was breaking? Shepherds in the streets of Bethlehem seemingly ranting and raving about the Messiah's arrival. Something about angels, a manger, a baby. As the people stepped out into the streets to hear, shepherds held audience about the Good News. Fear was replaced by Truth. The rejected proclaimed the praise. The humble declared the news of the Most High. After the night they experienced, life would never be the same. No longer would no one want to speak to these shepherds. Everywhere they went, they probably found an audience waiting to hear the first-hand account of that glorious night. Do you think that lasted a month or two? Or as old men did they still share the story that changed the world?

The message of hope, peace, and love that the shepherds told is the same message we have to share today. As new believers, we tell everyone we meet the Good News. We tell of the change. We tell of the joy, peace, and love that we have found. But sometimes, we get to the point where we stop sharing that Good News. The message of the Messiah, the Savior, is a message all need to hear. It isn't old news about angels, a manger, and a baby. It is the life-saving, life-giving news that everyone needs to hear. Continue to go tell it on the mountain. Continue telling of the Good News of God's salvation plan. Go tell of your encounter with the Lord of lords and King of kings. It's a story that never grows old. It is a story still relevant today. A message all need to hear.

Father, You commanded us "Go therefore and make disciples of all the nations, baptizing them in the name of the Father and of the Son and of the Holy Spirit, teaching them to observe all things that I have commanded you; and lo, I am with you always, even to the end of the age." (Matthew 28:19-20) Reignite a passion in us to go and tell. Amen.

Inspired by "Go Tell it on the Mountain" by Lynda Randle

What's in a name
Matthew 1

When the angel visited Joseph in the dream, he received the name of the Christ Child. "And she will bring forth a Son, and you shall call His name Jesus, for He will save His people from their sins." (Matthew 1:21) He was also informed that this Child was the One that the prophets had foretold would come. Matthew 1:23 is quoting Isaiah 7:14 "Behold, the virgin shall conceive and bear a Son, and shall call His name Immanuel." The verse in Matthew goes on to say, "which is translated, "God with us." From that angelic encounter, Joseph received the message that the Child was coming to save, and He would be "God with us." What moment, as he watched Mary carry the promised Child, did Joseph recall all the prophecies surrounding the Messiah? In Isaiah, we seem to find a contrast. We love to quote Isaiah 9:6. This birth announcement brought hope, power, and excitement. "For unto us a Child is born, unto us a Son is given; and the government will be upon His shoulder. And His name will be called Wonderful, Counselor, Mighty God, Everlasting Father, Prince of Peace." (vs. 6) That's what the people in Joseph's time were longing for, and it is what we long for even today. We want that Mighty God to come and make all things right. We need that Prince of Peace to come and calm our life's storms as He also brings peace to the world. Even though we don't always recognize it, we experience that to a certain degree even in today's world. But our hope is found in our Everlasting Father, who has promised that someday we will live in our eternal peaceful Home. Isaiah 53, on the other hand, creates disturbing imagery that is not exciting and promising. Can you imagine the first time, after the angel's announcement, when Joseph again hears or recalls the message from Isaiah 53? We have the images of the cross as we read this chapter. However, Joseph did not know how this prophecy would be fulfilled in Jesus' life. But imagine what he felt as he thought of Mary's precious Son in relation to "But He was wounded for our transgressions, He was bruised for our iniquities; the chastisement for our peace was upon Him, and by His stripes we are healed." (vs. 5) Each time Joseph holds the Infant Jesus does he feel the weight of the many names of Jesus? Does he bow as he thinks about the fact he is holding the Mighty God, the Everlasting Father, the Prince of Peace, Immanuel? Does his heart break each time he says the name of Jesus, as he realizes the pain Mary's Son will suffer since He came to save all of humanity? Such a small baby to have to bear the names that define why He came. But thanks be to God, Jesus, our Savior, Immanuel, God with us, came!

Father, thank You for a perfect redemption plan. Amen.

December 25
Happy Birthday, Jesus
Luke 2

Happy birthday, Jesus! It's all about You! We thank You for the countless gifts You have given us. Without You, we are just wandering around hopeless and lost. Without You, life has no purpose. Without You, life becomes unbearable. Without You, we are lonely and afraid with no one to rescue us.

But with You!!!!
You are our anchor in our storms.
You are our peace amid the chaos.
You are our reason for living.
You are our hope when our world falls apart.
You are our joy even in our sadness.
You are our Redeemer.
You are our Provider.
You are our Protector.
You are our Comforter.
You are our Faithful Friend.
You are our Savior.
You are the Lover of our soul.
You will lead us to our Eternal Home.

Thank You, Jesus, for leaving the glories of Heaven to come to earth. Thank You for living among us. Thank You for teaching us how to love one another. Thank You for paying the ultimate sacrifice for us. Thank You for Your victory over death, hell, and the grave! Thank You that You have promised to return someday. Thank You for always keeping Your promises! Happy Birthday, Jesus! Jesus, I love You!

December 26
Joy to the world, the Lord has come
Luke 2

Do you ever wonder about what happened after the news of a Babe born in a manger died down in Bethlehem? When life returned to normal? We know that the lives of the people of Bethlehem would forever be changed. But did they? Did they carry the impact of that first Christmas for the rest of their lives? Did they recognize that God was doing something in their midst? Or did they just return to their jobs, their homes, their routines with the same mindset and attitudes that they had before hearing about the glorious birth?

We can probably safely assume that the lives of the shepherds, Simeon, Anna, and the wise men would forever be changed. But what about all those we don't read about that listened to the first-hand accounts? Did they allow the news that the Messiah had come change their world?

What about us? Now that Christmas is official over, are we going back to the routines and attitudes we had before the season began? Or has the Message of Christmas brought change in our lives? Even if you have been a Christian for many years, is there some way you discovered you need to change this season? Some area where you are not allowing the Prince of Peace to come in and calm? Some mindset you need to adjust to align more with that of the Everlasting Father? Some thought patterns that needs to be changed so you better follow the Word of the Wonderful Counselor? Are we sharing the Good News? Let's continue to share the Christmas message of peace, hope, love, and joy throughout the year. As we spend time with our Father, ask Him what part of that message do we need more of in our own lives? What Truth needs to be spoken into the lives of those around us? How can we do better at Go and Tell? Part of the Good News is that we don't have to do any of that on our own. Our Mighty God will direct and strengthen us.

Father, what areas in our lives do we need to allow Your peace, hope, love, and joy to bring change and healing? Who in our sphere of influence needs to hear a Word from You? How do you want us to continue sharing Your redemption plan? May we spread the message of Joy to the World; the Lord has come. Amen.

Jesus' "first" breaths
Colossians 1

Jesus. The King of kings and Lord of lords. The Maker of Heaven and Earth. The Alpha and the Omega. The Great I AM. When He took His "first" breaths, the world would forever be changed. In Genesis 1:26, "God said, "Let Us make man in Our image, according to Our likeness." From this Scripture, we recognize that Jesus was there in the beginning. He was a part of Adam's first breath. "He is the image of the invisible God, the firstborn over all creation. For by Him all things were created that are in heaven and that are on earth." (Colossians 1:15-16) When God breathed into Adam the breath of life, mankind was born. Adam was not created like the angels. Adam was given free will so that he had the choice whether to worship God. But mankind chose not to listen to God. Sin was born and began to reign in their hearts and minds. So, God created a redemption plan. The first mention of this plan is in Genesis 3:15 when God spoke to the serpent. "And I will put enmity between you and the woman, and between your seed and her Seed; He shall bruise your head, and you shall bruise His heel." That plan begins to unfold when Baby Jesus, the Infant Emmanuel, drew His first breath in the manger. The breath that brought God down to man. "And the Word became flesh and dwelt among us, and we beheld His glory, the glory as of the only begotten of the Father, full of grace and truth." (John 1:14) The breath that showed how much God loved us. The first breath of the One who came to save us! Throughout His life here on earth, Jesus showed us how to love one another, how even the least of us was worthy of His love and forgiveness. Jesus knew that His final breath would be as a sacrifice for the sins of the whole world, past, present, and future. And yet He willingly came to offer His every breath for us: to teach, love, heal, provide and finally to redeem us. But the story doesn't end with His final breath on the Cross. Three days later, Jesus again drew a "first" breath! Death, hell and the grave could not defeat Him! The Resurrection of our Lord and Savior Jesus Christ again gave mankind life. We now have Hope in this life. We now have a Promise of Eternal Life. Hallelujah! Lord Jesus, thank You for those first breaths!

Lord, I pray Paul's prayer over all of us today: that "you may be filled with the knowledge of His will in all wisdom and spiritual understanding; that you may walk worthy of the Lord, fully pleasing Him, being fruitful in every good work and increasing in the knowledge of God; strengthened with all might to His glorious power, for all patience and longsuffering with joy; giving thanks to the Father who has qualified us to be partakers of the inheritance of the saints in the light." (Colossians 1:9-12) Amen.

December 28
Prince of Peace
John 14

How many days do we spend in chaos whether it is in the world around us or inside our own heads? How many days do we just want relief? We want the answer to come. We want the pain to stop. We want something to feel like it is going right. We want to cry out "It's too much." Our fallen world often seems like it's "burying" us with all the troubles that we face. We go to church on Sunday and paint a smile on our face. We tell everyone we meet that we are fine. But inside, we feel anything but. We are barely holding it together. But no one is supposed to know. My friend, there is Someone who already knows. Jesus is Everything to us. But sometimes we don't fully comprehend what that means. We praise Him for being our Savior. We accept Him as Lord. But how often do we allow Him to be our Prince of Peace? Jesus suffered. Jesus saw the brokenness of humanity. Jesus experienced pain, rejection, heartache. How often do we allow the Jesus who lived here on earth to come and "sit with us?" How often do we "cry on His shoulder?" How often do we cry out for His peace? How often do we cry out just to be held? Some of us experience those stormy days, especially in different life seasons, more often than others. Some of us can say "yes, I have experienced Him as my Prince of Peace" while some of us are still struggling to get through each day.

If Jesus was not real, if He was just sitting on His throne watching from the sidelines, then these are just empty words. But Jesus is real and active in our lives. He loves us as much now as He did when He sacrificed His life for ours. I don't know how He will show Himself as your Prince of Peace. I don't know how He will choose to comfort you throughout these days. I don't know if you will even sense Him there. What I do know is that He is there with you. I do know that He will answer when you call. Just cry out to Your Prince of Peace.

My loving Father, You know exactly what we need. We often expect You to speak "Peace, be still" and the storm will go away. However, You can still bring us peace even when the storm still rages. Jesus, right now I pray for those who feel like they are drowning in those storms today. I pray that they experience You as their Prince of Peace. Thank You for still being active in our lives today. Thank You for not leaving us to face life on our own. Amen.

Inspired by <u>"Hold me Jesus"</u> by Big Daddy Weave

Remember
Hebrews 12

At this time of the year, we see the "review highlights" of the past year: the top 40 songs, the top movies, etc. We also are reminded of those "celebrities" that we lost during the year. How often do we take time to reflect on our own highlights of the year? To recall those things that brought either blessing or heartache? How often do we take the time to remember how God has been with us every step of the way? As we read through the Bible, we find time and time again where writers retold how God had moved. It is important to remember from where God brought us. It is important to remember how He has delivered, provided, showed His love toward us. It is important to remember those times He made a way when there seem to be no way. As you read this, can you recall those times in your own life?

Not only should we take the time to thank God for all those times again, but we should also reflect on who may need to hear how God has moved in our lives. The Israelites were often reminded about how God delivered them from the Egyptians and how He brought them to the Promised Land. David often wrote about how God was with him throughout the years he was running from King Saul. Think about what an encouragement it is as we read about how God delivered in so many ways from so many different circumstances. Think about how reassuring it is to read about how, even in the most desperate times, God sustained. Do you know how many people are looking for something to give them that kind of hope?

People need to hear your stories too. They need to know that the God from the Bible is still active in our lives today. "And if someone asks about your hope as a believer, always be ready to explain it." (1 Peter 3:15 NLT) My friend, take some time to recall those moments in the past year and throughout your Christian journey. Those moments when God moved in a mighty way or was with you in your darkest days. Then you and I will be ready to give a reason for the hope that is in us. Those times will also serve as a reminder for us, as we head into a new year, that God will be faithful no matter what the year brings.

Father, as we take some time to count our blessings. We recall how much You have done for us: how you have shown Your love, how You have brought peace and joy, how much we need You. Father, may our lives be a reflection of the mercy, love, and grace that You have shown us. Let us be witnesses of Your goodness. Amen.

December 30
Living in Hope and Victory
Isaiah 53

Sometimes we forget to live like we have hope and victory. We go to church on Sunday mornings and praise God. Then we seem to leave all thoughts about that hope and victory until the next Sunday. When we step out of the church building, we step back into our "real" world filled with problems and routines and let the weight of it dim our hope and victory. We don't have to be happy all the time. There are many circumstances that shake our world. Problems too big for us to handle. Heartache we wish no one had to suffer. But still, we have Hope. But still, we have Victory. Jesus. Hope and victory are not based on how we are feeling. They are not just a reality as we worship on Sunday. They are living within us even when we can barely see their light. Jesus suffered on this earth so that He can be with us through our suffering. "He is despised and rejected by men, a Man of sorrows and acquainted with grief. And we hid, as it were, our faces from Him; He was despised, and we did not esteem Him. Surely He has borne our griefs and carried our sorrows." (Isaiah 53:3-4) Maybe we have been in a battle for a while, and it seems there are more defeats than victories. Maybe it seems we are fighting alone and we cry out "God, where is our help, our hope, our victory?" Most of the time we only see through our natural eyes. We may not be aware of what is happening in the spiritual battle. We may need to be like Elisha and pray that God opens our eyes. When Elisha and his servant were surrounded by the Syrian army, his servant cried out: "Alas, my master! What shall we do?" So he (Elisha) answered, "Do not fear, for those who are with us are more than those who are with them." And Elisha prayed, and said, "Lord, I pray, open his eyes that he may see." Then the Lord opened the eyes of the young man, and he saw. And behold, the mountain was full of horses and chariots of fire all around Elisha." (2 Kings 6:15-17) Maybe we need to remember that we don't leave Jesus in the church building on Sunday mornings. Maybe we need to trust that we have more hope and victory than we can currently see. Maybe we need to learn to praise throughout the week. Praise Him for what is true on Sunday mornings is true throughout the week. Because of what Jesus did for us, our current situation is not our permanent situation. There is nothing we face alone. Our lives have a deeper purpose.

Father, open our eyes to see our living hope and victory every day. Help us to remember that life is so much bigger than what we can see. Remind us that our current situation does not take away from the Everlasting Truth. Your Holy Spirit is actively living inside us to comfort, to guide, to provide. Thank You, Jesus! Amen. Inspired by "Living Hope" by Phil Wickham

December 31
Old things will pass away
Revelation 21

"For the former things have passed away. Then He who sat on the throne said, "Behold, I make all things new." (Revelation 21:4-5)

We have such high expectations when the ball drops every New Year's Eve. We seem to expect all our problems will suddenly disappear as we ring in the New Year. Our habits and hang-ups will stay behind as our resolutions will fix all our issues. We want to forget everything that went wrong and believe that the new year will bring more hope and joy. People will make better decisions. Conflicts will cease. Every year, those are our prayers, our hopes, our dreams. And every year, most of those hopes and dreams do not make it through the first day. We are not living in a world that is going to get better. We are living in a sinful world that had been prophesied to only get worse. However, there is good news! There is coming a day when this world will pass away. There is coming a day when we will spend eternity in Heaven. A peaceful land where there will be no more pain, no more sorrow, no more goodbyes. But there is good news while we are here in this life. Those hang-ups and habits that you would like to break, ask Jesus to help you break them. "Therefore, if anyone is in Christ, he is a new creation; old things have passed away; behold, all things have become new." (2 Corinthians 5:17) He is not a genie who will make them magically disappear when the ball drops. However, He has promised to be with you, guiding you along the way. It may not be easy or quick. There will be some failures. But He won't give up on you. We also need to pray for one another, for our country, for our world. "Praying always with all prayer and supplication in the Spirit, being watchful to this end with all perseverance and supplication for all the saints." (Ephesians 6:18) If you want to make a resolution, resolve to pray more. Pray for your family, friends, church, leaders, the requests on your social media feed. Remember "the effective, fervent prayer of a righteous man avails much." (James 5:16) This world needs your prayers! "Let us therefore come boldly to the throne of grace, that we may obtain mercy and find grace to help in time of need." (Hebrews 4:16) *Father, as we close out another year, most of us will look back and reflect on what this year has brought to our lives. Blessings that brought joy, heartaches that brought sorrow. Thank You for being there through it all. Father, I pray that this upcoming year will be a year of prayer. You have promised, "if My people who are called by My name will humble themselves, and pray and seek My face, and turn from their wicked ways, then I will hear from heaven, and will forgive their sin and heal their land." (2 Chronicles 7:14) Our Holy God, forgive us for leaving our post, for allowing the world to redefine what is right and wrong. Remind us to be a people on our knees! Amen.*

Bibliography

BibleGateway.Com: A Searchable Online Bible in over 150 Versions and 50 Languages. https://www.biblegateway.com/. Accessed 1 Aug. 2019.

Butler, Trent C., and Holman Bible Publishers (Nashville, Tenn.), editors. Holman Bible Dictionary: With Summary Definitions and Explanatory Articles on Every Bible Subject, Introductions and Teaching Outlines for Each Bible Book, in-Depth Theological Articles, plus Internal Maps, Charts, Illustrations, Scale Reconstruction Drawings, Archaeological Photos, and Atlas. Holman Bible Publishers, 1991.

Dictionary by Merriam-Webster: America's Most-Trusted Online Dictionary. https://www.merriam-webster.com/. Accessed 1 Aug. 2019.

"Dictionary.Com Is The World's Favorite Online Dictionary." Dictionary.Com, https://www.dictionary.com/. Accessed 1 Aug. 2019.

Lotz, Anne Graham. Daniel Prayer: Prayer That Moves Heaven and Changes Nations. Zondervan, 2018.

Stevenson, Angus, and Maurice Waite, editors. Concise Oxford English Dictionary. 12th ed, Oxford University Press, 2011.

Tyndale House Publishers, editor. Life Application Bible: New King James Version. Tyndale House Publishers, 1993.

Author's Playlist

"Boasting" by Lecrae
"Come to the table" by Sidewalk Prophets
"Courageous" by Casting Crowns
"He's Still Working on Me" by The Hemphills.
"Give me Your eyes" by Brandon Heath
"Go Tell it on the Mountain" by Lynda Randle
"God of All My Days" by Casting Crowns
"Grace Got You" by MercyMe
"He set me free" by Bill and Gloria Gaither
"Hold me Jesus" by Big Daddy Weave
"How can I keep from singing?" by Chris Tomlin
"I Can't Even Walk (Without You Holding My Hand)" by Charles
    Johnson and the Revivers.
"If It Had Not Been" by Lynda Randle, Andrae Crouch
"Just Give Me Jesus" by Unspoken
Laminin by Louie Giglio
"Living Hope" by Phil Wickham
"My God is Awesome" by Charles Jenkins
"My Redeemer Lives" by Nicole C Mullen
"Nobody loves me like You" by Chris Tomlin
"No Matter What" by Ryan Stevenson
"Not Today" by Hillsong United
"O Come to the Altar" by Elevation Worship
"Praise the Lord" by Russ Taff
"The Proof of Your Love" by King and Country
"Reckless Love" by Cory Asbury
"Say Amen" by Finding Favour
"Speak Life" by TobyMac
"Surrounded (Fight My Battles)" by Michael W. Smith
"That's My King" by Dr. S. M. Lockridge
"War Room" clip
"The Way" by Pat Barrett
"What If" by Blanca
"Where Could I Go" by Gaither Vocal Band
"While I'm Waiting" by John Waller

Made in the USA
Lexington, KY
09 December 2019